TANGENTIALLY READING

WITH CHRISTOPHER RYAN

For Gabor,
Many thanks for sharing your story.
CR

Edited by
M. M. Owen

Designed by
Michael Aliposa

Illustrations by
Adam McDade

TANGENTIALLY READING

with Christopher Ryan

Printed in the United States of America

First Printing, 2017

ISBN 978-0-9956848-1-2

MISFIT PRESS

Vancouver, Canada

www.misfitpress.co

TABLE OF CONTENTS

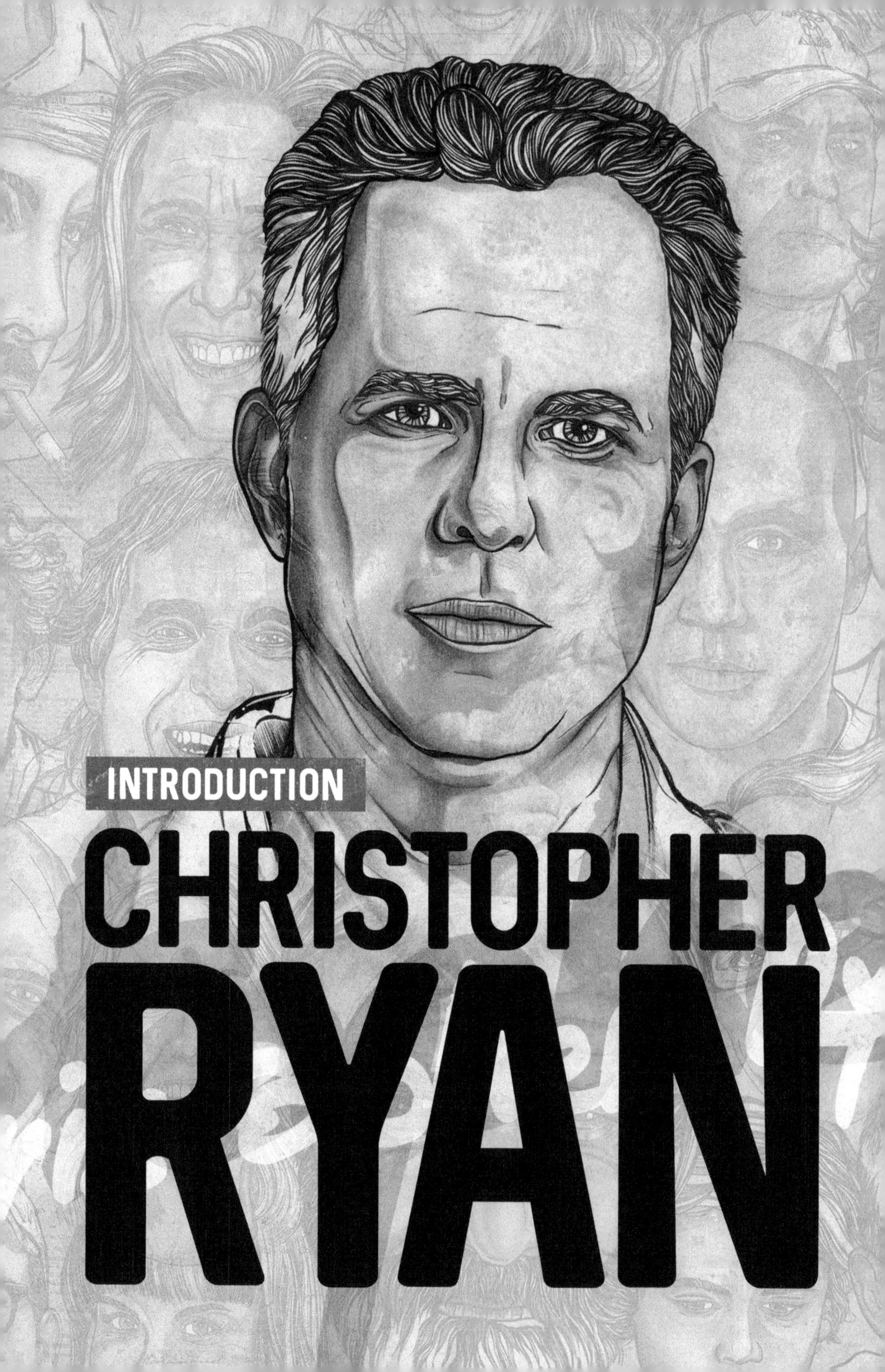

INTRODUCTION

CHRISTOPHER RYAN

Revolutions are like dogs. The small ones make the most noise. Bombs explode, crowds chant, leaders proclaim, sirens wail, and helicopters hover. But more often than not, loud revolutions don't amount to much. "Meet the new boss - same as the old boss." Quiet revolutions however, like truly dangerous dogs, tend not to announce their arrival. They sneak up on you. They come in tsunami-slow and unstoppable. By the time you notice that something very important is happening, it's too late to do anything but try to ride the wave.

We live in a historic moment ripe for revolution. The old world is dead, and it's high time we buried it. The playwright Arthur Miller once said, "an era can be considered over when its basic illusions have been exhausted." Here in the dog-days of 2017, our basic illusions lie sprawled about like spent marathon runners at the finish line. Wall Street is a safe place for your retirement fund? Ha! A university education is a ticket to prosperity? Right. Modern medicine? Please. Government? Religion? Consumerism? The American Dream? Wake the fuck up already.

The invention of the printing press in 1440 allowed the spread of unconventional ideas on an unprecedented scale. This quiet technological development changed the world far more dramatically (and lastingly) than any number of *bloody* revolutions, punctuated by screams, explosions, and speeches. Podcasting may one day be seen as equally revolutionary in its impact on the path of civilization - if not more so. While books are expensive to produce and distribute, podcasts are normally free - and distribution is nearly effortless.

I've been making podcasts for about four years now, and I'm still amazed by the unobtrusive power of the process. I sit down with someone, clip on a couple of microphones, and push a button. After an hour or two of conversation, I thank them and push another button. A few weeks later, when it's time to upload the episode, I record an impromptu introduction, push a few more buttons, and it's done. Within a few days, the equivalent of a stadium-full of people will have listened in on our conversation. Dan Carlin, Joe Rogan, and Duncan Trussell are talking to the equivalent of entire towns or cities of people. And because every episode is archived online, there's no telling how many people will ultimately hear these conversations.

This reach is nearly free for the producer as well as the audience. All my podcasting gear cost me less than $1,000, plus the computer, which I already had. A hosting service runs about $20/month. No studio to rent. No technicians turning things on and off. No producers, assistants, or publicists. Just me, a recorder, some microphones, a laptop, and a guest. And because this process is so cheap, there's no need for big corporations to get involved, looking over my shoulder, telling me to avoid this word, skirt that issue, or disinvite a potentially controversial guest. My goal is simply to have a conversation that's as organic as possible with anyone who interests me.

In addition to being so simple, podcasting is mobile. In addition to the U.S., I've recorded episodes in Mexico, Thailand, South Africa, Botswana, Costa Rica, Canada, Holland, Spain, and probably a few more countries I'm forgetting. I spent last summer living in my Sprinter van, cruising around the western U.S., uploading episodes from cafes, libraries, restaurants, churches, and any place else who will let me use their wifi. (#vanthropology2017)

The main reason I keep making *Tangentially Speaking* is that podcasting has revolutionized my own life. A lot of people think of me as a writer, but I don't really love to write; I love *having written*, as they say. This podcast, on the other hand, I love doing. For a while, I recorded remotely, but I stopped doing that because I missed the simple, essential joy of being in a room with the person I was speaking with. Their eyes and body show me where the conversation can flow most naturally. There's an intimacy created by a good conversation, and it never felt right to just hang up after having shared that connection. Thanks to the audience I bring with me, even very busy people can sometimes find the time to invite me into their lives for a bit.

Lastly, a few words about the *Tangentially Speaking* audience, which probably includes you, who bought this book – or the person who gave you this book – as well as the people who created this book. I initially met Matt Owen and AJ Leon (of Misfit Press) because they were visiting Portland, OR, where I was living at the time. Matt had sent me an email: "Hey Chris, Big fan of the podcast. I'm coming to Portland. You have time for a beer?" I did, and one thing led to another, which led to the book you're now holding in your hands. The illustrations were all done by Adam McDade, a listener who had to be threatened with bodily injury to accept even a token payment. (Prints are available via his site: http://adammcdade.weebly.com.) The transcriptions were done by a team of volunteers who heard me talking about the possibility of a book like this and sent an email offering to help. *That* is the kind of community that's gathered around *Tangentially Speaking* and this book, like layers of pearl around a grain of confused – but very grateful – sand.

I've met a lot of you. That's one of the reasons I wanted to spend this past summer in the van. I got to float down the Flathead river in Montana, with Jonathan, Jillyn, and their pal Connor. I did three loads of laundry in Bend, Oregon while getting to know Tom and Judy (and then we ended up going to Burning Man together). I've met you in bars, supermarkets, gas stations, airports, walking down the street. Hell, travelers recognized me on five separate occasions in a little town called Pai, in northern Thailand! If it sounds like my tiny sliver of fame is going to my head, please forgive me. I'm just mystified by it. More importantly, the people I've met have all been fantastic. When there was time to hang out, we became friends. Every time. So, while I wouldn't presume to say exactly what listeners get from the podcast, I can tell you that I get a hell of a lot from it – including introductions to some of my favorite people.

What will it all add up to? I don't know. But it's clear that we're all seeking profound, radical changes in how we live on this planet (or off it, Elon). Western civilization is due for a cleansing, renewing revolution, and I've come to believe that the deepest of these sound like unscripted, uncensored, uninhibited conversation.

CHRISTOPHER RYAN

OCTOBER, 2017

TOPANGA, CA

WHAT WILL IT ALL ADD UP TO? I DON'T KNOW. BUT IT'S CLEAR THAT WE ARE ALL SEEKING PROFOUND, RADICAL CHANGES IN HOW WE LIVE ON THIS PLANET (OR OFF IT, ELON). WESTERN CIVILIZATION IS DUE FOR A CLEANSING, RENEWING REVOLUTION, AND I'VE COME TO BELIEVE THAT THE DEEPEST OF THESE SOUND LIKE UNSCRIPTED, UNCENSORED, UNINHIBITED CONVERSATION.

CHAPTER 1

JOE ROGAN

&

DUNCAN TRUSSELL

WHY DO WE ALWAYS HAVE TO BE FUCKING HAPPY? WHAT IS THAT?

I LOVE TODAY. I THINK THIS IS THE GREATEST TIME EVER TO BE ALIVE.

EPISODE #54 (FEBRUARY 13, 2014) & EPISODE #72 (MAY 19, 2014)

Joe Rogan is a stand-up comedian, MMA commentator, and host of the popular podcast The Joe Rogan Experience.

PERFORMANCE | COMEDY | LIFE | TECHNOLOGY | FREEDOM

Duncan Trussell is an actor and stand-up comic who hosts The Duncan Trussell Family Hour podcast.

DEATH | CIVILIZATION | U.S. SOCIETY | REALITY | FUTURE

BEGIN TS #54
W/ JOE ROGAN AND DUNCAN TRUSSELL

CHRIS RYAN: So we should come up with a title for our group podcasts. Three Musketeers is too easy. Circle Jerk.

JOE ROGAN: Tripod?

CR: Triangular.

JR: I like the Three Amigos. It sounds unpretentious.

DUNCAN TRUSSELL: How about the Lords of Truth?

CR: That's not pretentious..

JR: The Spiritual Arbiters of the Western World.

DT: How about Shrimp Parade?

JR: What is a Shrimp Parade?

DT: I have no idea but I would go to one though.

CR: I thought that was some sort of reference to penises.

JR: That's 'cause you always think about penises.

CR: You were saying that your podcast was a sausage fest, Duncan.

DT: I didn't mean phallus. My podcast reminds of a package of old salty, briny, withered sausages you might find at a secondhand meat store.

JR: What the fuck is a secondhand meat store?

DT: Discarded old sausage.

CR: A guy named Jack – one of my listeners – he lives

in New Zealand, had a shitty job. He wrote to say " I emailed you last year asking for advice, you said the only way to fly is to jump, so I thought I would email you again and tell you that because of listening to you and Duncan and Joe..."

DT: "I'm now paralyzed from the neck down."

JR: "I found out about airplanes. You're full of shit. The only way to fly is to get on a fucking airplane."

CR: "So I quit the job I hated, I sold my car, and I'm leaving New Zealand and going to Southeast Asia to travel for six months. I thought you'd like to know you guys helped me and I'll be listening to your podcasts on the planes, trains and buses in Asia."

JR: Do you get a lot of those?

CR: Yeah, 'cause you know, my thing is that I traveled a lot, so I get a lot of emails from people saying, "I don't know what to do. I'm with this woman, I don't know if I love her. I've got this job, I kind of hate it and I was thinking, maybe I should go travel. I don't know, what do you think?" I'm like "Dude, you're writing to me? Your answer is in the fact that you chose *me* to write to."

JR: It's real hard to give someone advice like that; you don't know them.

CR: Yeah, it's impossible.

JR: I see what they're doing though. They're just trying to reach out to you. But what I get a lot is, "the podcast changed my life" story. I get that fucking thing like, "I decided to take a chance, I decided to live with passion, I decided to abandon my job, lose my burdensome relationship, get my shit together, stop eating sugar." I've heard all those things. All the time, constantly. Completely unintended side effect of something that I thought was just going to be fun. I just have a bunch of funny friends, and that's how we started doing these podcasts: in the green rooms of comedy clubs. We just set up a webcam and started talking. The idea that it would, somehow or another, change who knows how many peoples' lives... I mean, I've lost track of how many people who came up and told me they lost 100 pounds, how many people came up to me and told me they started exercising, they got off antidepressants. They feel better than they've ever felt in their life. Their whole life is super positive now. They realize that you can get a pattern going, where you are just constantly nice to people. It can really enrich and change your life. I get those emails every day. I get those emails *all* day, it's bizarre.

CR: It's fantastic.

JR: But it's weird. Because it's totally unintended. Unforeseen. I never saw it coming.

DT: It's a tuning fork.

CR: It's a resonance, isn't it? The theme that keeps coming through for me is that people feel like they have connected with a community that they haven't found in the town they live in, or whatever. It's not that we're doing anything that's so unusual, it's just that it resonates with people around the world. And that's wonderful.

JR: We got lucky when the three of us found each other. We got lucky that we found each other physically, and we can all hang out together physically. We can go to dinner and joke around. But if you are stuck in Hammond, Indiana, and you're in a small town... maybe your neighbor is a douchebag, maybe the kids

“” BECAUSE WHEN A PERSON DIES THAT IS AN INCREDIBLY STRANGE THING: THEY DON'T EXIST ANYMORE AND IT MAKES YOU REALLY TRY TO CONCEPTUALIZE WHAT IS BEING ALIVE.

you go to school with are assholes, maybe everyone's stupid, maybe they throw rocks at gay people. Who knows what the fuck the issue is? But you are stuck in that geographic spot. But because of podcasts like this, they are interacting with people that aren't stuck. We've all been in bad spots.

CR: I know Bill Maher sometimes says he loves playing gigs in shithole conservative towns, because the cool people who live there in the shadows all come out to see him. That is their one chance to not be in the minority.

JR: That make sense. I heard Salt Lake City is like that. I still haven't done Salt Lake City but I need to. I keep hearing that about Wise Guys Club; I heard it's fucking fantastic. Joey Diaz just came back; he was there a couple months ago and said it was amazing.

CR: Duncan, are you on the road again? What are you doing these days?

JR: He's coming on the road with me.

DT: I'm going with Joe. I've started doing comedy regularly again. It's great. I was going to do a podcast tour, but now I'm thinking I'll just keep building this new set that I'm working on, and just go on the road.

JR: Just have some fun, Duncan. Get back on the horse. You are too good to *not* be doing comedy.

DT: I'm definitely doing it again, and it feels good. I've never been one of these industrialist artists who's like, “I'm going to go up no matter what, never a sick day, always go up.” I can't do it like that. I need to be drawn to it so I feel excited about it. Because otherwise you are up there and you just feel like you're some kind of automaton, sort of rolling through some nonsense. For what reason? It's not fair to the audience; even if they are laughing, it's still no good. I think it's better to do things when you're inspired. Not that you're always going to be inspired, but you need to just trust that if there is a pause in your desire to do some art form... you don't want to apply the same way you build a car to the way you try to communicate the deepest parts of yourself to the world.

JR: Especially considering that you went through a very emotional and a really powerful, profound experience. The loss of your mother, one of the most important people in your life. That's something you don't get over very quickly. Phil Hartman was a very good friend of mine, but he wasn't as close to me as your mother was to you. When Phil died, I was fucked up for a long time. I went on stage too soon and had two really bad sets because of it. One was unbelievably bad; I couldn't be funny if my life depended on it. I was unbelievably bummed out getting onto stage. Everything that came out of my mouth felt pointless. It was a terrible experience, only two weeks after Phil died, and I had no business being on stage. I think what you did was really smart Duncan: you took a long time, and you let your emotions settle. Loss is a big thing, it's not to be taken lightly. There is no shame in wanting to rekindle your desire to do something that you love doing. Do what you do.

CR: And also Duncan, the way you went through the experience and *still* are going through the experience: with your eyes open. By interviewing your mother on your podcast before she died. By being completely conscious as everything was happening. I have so much respect for you for doing that.

DT: Thanks. It is intense, but it is totally normal. That's the other thing you have to realize is that your mom dying...

CR: ...it's going to happen.

DT: It's definitely going to happen, there is no way around it. I appreciate what you guys are saying, and I'm not trying to underplay it. It sucked, I had grief. Grief is like getting the psychic flu. It's like the worst heartbreak of your life times ten. You go crazy in some weird way. What's really interesting, is when you start to realize that this is not abnormal. This is *normal.* Then, you realize society is built on not acknowledging this *thing* that will happen to every single one of us. They don't teach it in class. There's no class in high school where they teach you, "Here's what's going to happen: your parents are going to die, and everyone you know is going to die, and everything you have is going to go away. You're basically a tenant existing in this dimension for only a certain amount of time. So definitely make sure you return those calls, and don't take this for granted." It sounds a little cliché, I know. But it's the fact that those things aren't taught to us, and instead, through TV, we get this kind of window into a very specific age range - 20 to 30 maybe - the height of virility in a person's life. That's mostly what we like to look at, we like to look at young, beautiful people. When your parent dies, or your friend dies, or whatever happens, it always blows your fucking mind.

CR: It's always a surprise.

DT: It's always a surprise. It's also, "Holy shit, holy fucking shit! We're all at the edge of a cliff!" You know what I mean? We've been walking along the edge of a cliff since we were born.

JR: It puts into perspective what life really *is.* Because when a person dies, they vanish. That is an incredibly strange thing: they don't exist anymore, and it makes you really try to conceptualize what it is to be alive. What is this exact experience? Am I just so accustomed to it, is it so normal to me, that it's seems like something that makes sense? But then, objectively, I think about death, and... you just disappear? Stop existing? What the fuck is going on there? It's not a rock, it's not water, it's not metal. It's a person. And then it stops being alive. Why? What the fuck is that all about? What's going on? Why does it disappear?

CR: But we still exist on Facebook.

JR: Yeah but your life just stops. Why should planned obsolescence be built into the system?

DT: Flappy bird. Have you played Flappy Bird? It's a fun fucking game. You only get one life.

CR: But does it stop?

JR: That's the question.

CR: Does a raindrop cease to exist when it lands on the ocean?

JR: Are you the same person today as you were when you went to bed yesterday? I'm not exactly sure. I don't understand what the fuck is going on when I go to sleep; I'm not pretending that I understand it. I know that I shut off and then I don't have any recollection or idea of anything for eight hours. And that's supposed to be *normal*. I think that's über bizarre.

DT: Getting back to death awareness... the point is that we're taught not to spend our time fixating on the fact that there is death in the universe, and that we're all going to fall into the void, and everything is going to go away. But it needs to be acknowledged, and the more that you escape from that truth, the more likely you are to take the people around you for granted.

CR: And take your own life for granted.

DT: That's why *Watership Down* and all those stories are so important: to teach you to appreciate what's happening around you right now, if you can. Because you haven't really looked at where you're at, which is that you're going to get sick. People think that you're being negative if you think like that. It's not like I am always thinking like that. It's just that I know, that the more that I digest that truth, the more interesting my life becomes. I'm not saying it becomes happier; I'm not saying my life suddenly gets blissful.

CR: Happiness is for idiots, let's face it.

DT: Why do we always have to be fucking happy? What is that?

CR: I hate when people ask me if I'm happy.

JR: I'm happy. I must be an idiot.

CR: It's a different form of happiness.

DT: Exactly, it's a different thing. I'm talking about a kind of numbed-out, blank-face, fucking emoticon grin. As you wander around like a little zombie. Not even aware.

JR: Or constantly happy.

DT: Constantly happy. What is that? That's not good.

JR: You're not paying attention.

CR: Honestly, Duncan, that's one of the things that keeps me away from the retreats that you go to sometimes. There are too many happy people there. They creep me out. Too many blissful smiles. I need sarcasm, I need nasty snark.

DT: You'd be surprised, A lot of the people I know that go to those retreats, they do snark and it's hilarious, and there's no bullshit happening. I've definitely been beautifully insulted there, but in a sweet way. The way *you* do it Chris, like a friend. At the wrong type of retreat, you will definitely end up with a bunch of phony shitheads wandering around. But I think if you go to the right one, that might not be a problem.

CR: Every time someone does that thing with their hands and says, "Namaste," I just want to slap somebody.

DT: I think that's one of the big problems: people confuse spirituality with being a pussy, because there's so many people who imitate being spiritual. Whenever you see imitations like that, that's when you get the sense that you're having some weird thing being run on you. But when you run into people who are really working on themselves, usually what you get from them is authenticity.

“”

WHEN YOU ARE WORSHIPING THE GODS, YOU'RE NOT JUST WORSHIPING THE GODS, YOU'RE ALSO OFFERING UP YOUR OWN HUMILITY.

JR: That's what's important about what you are saying. People that are *really* working on themselves undertake a struggle; it's a quest. There's not really a final destination, where all of a sudden you're enlightened. These people that are pretending to be constantly spiritual – "Satnam; Namaste" – what they're doing is putting on a show. By doing that, you're avoiding all the work. You're not really being a person. Not all of them anyway. That feeling that you get from the phony ones is like, "You've sort of adopted this predetermined pattern and now you're claiming spirituality."

CR: Off-the-rack hippies are so irritating.

JR: Off-the-rack: that's the best way to describe it. Typically unique.

* * *

JR: When you are worshiping the gods, you're not just worshiping the gods. You're also offering up your own humility- that you don't compare to the gods. When you are experiencing a hunter-gatherer lifestyle, you are getting the exact programming and set of rewards that your body has been programmed to receive in order to stay alive forever. We are going through a transitionary period with our bodies, because our bodies have all these reward systems built in – and there is no need, whatsoever, to feed them these days. There's no need to feed the "fight and flight," to feed the hunter-gatherer. Instead, you're going to the supermarket to get your food. You're going to work and sitting down all day. None of it makes sense to your body. Your body is absolutely baffled. You're not doing something that you absolutely love, when you're there sitting in that studio, designing art or whatever it is you're doing. You could *conceivably* find the most amazing job ever. But if it's not the most amazing job ever, if you are just sitting there doing nonsense that you don't give a fuck about all day... there's nothing like that in all of nature. Gathering food is exciting, hunting is exciting, fishing is exciting, planting crops is satisfying. If you pull a tomato off of a vine and you eat that tomato, there is a visceral – almost genetic – excitement that you get from that. We're not getting any of those rewards, all day long. But we are forcing ourselves to live in this other way. It's not like it's impossible to live in a way where we could get those rewards. But society almost engineered itself to make it so we can innovate and make new things easier and quicker. That's what society did. It pushed people into large groups. It's almost like the machine wants to be born, so it reprograms society to live for the machine itself, rather than live for its own need system, its own wants and desires. If you could tell someone, "You are going to live a finite life, you only have this amount of life, so let's manage it and see how you handle it." How much time do you think you'd spend sitting in a fucking box, doing some shit you don't like? You wouldn't. You'd spend none that way. You'd give zero time to the box. Zero. When you're engineering your life to live for your needs, to exist for what would make you happy, what would make you feel satisfied and feel thrilled by life? But that's not what society wants. Society wants us to feed our reward systems with material items. Because if it's not based on material items, then we can't make more material items. We want to make sure that you always need the newest, craziest shit. So we are going to put you into a society where you are inundated by visual images of things that are way better than the things you possess. Your main focus will be possessing those things, because they will equal happiness for you. Of course, you'll never *receive* that happiness, because if you did, you'd drop out of the game. If having a '69 Mustang is the thing that would make you really happy, you'd get that '69 Mustang, and you'd be good to go. But it's not good, you're not done. Next you want a '70 Firebird. You want a *this*, you want a *that*, you get caught up in this path of collecting items. This ensures that these items get produced. So, we are living our lives for this system, more than we are living our lives for humanity. The system is tricking us.

CR: Fuck! That was what my next book was going to be about. Now I have to think of something else to write...

JR: That *is* what it *is*, right?

CR: We're rats on a wheel.

JR: There is an intelligent life that is waiting to be born out of human innovation. It's making us create itself.

CR: It's already born, and we are slaves of it. That's what my next book is about. All this talk about Frankenstein, and the Singularity, and whatever. Frankenstein *exists*. And Frankenstein is the economic system that enslaves us in order to keep the economic system running. You're right, it's not designed for human satisfaction, it's designed to perpetuate itself. Profit is the central engine in this whole thing. When I see a commercial that says "BP believes," I think, "BP doesn't believe anything. It has no brain, it's not a being." I don't give a fuck what Mitt Romney says, corporations are not people, my friend. Corporations are artificial structures that have taken on life like the fucking Frankenstein monster. And they've turned against us, and now they rule the world. They don't give a fuck about the plastic in the ocean, and overfishing, and cruelty to the fucking pigs, and the industrial farms, and whatever else. They don't care because they *can't* care. And this is the problem.

DT: There's this primitive anarchist guy, John Zerzan, and he says that the whole problem started when we began to use symbols to represent life. Then we got confused with the symbols, and started thinking the symbols were life. So that's the big problem. The Frankenstein is fact that people don't experience *reality* anymore. They experience the secondhand reality composed of all these man-made symbols only that *represent* what reality is. Like the clock. The clock represents the sun. We still worship the sun, but now we worship it in the form of this re-creation of the day-and-night cycle that we put into a fucking clock. We *worship* that fucking thing and it modulates society. The pulsation of society is all based on this symbolic *representation* of the light and dark we all exist in. The clock is not life. Life is the experience of being out in the sun, and the sun is going to be there for a certain amount of time. And while it's there, there's certain things you can do. When it's not there, there's certain things you can't do. But establishing a connection to that light, and not to the fucking weird sundial thing on your wall, would be so much healthier. There are so many other examples of people getting addicted a symbol of something else. Saying, "I love you" does not mean that you love me. Completely embracing me, and forgiving me, and being in the moment with me... *that's* love. Not some random sentiments you muttered. But, again, once you get caught up in those fucking symbols, your feet aren't touching the ground anymore.

CR: The thing where you were talking about earlier, about being on the wheel (basically this whole rant we're on here)... do you think that's the reason psychedelics are so heavily penalized in this country?

JR: I think there is always a push and a pull to life. There's always good and evil. It sounds cliché, but I really do think that there may be forces in the universe that are what you would describe as "natural." I think that we look at natural behavior in other systems: whether it's bees' bizarre behavior building honeycombs, and gathering honey, and the infanticide where the female bees find the other female larva and stab them with their stinger. We look at all these things as being completely normal, although very complex, for these relatively simple life forms like bees. With humans, when you factor in the fact that people with different languages, different cultures, and different geographic origins interact with each other, and change each other in all these ways... you have to think of it as natural. I mean, I don't see how it could be anything but natural. If I look at it as natural, what is the thing that is going on? If I step away from culture, step away from language, and try look at this objectively – so objectively that I am not even a human being – I'm analyzing it mathematically. What's going on here? It's *making* things. It's constantly making things. Not just things, but different things, and more innovation every day.

CR: But also *destroying*.

JR: Sure. The process of making those things kills the mother itself. That's universal. The process of making those things, whether it's through coal, whether it's digging into the ground to get minerals for an electric car, whether it's dropping plastic into the ocean. Whatever it is, the process of this nation's industrialization is destroying its mother. But it doesn't give a fuck about destroying its mother, because what it's trying to do is *make* something. It's trying to make some ultimate piece of technology, most likely a technological life form. If you talk to the people that we talked to when we did that 2045 conference, those guys are all thinking that there will be artificial life. It's not like only one guy thinks it, and every other guy thinks he's a quack. They all think it. They all think there is going to be artificial intelligence (AI) that is so intense, and so powerful, that it's going to be sentient. And it's going to be able to create copies of itself, and it's going to be able to improve upon whatever design it has.

CR: We're the larva stage of this being.

JR: It's alive. We just don't think of it as alive, because it can't die like we do. It doesn't have the same issues that we do, as far as our body having a ticking time bomb inside of us, an expiration date.

CR: Do you think tadpoles get pissed off about the transition to becoming frogs? Because if that's what is happening, as the tadpole here, I don't like this process. I mean the fucking Earth was great. We're fucking it up.

JR: It's still great!

CR: It's less great than it was before we got here.

JR: I'm not sure. I don't even want to think about that. I don't think you can stop it. I think it is what it is. I think it's nature. I think it's just like getting wet when the rain comes down. It just happens.

CR: Well, certainly when Duncan was talking about Zerzan, and his idea that symbolic intelligence is the beginning of the problem, I was thinking the same thing. *Okay*. But how do we avoid symbolic intelligence? We are, in our very nature, symbolic beings. There's no culture in the world that doesn't have language.

DT: We just need to get a little closer to the source. For example, when you say you've accidentally killed a bunch of people with your robot flying machine, don't call it "collateral damage." Call it, "we killed a bunch of people, we murdered people."

CR: Call it, "they were the enemy." It's the same thing. Dehumanize them in one way or the other.

DT: I'm not saying we all just stop talking and wander around in some kind of open-mouthed, gurgling bliss state.

CR: Namaste.

JR: The secondhand meat factory.

DT: I'm saying we zoom in a little. Just try and get a little closer to the experience itself, and then a lot of these things we think are going to be great - a car, a nice house - all these things are just symbols. So we are seeking to obtain these symbols, and forgetting that it's *not* the symbols we want, it's the *feelings* they give us that are what we want.

CR: But isn't that like dragging your feet in the parade of history? If I understand what Joe is saying, that's where we're going. So maybe we should just say, "Fuck it, let's go."

JR: I think we should enjoy the moment. We should enjoy life. We should be really cool to each other. This doesn't necessarily have to be a negative thing. I think all of history, as far as human beings go, points to the fact that things get better. People romanticize times like the Dark Ages, but I say fuck them. Those people are crazy. They were all getting syphilis and smallpox.

CR: You and I disagree on that. That's a fundamental disagreement.

JR: I love today. I think this is the greatest time, ever, to be alive. Because of the internet. I think without the internet, my life would not be nearly as rich and rewarding. I wouldn't know as many things. I wouldn't be in touch with as many people. I wouldn't be influenced by as many sources.

CR: You're happier living now than you would have been in the 60s?

JR: Fuck yeah. I wouldn't want to live in the 60s. How hard would it be to do a podcast in the 60s? It'd be fucking impossible, and they'd arrest us if we said half the stuff we said during your commercials. All the shit that Lenny Bruce went to jail for? Fuck that. I like being alive today. All the forefathers have already done the work. I pick up where they left off.

DT: But you're kind of utopian, Chris. You're looking to the past.

CR: We're all utopians here. That's the funny thing. We just locate it in different places. But before we move too far away from utopia, I just wanted to add a little trivia here. Do you know what the word "utopia" actually means, the root of the word utopia?

JR: I Googled it once, but I forgot.

CR: It means, "no such place exists."

• BEGIN TS #72 •
W/ JOE ROGAN AND DUNCAN TRUSSELL

DT: Let me tell you my theory about selfies being the precursor to the time machine. This is really interesting, I've been thinking of writing an article about this for *Vice*: you can take virtual reality (VR) goggles *right now*, go into Google street view, and look around the street from a 3D perspective; it will interpolate that stuff. You can do that now. But in ten years, a computer will be able to scan the environment, and see that there is a tree here, and know the behavior of a tree in the wind. So, all of a sudden, it can scan the environment and locate trees... okay, let's make these trees move as if they're really blowing in the wind. And then there's a dog – you might see an image of a dog in the goggles. You know what a dog acts like, so you can assign a generic AI to the dog and separate it from its background. Now, the dog is running around in 3D space. It goes from our current time, where you put on the VR goggles, look around in Google Street View, and it's kind of shitty. But you could do the exact same thing in five years, and stand in the street looking up and down and around. And the next step is to take all the elements of the scene, animate them with artificial intelligence, and now you're not just standing in a static three dimensional Street View... now you're actually in the fucking neighborhood looking around. And then the next step is – this is where it gets really weird – with facial recognition you will be able to key in on the faces of other people in the Street View, scan through all their social data on the cloud (tweets, Facebook posts, anything that's accessible), and you will be able to assemble an artificial intelligence that would mimic their personality. So you will instill still images of people with an artificial intelligence based on their social fingerprint. What that means is, a hundred years from now, you're going to put in GPS coordinates, temporal coordinates (where your parents were, at that baseball game or whatever), and you will be able to have an animated conversation with avatars of your parents, based on their social thumbprint. That's *going to happen*, man. So every time you're taking a selfie and uploading it the cloud, you're filling in a tiny little piece of this digital time machine. It's wild, because what we're doing with our phones is literally digitizing everything: sucking reality in, converting it to data, and storing it in these incredible storage units called hard drives. It's like granaries for time, and in the future, it's all going to get taken out, and interpolated, and refined, and recreated.

CR: Wow, that's an interesting idea.

JR: There's this idea I've come up with, and toyed around with, and it sounds completely insane given the computing power that exists today. But I think in the future, what they will be able to do – based on

"

WE'RE ALL UTOPIANS HERE. THAT'S THE FUNNY THING. WE JUST LOCATE IT IN DIFFERENT PLACES.

what we know so far – they will be able to go back in time, into a re-creation, and map out every single rock that moved in every single direction. If your computer processing power is significant enough, and the capturing of reality is accurate enough, they could possibly extrapolate back into the past.

DT: That's a time machine.

JR: That's a time machine. You would be able to re-create events based on the data. If your process was complex and accurate enough, you could – with a significant amount of data – go back in time.

DT: That's right, man. We are in the merging between history and prehistory. We are in this liminal phase in-between. We, as we are now, will end up being the low-resolution humans – in the same way we have black and white photos. When the future we travel back in time, what we are now will be the avatars you will visit, that just aren't quite right.

CR: Yeah, because we didn't give up enough data while we were alive.

JR: They might be able to go back and de-age you. They've done that with abducted kids; they show you what they'd look like seven years later, by running it through some computer program. It's fairly accurate, apparently.

DT: You think about all this shit and then you think, "Alright, every human life – as it eventually becomes more and more recorded – will become a form of riverbed, that people from the future will be able to send their consciousness down, to re-experience all these lives that have happened." Which means that this *thing* that you think you *are*, and this *thing* that I think *I am*, is in fact just a river of consciousness... flowing through a pre-existing riverbed, and it always kind of works out this way, again and again and again. And then the attention of some futuristic being beams down into it, and lives that life, again and again and again. That's déjà vu.

CR: That's Nietzsche's theory of eternal return, of infinite lives.

DT: Yes! So this thing you find yourself in, is just like an apartment. You're in a rental unit right now. You think it's *you*, Joe Rogan. But in fact, you're just existing in this kind of *life* that so many other consciousnesses have already inhabited. You're just getting to experience it like they did.

CR: So do each of those consciousnesses live the exact same life? Or do they just have the same identity? In other words, are they all married to Joe's wife, with Joe's kids, and Joe's job? Or are they just here as Joe's *essence*, making different decisions?

DT: I don't know. Based on this theory, part of me thinks, no: it's the exact same thing happening on repeat.

CR: I think that's Nietzsche's idea: that you don't really have any choice. Because your life is always going to be what it was, and always what it will be.

I'M HONESTLY CONVINCED THAT WHAT'S BEHIND MY SUCCESS – HOWEVER MUCH SUCCESS I HAVE – **IS THAT I'M CONSTANTLY KICKING MYSELF AND PUSHING MYSELF TO NOT BE SO LAME.**

MARY ROACH

CHAPTER 2

EPISODE #59 (MARCH 4, 2014)

Mary Roach is a popular science author, having written books on a wide range of topics including death, sex, and the race for Mars. Her latest book is Grunt: The Curious Science of Humans at War.

BODY SCIENCE | WRITING | AGING

CHRIS RYAN: I've got an idea for a podcast that I haven't put into motion yet, but the idea is to interview old people. And the catch is this: it won't be posted until you die. So you can say whatever the hell you want! This is you speaking from the grave, and that could be kind of morbid.

MARY ROACH: That's perfect. That's great.

CR: But I want to do it – I want that sort of like, "Yeah, I'm old and I don't give a shit!" kind of person. I don't want someone who's whining and feeling sorry.

MR: Well, you know, when the prefrontal cortex starts to go, they say anything. Just plug in the microphone!

CR: We could call it "Old People Say The Darndest Things."

MR: I remember when my mother was in her 80s – and my mother was a very good Catholic; New Englander Germanic background, as uptight as they come – I was sitting in her senior facility, and I asked her about the span of years between my brother and I. I said, "So six years is quite a span for someone not using birth control." And my mother said, "Well, your father had difficulty maintaining an erection"! I realized later, it must have something to do with the prefrontal cortex, which starts to disintegrate causing you to lose your impulse control.

CR: Too much information, mom!

MR: I'm convinced she answered like that because of changes in the part of the brain that normally causes you to keep that information to yourself. But at least I got an answer!

CR: It's a blessing. And you have to wonder if – and I don't want to get into intelligent design and all that – there is some sort of justice, or balance, or beauty in being old enough not to give a shit, and to just say whatever the hell you want to say.

MR: For a long time I wanted to believe that this was my mother – having held everything in all those years, dealing with my father, me, my brother, and all the hassles of life – that she had reached this point where she was just like, "Fuck it! I'm going to say anything! You ask me a question... I'm going to give you the answer you deserve."

CR: Do you have a Fuck It List?

MR: Did you make up the term "Fuck It List" just now?

CR: Not right now, but I've been toying with it for a while.

MR: I love that. A Fuck It List!

CR: I shouldn't talk about it publicly because other people will steal it. But the idea with the Fuck It List, is that you've got things that used to be on your Bucket List. And then you get to a certain age and you say, "Fuck it, I'm not going to bungee jump. Are you kidding me? Fuck that." So yeah, bungee jumping is high on the Fuck It List for me, as well as... well, my Fuck It List is pretty humble. But bungee jumping, for sure. And tattoos.

MR: I *did* bungee jump.

CR: How was it?

MR: Bungee jumping was interesting. I did it in New Zealand, where they don't give you a harness. They put a frayed-rubber-band woven thing around your ankles with an old towel, and they have you swan dive off a tiny plank. You hop out on it like you're on a pirate ship about to be pushed off the gangplank. And you jump. It took me a couple of tries; I couldn't do it. Finally I was shamed into doing it.

CR: You couldn't do it *physically*, or... ?

MR: They counted down, and I just stood there, and everyone was like "Oooh... "

CR: 3, 2, 1 – Nothing! Not jumping!

MR: Yeah. The second around, I did it. But I screamed without intending to, which I had never done in my life. I didn't know until I saw the videotape, that there was this blood curdling scream that was... *me*.

CR: Audible all the way to Australia!

MR: And my brain... you know when the station sign is off, and there's this fuzzy gray? My brain did that for a second. And then it came back on, and I'm looking at this river down below. And, of course, the survival instinct is to take in all the detail; so I have this extremely detailed memory of the whitecaps on the river. Of course, my brain was like, "There must be a solution here! Perhaps we can figure a way out of this!"

CR: Did time slow down?

MR: Yes! It felt like I had a lot of time to look at the river, and to contemplate the river; but of course, it was only a matter of seconds. So, from a neurological perspective, it was fascinating.

CR: Have you ever read Tim Cahill's essay called "The Scream of the Eagle" about parachuting? I think it was in *Outside* magazine about 20 years ago. What I remember about it, was not only did he scream involuntarily, but there was a videotape that someone had taken of him, and he could see himself trying to run in midair. His legs were like "Where you running man? You're at 9,000 feet, falling through midair!"

MR: Someone just survived a 3,500 foot fall. A young woman. There's a photograph of her doing a press conference. How is that possible? To survive?

CR: Did she land in a haystack? At least she didn't do it from a crane over a parking lot.

MR: That's actually the most brutal, because it's so low that there's very little "bouncy-bouncy." So the thing whips you around, grabs you, and stops you. People rupture blood vessels in their eyes; their eyes pop out, and they get little broken red spots. It's brutal. The higher it is, the more gentle the bounce. So it's actually very fun to jump from a high one.

CR: I think there's a metaphor there.

MR: There's gotta be a metaphor there. I'll leave that for you.

CR: It reminds me of one time I was speeding, and I went through a speed trap on some French highway. It was two in the morning and I was going 220km/hr in my friend's BMW. And we went under this bridge, and the flash from the camera was so bright that it woke him up. It was like BOOM! And so we're like, "Oh we are really screwed." But we got up to the next pay station, and nothing happened. We went through no problem. Then, later, I was talking to a cop about it and he said, "Yeah, you were going too fast. The cameras are set up to catch people who are going 10, 15, 30km over the limit. You guys were like 50km over the limit." Yeah, more like 100km over the limit.

MR: And you were encouraged and rewarded.

CR: Yeah, exactly. So, if you're going to go for it, go for it. If you're going to rob a bank, don't ask for just $10,000. I mean, come on.

MR: I used to share an office with a former bank robber who became a writer, and one day he robbed several banks in a row. And I said, "Joe, what was up with that? Were you just particularly moved that day?" And he said, "No, here's what it was: the woman pushed the button in the first bank, and I knew they were coming for me. So I'm going down the street, and there's another bank. And I thought, 'the last place they're going to look for me is in another bank.' So I went in another bank, and I robbed that bank."

CR: And they caught him.

MR: No, they didn't catch him that time. They caught him years later; I forget how, but it wasn't in a bank. And the thing that I love is that he's Latino; his name is Joe Loya. But the person who looked at one of the security cameras thought he looked Arab, so they called him the Beirut Bandit. So he felt that he could move through the world kind of immune, because they're looking for the Beirut Bandit. And he's Joe Loya.

CR: Always blame it on the Arabs. Was this pre-911?

MR: I think it was. Even back then.

* * *

CR: Do you ever have writer's block? Do you ever deal with that?

MR: Daily.

CR: Yeah? Is it really writer's block or is it just that writing's a pain in the ass?

MR: It's neither. It's just mild self-loathing. When I read, I'm constantly reading other writers and kicking myself that I'm not as good as them.

CR: This is your New England upbringing coming through here.

“” I'M HONESTLY CONVINCED THAT WHAT'S BEHIND MY SUCCESS – HOWEVER MUCH SUCCESS I'VE HAD – IS THAT I'M CONSTANTLY KICKING MYSELF AND PUSHING MYSELF TO NOT BE SO LAME.

MR: I'm honestly convinced that's what's behind my success – however much success I've had – that I'm constantly kicking myself and pushing myself to not be so lame. I sit down and I just kind of put it down in a crappy way, and then I'll go back and fix it up, and I'll do it over and over and over. And I'm constantly massaging it and trying to make it better.

CR: Do you take pleasure in it when you read it years later?

MR: Often, yeah. But I don't take pleasure until it's out there and I get good feedback from the outside world. I usually think it's horrible: with every single book I think, "This one, they're not even going to accept it."

CR: The publisher?

MR: Right. It won't even be a failure, because they're not even going to accept it. When I turned in my first book, I didn't hear from my editor until two months later. And I didn't want to contact her, I didn't want to know what was going on. I automatically assumed that she was saying, "Well, I'll just put it off, because it's going to be a difficult phone call. I'm going to have to tell Mary that we're not accepting her book." When I finally got the email, it took me two hours to get the courage to open it. And it said, "Hi Mary, sorry I haven't gotten to your manuscript yet. I'm hoping to in the next few weeks."

CR: You were talking about your motivation and how this feeling of "never being quite good enough" motivates you. Does that then prevent you from ever really enjoying it? Because it's never good enough?

MR: No, no. With me, I'm starting over every chapter, because I have a very short attention span, and I'm completely changing topics in every chapter. So I go through two days of beating myself up, trying to figure out how I'm going to frame the chapter, how I'm going to open it, what's the structure going to be – and wanting to write up a few really good paragraphs. There are always two days where nothing seems to work, and it's just misery. And then I break through that and have a sense of where things are going, and how the chapter is going to look. And then suddenly it starts to become fun. Today was really fun. I have this great chapter, I have a lot of good material, and it's really fun. But there are always two days where I think, "I can't do it! I don't know what to do, I don't know where to start, this isn't going well." It's just a pattern that happens over and over. And I'm powerless to change or eliminate the two days of torture. It's a process.

CR: It's interesting to hear about that, because your writing is so joyful and humorous. To imagine you suffering somewhere, and then coming up with all these great lines and these quirky ways to talk about stuff.

MR: Yeah, there's never a time where I'm sitting there chuckling...

CR: Chortling to yourself?

MR: Yeah, chortling at the keyboard over my own wit! No, I would say I crack myself up once per book. And it's almost never something I've written; it's somebody else's line. I remember in Spook, there's a chapter about ectoplasm, which emanated from the medium, and which spiritualists believed was the spirit made physical. Often the medium would regurgitate cheesecloth, and that was the "ectoplasm." There's a transcript of one of the scientists trying to communicate with the "beyond," and because he had this wad of wet cheesecloth – which he believed to be ectoplasm from the spiritual world – he says through the medium, "The material appears as if woven. Have you a loom in your world?" [Laughs] It just cracked me up! This really serious guy – in a tie, in a suit, communicating to the beyond – kinda just trying to figure it out. "Have you a loom in your world?" It's freaking cheesecloth dude, figure it out! Anyway, there's typically one moment per book where I'm cracking myself up.

CR: Well, your process sounds a lot nobler than mine. Someone asked Cassie (my wife) one time about my writing process. She described it quite accurately; she said, "Oh yeah, Chris writes the way a dog shits: he gets all agitated and goes around in circles for a long time and then he squats and it all comes out." That's pretty much how it works for me.

MR: One of the women I work with, her classic line is: "Poop it out! Just poop it out, Mary! Just poop it out!"

CR: Now does a book come together in your head before you start writing or do you work it out on the page?

MR: I work it out. I start writing before I even know what all the chapters will be. Sometimes I even start writing before I've got enough material for the chapters.

CR: Are you still writing proposals at this point? Or do you just go ahead and write?

MR: I *do* write proposals, but they're very basic.

CR: You've had so many walloping successes, that the publishers will take whatever you give them.

MR: I do feel a need to put it down on paper. And partly I think that's a tactic. My agent encourages me to do that, I think, because if you have a proposal, it does suggest that you have something you could take elsewhere.

CR: Ha! It's a negotiating tactic!

MR: But it is so perfunctory, and such a crappy document. Honestly, I couldn't take it elsewhere; people would laugh at me. "What is this? This isn't a book proposal! It's scrawled on toilet paper!"

CR: Well they wouldn't laugh at you, they'd laugh at someone who they *didn't know*, who didn't have a track record of success. I've noticed from my first book to my second book, it's a massively different experience.

MR: There are lots of authors who don't do proposals. You just call your editor up and say, "So how about..." And with Bonk, I essentially did just that. I was in a restaurant with my agent and my editor, and I told an anecdote about Masters and Johnson and the penis camera, and I said the next book will be about sex research. Physiological sex research. And they got all excited and said, "Sign us up!"

CR: Is that your bestselling book to date?

MR: Surprisingly, no. I thought it would be. *Stiff* has been the bestselling book. Stiff has been around the longest. Stiff – and I don't understand how this happened – got picked up as high school and college reading, and once you're on those lists, everybody looks at everybody else's list and cribs from everyone else's list. There's a wonderful lack of imagination and creativity that goes on there. It's like, "What do you have? I'm going to do that too."

CR: So what class is teaching using *Stiff*?

MR: We got English classes. We got Anatomy classes. Science classes. Summer reading. Common read programs for the particularly adventurous college or university; every now and then they choose *Stiff* as the common read.

CR: *Stiff*, by the way, is about death and how we deal with cadavers.

MR: It's kind of about postmortem careers, and interesting things that dead people have gotten up to over the years. Practical uses for dead bodies.

CR: Do you work on deadline?

MR: I do.

CR: Do you need a deadline to get it done?

MR: No. But it's good to have one. You know how that is: a project expands to fill the amount of time that you give it. So if you give it ten years, it'll take ten years. I guess do need it in that sense, but it's a pretty relaxed deadline. Some of those young adult authors are cranking out two books a year. Or if it's a timely subject matter, and you've got nine months or three months... Wah! I couldn't do it.

* * *

CR: Are you best known as a science writer, or a humor writer?

MR: Neither. People apply the term "science writer," but I don't feel comfortable with that. I don't have a science degree; I don't know what the hell I'm talking about. I know what I'm talking about to the extent that I need to know for each chapter, but it feels belittling to a *real* science writer to call *me* a science writer. And likewise, "humorist." I'm no David Sedaris, or Dave Barry, or any of those people who only do humor, and do it so well. I could never do that. I'm kind of just a science goober.

CR: So you focus on science just because you're fascinated by it?

MR: Yeah, it's very interesting subject matter. And I kind of like the fact that people learn something. Mostly my books deal with the human body, because it's endlessly interesting for me that we go through this world inhabiting these things – our bodies – and we manage to ignore them most of the time. We sort of think of ourselves as our minds.

CR: As spirits,

MR: Yeah. But you are this amazing pile of mucus, and bone, and blood, and it's amazing that it all works. I like the idea that people read my books, and they get a bit of respect or awe for that bag of guts and bones.

CR: I prefer to think we're made of stardust.

MR: Stardust!

CR: And mucus.

MR: Stardust and mucus! That'll be the title of my memoir.

CR: So if you hadn't become an author, what would be your second career choice? Would you be a doctor?

MR: No, no. I didn't take any math or science in college.

CR: Your fascination with the body doesn't extend to wanting to cut it open?

MR: No, not at all. Because science and medicine occurs at the molecular level; it's all protein receptors, and enzymes, and genetics. I think when you dive into that, it becomes as interesting as it is to me at my level, but it's so focused. I like to skate around, and keep myself in a perpetual state of wonder.

CR: So is writing one of the few ways to remain a generalist?

MR: I guess it is.

CR: Because we're visiting all these specialized worlds.

MR: Yeah. I'm very wedded to being a generalist. I have a very short attention span. And I don't want to study hard. And I don't want to go deep. I want to stick with it just as long as it's interesting, bring the reader along, and then skip on to something else.

CR: That describes my love life throughout my 20s, 30s and 40s.

MR: My 20s and 30s, yes. Definitely.

“”

IT'S ENDLESSLY INTERESTING FOR ME THAT WE GO THROUGH THIS WORLD INHABITING THESE THINGS, OUR BODIES, AND WE MANAGE TO IGNORE THEM MOST OF THE TIME.

CR: Do you ever feel like your job is to do homework for a living? Like, every book is the biggest fucking homework assignment ever. I feel that way sometimes. Instead of a 15-page term paper, it's a 300-page book.

MR: No, I don't feel that way because so much of it goes out into the world. I do twelve or more trips, and then there's an archive trip sometimes. I'm spending so much time out in the world, that it feels like I'm getting away with something.

CR: Right. People are paying you to cruise around and meet interesting people.

MR: Paying me to say, “This is really interesting, I'm going to go here and hang out for three days.” It's a wonderful privilege. Although there definitely are moments where it feels like the worst possible homework assignment. And then there are the revisions. My editor has a great instinct on how to start a book, and invariably she'll say, “This chapter back here, chapter seven, I think you should start with that.” Which means pulling the whole thing apart.

“”

I LIKE THE IDEA THAT PEOPLE READ MY BOOKS AND THEY GET A BIT OF RESPECT OR AWE FOR THAT BAG OF GUTS AND BONES.

And my initial response is always, "Fuck no! You don't understand!" Then I go, "Oh, wait a minute, that could work. I see how we could do that."

CR: So do you like taking direction?

MR: Although I have an initial reaction of horror... when I dive down into it, I kind of like the puzzle of revisions and reworking a book.

CR: And you have faith in your editor because you've worked with her a lot.

MR: She's got a good instinct and she's never wrong.

CR: It's a difficult thing as a writer - and you know this way better than I do - but my feeling is this: you have to really trust your opinion. Because it's you who's doing it; it's your voice, your ideas. Whatever direction you move, you're taking that step. But you also have to keep in mind, that because you're so immersed in it, your perspective is invalidated in a way. So if someone you really trust says, "No it needs to start with this" - that's a great gift. To have someone like that.

MR: Or somebody that says, "This goes on too long, I'm bored." There's a trap that you fall into - I think this happens a lot to people who spend time in archives - where you go, "I spent a week in this archive, therefore I've got to use this material. I've worked really hard to get this, I've got to put it in." But maybe there's a possibility that it's not very interesting, and therefore it doesn't go in. And that's what your editor does. As a writer, it's hard for you to pull back enough to see that; you have too much invested in it.

CR: Just because you spent a month in the mine, doesn't mean you found gold there.

MR: That's right.

CR: That's what Cassie did with *Sex At Dawn*. Every day she would come home from running the mental hospital and read what I had written (in her sixth or seventh language). I think it helps that it's not her first language, because she would truly read it word by word. She was the one who said, "Yeah, this isn't funny. I get it, but it's not funny." Very few people can say that to you, and that's really important.

MR: My editor will just draw a line through a sentence and just write, "No." Not I'm not sure or maybe reconsider, just "No."

CR: That's great. No ambiguity there.

MR: I may initially say, "Wait. That was my favorite line!" But eventually I come around and say, "Oh yeah, that was stupid. That was dumb."

CR: In *Sex at Dawn*, there was this extended dialogue where a scientist was sort of explaining the distillation of what I was arguing *against*. It was about two pages. So without omitting anything, I would have a paragraph of his and then I would respond. And in the margin, my editor wrote: "I can't begin to tell you how much I despise reading this."

MR: Sometimes you need that bluntness. I had an editor when I worked at the zoo, and in one of my books, I had a description of an insect zoo. I was describing katydids, and I wrote, "Itty-Bitty Katydids," because I thought that sounded cool. She wrote, "Ugh." And she was right!

CR: I used the phrase "penguin poontang" in *Sex At Dawn*, and I was unsure about it. I sent the section to my dad, and I said, "Do you think that's pushing it a bit far?" And he was like, "Hell no! Fight for that one! Keep that one in there!" A lot of people have written to me saying, "Penguin poontang, you cracked me up with that one!"

MR: There are times when you need to fight back. There will always be times when you're like, "No, you're wrong! That's one of my favorite lines, and that's staying!"

CR: Can you talk about what you're doing now? Or what's coming next?

MR: I can, legally, but I don't like to.

CR: Good. You know, I wonder about that. Because people ask me about my next book, and I talk about it, but I don't like to. I'm wondering if maybe I shouldn't?

MR: I work really, really hard to find things that aren't already over-exposed on the internet, things that are fresh and surprising, and will make people go, "Holy shit! Where'd she get that!?" And if I go around for two years spilling all the beans...

CR: So you keep your powder dry, and don't talk about it.

MR: Because of the internet. Because if there's something interesting that people would like to share, it's suddenly all over the internet. And it gets old and stale, and your book comes out in two years, and people go, "Oh yeah, I read about that on the internet." So I'm very paranoid.

CR: That's what's going to happen to me. I've already got t-shirts promoting a book that I haven't even started writing yet.

MR: But you haven't handed them out yet.

CR: They're on order. Someone else is going to write a book with that title, and everyone is going to be like, "Oh it's out!" And everyone's going to buy it, and I'll be like, "No! It's not the right one!"

MR: But there *is* a very valid argument that says you do want to be building the case through social media for the two years leading up to the book. Then when it comes out, everyone has just been chomping at the bit to get it.

CR: But with your next work, you're just going to leave us hanging here?

MR: I'm going to leave you scratching your head.

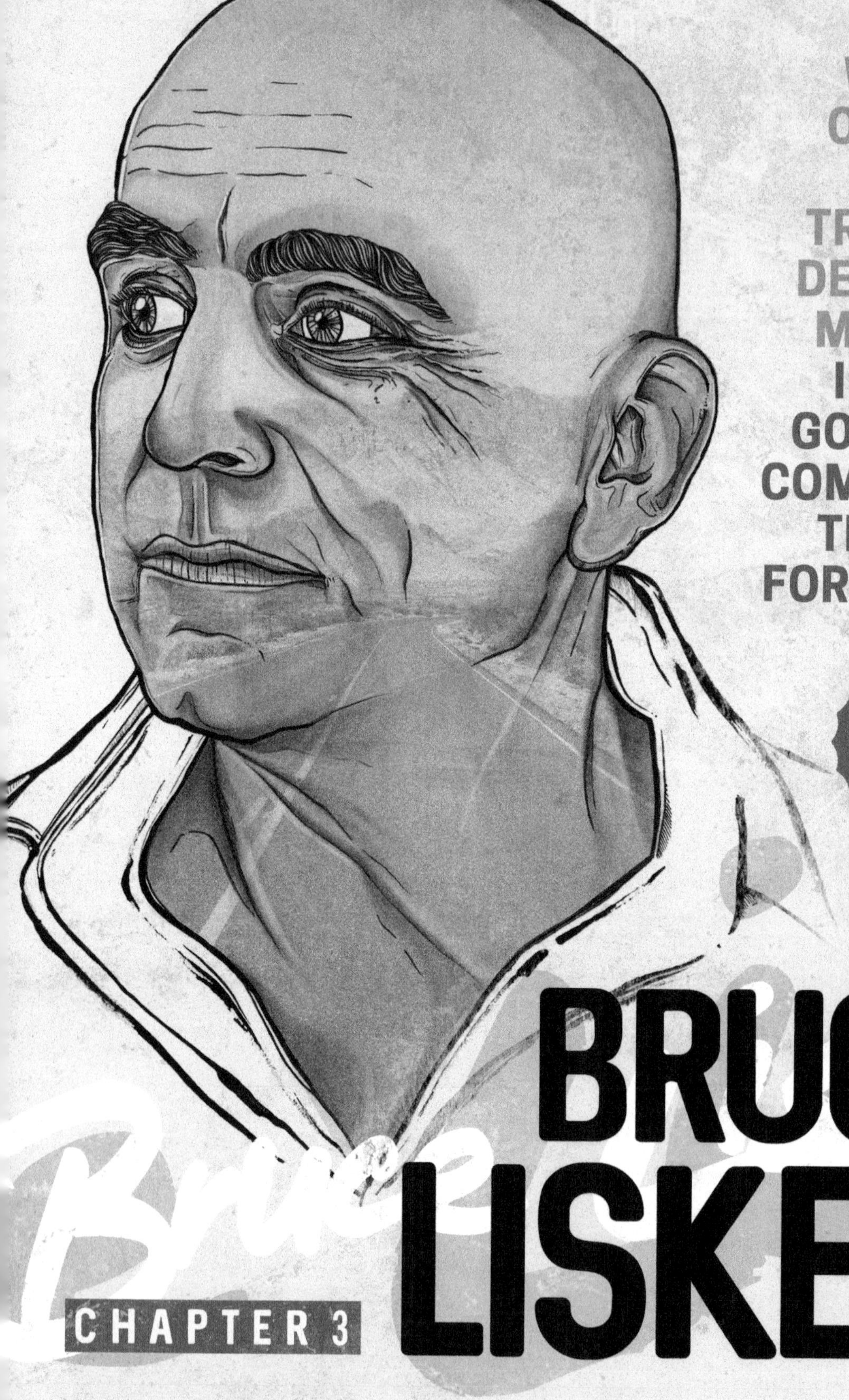

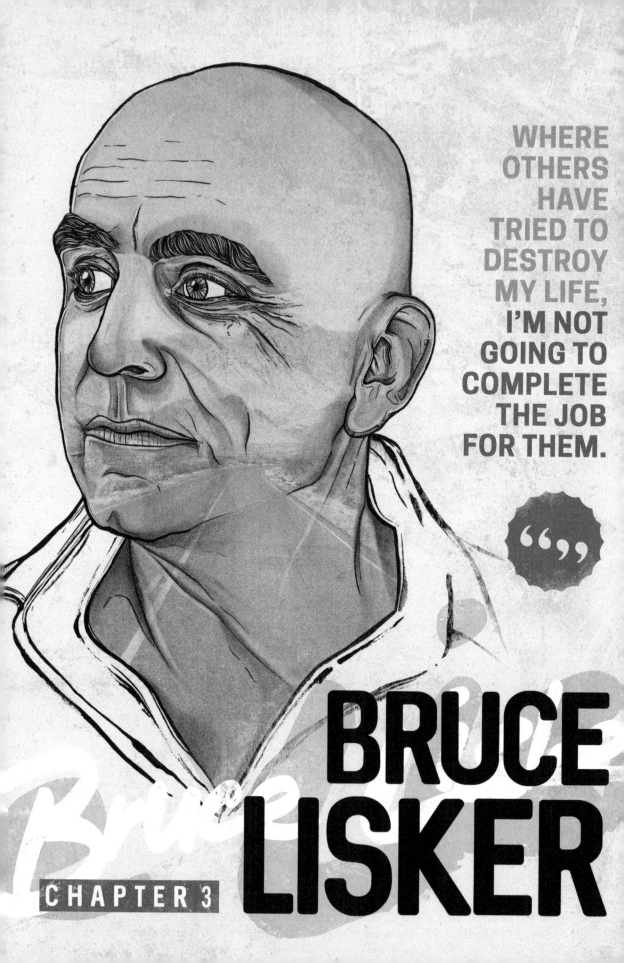

WHERE OTHERS HAVE TRIED TO DESTROY MY LIFE, **I'M NOT GOING TO COMPLETE THE JOB FOR THEM.**

CHAPTER 3

BRUCE LISKER

EPISODE #53 (FEBRUARY 11, 2014)

Bruce Lisker was seventeen when he was sentenced to prison for the murder of his mother – a crime he did not commit. He served 26 years, until California finally admitted to his innocence.

PRISON | LAW | PSYCHOLOGY | U.S. SOCIETY

CHRIS RYAN: I heard about your case from my aunt about two years ago, and I immediately thought I'd like to meet you, to hear the insights you've gained from your very unusual life. I don't want to say *tragic*, because you don't seem like a tragic guy at all. But your case is so full of tragedy, whether or not we want to frame it that way. When someone's mother dies, that's always tragic. You discovered your mother's body, which is even more tragic. And then you get accused of committing the crime. There's no way *not* to see that as tragic. But what my aunt said to me was that you're relaxed, cool, and not angry. And I didn't quite believe it until I met you yesterday.

BRUCE LISKER: I find it interesting, the way you frame that. It's so important because, as individuals, we create for ourselves the way we're going to respond to life. Good and bad things happen to all of us; to some of us it's more extreme on the bad or the good side. How we set ourselves up, how we determine how we're going to respond to everything that comes our way... all of that informs how happy we are throughout our lives. Where others have tried to destroy *my* life, I'm not going to complete the job for them. Life is ten percent what happens to us, and ninety percent how we react to it. And I'm just not going to hold a grudge.

CR: You should read *Man's Search For Meaning* by Viktor Frankl. Frankl was a psychoanalyst living in Vienna when the Second World War started. Being pretty well known, he was offered opportunities to leave, to get out and go to America. And he didn't, because he felt he should stick around and take care of his parents, who couldn't get out. So he stayed. Of course, both he and his parents were sent to concentration camps. His parents and wife died there, while he survived. In the first half of the book he writes about the concentration camps, and in the second half of the book are life lessons he took from the experience – and how he applied those to his psychotherapy. One of the things he keeps coming back to is exactly what you just said: we choose how we frame our experiences. We don't choose our experiences, but we choose the story in which they're embedded. That's the story we tell, and that's what we can control. It's kind of Buddhist-like. Have you studied Buddhism at all?

BL: Spiritually, I'm kind of a mutt. There are far fewer atheists in prison than there are out here. When things get extreme, we look for some sense of meaning. Our minds are wired to pattern-match, and to say that things happen for a reason. Especially if you're innocent: you look for some type of higher meaning, purpose, and rationale for what's going on. So I became a born-again Christian. Then I fell away from that, and attended some Buddhist services along the way. I pick

"IN PRISON, THERE'S THIS GREAT CONFUSION ABOUT RESPECT. PEOPLE MISTAKE FEAR FOR RESPECT."

and choose what resonates with me; I'm really not a devotee of any major religion. I think man's influence on religions has spoiled any kind of raw goodness that might have been there. But I do think that if, at the individual level, we stop considering ourselves the be-all and end-all – but instead have a more egalitarian and global view of things (i.e. that other things matter) – that would benefit us all.

CR: One of the things I want to ask you about is what it's like to be in prison for 26 years, after being arrested at 17. Because the American prison system feels like a country we all know exists, one in which five to ten percent of the public spends a lot of time throughout their lives, while the rest of us never go there, even to visit. We're exposed through TV shows, but that's about it. But it's still this huge presence in society. How accurate do you think people's sense is, of what it's like?

BL: If I was to generalize, I'd say most people have about a ten or fifteen percent awareness of what it's really like to be in prison, because their exposure comes from TV and movies. The creative minds behind the media are trying to cram the entirety of the prison experience into such a small amount of time. You wind up with a lot of stabbings, assaults, and rape – when in fact, the inverse is true: there's a lot of boredom. When you take a human being who has all the trappings of freedom – a car, clothing, relationships, everything – and you strip them naked, it takes a long time for them to adjust to it. One of the first things you notice is the boredom, it's the stock-in-trade. Boredom, apathy, lowered expectations, and a constant thumb on your tail. You can't really succeed, or do very much in there. It's the nature of the beast. It's not what you expect, because what we expect comes from what we've been taught – through the limited exposure we've had.

CR: Were you in medium-security, or maximum?

BL: I started off in maximum as a 187 – the California penal code for homicide. I started in Sylmar juvenile hall, then I was in East Lake, then Youth Authority, then San Quentin for three years, and then I was in a place called Mule Creek, 30 miles southeast of Sacramento for nineteen years. So I was in maximum-security. In San Quentin, I was level four. In California, the prison is segregated into tiers: Level one, which are the lowest security, where you go out on day crews to do work in the community. Those guys are largely told to stay behind the fence and sleep there at night. Level two is behind the walls, behind the fences, but they're lower security. Level threes are higher than that, and fours are maximum. Level four, you're in a concrete cell.

CR: Did everyone know what you were in for?

BL: Pretty much. Most people know what an inmate's there for, in terms of the penal code that was violated to put you there. But specifics about individual cases? Sometimes yes, sometimes no. If it's a notorious case, it's in all likelihood been in the media, and the inmates with TVs will have heard about it.

CR: Did you ever find yourself in solitary? Or did you get into any fights? Or were you always this Zen character we find today? You must have gone through a lot.

BL: Yeah, I've been through bits of turmoil. I think I got in a total of three fights throughout the years I was in, and I lost most of those. But you *have* to fight, you have to stand up. The biggest individual in the prison yard could be picking on you, but you can't run away. Because then you're an easy target, and they'll take your radio and your stuff. You have to stand up for yourself. There *will* come a time when somebody will test you in there. Somebody will think, "This guy is weak, and I can take something from him." And you have to stand up to those people. One thing I've grown a great distaste for, over the years, is bullies. So standing up to them, even if I knew I was going to lose a fight, was something of a source of pride for me. You could look at Mike Ryan - the person who killed my Mom - as a bully; he always was. In a way, I was standing up to him.

CR: What do you think about the different views about "bad" people? The liberal view being that people end up in prison because they're unlucky: they've been abused as kids, they didn't have educational opportunities, racism that pushes people in certain ways... And, the right-wing view that some people are just *bad.*

BL: I don't agree with the right-wing view, because it's too black-and-white. And life isn't black and white, there's a lot of gray area. I'd say all of the above are factors in putting a lot of people in prison. People who feel disenfranchised, people who feel wronged, hurt people. We know this. Everybody has a light and a dark side, and it's in understanding this as individuals that we come to be more holistically in tune, in balance.

CR: There's some line about how we judge heroes by their finest moments and criminals by their least fine. It's like Obama with all the cocaine he did; he never got caught, and now he's president. But, another black kid gets caught and gets twenty years, minimum mandatory. He will never be president, he will never vote, he will never have a job. And we judge him by that. What's the difference? One guy got caught, and the other didn't. That's the difference. And what determines whether or not you get caught can come down to what color you are, what neighborhood you're in, whose car you happened to be in. It's so random, and yet we act as if there's some logic underlying it.

BL: Yeah, it's very easy to not have a disadvantaged youth, and then to sit in an ivory tower judging the people below you - when it's probably 75% sheer luck. Certainly, we were lucky to have been born in America, this nation of prosperity, and made it to 15 without starving. That's luck! A lot of people don't get there. When you get introspective, you get away from judgment, and you gain a big-picture view of things. And you have a lot of time to do that when you're sitting in a prison cell. You come to an understanding that people are products of what they've been through. Give them a break whenever possible.

CR: Ironically, such a worldview doesn't align very well with prison as a rehabilitation center, because you're killing their intellectual capacity by boring them to death. And putting them under the influence of generally not-so-great people – or at least, people who aren't going to teach them ways to become productive and to get a good job. And still, I was amazed at how kind people were when I was in. I was in for stealing a Snickers bar; that's what happened. My friend was saying the we should tell people we killed someone, just to keep others away from us. I didn't think it was a good idea; you don't lie to professional liars, they'll know it's bullshit. So we told the truth, and everyone just thought it was hilarious. I remember this big black dude who was in for rape, I think, who put his arm around my shoulder and was like, "You're gonna be alright, little man." And I just remember feeling like I loved that dude. My point is, that I was surprised at how kind people were. So I imagine, in 26 years, you've met some incredible people.

BL: Oh yeah, you meet all kinds. People are aware at a visceral level: stakes are high, stress is high, nobody wants to be there, and you might inadvertently say the wrong thing to the wrong person – which might make it your last day. The stakes are exactly that high. It's really stressful to walk around with these thoughts in your head, so you just adopt a posture, and you try to get along by treating people the way you'd like to be treated. At the end of the day, it's a pretty good lesson, it's a pretty good thing to do. But in prison, there's this great confusion about respect. People mistake fear for respect. Respect is earned; fear can be enforced, but it only goes so far. Because if you dominate somebody, and you crush his spirit, thus invoking fear, he might behave the way you want him to behave, but you've also created a powerful enemy.

So, there were a lot of people I didn't respect, but there were also quite a few who I did. Although they were dealt an unfair hand in life, they managed to treat others around them with dignity. They understood that nobody wanted to be there, and they tried to make the best of it. You know, the best way to survive when you're in prison, whether you belong there or not, is to find people who are like-minded, who are rehabilitation-minded – and surround yourself with them. They are people who have learned lessons, from whom you can learn without going through it the hard way. I hung out with mainly older people when I was in, because they had learned these hard lessons. I didn't start gambling, I didn't get into drugs, I didn't do all this other stuff a lot of people do thinking, "I'm gonna hang with the fellas and be a cool guy on the prison yard." It's a dead-end road; you're going to get yourself on a rack. I managed to get into computer class, and hang out with the older cats who were more mellow, and more mature, and more respectful. And it served me well.

* * *

CR: Did you have to join a gang at any point?

BL: I didn't. When I went in, it was a window in time when, if you were accused of homicide – if you were a lifer – people would leave you alone and let you write your own ticket. You were left to act however you wanted to, join whatever trade you wanted to, hang with whoever you wanted to... within reason. But there is a lot of racial divide you sort of have to go along with, even if you don't agree with it.

CR: Are you asking for trouble if you become friends with a black guy?

BL: It depends how close you get... everything's relative. I don't have a racist bone in my body, but if you see all the white guys hanging out with each other, then you kind of have to do that – otherwise you make yourself a target. I had friends of all races. I didn't look at race as any barrier to me making a connection with

“PEOPLE ARE AWARE AT A VISCERAL LEVEL: STAKES ARE HIGH, STRESS IS HIGH, NOBODY WANTS TO BE THERE, AND YOU MIGHT INADVERTENTLY SAY THE WRONG THING TO THE WRONG PERSON, WHICH MIGHT MAKE IT YOUR LAST DAY.”

somebody in terms of a friendship. But you just have to be careful. That's the worst bit about prison: you have to constantly think, "Where am I? Am I safe?" All this stuff that just wears you out, it's exhausting.

CR: There's so many parallels between the experience you're describing and what I hear from people who are in war zones. The keeping your head down, and getting along in a situation you're thrown into with people from completely different experiences and worlds. And what you said about fear and respect also reminded me of the military. The United States foreign policy seems to be based on making other nations fear us, rather than respect us. And as you perfectly put it, it creates enemies. And here we are. Look at the world as it is right now. So getting back to when you were in: you're innocent, you know you're innocent, you've been insisting you're innocent... I know at one point, in a probation hearing, you agreed to say you were guilty in exchange for getting out. And then they still didn't let you out. So how did they pull out of that deal?

BL: They sent me to Youth Authority where you have to talk to psychologists, and my attorney told me I had to tell them I did it, to maintain the illusion. So I'm talking to all of these psychs, and they say I don't show any signs of authentic remorse. So they sent back a report saying I wasn't amenable, and they didn't think they could change me. When the judge got the report he said he didn't realize "my problem" was this deep, and that he was going to allow me to take back my plea and go ahead with a trial. The nightmare just never stopped: it's like a snowball, it just kept getting worse and worse.

CR: So you were in a situation where, if you had gone into the psychiatric interviews, did a fake cry, and said, "I did it, I'm so sorry." You would have been going through the motions, but not showing the emotion they require. With those parameters, the only person who could have done what you were required to do would be a psychopath. It's a Catch-22.

BL: Exactly, right! This whole thing has been like the world on its ear. Black is white, white is black. Through-the-looking-glass stuff. A lie is the truth, and the truth is held to be a lie.

CR: Did people believe you, all those years when you were in? Did other prisoners just roll their eyes and go, "Yeah, man, we're all innocent."? Did you even have a chance to talk about it much?

BL: It went in waves. When I first went in Juvenile Hall I was telling every single breathing soul that this was a mistake, that I don't belong here; telling this to inmates and staff alike. And the staff were like, "Yeah, listen, you really need to say that to your attorney, I don't care." And prisoners would listen, and some of them would say, "Fuck you." Who-do-you-think-you're-better-than-me kind of thing. And then there are others who say, "Yeah, I'm innocent too." Then they start talking about their situation and you find out they're not. There were also the jailhouse snitches who would say, "Oh, really? Well, what did they say you did? I believe you." And in the case of murder, they're really interested, because if they can testify that you confessed to them, then they can get out early. This type of thing was a huge conspiracy in the L.A. County Jail system in the late 80s, and it culminated in the Grand Jury being convened in L.A., and issuing a scathing 150-page report about the practice of using jailhouse-informant testimony in criminal convictions. Once a jailhouse informant claimed I had confessed to him, lying his ass off and getting a time cut for it, I learned to shut my mouth. If it comes up in conversation with somebody you really trust, then you can share. But you don't always wear it on your sleeve.

CR: If you had to guess, what percentage of the people you met inside didn't deserve to be there?

BL: If you include everything from people framed, to trumped-up charges, to those wrongly charged... Amnesty International says it's 10% of the prison population. When I left prison, we were incarcerating 170,000 people in the state of California alone. So even if it's a tenth of what Amnesty claims, that's 1,700 people who don't belong there.

CR: I think I read it was about 1,300 people who had recently been exonerated by the Innocence Project – just by using the DNA technology that has become available.

BL: I don't know the exact number, but every one of those is such a victory for humanity: that we're able to take science, and apply it to forensics in a way that not only puts deserving people in prison, but also corrects the wrongs that have been done.

CR: How did you eventually turn things around?

BL: I had my dad send me every single page of every police report, every page of trial testimony, and every page of the Fitness and Detention Hearing (which is like a mini-trial in Juvenile to determine if there's a reason to continue to hold you). Then I had a prelim, then I had a trial, then another trial. I got every page, every paper, every scrap of documentary evidence, all into my cell, and I started to pour over it. This was shortly after I got to San Quentin prison and settled in. I started to note discrepancies, and I documented them. "This detective said this in the police report, but then in the other police report he said that, and in the prelim testimony he said something else." None of that reconciles. You can't make sense of these things. So, I documented it with footnotes, and slowly made some ground. Eventually, the list of discrepancies wound up being 100 pages with 700+ footnotes. It took years, because it's not easy to write in prison; they don't let you store stuff on computers, there's no internet access, no modern implements of productivity – I had to do it with a typewriter, where making an edit meant retyping the page. Everything was sent out and then scanned in by somebody out here, and put together into the site www.freebruce.org. It's a glacially slow crawl.

CR: Did it make it more painful, the fact that you were struggling to get out? Did you ever just feel like, "Fuck this."

BL: Oh, yeah. Hope is the biggest blessing and the biggest curse to the prisoner. It's kryptonite. You have to play it in and play it out. If you keep it too close to your vest, you're going to be depressed all the time.

CR: It's like a starving man smelling food: you just don't want to be near it.

BL: Right, but you need sustenance. Hope, like food, you can't let it go, you have to keep it there. It is the lifeblood of anybody who's doing what I was doing.

CR: Did you ever think "Fuck, maybe I did it?"

BL: No.

CR: No false confession? I mean, when you were being interrogated, you went through the motions, right? I recently read an article in *The New Yorker* about this guy who developed an interrogation technique that's used all over the world. Some people started studying it, and they found that it elicits about 25% false confessions. That's incredible, because even when the police don't mean to do it, they're supplying the information for you to give back to them, to substantiate the crime you didn't commit. It's an amazing interaction. I imagine you were being interrogated mercilessly.

BL: Yeah, it was intense. I was at the police station from about 1 PM. Interrogated by Detective Monsue who was sitting across from me with his swagger, being very accusatory. Then dad and I demanded I be given a polygraph. And by 1 or 2 AM the next morning, I was driven to Parker Center for a polygraph. I state my innocence, but they say I'm not, that I'm horribly deceptive. They were just trying and trying. And I understand the techniques they use – I've read about them in subsequent years – you're never going to get a 100% success rate. With these techniques, you are going to put more people in prison, and not all of them are going to be guilty. If you did it the other way, you'd be letting more guilty people go. So I'm not at all surprised by the 25%; the interrogation tactics are designed to elicit confessions.

CR: Right. It's not designed to elicit only true confessions. Especially with juveniles; you can get kids to say anything. I can imagine at some point you'll have enough of all of this defining your life. Your life is also about other things, right?

BL: Of course it is, but it's also about this. I think it's incumbent on people who have had unbelievable shit happen to them, especially if it's bad, to address those things, and to carry them into the present. To discuss it, and to speak wisdom and truth. To try to fix some of this stuff.

CR: In the cafés in Thailand, there are a lot of signs that say, "Go visit Americans and Europeans who are in jail here." They got picked up because they had some heroin, or marijuana, or whatever, and they end up doing five or ten years in a Thai prison – and they don't speak Thai. It's something a lot of travelers do: bring them some books, or some money, or whatever they can. Is there something in the US people can do? Should we go visit people? Should we become pen pals? Does that shit matter?

BL: Actually, I do think it matters a lot. Having sat in there for as long as I have, I've seen a lot of people go home, and I've seen a lot of people come back. One of the common denominators among the people who stayed out seemed to be viable social contact – having people who can help them. Here in California, you're given $200 at the end of sentence, after they've taken your entire life. So I've started a website called www.cellblock-services.com, which seeks to bridge that gap. Inmates send me their ads, I post them, and I connect my clients to pen pals on the outside. It costs nothing to anybody out here, but by writing to somebody, you're not only brightening their dismal day, but you're making it that much less likely that a person will reoffend.

CR: Let's swing that 180°. Are worried about people you knew inside showing up on your doorstep?

BL: Yes and no. Of course, there are people in prison who absolutely belong there and who you don't want to trust, because if you do, it might be to your own detriment. But they're the minority. True sociopaths, and people who are constantly looking to victimize innocent people, are definitely the minority in prison. Most people in prison come from a disadvantaged background, have dropped out of school, and thus have lower educational levels and perhaps lower IQs. Mentally challenged is no longer a defense to a criminal charge, so there's a lot of folks like that in there. We can thank Ronald Reagan for closing the psychiatric hospitals. Inmates are also products of what they've been through. Writing to somebody doesn't mean I'm inviting people over to my house. I have a PO box. With a bit of rational protection – which you would exercise with anyone else you might meet, even out here – I'm not worried.

The prison and criminal justice system, as it exists, is designed by those people who benefit from it being a black box. "Let us tell you what prison is like, what prisoners are like, how scared you should be of all those people in there. And by the way, give us a buttload of money so we can continue perpetuating this thing." In reality, if you gave somebody a chance, and gave somebody some rehabilitative tools, they won't want to come back. It's nicer out here than it is in there. They want to be out here.

CR: And this kills me: the same amount of money they spend per prisoner could give a guy an apartment and some basic education. In the end it would cost less than what you're spending on the prison. Especially now with the private for-profit prisons, where they guarantee a certain occupancy rate – it's incredible.

BL: Where's the motivation? If I was king for a day, I would give bonuses to every staff member whose prison exhibits the lowest recidivism rate at the end of each year. You'd have staff coming up to inmates at the tables in the day rooms saying, "Can I give you some college brochures? Can I help you out? I'll be your tutor!"

“” IF I WAS KING FOR A DAY, I WOULD GIVE BONUSES TO EVERY STAFF MEMBER WHOSE PRISON EXHIBITS THE LOWEST RECIDIVISM RATE AT THE END OF EACH YEAR.

CR: Right! The incentives are all wrong. I know there's an automatic payout in some states for a case like yours, if you're exonerated. In other states, you get shit.

BL: California is one of the ones that has a program. If you look in the penal code, you can get $100 a day for every day you were wrongly convicted. In my case – with 26 years, five months, three days (but who's counting?), or 9,653 days – that would add up to a sizable amount of money. However, I didn't even apply for it, because in essence you're applying to the D.A. And in doing this, you give up any right to sue. It isn't automatic; there's this common belief that it is, that society will compensate. But it's a pittance. The legislators who passed that legislation clearly wanted to look like they were doing a great thing for people who get screwed over by society, but they were not. It's a drop in the bucket to say, "Rather than $100 a day, we make it $10,000 a day." The number of people who were able to prove they were screwed over and wrongly convicted, like I have proven, is tiny. It's a fraction of the people who were actually screwed. It's such a minuscule number that it's a drop in the bucket budget-wise.

CR: The cop who screwed you over, Detective Monsue... is anyone looking at his other cases?

BL: I would hope so. I forget the number, but he boasted once that his testimonies, or his depositions, were in the thousands or more. I don't know, maybe I'm getting the number wrong, but it's a lot of homicide cases he's worked.

CR: It's not likely yours is the only one where he played games...

BL: No, you don't act like that in a vacuum. You don't just do this in one case, and then you're suddenly a fine, upstanding officer in all the rest.

CR: Have you ever run into him since you've been free?

BL: Yeah, I've seen him at depositions. I've actually been right across the table from him several times.

CR: How does it feel?

BL: Like I said, I'm not going to harbor resentment. I'm not going to let him rent space in my head. I'm not going to let him continue the job he did in trying to screw me over, when he tried to kill me with the weapon of prison so many years ago. I'm not going to destroy myself.

CR: How does he seem? Are you calm enough to be able to judge his behavior?

BL: He's arrogant. There's a sort of group thing that exists among his ilk at LAPD, from his generation. They slap each other on the back; it's the "you didn't do anything wrong" kind of generation. So I imagine he has no shortage of support. "If that scumbag didn't do this, he did something else. Don't worry about it. You're alright." And the hubris continues. When you're dealing with maniacs who run wild with their power – megalomaniacal people – you have to give them a wide berth.

* * *

BL: In prison, you'd see some of these guys who are just trumpeting steam out of their ears about "those faggots." And you just wait a year, someone will walk past their cell and find that same person doing something with their celly.

CR: Mentioning the homosexuality, is the situational homosexuality in prison as common as it's depicted?

BL: No, it's not. There's a lot of guys who are just like, "I'm lonely, but I have my magazines and I could just take care of myself." You don't do it in front of other people, but you give your celly some personal cell-time, and they do the same.

CR: What was your sentence, initially?

BL: Sixteen years to life.

CR: So you were considered a lifer?

BL: Yeah, I was a lifer.

CR: So what happens next? Are you going to write a book? Are you going to try to do something public with this?

BL: I speak publicly at Innocence Project. I'm always

happy and willing to do it when asked. It could have been worse, I could have been killed. The fact I'm alive and able to tell the tale, to explain how this crazy thing happened, makes it incumbent upon me to speak out. Because it makes it much less likely to happen again when you have somebody saying, "Look there! What we're doing right now is what we were doing back then!" I know we don't have the best track record as a society for learning from history's lessons, but at least the possibility's there. So I'm compelled to try, and every time I'm asked to speak, I speak.

CR: That's great because you're not only unusual in the sense that this happened to you, and you've found a way out, but you're also unique in the sense that you're articulate and well-spoken. That might not be the case for others who are innocent and find a way out. You're not a threatening guy. I wouldn't be as sympathetic to a bad-ass motherfucker covered in tattoos, even if he was innocent.

BL: Which is why it's all the more incumbent upon me to put together cohesive sentences and say, "Look. This is how it happens. I can draw you a road map. We need to change this."

CR: Well, I hope the rest of your life is filled with happiness.

BL: Thank you.

CR: Thank you for doing this.

> I THINK THAT THE CORE RESISTANCE TO PSYCHEDELICS IS THE FEAR OF OURSELVES.

RICK DOBLIN

CHAPTER 4

EPISODE #98 (NOVENBER 9, 2014)

Rick Doblin is the founder and executive director of the Multidisciplinary Association for Psychedelic Studies (MAPS). MAPS is a nonprofit that seeks to raise awareness and acceptance of the therapeutic potential of psychedelic substances. MAPS assists scientists in designing, funding, and obtaining regulatory approval for research involving controlled substances.

PSYCHEDELICS | WESTERN MEDICINE | MIND-BODY CONNECTION | PSYCHOLOGY | U.S. SOCIETY | SHAMANISM

CHRIS RYAN: I am honored to have Rick Doblin with me here, the driving force behind MAPS. Your persistence is just incredible. You just kept plowing and plowing, banging your head against a wall. Amazingly, it's the wall that's breaking before your head. It's incredible.

RICK DOBLIN: It's true. At the same time, I don't have that many good ideas, and I thought this was a really good idea. Nothing else seemed any more important or better. The crucial thing for me was to be able to enjoy the process, even though the outcome was unclear and there just was so much opposition. It just felt like this is what I needed to do, so I'm able to just keep on doing it. I had this kind of 60s hippy idea when I was 18 to become a psychedelic therapist, and try to bring back psychedelic research, and integrate psychedelics into the culture. It still seems like a really good idea: I've not had a better idea in 42 years.

CR: It's good that you had your best idea early in life and that you recognized it. Imagine if you'd been chasing second-best all this time.

RD: There was actually one moment at Esalen in the late 80s, when I was standing at the cliff overlooking the Pacific Ocean, and I just entertained this idea for a moment. I thought, "Who would I be if I wasn't interested in psychedelics – if that wasn't what I organized my life around?" I'd never thought of that since 1972, and I felt this kind of whirlpool, like a fear of not knowing who I'd be if I didn't have this organizing principle. Almost like it was pulling me over the cliff to destruction. Since then, I've not asked that question, and it still continually seems right. I think for many of us, psychedelics have stood the test of time, and they serve different purposes throughout our lifespans. It's not just something that young people do, only to give up in their 20s when they start jobs and families.

CR: Yeah, when they get "serious."

RD: There was this crucial crisis of confidence perhaps about ten to 12 years ago, when it was clear that what I was going to do was not going to be accomplished in my lifetime; that this was a multi-generational effort. In a way, I see it as being centuries in the making – from when Copernicus and Galileo were censured by the church for their new ideas, when religion and spirituality and science went off into different directions. And now it feels like they are coming together. Once I realized that my hopes at age 18 were not going to be fully realized in my lifetime, I was beset a little bit with this question: "Is this vision of integrating psychedelics into culture, and the importance of doing that, something that the younger generations would appreciate? Or is it just this historical anomaly that created all this enthusiasm in the 60s, but then once the crackdown happened, young people would begin to see it as a naïve – that in reality, psychedelics don't have this power and potential that I thought they had?"

Fortunately, right around that time, I taught a class at New College, the school that I had graduated from. After I got my PhD, I went back and taught an independent workshop and realized that some people within the new generations *did* share this view; that it wasn't just this idealistic, yet wrong-headed idea of the hippies from the 50s and the 60s. I saw that the work would be carried on by the next generation. Then I started realizing how foolish it was that I even doubted it. These drugs had been around for thousands of years, and people have valued them in innumerable ways. Our culture is actually an anomaly in the way that we've suppressed them; The Drug War, and this whole prohibition instinct, is not the natural state of being; it's more of a weird and counterproductive cultural overreaction. So now I feel a lot more relaxed about it – that the work will continue on through the generations.

* * *

CR: Is there an essential conflict between psychedelics and civilization?

RD: That is a great question, and I absolutely think the answer is no. I think that was one of the key mistakes of the 60s: this idea that those people who were advocates and involved with psychedelics were inherently counter-cultural. That set up an opposition that was destructive; you end up sort of defining yourself as the outside rebel, the counter-cultural rebel, waging war against the system. The system is bigger, and they would resist it in such a way that was destructive both to the counterculture and the culture.

I think the arc of my life has been that, at age 18, I was a counterculture, drug-using criminal. I was a draft resister to Vietnam. I was using illegal drugs. I did see myself as being on the outside. Over the last 42 years, these "us and them" dichotomies have collapsed. I think a big part of it, of course, was my getting accepted to the Kennedy School of Government at Harvard (a sort of center of establishment thinking and credibility), and getting my Masters and PhD there. But I think that the kind of forward-looking, challenging of status-quo thinking that can be generated by psychedelics, and the ways in which Timothy Leary and others talked about it as challenging existing systems – that a healthy society has people that are considered scouts, who go out and survey the new territory and report back – helps the society decide which ways to go. We've kind of, at least in the 60s, criminalized these scouts. You could say that psychedelics don't go well with unhealthy civilizations that have become too rigid and fundamentalist. I am strongly and firmly of the belief that we can integrate psychedelics and psychedelic experiences into our culture, and it will be healthy for the civilization and healthy for the scouts, and that there is no inherent contradiction. Timothy Leary went to West Point; he was part of the mainstream but rebelled against it, and was kicked out of West Point as a result. He could have chosen to stay at Harvard, but he felt more comfortable leaving.

So certain personalities like Leary helped to frame the use of psychedelics as somehow inherently corrosive of establishment thinking.

CR: Isn't there something innately contradictory in the sense that civilization relies upon hierarchies and upon a lot of mindless order-following, whereas psychedelics lead you to question all authority, and to seek a direct relationship with the transcendent, etc.? I see what you're saying about how they can be a healthy input to a thriving society, but I also feel there is something fundamentally inhuman about civilization on a scale of which we are talking about now. And psychedelics rebel against that.

RD: I do think there are really negative aspects to our civilization: we see the extinction of species, the degradation of the environment, the rise of fundamentalism, the incredible persistence of violence as a way to mediate disputes. There are a lot of things in our civilization that I think are destructive and need to be corrected. But to hold the view that this will always be the case, and that somehow there is an inherent aspect to this questioning that belongs outside of the civilization process - that civilization can't handle it - I don't think it's true. I think if we reflect on our own lives, there's so much we've got on autopilot. Even just the functioning that we do physically... think of the abilities super athletes have developed: their motions, their reactions, their responses are below the level of awareness. But they are just on autopilot, and that helps them to do higher functioning things. I think we need to ask ourselves, "What are those things that are on autopilot? Are they healthy? And do they have feedback systems that allow you to respond when something changes? So I think that civilization as a whole clearly needs a course correction.

I go back a lot to Albert Einstein, who said that the splitting of the atom has changed everything except our mode of thinking. Hence we drift towards unparalleled catastrophe. What shall be required if mankind is to survive, is a whole new mode of thinking. And what is that mode of thinking? In my view, it's this sort of mystical sense of connection and oneness that will lead us to appreciate shamans and have shamans as the core. I don't think it's a doomed quest, that because we have these tools of transformation, that there's always going to be this conflict. I would say that these tools are not as powerful as we think that they are, and that culture is more powerful. It's the context; the set and setting. If you look at some of these ayahuasca churches, they use this incredible plant tool for opening up, yet they are often encased in syncretic religious contexts that are heavily Catholic. These ayahuasca religions have emerged from hierarchical, homophobic, and patriarchal systems.

CR: Are you concerned at all about the rise of ayahuasca tourism, and the commercialization of this sort of experience?

RD: There has been a growing concern about the abuses that are taking place: sexual abuse of mostly women who travel to Peru for ayahuasca tourism. There's a lot of profiteering, and there's competition among the shamans for the business. There have been even cases of people dying from ayahuasca, then the shaman burying their body and not telling the family. There's this other tragic situation where a Charlie-Manson-like cult, who used ayahuasca, also committed murder - and in the court case, everyone is blaming ayahuasca. And at the same time, there's just been an amazing number of people who are part of what you would call this conventional civilization - some of the leaders of this conventional civilization who've been inspired by their ayahuasca experiences

A HEALTHY CIVILIZATION HAS PEOPLE THAT ARE CONSIDERED SCOUTS, WHO GO OUT AND SURVEY THE NEW TERRITORY OVER THE HORIZON AND THEN REPORT BACK.

to become more philanthropic rather than monetary. There definitely are reasons to be concerned about ayahuasca tourism. On the other hand, if you look at the good that's being done, I think it outweighs the bad.

MAPS is actually a fiscal sponsor for this group called the Ethnobotanical Stewardship Council. It's an attempt to create a self-regulatory process, like fair-trade, that industries create to protect what they are doing. In the absence of full social acceptance, we need to be moving forward with these self-regulatory processes to try to educate people about where to find shamans, clinics and centers in a responsible way. And where these clinics are not so responsible, to provide feedback and ratings so people can have more information about where they're heading. And I do think there is this naive sense that if something is from the plant, it's better than if it's synthetic. People from our own culture, where we've largely lost track of spiritual experiences, go to other cultures and somehow think that they'll suddenly become more genuine and more spiritually profound, even though it is a completely different cultural context than they grew up in. We don't often give full acknowledgment to the fact that these cultures really are different from ours, in quite a lot of different ways. We need to find ways within our own cultural context.

Personally, I *am* somewhat concerned about the problems that are coming from ayahuasca tourism. But I think the spread and diffusion of ayahuasca from the Amazon throughout the Western world has been incredibly positive. There are always risks and benefits mixed together. How do we address those risks in a way that forestalls the criminal justice system from just prohibiting the entire thing, which is pretty much where we're at.

CR: Yeah. You mentioned someone died from ayahuasca – I hadn't heard that was possible. Can you die from an overdose?

RD: It's not exactly clear what happened. This young healthy guy – a teenager, actually – went down to an ayahuasca treatment center, and their approach was for people to take ayahuasca, go into these little huts, and spend the night by themselves. The next morning they found this guy dead. How he died isn't exactly clear, but the shaman, in a panic, buried him and didn't tell the family.

CR: It could've been a snake bite or anything.

RD: Yeah. We don't hear anyone dying from LSD or psilocybin. We do occasionally hear about people dying from ibogaine and iboga, so I would say *that* is the most dangerous of all these plant-based psychedelics so far. Ayahuasca is tremendously safe in the sense that many, many, many people have taken it. When you use these drugs, there's this ego death experience, this kind of movement to the transcendent, from the personal to the transpersonal. And it's often experienced as a sense of physical death. People feel that they are physically dying, and it's rather difficult to relax and to recognize it as the symbolic death that it is. It's the idea of the ego no longer being the center of the universe. The ego doesn't really die because we are who we are, but it becomes a minor player in a bigger universe, in the sort of infinite spiritual self of this more primary mystical connection – with the ego being subsidiary to that. I think there's this very, very rare situation where people may be able to consciously choose death in these powerful altered states. What I wanted to know was how to choose the ego death, how to choose this "surrendering to what is" without it leading to *actual* death? I concluded for myself that if you are willingly going into it, even though there is a lot of fear... if you're choosing to explore rather than choosing to escape, then you'll come out of it fine.

CR: You mentioned ibogaine. I have a friend who, just last week, had an experience with a shaman. And my understanding of the situation is that probably 12 or 15 hours later, he seemed to be fine and the shaman left. And then my friend collapsed and was unconscious for two days in his apartment, and he collapsed in a way that cut off circulation to his legs. So when he was found two days later he was taken to the hospital, put in an induced coma for over a week, and they don't know if he's going to lose his legs at this point. And as you say, this is a young strong guy - and I'd never heard of anything like that. It certainly seems like a bit of malpractice to be leaving someone alone like that. Especially with ibogaine – we're talking a 72-hour experience.

RD: Just to contrast that with the psychedelic research we're doing with FDA and other research boards across the world, our sessions usually start at ten in the morning and end usually around six. But then people are required to spend the night at the treatment center. The therapist might leave then, but the night attendant comes in. The very next morning there's hours of integrative psychotherapy, reviewing what happened the day before, and really trying to do even deeper work by looking closer at some of the issues. The integration process is really important. In the afternoon people can go home, but they can't drive. Even after they're home, we have a phone call with them every day for a week – sometimes five minutes, sometimes 15 minutes, depending on the need – just to help continue the integration process. We're very careful in the research setting not to have gaps where people are unsupervised.

And to really highlight one of the fundamental differences between the recreational use of psychedelics and the therapeutic: in recreational use, people are looking for a really fun and wonderful experience, and what happens while they're under the influence is what is the deemed most important part of the experience. But in the therapeutic experience, the important element is what people bring back from the experience, and how they integrate that into their daily lives...how they're changed on a long-term basis, hopefully with the clinical problems we've been addressing with them being reduced over time. I think it's that focus on what people bring back that really keeps us grounded in safety, because there's so much contact after the experience is over – just checking in with people on a frequent basis.

CR: When you're talking about the therapeutic measures that you take, and the care and the structure that you've designed around these experiences in your research settings... it strikes me that, in a way, that's the way our culture expresses respect and sacredness – with structure and care. It's ritualistic in a sense.

RD: There is a roll for structure, there is a roll for trying to standardize things that we've learned in these moments of creation where everything is fluid – and where people are open to the new and novel, and are *really* exploring. And then trying to bring back things that become ritualized, and standardized, and can actually add structure and strength to what one is doing. It goes either way: it could be positive, or it could be negative. For me, there is a very sacred aspect to scientific procedures: that science and spirituality aren't disconnected.

* * *

RD: With the prior non-profit before MAPS, we were funding studies on the dog and the rat – toxicity studies that were the baseline FDA requirement before being able to conduct studies on humans. I happened to feel responsible for the killing of a bunch of these dogs, so I went down to the lab where the study was being done. It turned out the day I went to visit was the day they were euthanizing and autopsying a bunch of these dogs. Here we were in the basement of this multi-story hospital crowded around all these dogs. They were injected, and after just a second or so, they would crumple over and die. A minute or so later, they are being taken apart on the autopsy table, four dogs at a time. At first I thought, "Wow, this mystery of life and death..." It was awesome. It was beyond all of our capabilities to fully understand. The procedures of science – of trying to weigh, and standardize, and understand what happened to the different cells in the dogs' bodies – felt like this pathetic attempt to try to come to grips with this awesome mystery.

And yet there was something sacred about the procedures – where we tried to get over our own biases to discover what was really there. It was also a search for truth, so I felt this scientific process had a sacred element to it; I think a lot of scientists feel that way as well. The kind of procedures we set up in the therapeutic settings are a way to show respect, and to make something long-term come out of it – an appreciation, in a way, for the transformative potential of these non-ordinary states of consciousness, and the recognition that it's really just a potential; it doesn't automatically come from taking the drug. There has to be the preparation work, the integration work, and the interpretation. And with all of that together, if we're lucky, people can grow and become healthier.

CR: This might be one of the areas where the substances can be very helpful in altering the course of civilization: by making it tangible that these things cannot be reduced to pills, or to a good time, or to an easy throwaway experience – where you're just going to have a blast and learn a bunch, with no work required. I guess what I'm saying is, the same way we have taken cocoa leaves and have turned them into cocaine, or taken so many other complex, nuanced plants and experiences, and tried to reduce them to something easily packaged, sold, and replicated... these experiences resist that, and it can be dangerous to approach them without the respect and holistic appreciation for, as you say, the whole process. Coming to it with respect, and integration, and caring for experience.

RD: The best example of this for me occurred about ten years ago, when I was approached by two different women within a relatively short amount of time of each other. One of these women said that she had taken MDMA at a rave, and a memory came back to her of having previously been raped. She was with a bunch of her friends, they were partying hard, and had done the MDMA for recreational purposes. Because her friends were there to party, she felt that she couldn't talk to them about this more serious experience that she was going through. So she suppressed those memories and tried not to deal with them. But once it emerged and she tried to suppress it, it upset her balance. It was almost like PTSD, in that she was unable to get past it and unable to forget it. And it had long-lasting negative consequences. That same week, I was approached by another woman who said a similar thing had happened to her, but that she was with friends who were supportive and helped her work through it. Within an hour or so, she came to a better understanding of what had happened to her, and realized that it *wasn't* happening to her now – that it was something that had influenced her emotions and didn't need to be carried forward as a template for how everybody will react. She ended up feeling healthier, much stronger, and more loving afterwards. Hers was the same kind of context as the first woman's, and it was the same drug. But it was the reaction to the complex material that was different in the two cases. That made all the difference.

CR: Are you supporting pure research into neurology? Or is MAPS focused on more of a clinical and/or therapeutic approach to these things?

RD: We're very focused on the clinical research. We don't do it all, unless there is some really strong political importance to it. Again, my background is a combination of learning to be a therapist, and studying the politics of how we move toward integrating this into our society. From the FDA's point of view, to make a drug into a medicine, we're required to prove safety and efficacy; every pharma company faces the same set of requirements. But you don't have to have the vaguest idea of how the drug actually works. Pure science has no end to it, it just goes on and on and on, particularly when we start talking about neuroscience, with the brain being one of the most complicated things in the universe. There are billion-dollar brain initiatives being talked about. NIDA, the National Institute of Drug Abuse, is talking about a 300-million-dollar initiative just to look at the brain scans of 10,000 young people, and then again when they're 21, to see if they've used marijuana and how their brains might be different. We don't have that type of budget as a small non-profit, so we have to be more strategic with our resources. It's going to take another 18-million dollars to make MDMA into a prescription medicine, and we have 5.5-million of that in the bank. So with an annual budget of around two-million, we have to focus our resources in ways that are most likely to bring about this transition between fear and hope on the part of the public.

We've been suffering from this massive propaganda campaign in order to justify the horrors of prohibition that has demonized these drugs, exaggerated their risks, and denied their benefits. There's been this enormous reservoir of fear from parents and from everybody, that only one dose of MDMA will put holes in your brain, or your child's brain. That's something a lot of people still believe. Or that marijuana leads to heroin use. Or that LSD leads to chromosomal damage. There's all this fear. So for us, the therapeutic approach is the best way to mitigate this fear... by providing good evidence that, in certain contexts, there are more benefits than risks. We're also here to give hope to people; that's why we've strategically chosen to work with patient populations that the general public really respects and accepts as being part of the mainstream. I'm talking about veterans, and soldiers, and firefighters, and police officers. We have our first police officer with work-related PTSD enrolled in our study. We've really viewed pure research as something for other people to do; we hope our research demonstrates the therapeutic benefits, and will prompt other people, other governments, and other major foundations to say, "Well, how does this really work?" For us, I don't really care how it works, and neither does the FDA. So, while we really appreciate the value that people place on understanding how something works, it's not essential. And since we have to be strategic about our resources, we have nothing to do with pure research.

CR: But the by-product of what you're doing is opening up the way for pure research, because you're opening up the possibility of even bringing these substances into a laboratory.

RD: That is true. But the strategic value of trying to move MDMA or other drugs through the system is much higher than figuring out how they work. For example, Paul Allen, one of the founders of Microsoft, donated 25-million dollars to the SETI project, the Search for Extraterrestrial Intelligence. I do think that's a really, really important question to ask, "Are we alone in the universe?" But then again, when I think about my life, it wouldn't be any different if all of a sudden some signal comes in from somewhere, and it turns out to be some entity from another planet. It wouldn't change in a minute what I'm doing with my life. So I hope those people with enormous resources devote those resources to the search inside the brain - the search for inner space. And yet we don't yet have those resources. It's easier and more socially acceptable, in a way, for people to fund the search for extraterrestrial intelligence, rather than the search for human intelligence - something that is sorely lacking.

CR: Which is strange, because psychedelics have had such a pivotal role in creativity.

RD: Yes, but I think it gets back to this question that we were discussing a little bit earlier: can a society successfully integrate psychedelics, or will psychedelics always be this countercultural challenge to civilization? I think we're still left with this hangover from the 60s that says this work is inherently corrosive toward social structures, causing it to always be marginalized.

CR: If you don't think that they are inherently corrosive toward social structures, then what is the source of the vehement fear? Because, as you well know, the criminal penalties for possession or distribution of these substances far outweighs many other substances. And, in fact, it is harsher under minimum mandatory sentencing than second degree murder in many states. So what's the source of that vehemence?

RD: I think we can look at some of your own work into monogamy, polygamy, and how people's desires have been channeled by civilization in certain ways. I think it's because psychedelics open us up to things that have been suppressed, and many of us have grown up in somewhat repressive circumstances where our core urges and desires - particularly when you're young and you're the center of the universe - are focused on what you really want to the exclusion of what other people want. We see civilization as a way to somehow tame these innate social desires that would cause us to get into trouble if we were to fully explore them.

I think that the fundamental resistance to psychedelics is that we're all scared of parts of ourselves, and how to integrate those parts of ourselves into our own personalities, and with the society that is trying to channel us in certain ways. When we take off this veneer of consciousness, or the veneer of civilization, and we're confronted with these raw desires that are really difficult to understand, or to manage, or to fit within these more narrowly constrained social circumstances... we become scared. We're scared of ourselves, scared of letting go, and scared of what that might do to us. Scared we'll become rampaging rapists or plunders. When we bring those kinds of energies to the light of day - our negative potential and our positive potential - and then learn to express who we are, then it becomes more about what we do then as we're struggling with these energies. I think that the core resistance to psychedelics is the fear of ourselves, and that we all have that fear to some degree. In a bigger sense, psychedelics really came into Western consciousness during the 60s, and were aligned with the challenges to the status quo. We had a very rigid society at that time. We had just emerged from World War II, the Holocaust, and the power of the irrational – when people's emotions were manipulated to dehumanize Jewish people, Gypsies, gay people, and disabled people, and then to murder them on a massive scale. The power of the unconscious, when manipulated by dictators and others, is truly horrific. And I think the sort of social veneer we create is a sort of safeguard against the power of the irrational, which can be enormously destructive. The 60s were all about rationality: meditation was weird, yoga was a strange cult, death was something you didn't talk about, women were tranquilized while giving birth, men were tranquilized in the delivery rooms. Psychedelics came into widespread use in a time when this rigid culture was still very much reeling from having to deal with the Holocaust (which came about in Western Europe, the "pinnacle of civilization," you could say). Yet the irrational was so powerful that it caused the warping of that entire civilization.. I think there was this incapable rigidity that caused this clash, and caused psychedelics to be seen as inherently countercultural.

That's what we're struggling to overcome: that there are ways to do this deep dive into the unconscious with sufficient support, so that we can purify our intentions and desires, so that we can understand them and be true to ourselves. And to find (according to the theory) an even deeper sense of connection – that mysticism is the antidote to fundamentalism. And if you go deep enough into yourself, you'll find we do have this commonality, or a shared mystical experience of oneness. And if we can get people, including ourselves, to really feel this and to act from this place, then I think we'll have a healthier world. For thousands of years, psychedelics have permitted people to take this deep dive. When our normal minds are defended against that (because of all the survival tasks that require us to stay focused), it's not inherently incompatible with the social structure we hope to create – we really just have to acknowledge the fears and energies within ourselves.

One of the biggest experiences of my first DMT trip was this blissful sense of being connected with the entire sweep of history, and it was just glorious. Then I had this thought, "Hey, you're just appropriating all of the good parts of history, but if everything is within you, then Hitler is within you too." It just caused me to plummet into this kind of deep, sour depression. But it was true, there is this Hitler in all of us. There are parts of me that want to control, and dominate, and not care about others. Acknowledging that, trying to work through that, and trying not to act from that place that resides in all of us... that is what we really need to do. I'm ultimately hopeful that integrating

I THINK PSYCHEDELICS REALLY HELP US APPRECIATE THE PRECIOUS AND FLEETING NATURE OF THE MOMENTS WE HAVE.

psychedelics into our culture can be done in a healthy way – through this bigger project.

CR: You are one articulate motherfucker, I'll tell ya. When you were talking about the various things that we are running from, you mentioned birth, you mentioned death... you mentioned so many things. And it occurred to me how ironic it is that I agree with you. I think a lot of the fear of psychedelics is the fear of life itself, the fear of mortality, the fear of that thing that we know, that no other animal knows: which is that we're all going to die. How ironic that is, in light of the fact that one of the only things that can actually lessen that fear of death, is a psychedelic experience.

RD: First off, I don't know that no other animal knows they're going to die. That is an attempt to say that we are somehow different than nature, and that we're some rarefied species. I get a sense that certain types of animals, when it comes time for them to die, go off by their own; they dig being in certain kinds of places.

CR: There is also a mourning that appears in some animals, elephants certainly.

RD: I don't know that we're that unique, but I do feel that what psychedelics can help people to do, and what it helped me to do, is to be more frightened of not living fully than of dying. That promotes a certain kind of courage and a willingness to try, even in view of the fact that we're going to fuck up, and make mistakes, and that it's not going to come out the way we hope. You hear about how at the end of people's lives, they often talk about how their biggest regrets are not about the things they did, but about the things they didn't do. I think the fear of not living the life we have, that we have this precious gift we didn't ask to be born with (again, it depends what you think about reincarnation and stuff)... it is a gift given to us, and we have a very short period of time to live, and do what we can. And I think psychedelics really help us appreciate the precious and fleeting nature of the moments we have. And they have helped me and others become a little bit more courageous about trying things.

WIM HOF

CHAPTER 5

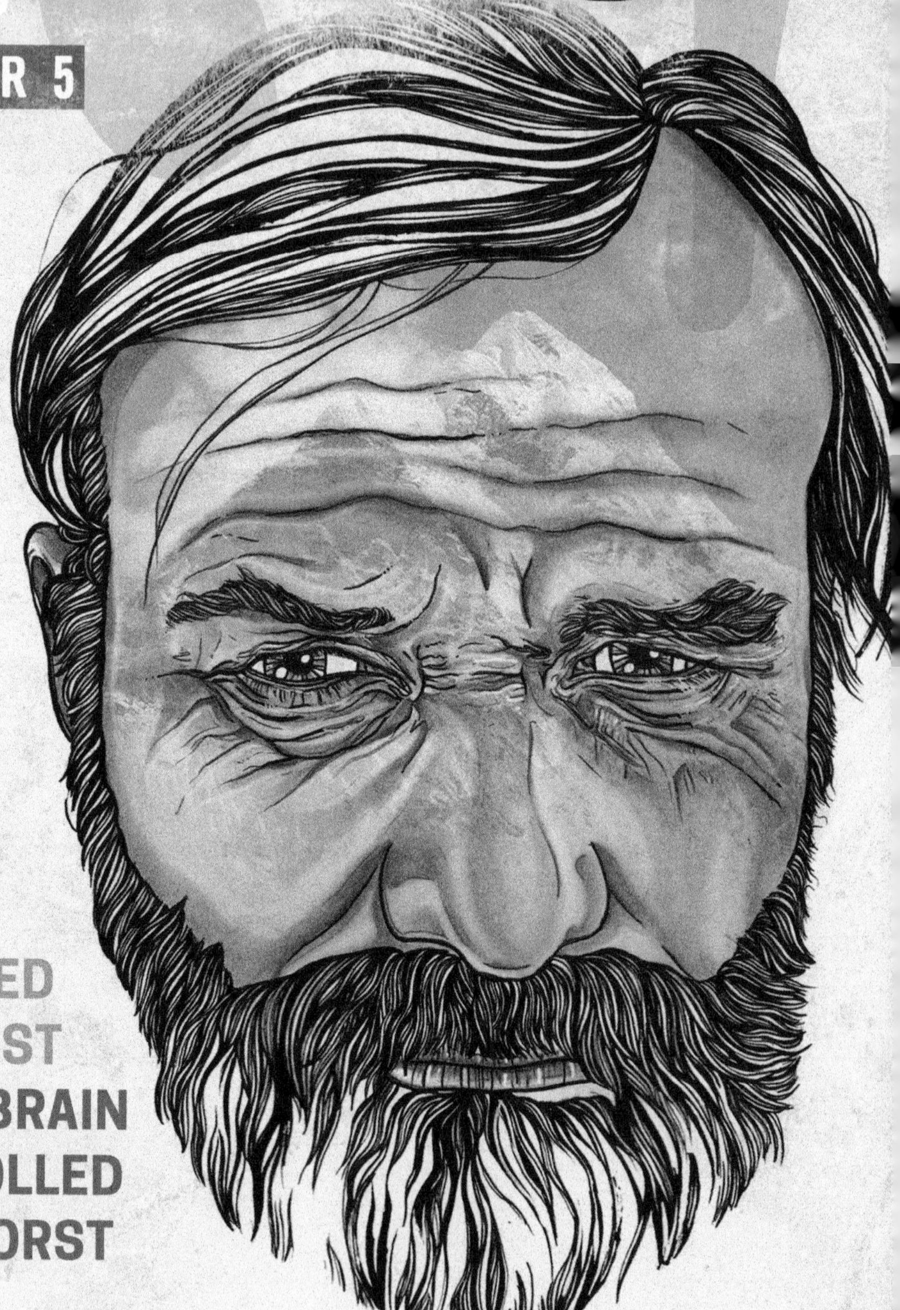

A BRAIN CONTROLLED IS YOUR BEST FRIEND; A BRAIN UNCONTROLLED IS YOUR WORST ENEMY.

EPISODE #204 (SEPTEMBER 22, 2014)
&
EPISODE 211 (W/ STANLEY KRIPPNER; NOVEMBER 7, 2016)

Wim Hof is often called "The Iceman" for his documented ability to withstand extreme cold longer than supposedly possible. Hof holds 26 world records, and is currently working with scientists to demonstrate the seemingly miraculous effects of his breathing techniques

MIND-BODY CONNECTION | WESTERN MEDICINE | SEX | SOCIETY | PSYCHOLOGY

CHRIS RYAN: I don't want to blow smoke up your ass but I have to say, when I talked to your son about doing this and he was like, "Oh we could do this over Skype or something." I said fuck that, no! Please let me come to Holland! I want to meet this guy. There are very few people who are going to be remembered by history, but I think you're one of them.

WIM HOF: Wow!

CR: You've talked about modernity. I've got this idea about modernity and comfort. I know a lot of what you work with, people would say it's about discomfort, right?

WH: Yeah.

CR: Well, I was staying with friends in Los Angeles recently and they said that in their guesthouse they had this beautiful bed with very expensive, latex technology. So I went to sleep that night, got up the next day, took a shower...and when I went to breakfast and they asked, "What did you think of the bed?" I said, "Oh, I didn't think anything actually, I just fell asleep." So I guess that was means it was comfortable. But then I thought: comfort can't be merely the absence of discomfort.

WH: Exactly!

CR: Right? Comfort is a positive thing. Comfort is pleasure! But I didn't really feel pleasure. I just felt the absence of displeasure. And I was thinking, that's the mistake of the modern world: that we're always trying to filter out every slightly negative sensation. And so we don't learn from it. But it kind of feels like your whole life, Wim, is like, "No no – I'm learning from this! And I can use this to teach people; this discomfort is full of meaning."

WH: Yes, yes! I was a soul searcher. And I didn't feel comfortable. I mean, look around. They say "comfort" and "the comfort zone," and that you can control nature, and that you can use technology. But you can't control nature by the mind alone. It's by your body and your mind together. The body has been neglected, because if we can choose between cold and warm, we always choose warm. But warm all

JUST GET BACK TO THE OPTIMIZATION OF BODY AND MIND. WHICH MEANS: USE THE ELEMENTS OF NATURE, TIME AND AGAIN. SIMPLE!

the time! Meanwhile, the cold could be a trigger for deeper mechanisms, for physiology to be stimulated. That makes us feel strong. For example, the vascular system: if you don't trigger it, like with any muscle, then the condition lowers and it becomes weak. It atrophies and the heart needs to compensate. So stress comes in. And not the right blood flow comes in. Thus the immune cells, they will get fat. So discomfort or cold is actually creating the optimization of comfort and strength for the whole body. Also, our breathing becomes shallow if we just make our minds, our environment, and our homes comfortable all the time. We not only ignore parts of our deeper physiology, but we also begin to breathe shallow.

And what happens if your oxygen is shallow for a long time? We become acidic. And where does it settle? It settles in the tissue. And now they found out that probably all autoimmune diseases are caused by being acidic in the tissue. What we do is, year after year, we get conditioned. And we think we are normal beings. And then we get sick: we get depression, autoimmune diseases, cancer, all those things – and we don't know how to treat them! Just get back to the optimization of body and mind. Which means: use the elements of nature, time and again. Simple!

CR: It is simple, and yet there's an arrogance to civilization, to modern medicine. There's a line I quote from T.S. Eliot: "We shall not cease from exploration, and the end of all our exploring will be to arrive where we started and know the place for the first time."

WH: And *consciously*.

CR: Yeah! And you're talking about cold, for example. We were talking about a teepee, about sleeping. Just recently research has shown that, if the temperature goes down ten or 15 degrees, you sleep better at night. But they call this *recent* research?! This is the way we've been sleeping for hundreds of thousands of years. It's crazy! It's like we have to go back to where we came from. And that's where everything makes sense. The diet... well, we eat what our ancestors ate. That's what we're designed to eat. The exercise patterns, the sexuality, the way we interact with other people, the way we depend on and share with one another. That's natural! Not, "Oh, this is mine! Stay away!" We've designed this world to be completely out of sync with the kind of animal that we are.

WH: Exactly. Alienation of our physiology by choice, by culture, by arrogance. Or creating a wrong mental attitude like, "We are the masters of nature, we got the technology." And this is culture, this is infrastructure, this is evolution. And humans are the best predators in the world, but then they forget themselves. They conquer everything outside of them, but inside they are deplorable and don't realize it. They don't know. So we got to wake everybody up, and the way I do it is by science. By scientific research – because nobody believes anymore.

CR: I watched the *Vice* profile they did on you and

there's a very moving moment where the question was how you felt when you were in the laboratory and I think you said you cried because you felt validation and recognition.

WH: Yeah, recognition... after 35 years of searching and stating that we are able to do so much more than we think. We are, by definition, more than we think! This connection is lost. I always stated that truth - in television shows, in challenges, in records, in everything I did - and they always told me I was crazy, mocked me... cynicism and all that. And then I lost my wife in '95 which was a lot of grief, a broken heart. And society just runs on, you know, you got to catch up all the time. I had to take care of four kids alone, and bring them up; I must say I did a good job on that. But in my heart, I was broken. But I went into nature anyway, because the only way I could get solace, or get rid of my grief, was by going into ice water or climbing steep rocks without gear, free climbing and... just nature! Nature had the answer to make me silent, to make me in tune again with myself. See for example zebras: they get attacked by lions, and ten minutes later, the herd is grazing again like nothing happened.

CR: Chill.

WH: Chill! Our minds can eat ourselves with grief! We weren't taught how to take care of ourselves in school.

CR: There's a great book called *Why Zebras Don't Get Ulcers* by Robert Sapolsky, and it's about stress. They feel acute stress, but not chronic stress.

WH: Stress oxidizes in the cell, and it deregulates the DNA epigenetically. And then yeah, you get all the problems. Deregulation of the DNA means the gene expressions become green instead of red. A cancer cell needs to become red, but it becomes green because it's deregulated. It's the stress... stress is doing that.

CR: Yeah and it goes through generations. You mentioned epigenetics: they've shown that when a man suffers from famine, his grandchildren are more likely to be obese. Even if they never knew him, even if they are adopted.

WH: Amazing! I am trying to solve all these problems now, as you do: you from your point, me from my point. And I use science for that.

CR: It's very interesting because you started with experience, and now you're moving into science. And I love that you shifted from merely demonstrating these things, into teaching people. That is so essential.

WH: And make it simple. You came up with answers as I see in your books. I directly see parallels between sexuality and in stimulating the deeper physiology because of the elements. And what do we do? We have taboos over sexuality, because we are twisted about sexuality. And we are twisted about our way to deal with nature. There's no harmony, there's no interaction. Thus the physiology is messed up, it gets into the brain, and then we get these mental attitudes - and it is creating stress. And it gets back into the DNA. I have shown, for example, with a cold physiological experiment at Maastricht University, how to combust five times more energy than another person with the same amount of brown fat adipose. I was exposed to around three hours in ten degrees Celsius (50 degrees Fahrenheit) - which is cold; it's fresh - lying still in shorts, and showing that I was able to create five times more combustion in the cell activity.

CR: So you're burning five times more calories?

WH: Ah, we talked about obesity. So famine, that's okay, it creates some affectivity in the body. But it also gets back into the DNA. So if the grandchildren become obese, it's because that has set into the DNA. Now we are able to tackle the same problem again. Now we got lots of food. But we do not know how to combust the energy. Just get back to nature.

CR: Also temperature control, right? We're living in temperature controlled environments; our bodies don't ever adapt. We're subverting all of these natural mechanisms.

WH: But also emotion, fear and trauma. We don't know how to deal with the subconscious because that organ in our brain is never stimulated. So we have no neurological pathway making us effective at influencing and dealing with our emotions, like the have. Thus we have grief, we cannot function, we live under stress. You know, stress comes anyway; if you do cold stress, it is stress. Heat stress, it is stress. When I learn things in the cold, I learn to deal with stress. Thus I learned to deal with emotions very well. I'm always optimistic, I love every day.

* * *

CR: Was this part of your plan, to attract enough attention that then you could then start get scientists interested? Was this all thought out?

WH: It was always my conviction. 25 years ago I wrote my first book, and I already stated that the autonomic nervous system and the immune system can be influenced far deeper than we think. Nobody believed it, everybody telling me, "He's crazy, he's a loner, no medical training." So in 2007, at the Feinstein Institute in New York, under the supervision of Dr. Kevin Tracey, they had me hooked up to take my blood and on the other side they had a heart and lung monitor, thinking, "Maybe this guy is able, where nobody is actually able, to influence into the vagus nerve. It's outside of our will, we cannot influence it, so let's test him." A week later I got a phone call. From Dr. Kenneth Kamler. He told me if I can reproduce this with a group of people, then that could mean huge consequences for humankind, because I influenced deeply into the vagus nerve. And the vagus nerve is responsible for so much grief and autoimmune diseases. Another professor came to me, a pneumologist, and he asked me if I could be subjected in an experiment with an E. coli bacteria, and I did it. And I showed I could suppress the effects caused by the E. coli bacteria on the immune system, which is fever, uncontrolled shivering, headaches, and all-over agony. I was able to have no symptoms at all, and to suppress inflammatory reaction of the immune system. And then they said, "Okay, you have shown that you are able to tap into the autonomic nervous system, but that's you. You are eccentric, you are so well trained, you are an exception that confirms the rule." So I told them, "No, let me train 20 people." They said, "How many days do you need to get them a little close to your results? A year?" I told them ten days!

CR: How did you know you could do it?

WH: Just a hunch! So I trained these 20 people in four days to withstand the cold, without prior experience, for five hours – from minus ten to minus 27 degrees – and to feel great doing it! And then I knew these guys are ready. In four days, not 10 days; it only took four days. So they were exposed the E. coli bacteria. Same experiment and same result: they all showed an ability to deeply influence into the autonomic nervous system and the immune system. Now there is a full chapter in the American university books about the Iceman.

CR: Wow. And all these things that they say, "No, no,

NATURE HAD THE ANSWER TO MAKE ME SILENT, TO MAKE ME IN TUNE AGAIN WITH MYSELF.

you can't control this." Of course we can control this, we control it all the time!

WH: Exactly! You can see the importance and the gravity of this all. And, talking about spirituality: we should be struck by awe, we should be in harmony with nature. It's happening every day, and we lost the wondering of it all. But besides that, being able to adapt to and tolerate cold, heat, and so-called discomfort... we got to bring this back. Because it is able to tackle not only disease to heal better, but it stimulates deeply the immune system. And brings about the right neurological pathway to learn to control the immune system, the green system, mood, and mood disorders. We are all very capable of doing that. And now we are saying depression is normal, cancer is normal, autoimmune is normal.

CR: "Take these pills."

WH: "Take these pills, take these pills." They never will make the solution, they just suppress what is acting as a signal. We suppress it and we don't remove the cause. So the cause, and the gravity of possibly reaching into the cause at will - it's there. The gravity of it is not spoken of, and we have to be very consequent on this point: that it is so simple! And now we do the science around it, so there is no speculation about it. We got to go back and live in harmony with nature, because our bodies are built that way. So we got this great brain. Years ago, NASA, control, control, rocket to the moon - great achievement! But now it's in an iPhone! The same bytes, and even more. I mean that's our brain! Our brain has evolved so much, but our body has been ignored. And now we have to bring this brain together again, aligned with the body! We got to stress this point to show the gravity of it. It's enormous! The connection between the mind and the body, and being able to create a neurological pathway - say in eight weeks - into the brain stem... from the surface of the brain (the neocortex, the thinking brain, the daily-methods brain, and all that) into that part that is primordial: the emotion, the trauma, the fear, the PTSD, the hormonal system...

CR: Right.

WH: ...the control chamber of ours which is the primitive brain, the brain stem. And so we are diving deep into that and showing that. So the gravity of your upcoming book, what you do, and what I do needs to be stressed! You got this point already figured out, but the whole world is suffering because of stress and having no way to control this stress. Because they always evade stimulation, or certain stress arises with its own neurological pathway in the brain and they're not able to directly act upon it. It's not trained, it's a muscle not trained, it's a pathway not trained, and the pattern is not there. So we are diving into that. And that will bring back the ability to intervene, to influence, and to control our mood. We have learned, and shown in hospital with people lying in bed doing this method, to create a sort of "high" from breathing exercises, and focusing to produce more adrenalin. That's control over the stress hormone; more adrenalin means being higher than somebody who's in fear for the first time doing a bungee jump. So we are able to control that. And that's what the world needs, and this should be in the schooling system from a young age: showing that everybody is able to do this from youth. Not to be alienated through the system, "Oh, mathematics are very important. And language. And history." No! Happiness too! And strength too! And health too!

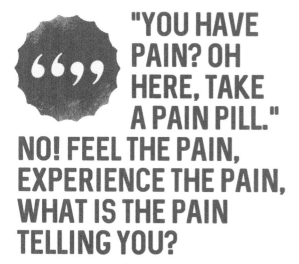

"YOU HAVE PAIN? OH HERE, TAKE A PAIN PILL." NO! FEEL THE PAIN, EXPERIENCE THE PAIN, WHAT IS THE PAIN TELLING YOU?

CR: You know you were talking earlier about how we don't address the very obvious core of the problem: we're always treating the symptoms and suppressing: "Oh, you have a fever? Take this!" And it'll cut the fever. Well, your body wants the fever because it's using the fever!

WH: It's a signal.

CR: Right, it's a signal. "You have pain? Oh here, take a pain pill." No! Feel the pain, experience the pain, what is the pain telling you?

WH: Yes!

CR: And I think about that in so many levels like foreign policy. "Oh, people are blowing themselves to kill us in Paris and New York? Oh, well let's go blow them up!" No! Why are they doing this? What is the source of the unhappiness? What is the anger? What is the injustice? People don't blow themselves up for the fuck of it.

WH: Exactly. What do you think a mother wants? Isn't it just happiness, strength and health for the kids? We are all the same! Why do we care? It's because of this system of power everywhere. We get lack of money and we get confused. It's all about the power and the money, and that's ridiculous because you cannot buy happiness, strength and health. And we need to go back to become in harmony with nature. We need to go back, or we need to make the next step in evolution.

CR: I think the next step forward *is* the step back. But I'm not saying go back to spears and spearheads; I'm talking solar panels.

WH: It's like you know with manual gear. First you got to retrieve to be able to go faster you know, before you can get it in a different gear, and to retrieve here in is becoming conscious that happiness, strength and health is actually within our dominion. We are able to control, not only the autonomic nervous system, we can do that consciously. And therefore enabling us to not get our eyes too much on what's the most valuable in life? That's health, strength and happiness.

* BEGIN TS #211 *
W/ STANLEY KRIPPNER

STANLEY KRIPPNER: The shaman will experience a personal illness, or a personal loss, and in many cases that is his or her call to shamanize. Very often they do a type of self-healing and the self-healing makes them able to heal others.

WH: I just stayed behind with four kids, you gotta keep on, and nobody is giving that power that is really helpful to heal this emotional heartbreak psychically within. So I resorted to nature and nature knows the answers yet. You have to open up toward it and there I found out not only that I was able to silence my emotional confusion caused by this broken heart and how to keep on and keep track with daily life and being alone – having no money and having four kids and going on – I learned that we are able as a human to solve this matter of emotion and grief, anxiety, fear, things that normally within our perception consciousness are not able to be tackled. Like nobody knows the way to tackle that anymore and – as you said, Stanley – a shaman needs a community. The shaman was the one who had time to heal, who have his focus and mind on that aspect – he had the talent for that empathy, took his time, tranquil, going in with his interests to people, and the rest was having food, gathering, and hunting. And that makes a tribe: caring and sharing and the shaman, everybody has this talent and it all functions as one. And we lost it and now it's a big industry with doctors and pharmacies and it's all very impersonal, you get pills and nobody knows about the inner power anymore, so the inner power and inner faculties we have shown up until now scientifically. And it needs to be scientifically otherwise the people are not going to be convinced that we are able to tap into the autonomic nervous system that related to the immune system and endocrine system makes a total different scope and dimension into what is our control over our physiology in the depth. We lost the belief to go within we go and resort to doctors and dependency and all no we got a huge power within our brain and breathing.

CR: Comfort. We build all these structures to protect us from these sorts of experiences. The hygiene hypothesis: we end up sick 'cause our immune system doesn't get trained to deal with the outer world. Or we protect ourselves from mortality. We think we're protecting ourselves by pretending no one ever dies, nothing bad ever happens. Dead people are all isolated and away from the rest of us and that robs us of the ability to develop these capacities.

WH: A brain controlled is your best friend; a brain uncontrolled is your worst enemy.

SK: The placebo effect. But the important thing is that the tribespeople believed this would help them, and as a result, they got well. Now if they didn't believe, or if they weren't suggestible, they would die and their genes would drop out of the gene pool. So over the millennia, humans have developed the capacity to be suggestible. And this is why hypnosis works. This is why self-regulation works. And now we are seeing the links between the physical body and, as you say, the autonomic nervous system, the immune system, and the endocrine system – and we can exert more control over this than we have in the past.

When I went to graduate school, we were told that the brain cannot change and that you have a certain number of cells; you can never get more. Now we know neither of those are true. Due to brain plasticity – a term that has come into vogue over the last several years – we know that many things can change the brain: meditation can change the brain, prayer can change the brain, good psychotherapy can change the brain, hypnosis can change the brain. The brain is plastic, we can change the brain ourselves with self-regulation exercises.

CR: Everything changes the brain. That's the joke. They've always taught that nothing can change the brain. But *every experience* changes the brain: orgasm changes the brain, sleep changes the brain, as you studied. Stanley, you're the senior person here, with the broadest historical perspective... when you look at the world now and relate it back to this podcast, do you think this is a unique moment for this sort of revolutionary information sharing - given that no company is directing the content of this podcast?

SK: It *is* revolutionary. However, we have to look at this in the broader context: how does all of this brain science stuff help people who are scraping by, day to day, trying to find a place to live, a place to sleep, and some food to eat for themselves and their children? As Charles Dickens says, this is the best of times, and this is the worst of times.

WH: I think so too. This comfort zone behavior is cultural conditioning, and people take it as a second nature now. And they relate to comfort, and warmth, and family, and money... but now I think we got a paradigm shift for that: to regain control over the most valuable things: our health, happiness, and strength. We actually do not have control over these anymore. We can use our new insights to help people be able to regulate these most valuables of life. Happiness, strength and health: those are the most valuable and they should be taught in the school. Right now people are homeless. Refugees come because they are into this money-mode of thinking. Power. Power is dependent on money, not on happiness. I think power, real power, is being able to maintain happiness, strength, and health. No mother in the world right now has the real evidence-based proof that we are able to tap into these systems of ours, guaranteeing our children happiness, strength, and health. No! They go and learn mathematics, history, and language - and this because you think you got to go after position and stress. And it distresses us in the moment. It gives a false sense of reality, that we have to follow a system instead of our own happiness, strength, and health. And then all the world is infected with this same mental virus of "Money is Power." I mean power or dominance? Where is the caring? Where is the sharing? Where is tribal consciousness? Where is the shaman?

CR: And when people talk about why are they pursuing domination... why do they *want* the money? In the final assessment, it's because they want to be happy, healthy, and strong. They think the money is going buy all that for them. But in fact, it's self-destructive. One of the things I was thinking while you were talking was: we're in a unique moment. I think there is a uniqueness to media, the way it's working now, in that an idea cannot be stopped, and it can spread so quickly and so rapidly. But I think another thing that may be unique, is that the Western medical paradigm has come to the end of the road. Life's not getting better anymore, we're not living longer. This is the first generation of Americans that don't expect to live as long as their parents. The Western medical model has been exposed as corrupt. So maybe that's the unique moment: that now, people are looking around for another path forward. Because this path has come to a precipice.

* * *

CR: Why is breathing so important?

WH: Breathing changes the internal chemistry directly. We learn the thinking systems of money and power instead of the basic, primordial control that we always had. But because of this culturally-conditioned way of thinking, we lost the deeper sense of ourselves. We begin to breathe more shallow. If you do that just long enough, you become acidic in the tissue and that affects our performance. You breathe deeper to cleanse yourself, in the deepest of the tissue - where all the emotion, trauma, fear, is stored chemically in the

POWER, REAL POWER, IS BEING ABLE TO MAINTAIN HAPPINESS, STRENGTH, AND HEALTH.

tissue. And we were not always able to get there, but now we are able to get there by this deeper breathing. And thus effectively change our chemistry the way nature meant to be. The neurotransmitters and electrical signals are suddenly able to connect with the cell, with the DNA - anywhere! That's the way nature meant it to be.

SK: When we talk about the body being involved, most people think that the brain has all the neurotransmitters. It doesn't! We have neurotransmitters in the heart, and we have more neurotransmitters in the gut than we have in the brain. So we actually have three brains - the gut, the heart, and the brain in our skull. And all of those work together in psycho-neuro-endocrin-immunology.

CR: When you do the cold stuff, you're focusing your mind, you're doing your breathing exercises, you're staying in a mental state... but what about when you do something like run a marathon in the desert with no water, how does that work? Do you train?

WH: No training involved, just mental power.

CR: Aren't there physiological limits?

WH: If your child is underneath a car. And you're there. You're not *thinking*. You're resorting to the inner power, and that's your unconditional love. Your mind is not in the way. And suddenly, you are able to lift that car. If your house is on fire, you run fast. If you just get the right reason or the right motivation, then the motivation will come.

CR: Do you ever have a moment where you think, "Oh shit, I'm not going to make it to end of this?"

WH: The experience of climbing without gear, steep rocks, is based on you looking at a rock. You read the rock and your body is involved in the mathematics. And you use your intuition, and you use your instinct, and the make the calculation far easier than "two and two is four." So that's the mind and the power of ours. I learned to confide therein, so much, that I played with the rocks. And 20 minutes later I was in, like, mortal situations, mindfully in peace. Why? Because intuition and instinct are able to tap into their physiology, and that together with our consciousness, that's amazing! That's a new world! And I want to bring that to neurology, and show that we are able to create a solution for those who suffer from PTSD, anxiety fear, depression, psychosis, autoimmune diseases, and even cancer! I just heard this book from Steve Curtis, who was cured completely of terminal cancer. After I talked to him and he writes in the foreword, "Wim, I am here because of you because you made me believe." I really think that we are able - with the *real* consciousness, intuition, and instinct, *together* - to have much more power in the cell, in the DNA, and in the brain stem than ever before was thought. So we got to show this. But, *people*... wake up! You got it!

“ ”

I REGARD THE LABEL PSEUDOSCIENTIST, WHICH IS FREQUENTLY APPLIED TO ME, AS A CHEAP AND EASY WAY FOR MY CRITICS TO AVOID ENGAGING WITH THE DATA THAT I PRESENT.

CHAPTER 6

GRAHAM HANCOCK

EPISODE #157 (DECEMBER 14, 2015)

Graham Hancock is a British writer and reporter. His bestselling* Fingerprints of the Gods *questions mainstream narratives of the ancient world.* Magicians of the Gods *brings more recent discoveries into the conversation.

SCIENCE | PREHISTORY | MIND-BODY CONNECTION | CONSCIOUSNESS

CHRIS RYAN: Let's start with a quick summary of what your new book is about, and how it relates to your first book, *Fingerprints of the Gods.*

GRAHAM HANCOCK: *Fingerprints of the Gods* was published in 1995, and what it proposed was that there is a forgotten episode in human history. Way back during the ice age, when our ancestors were supposedly just hunters and gatherers, we lost a civilization. I'm talking about an advanced civilization. I propose that it was destroyed in a global cataclysm between 13,000 and 12,000 years ago. I looked around for a number of possibilities to explain that cataclysm. It clearly was associated with the end of the ice age, but there was no hard science at the time. One of the reasons why I have written a new book 20 years later, is that the science on the cataclysm is still controversial.

There's a large group of very mainstream credentialed scientists who have been presenting evidence since 2007 that the earth was hit by several fragments of very substantial comet, back 12,800 years ago. There might have been a second series of strikes 11,600 years ago. And this was an extinction level event on a scale almost equivalent to the extinction of the dinosaurs 65-million years ago. This event was more than big enough to account for the loss of a civilization from the archaeological record – particularly since sea levels rose about 400 feet at the end of the ice age. I think it's a reasonable inquiry to go back into this story and to look at the new evidence that has come out. Not only the global cataclysms, but the archaeological sites that date back to that period that can't be explained.

CR: You and I have so many things in common. We'll get to some of the disagreements in a bit. But you know, thinking about this on the drive over here today, I heard you say on Rogan's podcast that you don't consider yourself a scientist. So people can't accuse you of pseudoscience, because you're not doing original research. You're a journalist who is reporting.

GH: I'm synthesizing data. If there is anything original in it, it's the big picture that emerges.

CR: You're telling a story. Which is what we did in *Sex at Dawn.* All that evidence was out there. I was actually

THERE IS A FORGOTTEN EPISODE IN HUMAN HISTORY. WAY BACK DURING THE ICE AGE, WHEN OUR ANCESTORS WERE SUPPOSEDLY JUST HUNTERS AND GATHERERS, WE LOST A CIVILIZATION.

paranoid that someone else would write the book before we got around to it. I get the same sort of criticism that you get, I think. Insiders who say: "Who the hell are you?" "What graduate school did you go to?" "How come I never... ?" What they don't get is that if I had gone through the same programs that they had gone through, or if you had, we would have lost the objectivity.

GH: Exactly. The only reason that you or I are able to tell stories like this is that we are on the outside. That is the virtue we bring to this kind of scientific issue. I regard the label pseudoscientist, which is frequently applied to me, as a cheap and easy way for my critics to avoid engaging with the data that I present. I think it is most unfortunate that it happens, but I see it happening again and again. It seems to be quite normal – as if one must have a PhD or be part of the club to be even able to discuss these issues. This is very arrogant and narrow-minded. I don't think it's helpful to science either.

CR: You're exposing the scientific community as the close-minded, insecure, highly defensive community that it is.

GH: In the broad scheme, science does eventually get rid of bad ideas and start to embrace new ideas. But, it can take a long time for that to happen.

CR: Wasn't there some quote: "science advances not because of new ideas but because of the death of old scientists."

GH: Most scientists have read Thomas Kuhn's *The Structure of Scientific Revolutions*. But they immediately forget the lessons in that book. This is actually how science progresses. The existing state of knowledge has to be completely overwhelmed and smashed to pieces by new evidence that can't be explained by the current paradigm, until that paradigm is discarded.

CR: Yeah, thanks to things like podcasts: the unfiltered access to your readers and other people with open minds.

GH: Yes, and people out there in the general public can do research faster now. They can check out information. We don't have to go to dusty libraries anymore and work our way along the shelves. The internet is an incredible source of good *and* bad information.

CR: So, one of the areas where we potentially disagree: When you say an advanced civilization was lost, what do you mean by advanced?

GH: I mean a civilization that is quite discontinuous with and out of character with the general population of the world during the ice age. A point that I often make, and I'll make it again now, is that the world that we live in today hosts an advanced technological civilization–our own. But it also hosts hunter-gatherer peoples. There are hunter-gatherer people in the Amazon that don't even know we exist, in the Kalahari Desert for example. So the notion of an advanced civilization coexisting with people of a different stage of economic development shouldn't be new or odd to us, because that happens today. And this is what I believe will turn out to be the case during the last ice age. That it wasn't just hunter-gatherers that we were taught in schools today, but there was an advanced civilization present

When I say advanced civilization, I don't necessarily mean flying to the moon or using a cellphone. I don't think that was what was involved. The evidence that I look at is, for example, ancient maps that are copied from older source maps, now lost. And in a number of cases where we have reference sources for these older source maps, the suggestion is that they came out of the library of Alexandria before it was burnt down, and made their way from there to Constantinople, and then went into a more general circulation. The thing with these maps: what we have are medieval maps, maps from the 15th and 16th centuries, which are copied or based upon older source maps. And it seems that, transferred from those older source maps is evidence of a global map-making project that was carried out during the ice age. So we can see features on some of these maps that were only present during the ice age and have been under water for 12,000 years. Suddenly they show up on these maps.

What these maps are accurately showing is the world as it looked during the last ice age. This suggests that someone at that time was in the position to explore the world, because these maps had very precise longitudes. We couldn't do longitudes until the late 18th century, and that's because a marine chronometer wasn't invented until then. When I see maps that show features of the world that were last seen 12,000 years ago, and these maps also incorporate accurate longitudes... that speaks to me of a fairly advanced civilization. A civilization that was capable of a substantial scientific feat.

Another aspect of this is the placement of very large blocks of stone, megalithic sites, where in some cases the workmanship boggles belief. For example, Saqsaywaman in Peru. What you have there are, in some cases, stones that weigh in excess of 300 tons, and which are multi-angled and joined onto other stones in a kind of 3 dimensional jigsaw puzzle. Many attempts have been made by archaeologists to explain how this has been done. I don't find their answers satisfactory at all. When I go and conduct research in the Andes, what I see is evidence of not merely one episode of culture, i.e. the Incas in the 1500s... I see the Incas building upon and respecting older structures. The character of the workmanship is such that, were it to be anywhere else, you would say obviously this is the work of different cultures. But somehow that seems to conflict with an archaeological prejudice. I think we are looking at much, much older material. Indeed we are now discovering very ancient megalithic sites where there is no argument about their antiquity... like Gobekli Tepe in Turkey, where again huge megalithic blocks are moved and set into position. In some mysterious sites like Baalbek in Lebanon... Baalbek is supposed to be entirely a Roman Temple. I don't think it is. I think parts of it are much older. I went there and

THIS IS ACTUALLY HOW SCIENCE PROGRESSES. THE EXISTING STATE OF KNOWLEDGE HAS TO BE COMPLETELY OVERWHELMED AND SMASHED TO PIECES BY NEW EVIDENCE THAT CAN'T BE EXPLAINED BY THE CURRENT PARADIGM, UNTIL THAT PARADIGM IS DISCARDED.

made a special study of Baalbek, and there is a most curious U-shaped megalithic wall. That megalithic wall incorporates 3 blocks that weigh 900 tons each, and that are raised 30 feet above the ground. My sense is that we are dealing with a civilization that had certain scientific abilities.

CR: What I was getting at is: my new book is a critique of civilization and essentially what I'm arguing for in this book is that civilization is sort of mass hysteria, analogous to the swarming of locusts. I don't know if you know this, but all locusts start off as grasshoppers. Same DNA. Same animal. But what happens is there's a tipping point where, if the population density is too high, it triggers a physiological change; their brains change, their legs change, their coloring changes, their behavior changes, and they begin to swarm. This is caused by the unusual rain patterns in the Sahara, for example. When the swarming is over, most of them die, and those that are left return to being grasshoppers.

It's similar to *quorum sensing*, where animals like salmon, at certain numbers, suddenly become a school and start behaving as a superorganism. So my argument is that civilization is a superorganism that operates according to its own agenda, its own system. And like any system, it tries to replicate itself to survive. And those interests often go against the interest of the individuals that make up the system. So, when I hear terms like "advanced civilization," alarms start beeping in my head.

GH: Well we shouldn't load it with value judgments. Advanced civilization doesn't necessarily mean good civilization, or that it's a good thing, or that it's good for humanity. That is not the case. That comes down to philosophical issues, like: what are we here for? Is there any purpose to human life? What is its function? The model we are operating on now, in advanced technological western societies, makes it seem that human life is utterly meaningless, a simple accident of biology and chemistry, and that our only purpose is to produce and consume material goods.

CR: By destroying the natural world.

GH: And by regarding the natural world as a dead entity that is to be exploited by human beings. And there is an aspect of science that comes into this as well: the materialist reductionist science, which is a very dominant voice in science today that says that everything can be reduced to matter, and that there is no more to reality than that.

Another proposition from many ancient traditions, is that we are spirits incarnated in human form; we enter this university of duality to learn, grow, and develop. This possibility is not considered at all by our society, but there is no reason to rule it out. If that were the goal and the game we are playing – that we are here to learn, grow, and develop – then civilization is not here to help us at all. It is devolving all responsibility onto large corporations, large states, and large bureaucracy – and leaving the individual in a place where there is very little responsibility.

CR: So that was my one point of disagreement, and you don't disagree!

GH: The paramount story of a lost civilization is Plato's story of Atlantis. Plato tells us in the *Timaeus* and the *Critias* that Atlantis was certainly advanced. It had mythology and it had all kinds of all kinds of incredible stone workmanship. It was a navigating seagoing civilization that could extend its power across the world. It was initially dedicated to the nature and growth of spirit, but over time, it became corrupt, wicked, and unkind. Interestingly, there is a very specific phrase that Atlantis "ceased to wear its prosperity with moderation". Plato depicts that as the ultimate reason as to why Atlantis was slapped down by the universe. It fell out of harmony with the universe. Hubris.

We see this today. We have a very fragile civilization. It appears to be strong, but it is based on specialization. It is filled with individuals who have no idea how to survive.

CR: Well, it only appears to be strong if you don't look beyond the surface.

GH: Indeed. Food not coming into the cities for three days. Break that chain of supply and you are into a horrific situation of rioting and starving. We do have a very fragile civilization. I spent quite a lot of my life in Africa, and I remember famine situations. The people who really get through famines triumphantly and are hardly touched by it, these are the hunter-gatherers, not the agriculturalists. The agriculturalists are the ones who starve. And many times the agriculturalists would be turning to them for support. It is a lesson worth learning.

CR: Right. I get this all the time: "If hunter-gatherers were so great, how come they are almost extinct, and we've taken over the world". Well, they lasted *at least* 200,000 years, and we've lasted a couple hundred and are teetering on the brink of destruction.

GH: Yeah, we're just a "pimple on the ass of the world" really. This modern civilization has no time-depth to it. It is very recent. How arrogant of us to think the way we are doing things is the right way and everybody else was wrong. This is again and again reinforced in ancient mythology. There isn't any account that I am aware of, of a global cataclysm in ancient mythology that wipes away a former age and allows a new age come into play, that doesn't in some way implicate humanity in that process. We are not distinct or separate from the universe. We are intricately interlinked.

CR: There's an incredible arrogance around scientific assumptions about materialism. I find it very frustrating when I deal with scientists who say they are not interested in something where the mechanism cannot be explained, like hypnosis. And yet, placebo is taken into consideration in every medical test that's ever done. No one's ever explained placebo! So they name it, put it in a file, and pretend that it is explained. There was a "Big Bang", but where did the "Big Bang" happen? Not to be disrespectful, because there is incredible scientific work being done, but there needs to be the humility of recognizing that science is a flashlight: where you shine the light, it illuminates. But there is a lot of darkness around that light.

GH: Perfect analogy, I bumped up against this a lot throughout my writing career. Take the issue of consciousness, which is regarded by an astonishingly large faction of credentialed scientists as simply an epiphenomenon of brain activity - reducible to a few pounds of jelly inside our skulls. It is a theory, a reference frame; it might be true, but it equally as well might *not* be true. What this does, is discourage inquiry into other areas of reality that do not fit that particular reference frame.

CR: Are you familiar with the aquatic ape theory?

GH: Yes I am. We've got this groove, here, under our noses, making me think there might be something to that theory. I think the suggestion with that thesis is that at some point, our ancestors evolved in an aquatic environment, and took on certain characteristics that animals that did not evolve in an aquatic environment do not have. Hence, our proclivity of living near water.

WE HAVE A VERY FRAGILE CIVILIZATION. IT APPEARS TO BE STRONG, BUT IT IS BASED ON SPECIALIZATION. IT IS FILLED WITH INDIVIDUALS WHO HAVE NO IDEA HOW TO SURVIVE.

CR: Just to give some other points to this theory: Humans are the only primate whose infants know to hold their breath underwater. Human babies are buoyant; they're born with all that fat; they float! The placement of our oil glands. The salinity of tears; we are the only primate that has salt-water tears.

GH: That particular thesis has been accused of being pseudoscience. Why? Because it goes up against an entrenched interest. It is a curious feature of the human creature... how much importance we place on ideas. Ideas are not things, but they behave like things. They act like things, and they can lead to enormous problems. Ideas about God lead to global conflict and to people murdering one another. There is no proof that any of those ideas are correct. Yet those the defense of those ideas will lead us to the most extreme behavior. That suggests that we become existentially attached to our particular ideas - and if the idea is attacked, then that is interpreted as an attack on us.

CR: So how do you deal with that? Being seen as an outsider by the scientific community?

GH: I've always been an outsider, since my first book. Probably even further back than that, as a child growing up in South India. I've never felt myself to be part of any mainstream trend, and I think that's partly what helps me to do what I do. As for dealing with it, I think the only answer is persistence. When you radically oppose the mainstream view, you can expect a lot of unpleasantness. Especially if you're writing books that are successful; my major crime has been writing successful books. I don't want to come across as feeling sorry for myself; I think it comes with the territory. Academics act like gangs of attack dogs, and that's a good test for ideas. If you're persistent, and your data is good, and you can defend against those attacks, then you're on the right track.

* * *

GH: I think a lot of the materialist faction of science would benefit from profound psychedelic experiences.

CR: Yeah. I love the period in the late fifties early sixties before LSD was made illegal, when it was marketed to psychologists and psychiatrists as a psychotomimetic. There is something very noble and beautiful about a psychiatrist taking LSD as a way to better understand the experience of their psychotic patients. It's very much in alignment with the shamanic practices where it is the *shaman* who takes the drug in order to better understand what you are dealing with.

GH: There was an interesting period of quite fascinating research that was stopped dead by the horrible, evil war on drugs, which by the way, is a terrible mistake made by modern society. It is quite out of step with the rest of the human story. It allowed centralized governments to create another witch

“”

I SPENT QUITE A LOT OF MY LIFE IN AFRICA, AND I REMEMBER FAMINE SITUATIONS. THE PEOPLE THAT REALLY GET THROUGH FAMINES TRIUMPHANTLY AND WELL AND ARE HARDLY TOUCHED BY IT, THEY ARE THE HUNTER-GATHERERS, NOT THE AGRICULTURALISTS. THE AGRICULTURALISTS ARE THE ONES WHO STARVE.

hunt, to hyperbolically portray drugs as some kind of existential threat to society. And now we have this war on drugs. It really gets my hackles up every time I hear the phrase "war on this" or "war on that". They are creating an internal enemy to attack and fundamentally strengthen their own position.

CR: To justify their own existence.

GH: The cost of this is the emergence of enormously expanded, armed bureaucracies that have a right to enter our deepest areas of privacy. At the same time, it has empowered and enriched criminal gangs all around us. It is so obviously, patently, painfully, a really bad idea. It is astonishing how long our society has stuck with it.

CR: I think this goes back to the idea of systems all wanting to perpetuate themselves and survive. It goes back to Thomas Hobbes' *Leviathan* and the whole founding of state machinery: the idea that we are chimpanzees with a tiny veneer of civil training, who need to be controlled.

GH: That's the myth they promote.

CR: That's the myth Steven Pinker and others are still promoting today. This idea that we are innately evil, or have bloodthirsty primate origins (e.g. original sin). But they never mention bonobos! One of the two primates we're most closely related to.

GH: It's not science, it's propaganda. Actually, hunter-gatherer societies are not big on warfare.

CR: They don't have accumulated resources; there's nothing to fight over!

GH: Exactly, and this has been the case throughout history. What actually does endanger us, and make the world very unsafe, is the behavior of states and governments, empowered by vast amounts of public money buying expensive and lethal toys. Their propaganda promotes not trusting the human creature. It's their view of what humanity is. But there's a whole other view that is not being allowed to flourish.

CR: Which happens to have the advantage of being true. As we see in Rebecca Solnit's *A Paradise Built in Hell*, we possess an innate sense of community; it's how we evolved to be.

GH: The way that human society is currently structured is deeply harmful to the human creature. Not to say it's all bad... I'm sitting here with an artificial hip, so obviously I don't reject technology.

CR: But if you'd been squatting to shit your whole life, you might not have needed the artificial hip.

GH: Quite right! Many of our current problems are a result of our current lifestyle. But I think if we're to move forward from this rather disturbing modern state of affairs, we're gonna have to find a way that doesn't reject technology; technology's going to have to be part of the story.

CR: Yeah. One of the arguments I make in this book is that we're not going back. Even if 90% of the human population disappears, we're not going back. So we are going to live in an artificial environment no matter what. But if you are a good person who owns a zoo (which is a problematic idea in itself), you will want to design the enclosures in ways that best replicate the environment of the animals. So if we are going to live in an artificial environment, which we are, let's at least study the animal that is us, the hunter-gatherers. And recreate to the best of our ability the natural environment: social, diet, exercise, everything.

GH: That is a very nice thought and a very practical proposition as well. It could lead to definite action in certain areas, instead of living in a soulless and really unpleasant urban environment, where we can't even see the sky. Our connection to the cosmos is blocked out by light pollution.

CR: In *The Marriage of the Sun and the Moon* by Andrew Weil, there is a chapter on solar eclipses. It talks about how different cultures react fearfully to the solar eclipse, including our own, telling us that you'll go blind by looking at it, which you won't; in a full solar eclipse, there are no gamma rays going into your eyes. The point that Weil makes is that the sun, which is so much larger than the earth, and the moon, which is a fraction of the size of the earth, have this bizarre relationship to the earth, where they appear to be the same size in the sky. There is no reason for this. On the surface of Jupiter, the moons don't block out the sun.

GH: It is a very odd thing. If the moon were 50,000 miles closer or 50,000 miles further away, this would not happen. I don't want to get all "woo woo" here, but there is a curious thing. In English miles, the diameter of the moon is 200,160 miles... and 200,160 happens to be part of the sequence of numbers that is found in ancient mythology all around the world. It's a multiple of 72 (72 x 30). It is the number of years that one house of the zodiac is considered to define the character of the age - by housing the sun on the spring equinox. All probably a total coincidence, but quite fascinating,

CR: Well there *is* something mysterious behind it, that's the thing. *Everything* is enveloped in mystery..

GH: Exactly.

* * *

CR: Are you familiar with Henry David Thoreau's line about the pyramids?

GH: No, tell me.

CR: Oh it's wonderful. He says this in *Walden*: "As for the pyramids, there is nothing to wonder at them so much as the fact that so many men could be found degraded enough to spend their lives constructing a tomb for some ambitious booby whom it would have been wiser and manlier to have drowned in the Nile and given his body to the dogs".

GH: Well unfortunately Thoreau – and I don't blame him – is buying into what has been the established views of what the pyramids are for the last 150 years or so. The established view being that the pyramids are tombs for egomaniacal pharaohs. What is not widely known is that there isn't a single pyramid in Egypt where an intact burial of a pharaoh has been found. Indeed, in some pyramids where they open seal chambers, they found the sarcophagus to be empty. It's an astonishing flimsy case to argue that the pyramids were built as tombs. There is no real evidence for it. Also, one hears again and again the old story that the pyramids were built by slaves. Such nonsense.

CR: Really?

GH: Complete and utter crap. I have had the privilege to climb the pyramid five times. I've been in every known nook and cranny of the great pyramid. I know it like the back of my hand, and there is no way on earth that slave labor was involved in that majestic construction. That is the work of master stonemasons at the peek of their skills, not the work of unskilled slaves whipped on by an overseer. And in any case, there is very little evidence of slavery in the old kingdom. Slavery occurred in the new kingdom.

So it's just one of those nonsense ideas that have spread around. I don't think we understand what the functions of the Giza pyramids are. Egyptology resists the notion that they reflect the patterns of certain stars from the ground such as the Belt of Orion. But anyone can see the resemblance immediately. The criticism is that anyone can pick any building, and line them up with stars in the sky. But then we have to remember that the constellation of Orion was highly significant in ancient Egypt. It was seen as the celestial image of the god Osiris, who rules over the afterlife realm.

So I think if the pyramids are anything at all, they are certainly not tombs. I believe they were part of an ancient system that the ancient Egyptians quest to transcend material life and to achieve spiritual mortality.

CR: Do you think the world would be very different if the Library of Alexandria had survived?

GH: I think it would. I think we lost a whole archive of the human story at that time, and it's partly why we are a species with amnesia, because we keep losing our records. Even the records that we're making today, can be easily lost. That's one reason why so many people are seeing connections between the way that our past is being told to us, and the way that our present is being told to us. We need to make changes in the present, and if we are going to do that, we are going to need to understand the past better.

THE KIDS IN THIS CENTURY, THIS DECADE, THEY HAVE ALL THESE IPADS AND IPODS, AND **IT'S HARD FOR THEM TO INTERACT WITH THE OUTSIDE WORLD.**

THEY'RE JUST COMING IN WITH WEED-WHACKERS **AND CUTTING DOWN THESE PLANTS THE NATIVES USE FOR MEDICINE.**

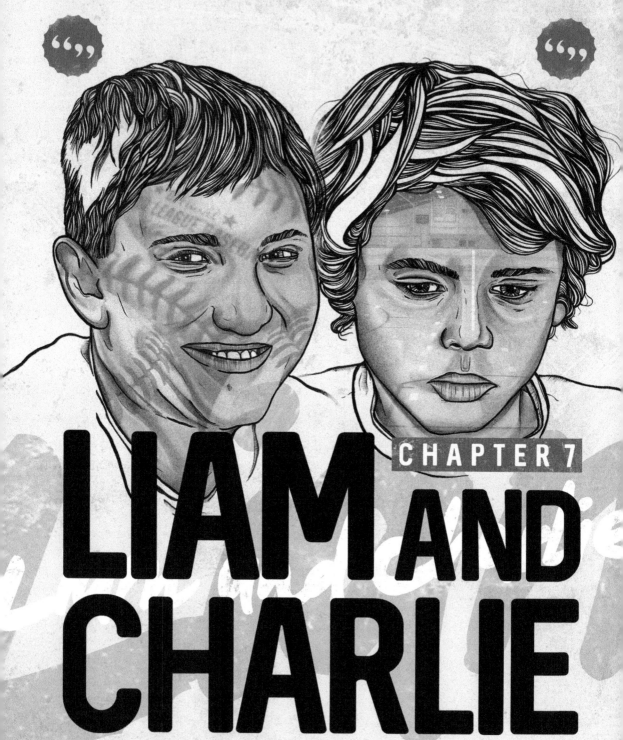

CHAPTER 7

LIAM AND CHARLIE

EPISODE #27 (APRIL 23, 2013)

Liam & Charlie, aged eleven and nine, are friends of Chris's. Despite their youth, they have lots to say on life, success, and travel.

HISTORY | LEARNING | CHILD DEVELOPMENT
RELATIONSHIPS | ENVIRONMENT | TRAVEL

CHRIS RYAN: How old are you?

LIAM: Ten. Wait no, eleven. Eleven, eleven.

CR: Changes every year, hard to remember right? Liam is an old friend of mine, as old you can you be when you're eleven. I've known Liam since the day after he was born, maybe two days after. Normally I interview doctors, film directors, and authors. People like that. I don't care if they're famous or not, I just care if they're smart and interesting. And talking with you the other night, Liam, you are pretty smart and interesting, especially for an eleven year old. First let's talk about you for a little bit: you're eleven years old, you live in Barcelona, your dad is American, your mom is Spanish Catalan. So you speak, what, three languages?

LM: Three languages but I'm currently studying French - this is my third year. And this year I started to learn German.

CR: So you speak three languages already, and you're working on fourth and a fifth. Why are you learning German?

LM: I don't know, I just think it's good to have as many languages as you can.

CR: Any other languages you want to learn?

LM: Not really.

CR: So we were talking the other night about hockey. You're a big hockey guy. We were talking about how you're growing up in this football culture. You're in Barcelona, which is like the center of the football world - football meaning soccer, for you Americans - and Barcelona is like the best team ever, year after year after year. But you prefer hockey - tell me again why you prefer hockey?

LM: Well, the feel is better for me. I don't know, I just picked up a stick and I liked it from the beginning. I kept doing it because I enjoyed it, first of all. And then I enjoyed watching it and one thing led to the next, and I think that's why I play every day.

CR: And you've got some natural talent for it as well.

LM: Yeah.

CR: So you enjoy it and you're good at it. Sometimes we enjoy things we are not very good at, or we're good at things we don't enjoy. I have a friend who is really tall and everybody always asks him why he doesn't play basketball. And he's tired of it, he's like, "Yeah, okay, I'm tall. That doesn't mean I have to play basketball." So maybe you have an advantage in something, but you're not so good at it. So you found something you're good at and that you enjoy. At eleven years old you've already got that worked out, and that's pretty good. Is there anything else that fits that category – that you're good at and you enjoy?

LM: I enjoy school, I enjoy many subjects. But with some, I just don't pay much attention. Because one thing after the next, some people don't get the first time, and they have to repeat it again.

CR: What's your favorite subject in school? If you have one?

LM: I'd say math and science, probably. And PE (physical education), if it counts.

CR: So you like math and science... you like things that have an answer.

LM: Yes.

CR: I was more on the other side, more into stories and literature and stuff. It's not like a math problem. But I do remember that sort of satisfaction when you get to the end of a math problem, and you get the answer, and it's right. That's a good solid feeling.

LM: Yeah.

CR: So you told me the other night about your backup plan if you don't make it to the big leagues in hockey – you'll go into engineering?

LM: Yeah, mechanical industrial engineering.

CR: Why that?

LM: Well, last year we went to see windmills, and they did a presentation on all that. And they said the profession for this is industrial engineering. And then I knew that that's what I wanted to do, because I found it very interesting and relating to math and science, which I both like. And it will involve experiments, which I enjoy a lot. And calculations, which I enjoy too.

CR: Are you also interested in for the ecological thing at all?

LM: Yeah, as well.

CR: So you like alternative energy sources?

LM: Yeah.

CR: That could be a good thing to be doing in the next 30 years.

* * *

CR: So, alright, I'm trying to remember when I was eleven. I'm 50, so that's a long way back. I remember a couple of things but not a lot. I remember a couple of vague stories. So if you had to guess, when you're 50, what do you think you will remember from this time in your life? When you were ten, eleven? Do you think there is anything you'll remember?

LM: Well, I will remember that I played hockey more so than normal, which isn't very usual.

CR: Right, that's true.

LM: And I will remember where I lived, probably.

CR: Yeah, that's true alright. I remember that.

LM: And, probably remember some of my friends, my closest friends, and teachers that stand out to me.

CR: What do you think about being your age – is it a good age?

LM: Yeah it's a good age. You know, you start to get more responsibilities. You start to, I would say, learn in a more efficient way. You start to be interested, you start to understand – just a bit, but not so much – about what's going to happen when you finish school; that you're going to have to do something with what you learn. You have to know what you want to do, and where you are going to study, or if you're not going to study, if you're going to be an athlete. So you have to keep this in mind always, when you are ten or eleven, and I start to panic a bit. Because all this life situation, crisis, it's kind of hard.

CR: Which life situation?

LM: For example the crisis.

CR: The economic crisis?

LM: Yeah, it doesn't affect us. Well, it does. Well, we don't understand most of the things that are happening. With crisis, it's kind of like problems, and money. Eh, you need it to move through life, that's how our civilization rose. And, that's pretty much it. Like, you start to think what will happen in the future, and you start to realize that you have to work if you want to make something work. One in many people will maybe have good grades. They want to have very good grades because they know in the future it will help them. So they think, "I want to have good grades! I want to have good grades!" But you don't have good grades just because you want to. You have to, when you go home, do your homework, and make sure you understand what you learned. And it's helpful to go over things on my own, to see if I really understand them. And if I don't, I ask the teacher the next day. Because if it pops up in the exam and you don't understand it, but you know it's in the book because you memorize it, but the exam is telling you to *explain* it, you don't know how to explain it. It's very important. Very important to *understand* more than to memorize.

CR: Very good distinction. I remember when I first started teaching. I started teaching something that I thought I understood perfectly. But as soon as I had to explain it to other people, I realized, "Wait a minute, I don't really understand this as well as I thought I did." Sort of like what you're saying – memorizing something isn't the same as learning it, and teaching it makes you know it even more deeply. So sometimes if you're not sure you understand something, and you're talking with your friend who you explain it to, then you can check to see how well you really know it.

LM: Yeah. And for me sometimes, it's a problem to study with friends. Because you don't study as well if you think, "Yeah, I already know this." They say the same stuff they already know and you say, "I know it,

I WAS LOOKING ON THE INTERNET AND I FOUND A PHRASE FROM VINCE LOMBARDI, THE POPULAR AMERICAN FOOTBALL COACH. HE SAID THE ONLY TIME SUCCESS COMES BEFORE WORK IS IN THE DICTIONARY.

I know it, I know it." Then it comes to test and it says, "Explain why *this* happens." And you go, "Whoa, I really don't know it." And then, sometimes it says, "Imagine you're explaining it to a little boy, and you have to summarize it." So you have to say important events, and importantly, what causes these. In history, they say, for studying, it is better to say cause and effect. We're studying the Hebrew kingdom and all that, Mesopotamia and civilization. So they're saying, for study guide, it is better to say cause and effect. Not to write down notes; instead of notes, you can make a t-chart and say, "This happened, and this is how it impacted civilization, how people lived their lives, or how the religion maintained itself – and what happened after that, and what affected the rest of people's lives."

CR: Yeah. So you're studying the rise of civilization now?

LM: Mostly. We have to study three things at the same time: Mesopotamia, Egypt, and the Hebrew Kingdom. So we studied Mesopotamia already, now we have to study the Hebrew Kingdoms, and then we'll study Egypt. Then we have to combine them all at the same time. It's kind of confusing because you don't study at the same time.

CR: Right. But they were all sort of *happening* at the same time, and they interacted. Certainly the Hebrew Kingdoms and Egypt, there were some important interactions there. Interesting.

* * *

CR: So you were talking about getting good grades as a way to prepare for the future. But that it's not enough to just want good grades, you have to really *work* to get good grades.

LM: In hockey, you only improve if you work. I was looking on the internet and I found a phrase from Vince Lombardi, the popular American football coach. He said the only time success comes before work is in the dictionary. Which I understood perfectly. So, you know, some people say, "I want this so bad, so bad, so bad." Then if you want it so bad, you prove it and you find a way to make it happen.

CR: You have identified talent, desire, hard work, but what about luck?

LM: Well, there's always luck if you work really hard. I think luck might come at the beginning when you start something new. And might come at the end. Because you might work really hard to beat a team, for example in sports; sometimes in my situation, you don't end up winning. But that just accumulates more desire to succeed. In the practices, you work even harder and take it even more serious.

CR: So maybe it feels like bad luck, but in the end it could be good luck?

LM: Yeah. Actually bad luck, kind of for me, should always come before good luck, because that shows me if I really want something. But if I don't really want something, that is how I identify what I need - or what I don't really need, but I want.

CR: So you like a challenge.

LM: Yeah. Sometimes it's better for me.

CR: Now speaking of challenges, you've got three sisters.

LM: Yes...

CR: So what's it like to have three sisters?

LM: Well, you always have company. So that's good. You're never actually bored, you always have something to do.

CR: One older sister and two younger sisters.

LM: Yeah because the younger sister is always offering for you to play with her, and you can play with her at any time. Sometimes she falls asleep, so you can't really play with her then. Brigitte, the one that's younger than me, I have to help her with hockey because she isn't as much motivated as me and my parents.

CR: But she wants to play hockey?

LM: She likes to play hockey, but she isn't as motivated as she should be. They ask me to help her, but it's hard to get her off the computer because with all this technology, the kids in this century, this decade, they have all these iPads and iPods, and it's hard for them to interact with the outside world.

CR: Yeah, I think you're right about that.

LM: Because all these video games and all this technology. It's okay to play one hour, or watch TV, or play your computer. But it's always good to interact with the outside world. Or do something and get moving. It's kind of like... you don't want to waste a day on the TV because that's useless. You have to get up and do something. Because that will affect your future. I still use my computer though; I use it an hour, maybe, a day.

CR: Are you tempted? Are you doing this from discipline or are you just not interested?

LM: Sometimes I like a video, maybe, and I watch it. Sometimes it just gets too boring for me. I wouldn't be able to stand spending my life in front of the TV.

CR: You need to move.

LM: Yeah, I need to move. I can't be sitting on a couch, playing my video games. I have to be up and doing something, because video games... I don't enjoy them that much. I'd much rather be doing any hockey activity, any athletic activity. Or, you know, it's always good to go to the park with your sister. They always like to go to the park to enjoy it.

CR: So living with three girls, do you think you're going to understand women better in life?

LM: Maybe. Because at the end, I think all women are the same. But they spread out in different roots, and all my sisters are different. They have some similarities, of course, but they are not exactly the same. So it just means there are more types of opinions than just three. So I think maybe some types...

CR: You know, I am sorry to interrupt you. You just said something that I think is already very insightful that a guy without three sisters might not understand. Which is that you can't generalize about women. They're all different. A lot of guys don't understand women. When they get older, they try to find out, "What's the best gift to give to a woman? What's the best thing to say to a woman?" Well, it depends on the woman, right? They're all different. So you've already hit on a pretty important point there.

LM: Like you said, it's not about giving. It's more about, evenness, I would say. I wouldn't want to be given everything. I think that with some couples, the man tries to control the woman too much, and tries to give too many things to the woman. And some women might take that, and keep it like that, but eventually they will say, "It's useless because all these things that you buy me – I can't wear 50 necklaces at once. I can only wear one. One or two or three. But, three maximum, I won't wear 50 necklaces because my neck will fall off!"

CR: So you're talking about couples, and men giving too many gifts to women, and women not really appreciating that because "enough is enough," right?

LM: Yeah.

* * *

CR: You're eleven now, but you know there is this whole new phase of your life coming in a year or two, right? What do you think about all that?

LM: I think it's going to be change.

CR: What kind of change?

LM: Well, I will eventually mature. Maybe some of my opinions will change. On how the government should be. But I don't think I'll change much. I think I am kind of straightforward.

CR: The government?

LM: Not the government, but how people should tell me what to do.

CR: Oh, are we talking about the same thing here? I'm talking about things like puberty, adolescence.

LM: Normally when you're in your teens you're like (and I learned this from my sister), "Why should I do this? Why should I do that?" You're kind of like, not doing what your parents tell you.

CR: Oh I see what you mean, you get rebellious.

LM: Yes, but I don't think I will too much. Because I think I am not as rebellious, I have never been. You can tell me something, one, two, three times maximum before I do it unless I'm in a bad mood. I don't think my thoughts will change, at all. When I say I am going to do something I am going to do it. It's never been different. It might change, but I'm pretty sure it won't. Because I already know.

CR: You think your relationship with girls will change?

LM: I don't think so. I think I'll prefer to play hockey. Hockey is my... it gets me happy.

CR: Hockey is your woman, right. Well, we'll see how long that lasts.

LM: It will last a lifetime!

CR: A lifetime? Well, you sound pretty convinced that you love hockey, that's for sure. That's good, that's a real luxury in a way – to have that kind of focus at a young age. I think that's really cool. Because when you get older – and we're talking about work now, and you know all these things can change so much. But I think it's crazy that people have to choose their career even when they're nineteen or twenty, you know? Much less ten, eleven, twelve – who knows. But if you do have a real sense of what makes you happy, there are problems you won't have to worry about later on. Then you can focus. That's cool.

* * *

CR: This conversation we're having is going to be on the internet; thousands of people are going to listen to this. One of those people, someday, could be you; ten years from now you might listen to this. Imagine you're 21 years old and you just finished college. Is there anything you want to say to that guy? Is there any message that you want to shoot into the future? Like something you don't want to forget? Do you ever think about that?

LM: I will never forget hockey. So I think that's pretty obvious for me. I think I would always thank people for what they've done. I will always thank, well, my dad for saying, "Play piano, it will be good for the future." So I will remember to thank him, because it will probably help me, because whatever he says probably happens. It normally does.

CR: He's a pretty smart guy, your dad. That's true.

LM: And he says, "Do this, do this, do this, this will help you learn more easily. And develop your brain more." And so it will probably be that way. And, hopefully, I will always thank people and be respectful, because I don't want to be disrespected. I want to be respectful and I want to be respected.

CR: Ah, right. You can't have one without the other. You know, one of the things I like about talking to you is that you seem to have a sense of life that is bigger than most kids'. Most kids are really focused on exactly where they are, and they're not really thinking about what comes later. It's hard for them to see a bigger picture. It's hard for everybody, but I think it's especially hard when you are really young. But you seem to have a bigger awareness of what's going on in life. So, when you look at life, and let's say most people live to 80 or something like that, is there any part of life that you are particularly looking forward to or worried about?

LM: Obviously when I go to Canada, I will leave my family and friends behind. I will always contact them. And yeah, that's basically it: that I will always miss whatever I leave behind, or whatever leaves me behind.

“” **IF YOU DO HAVE A REAL SENSE OF WHAT MAKES YOU HAPPY, THERE ARE PROBLEMS YOU WON'T HAVE TO WORRY ABOUT LATER ON. THEN YOU CAN FOCUS. THAT'S COOL.**

CR: Yeah, that's the truth. But, that's the price of movement right?

LM: Yeah, well you have to make sacrifices in life. If you're sure of it, you should take a risk, you know? I mean that's what you have to do.

CR: Alright, well thanks for doing this. Liam says that if you are sure, and you know what you want to do, then take the risk. That sounds like good advice to end on.

* BEGIN *
INTERVIEW W/ CHARLIE

CR: How old are you, Charlie?

CHARLIE: Nine. I'm turning ten in twenty-five days. Today's April Fools.

CR: So tell me about Ecuador. That was your second time to Ecuador; the first time you went to the Galapagos. What was that like?

CH: Really amazing. Just really beautiful. There was lots and lots of animals. There were a ton of species that you can't find anywhere else. Like half the animals there are native to Galapagos and Galapagos only. And I think I'm going to go there again with grandma next year.

CR: Dude, spread it around a bit! I've never been to Ecuador, the Galapagos, the Amazon. Hey Grandma, what about Chris?!

CH: Grandma invited me! But I was trying to go snorkeling and it freaked me out so much. I saw a shark below me, "Oh look, it's a shark." At that exact same second, my mask tipped and all this water flooded into my right eye and I'm like, "Ow, ow." And I'm feeling for this rubber dingy following me, because that was my first time really snorkeling. So I jump into the dingy and I'm like, "Shark, shark!"

CR: Was it a big shark?

CH: Yeah. Like my size.

CR: And the animals in the Galapagos aren't afraid of people, right? Some of them just ignore you.

CH: Yeah. There was this baby seal that I would just run around in circles, and its neck would literally revolve, watching me. One time I was building this sandcastle right by the water, and this seal just charges up and knocks it down. It leaves me alone, but just doesn't like my sandcastle. Then goes back in the water.

CR: It just didn't like the sandcastle.

CH: "People I can handle. Sandcastles, that's too far over."

CR: So I guess it's fair to say you like traveling. Why do you like traveling?

CH: Just because it's interesting to see how the world is, what the world is. I'm going to Ireland this summer, and next summer I'm going back to the Amazon to live with a tribe for a month. When I was in Ecuador, I met these two guys from the Cofán tribe. And to get to their tribe, it's a four hour flight, two hours by motorized canoe, and then it's an hour hike through the jungle. But then it's kind of modernized: they have stoves. But there's no lights; when the sun goes down, you don't have any light unless you bring a flashlight.

CR: Y'know, I've written a book partially about Amazon tribes and I've never even spent a day in an Amazon tribe. And you're going to live with them for a month!

EVERYONE THINKS, "OH, IT'S JUST A RAINFOREST, THESE ANIMALS CAN LIVE SOMEWHERE ELSE." THEY CAN'T! THERE IS NOWHERE ELSE.

CH: You could probably come too. I wonder how hard it will be to use the stuff they use. They use, like blowdarts, and bows and arrows. Hugo has lived in Seattle since he was ten, because they sent him up with a ton of money to get into school, and he brought back all this stuff – like a pump-action shotgun and a .22 rifle. For hunting purposes only. Because it's kind of hard to kill a jaguar with only blowdarts and a bow and arrow.

CR: That'll be fascinating. I'm really glad you're doing that; it's amazing. So do you know about the environmental stuff that's happening in the Amazon? That they're cutting it down?

CH: Yeah, they're cutting it down. And these tribes, lately, have been just standing there with spears, like, "Come any closer and you die." Everyone thinks, "Oh, it's just a rainforest, these animals can live somewhere else." They can't! There is nowhere else. This has one of the densest populations of animals in the world.

CR: And plants – a lot of the medicines we use come from the Amazon. And they haven't even begun to investigate all the different medicines that they can make. So we might be shooting ourselves in the foot by destroying all these plants.

CH: They're just coming in with weed-whackers and cutting down these plants the natives use for medicine.

CR: So, when you look forward to the rest of your life, what do you see coming? Are there things that you're really looking forward to, or things you're really not looking forward to?

CH: Yeah. Some of both. I'm looking forward to getting a car and driving.

CR: Being independent. And what are you *not* looking forward to?

CH: Bills. Taxes.

CR: Those are pretty adult concerns.

CH: The boring stuff.

“”

DEATH BOTHERS ME EVERY DAY. PEOPLE’S RELATIONSHIP WITH DEATH, AND THE WAY WE INTERACT WITH DEATH.

CAITLIN DOUGHTY

CHAPTER 8

EPISODE #25 (APRIL 11, 2013)
&
EPISODE #90 (SEPTEMBER 16, 2014)

Caitlin Doughty is a mortician, blogger and author of the bestselling book* Smoke Gets in Your Eyes & Other Lessons from the Crematory*. She advocates for an end to the culture of death denial and the reformation of the Western funerary industry.

DEATH | SEX | MORTALITY | WESTERN MEDICINE

CHRIS RYAN: You were saying that people dismiss this and say your interest in death and the processes involved with death are just a way of trying to work through stuff or to explore issues from childhood. But isn't every adult life, at least any adult life that's well lived, in some way trying to explore things that bother us? I remember in Carl Jung's autobiography, it essentially said to pay special attention to people and ideas that really bother you. Because that's where you will find yourself. There's a reason that stuff resonates.

CAITLIN DOUGHTY: Death bothers me every day. People's relationship with death and the way we interact with death. And I look at it and I'm just like, "Ugh if I could just get in there and tell you what to do." And then sometimes, if I could get in there and just figure it out myself - because I have no clue and I'm just bumbling around the universe like an idiot as well. But yes, if something *bothers* you...

CR: Yeah, don't run away from it. On a cultural level, I definitely agree with you. Our culture is sort of characterized by our avoidance of death.

CD: American culture, especially, has been so successful because of the denial of death. Death is a very humbling experience. If you really accept death into your framework, it's kind of a really humbling experience. But if you're just bullishly going through life denying death, there's a lot of hubris involved - so you're able to create this whole "American freedom and expression!" A lot of that (not to be unpatriotic) comes from a place of bold-faced, death-denying consumerism. It's all really connected to, "I'm not going to die. I'm optimistic. The world is great! I'm a powerhouse!"

CR: "I'm a god! Gods don't die!"

CD: "I'm an immortal thing. America's the best!" I think it comes from that.

CR: I think you're right. It's also ironic in a sense, because the stronger that impulse and that sort of belief system becomes, the more that short-term thinking takes over our politics, economics and everything else. I think of the famous thing the Iroquois did: every time they had to make a major decision, the seven different tribes of the Iroquois nation got together. In fact, the Iroquois political system is thought to have been the inspiration for the bicameral legislature in the United States government. Benjamin Franklin knew about the Iroquois and liked the checks-and-balances system that he saw there. But anyway, when they had to make a major decision they would say, "Okay, how is this going to affect seven generations into the future? That's how we need to make this decision." Even in our culture there is still lip service paid to, "our children and our children's children." But look at what people actually do: "Uh, we don't know what to do about nuclear waste... don't worry about it, we'll figure it out. Oh, the ice caps are melting? Whatever, it's not going to affect me. I'll be dead in 30 years."

CD: And having to admit that you're responsible for nuclear waste, or climate change, or any of these things – it diminishes us as humans presently alive. Ernest Becker, whom we are both acolytes of, writes in *The Denial of Death* that death is fundamentally affecting all of our desires to achieve, and to create, and to feel like we are contributing. So if you build a building, or if you build a nuclear weapon, or you start a war – these are all incentivized by death, these all come from death.

CR: Because we are trying to create something that will outlive us?

CD: Right, we are trying to create immortality symbols, we have our hero complex going on. We are trying to create something that demonstrates that we are a power. So if you're trying to do that in your lifetime, you're not really going to think too much of the future because you're thinking about your immortality vis-à-vis what you can actually experience in your own life – which is very short term. When you think about the people who have lived on this planet, our lives are tiny, like an ant you washed away in the sink yesterday.

CR: I know! I just turned 50 this year, and my sense of mortality grows much more intense. Everyone has heard this story, but there are all of these things you don't think about when you are young. You look at someone like Mick Jagger; he's *old*. When I was a kid, Mick Jagger was a little older than me, but he was the symbol of virility, sexuality. Now he's old. When did that happen?!

CD: Even the boy bands when I was in middle school... you look at them now, and you're like, "Ooooh, what has life done to you?!"

CR: I've been out of the U.S. for 25 years until recently, so I wasn't paying attention to these people.

CD: It's interesting because that was when I was growing up. It's like you went away, and I was living in it and becoming cognizant. It really influences you, and I'm discovering more and more how much that influence gets filtered. An anthropologist (I can't remember who) said, "we are all just caught in webs of significance."

CR: Sounds like Wade Davis.

CD: Might be, actually. Even if we can see through it, we still just completely get caught in these things, the cultural things that trap us. So when people are always like, "I hate how afraid of death I am. I hate how afraid of mortality I am." You've got to forgive them because they are caught in their culture, in what we've been taught.

CR: I have a friend who is a tattoo artist and we used to talk a lot about how pain exists as a cloud around the person who is suffering, and if you're near that person, you suffer too. So his contention was that tattoo artists spend all day suffering, like a dentist, and this leads these people to be depressed or suicidal because they are in this toxic environment. Do you feel that way when you're around people who are suffering so much emotionally? Is there a way you process that or protect yourself from it? How do you deal with that?

CD: That's a good question. I know an embalmer who worked for the mafia, and he used to always say, "That's why people have drugs and alcohol and strip clubs, that's why they do all this!" That's kind of true; there's a really high rate of alcoholism among funeral directors and embalmers, because it's a way to go home and forget seeing this pain and death. I do it differently, I think, because I worked extremely hard on my mental health. I've decided to take my mental health just as seriously as my physical health. So I really have things in place to prevent that from happening to me. And absolutely, I still have some things that really affect me – I don't think I have to become less empathetic. I still think I can understand their pain, but what has helped me to survive in the industry and keep going doing what I'm doing is not having a problem with my own death, and not having a problem with death in general as a concept

Let's say my father died. When my father dies, I'm going to be able to focus on his death, his specific death, the fact that he's gone; my issues with his death are gonna be very specific, but I'm not going to be thinking, "Oh death, what does death mean? Am I going to die? Why do people die? This is so unfair!" I'm not going to have any of those questions, because I worked so hard every day to answer them and to work towards them. So when I'm in a situation where I'm working with a family, my focus is on their specific problem, and their specific family member, and their specific desires. I'm not sitting there with the weight of these existential questions sitting on my shoulder. There's no way to not have those questions affect you, if you're not dealing with them. And a really good saying in the funeral industry is, "The only way out is through." Which is true; I've really been through it. I've worked so hard to dive right into the muckiest muck I possibly can, and to come out the other side. Or at least I'm starting to come out the other side. So that's kind of a highfalutin answer for that. I think I'm able to do this because I'm not bringing my own mortality fears into the conversation.

CR: You're reminding me of something I come back to time and time again, and I'm going to try and write about it in this book I'm working on. I think the culture is finally ready to hear this kind of stuff... You said "there's no way out but through," and that reminds me of psychedelics, and how psychedelics and altered states of consciousness are a central part of pretty much every traditional culture in the world. Sacred substances like magic mushrooms, ayahuasca, peyote, and others have been seen as the greatest gift from the gods. And here we are in this culture, where if you get caught with half a pound of mushrooms, you go to prison under mandatory minimum sentencing laws for a longer time than if you kill someone in second degree murder. What the hell is that about? Why are we so afraid of these substances? And I think one of the reasons is that these substances force you to confront your monsters, they force you to focus on your fears. People say, "Well people go crazy." Well, yeah, because they haven't faced their fears and suddenly – boom! – there they are, right in front of them. They can't take it, they've got an unstable personality structure and everything comes crashing down. I'm not advocating the use of psychedelics for anyone who is listening to this, but what I am saying is that a culture that incorporates them into the culture, and honors this process is, I think, a healthier culture.

* * *

CR: Is there some inherent link between sexuality and death or is it that we just deny both of them?

CD: I think there absolutely is! First of all, when you have sex, there's the idea of sublimation: that you don't need to be this person who lives all on your own. Because living on your own is a kind of cruel experience: the fact that we are all on this planet, but we're still individuals. It really sucks. We're trapped in our brains, trapped in our physical flesh, trapped in our own experience.

CR: Trapped in our own individuality, which is what America is all about.

CD: Which is a huge burden in a lot of ways. So, when you have sex, there's the idea that, for that moment, you are psychologically joined with another person – and they share your burden in a way. So even if you can't get inside each other's brains, you can at least get inside each other somehow, even just physically. And that emotional and mental experience can be a release, in that way. There's also the broader connection that you have sex to create life, and when you create life you create death. Women and fertility, and all those issues. I'm a woman; if I give birth to a child, I'm mother earth, I'm Gaia, I'm creating life. I'm also creating this little creature that's going to die, that's doomed to decay. That only lives by consuming, and destruction, and death. There's sex for pleasure, but there's also sex for the creation of life and death. And all those big issues are kind of at stake every time.

CR: You reminded me of this whole thing I experienced – I spent about a year in hospitals doing research, interviewing people, hanging out. One of the things I noticed was that there was this turbo-charged sexual atmosphere among specialists in areas like oncology and intensive care, and I think it's because of the phenomenon you're talking about. When you are around people who are dying, when you are reminded that death is there – no matter how much you try to avoid it, it is right over your shoulder every day. That changes the way you deal with things. The way I interpreted it, is that for the specialists in these situations, this whole impulse to put things off until later goes away. There is no later, you just do it. You want to have sex with her? Do it. Whatever it is you wanna do, do it. Don't think that you're going to do it tomorrow.

CD: Yes. Coming to that understanding, for me, felt very "Now!" Which is incredible. But there was also a pathological desperation and urgency behind it, because I hadn't been dealing with it. It's not something I struggle with now, but it's something that I struggle with defining.

CR: What's that? The sexuality?

CD: Yeah, even things that are complex can be broken down and explained pretty easily. But this one is a little bit harder to explain: the connection between Eros and Thanatos, and sex and death, and how it works for humans and how it works for me... it's still a little bit hard to define and explain to people who haven't necessarily experienced it.

CR: Yeah. Experienced whatever "it" is. We are talking about being alive while having awareness of death, which is what being alive is actually all about. I almost feel like Western society, by isolating us somewhat from death, has numbed us.

CD: Something that I came up with in an attempt to explain this phenomenon, is what I call the "ecstasy of decay." What the ecstasy of decay is, is that if you're faced with the most grotesque parts of life – with decay in the universe, with death, with sorrow, with grief – it opens you up on either side of the spectrum. So most people are living in a middle world; they are living between two bars, bumbling between those two things. And when all of what we've been talking about happened to me, all of a sudden the range expanded.

CR: Thinking back to psychedelics, that's exactly the sensation.

CD: I think it's a similar effect. All of a sudden there were higher highs; I would see a sunset and just burst into tears. And then comes the opposite side of the spectrum: I'm staring at the base of the abyss, into the nothingness, the nihilistic horrific existence of humanity. It was sort of like you had to have one with the other. I've worked my way back into the middle now, but I can still see it in the distance on both sides.

CR: It reminds me of the Tibetan monk Chögyam Trungpa. He wrote a bunch of books, and I remember he writes in his book *Shambhala: The Sacred Path of the Warrior*, that people think that enlightenment is constant bliss. But it's not, it's much more complicated than that. The state of enlightenment is a state of balance: you're in a center, and no matter how happy you are, you never forget the suffering in the world. And no matter how much you suffer, you never forget the beauty, and joy, and wonder of the world. Your range is huge, because you've been to both of those extremes. Now you're just trying to keep your balance, but your balance is in the center of a much larger range than most people can deal with.

* BEGIN TS #90 *

CR: Is death-positivity really a thing?

CD: Well, I pulled it out of my ass like a year ago, it is one of those words I made-up.

CR: I like it.

CD: It's blatantly stolen from "sex-positivity," the idea that (and you will probably agree with me on this) we need a redo or a societal "re-up" on how we perceive the role of sex and the role of death in our culture. Viewing at it as a positive force on our psyches is probably a healthier way to look at it than just assuming that it is this negative monolith that is hurting us.

CR: Indeed, you are right, although I am wondering if maybe "demise-positivity" would work better, since "death" also includes war, and murder, and genocide, and all these things I think we should try to avoid when possible.

CD: Well, people really like the term 'death-positive.' I said it as a joke a couple of times, but there is something to be said about it being a little bit sexy, or a little bit scandalous – so people have to say, "Wait, I don't know. Those words could never go together!" And they have to get indignant. Then you follow up by saying "We're not saying that when your mom dies you have to be like, 'You know what? No big deal, I'm death-positive.' All we are saying is that if you do some serious work on her death before she dies, and you think about mortality, and you think about what you want to be done with her dead body, and you think about how you feel about your own death – when she actually dies, it can be a beautiful experience, and it can be a better experience for you. And you can focus on the death as opposed to being completely wrapped up in the bullshit of fear.

CR: One of the things I get into in my next book, and which is a point that I'm sure is obvious to you, is that there is a big difference between prolonging life and prolonging death. And so much of what we do with our medical technology is to make the process of death take longer, draining it of its dramatic and emotional beauty and import. We take something that should happen in a few days, maximum, and we spread it out over five or six years, or even ten years. And then you ask, "When did that person die? Because he doesn't

> **SO MUCH OF WHAT WE DO WITH OUR MEDICAL TECHNOLOGY IS TO MAKE THE PROCESS OF DEATH TAKE LONGER, DRAINING IT OF ITS DRAMATIC AND EMOTIONAL BEAUTY AND IMPORT.**

know me; he doesn't know *anyone*. Is that even him anymore, or it is just his body? And if it's just his body, what does it really matter if he's alive or not?"

CD: And even beyond that, in the coming years, as the baby boomers get older, we do not have the resources to take care of them – either financially or through the physical presence of caregivers. And as we get more and more afraid of death and afraid of talking about death, we get more and more afraid of even addressing that problem in any way. So we need palliative care, we need hospital care, we need death with dignity, we need all of these things. We need this multi-pronged approach in place, and we just don't have it.

CR: We don't even have one prong! But you were talking about how the death of a loved one can ultimately be a beautiful experience, if you have already prepared for it.

CD: Yeah, if you've already done the work, especially in regard to your own life. When people die, it's too easy to make it a lot about you. If somebody dies, and you haven't dealt with death and mortality, it becomes, "Does this means I am going to die?" Well, yeah, that is what it means. But if you've already dealt with that in your own life, you can focus on your relationship with the person who is dying, and in grieving *that* specific loss as opposed to bringing in your own shit.

CR: Because you are experiencing the death of that person, as opposed to experiencing death itself.

CD: Yeah, and most people in this culture right now aren't able to do that. If you go through your life experiencing very little death, and very little threat to your own life, then when death does come up – even if you really love the person dying – you will immediately bring your thoughts back to your own mortality instead of theirs. And you are way out of shape; that part of your brain that processes death suffers severe atrophy. The death industry needs more presence, more involvement, more sense of responsibility around death. We don't want to say, "Hey, this person died, I know what to do. Call the funeral director, have him pick it up straight from the hospital, take him away, and we will get the ashes in the mail two weeks later." But instead, to say, "This is my loved one, my mother, my spouse, my partner, whoever it is, they are my responsibility. They are my community. Their death and their dead body is now my purview."

CR: I have to say... when I'm watching the news about the plane that was shot down in Ukraine, and they are interviewing some of the relatives who say, "I just want to get my daughter home," I get a little weird about that. It creeps me out a little, because you're referring to a dead body as your daughter. It's not your daughter...

CD: It is and it isn't, and it completely depends on cultural perception. The dead body is simultaneously sacred and profane; on one hand, it is merely a shell; the person is gone, is not there anymore. But the symbolic weight of that shell is heavier than the symbolic weight of just about any other inanimate object.

CR: If we are only talking about the symbolic weight here, can we then not shift that symbolic weight away from the body into, for example, a photograph of the person when they were younger and healthier – like you see in a lot of cemeteries in place of a tombstone?

CD: Well, that is what we had been doing, shifting the symbolic weight away from the body to just the memory. We have a memorial service where we think nice thoughts, drink punch, and listen to Steely Dan – which we will play at your funeral, Chris, because you like them. And I think that is a big part of the problem: death in the abstract, or death that exists only in memory and in hypotheticals. That there are these people who work behind the scenes to take care of the body, and we just don't want to know about it. And the person who actually dies is just an abstract loss. We know they're gone but we don't know what that means exactly. And that lack of tangible experience with a dead body is *absolutely* the problem.

CR: Do you think that having that tangible experience is *solving* the problem, or *clarifying* it somehow?

CD: It's not like that, but I think it's a call to self-awareness for people. It's not like putting corpses back into culture will fix society. But I think the corpse is the best way to open up to self-awareness. We are lacking self-awareness right now in our actions: the way we can live without a lot of sense of where our food comes from, or where our medicine comes from, or where our wars comes from, or where our waste is going or coming from. When you don't have that sense, you are not self-aware. Exposure to the physical corpse creates a big shift to that way of thinking; it certainly was for me and for other people I talked to who had a very similar experience.

CR: One of the pivot points in my book is that the Spanish word *aislar* means "to insulate," but it also means "to isolate." And by trying to insulate ourselves from every sort of discomfort, we are also isolating ourselves – feeling lonely, and lost, and so on. But I am stumbling a bit about the fact that we are focusing so much on the body as the source of this discomfort, because I feel that in a sense, life and death are abstractions.

CD: They are, but they are real enough. To say that death is an abstraction, doesn't that demean grief and demean the mourning process in a way?

CR: No, no. Because *love* is an abstraction. I mean, show me love... what does it looks like?

CD: But love is *way* more an abstraction than death.

CR: You think so? Okay, let me then play devil's advocate then. First of all, who dies? When a body dies, what's dying?

CD: The person's symbolic relationship to their world, and their community, and all the people they know.

CR: Okay, so if we are starting with symbolic, then it's already pretty abstract.

CD: It is, but the actual dead body is an incredibly powerful reminder that this person is dead. We are not just not losing people into the ether.

CR: Well, maybe we are though.

CD: I understand that from the spiritual perspective, but I don't think a lot of people have that mindset. And you can argue that shifting towards that mindset, as a whole culture, will be really helpful... but you could put the dead

“”

THE DEATH INDUSTRY NEEDS MORE PRESENCE, MORE TRANSCENDENCE, MORE INVOLVEMENT, MORE SENSE OF RESPONSIBILITY AROUND DEATH.

body into the home in almost any religion or secular family, and that body can mean something, and it can fit in with the world view. As opposed to trying to teach a different perception of what the body is, and what death is, and what transcendence is; I think that's a harder sell. Part of bringing the corpse back into our lives, is also about accepting that this dead body doesn't have to be preserved; you're taking your two days with the body, and then putting it in the ground to decompose, or giving it to animals to eat, or to take the next step and say, "I'm not going to chemically preserve this body, and then put it in a heavy casket, and then put in the ground, because it is so important that we need to keep it forever."

CR: Ah! So you are actually *minimizing* the body in some sense.

CD: Yes, I'm saying take the important two or three days to symbolically engage with this corpse, understand your own death and mortality, understand that this person is no longer part of the community, and then let the body go and do what the body is designed to do – which is to decompose, go back into the universe, and be consumed by other animals.

CR: Before I forget, let's talk about your projects.

CD: I do two things. I have a larger project called The Order of The Good Death, which is a community of writers, academics, and funeral professionals who are trying to do exactly what we are talking about: bring the conversation about death back into society through various means. Then another thing I do is a web series called "Ask a Mortician," which is just me sitting in front of a camera, kind of being a goon, answering questions people have about the funeral industry.

CR: So are you sort of a death nerd?

CD: Definitely a death nerd. We've talked about being a jack of all trades; I think I'm a bit of a jack of all trades when it comes to death. There are certain things I would consider myself very, very well versed on, but more importantly, I consider it my job to be able to talk about anything within the realm of death and dying. For example, with the Egyptians, I can tell you about canopic jars, and how they pulled the brain out with a little hook through the nose... I can give you a conversation about it without necessarily being the guy at the Smithsonian who is the expert on ancient Egyptians.

CR: A hook would pull the brain out through the nose?! I assume it would just cut right through the brain. Did you know the only Nobel Prize in science that was ever given to a Portuguese, was to the doctor who invented the frontal lobotomy? You know how they did that? They had this thing, sort of like an ice pick that went in through the eye socket; it curled up into the brain and they would just move it around and kill stuff.

CD: So in embalming, there's a thing called the trocar – and embalming is interesting because it has a scientific aura about it – but the trocar is just this long, pointed metal stick that goes in right above your belly button, and it just indiscriminately stabs at all of your internal organs. So you go up, *stab stab stab stab stab*, then you point down, *stab stab stab stab stab*, and then it sucks everything out with a little vacuum at the end. So it sucks all of the fluid out of your thoracic and internal cavities. Then you reverse the process and pour chemicals into it, for the preservation. I love the idea of something that's perceived to be some great Nobel Prize winning, scientific achievement – when really it's just something indiscriminately stabbing the human body. It's like scorched earth technology.

CR: Something that often strikes me when you hear things like, "a 72-year-old man lost his life in a car accident." He didn't lose his life; he lost what was *left* of his life, which probably wasn't much anyhow. It's such a funny expression. You were talking about emotional engagement and your defenses... do you feel that when someone young dies, it affects you much more?

CD: It definitely does, because there's an aspect of *memento mori*, of like, "Oh, look at this young person. It's you." And that's what you try to stay away from: over-identifying with anybody.

CR: Have you ever worked with a body that really looked like you?

CD: Not somebody who really looked like me, but definitely somebody who really did look like somebody I knew. These were mostly young men who looked like friends of mine, men I knew from college. It raises questions: do I want to take care of these friends when they die? Would I be able to do that?

CR: I was going to ask you that: do friends say to you, "Hey, if I die will you..."

CD: Yes. Strangely, in the industry, it seems to be the party line that you don't take care of your own.

CR: Because it would be so much harder to protect yourself emotionally, right?

CD: Right, but I completely disagree with that. Maybe it's because I don't practice primarily embalming, which is such an invasive process. The thought of my mother, or my father, or any of my close friends being handled by somebody else, is really abhorrent to me. Knowing what I know now, I want to be the one who does it; it's a great honor for me, and it's a great ritual for me. Which is something I'm trying to bring to other people too. I work in home funerals, and the idea there is that the family takes care of the dead person. So if you die in *your*

“”

WE'RE NOT GOING TO BURN DOWN THE ENTIRE DEATH SYSTEM IN AMERICA AND WALK AWAY AND START ANEW LIKE AN OLD GROWTH FOREST. YOU HAVE TO DO SOME CHANGE FROM THE INSIDE.

home, your friends and family come in and it's *they* who wash you, and shroud you. And they are in charge of the physical, tangible preparation of your body.

CR: I'm sure you get a lot of enthusiastic support from people who see your videos or read your blog. But do you get support from anyone in the business that you're in?

CD: I do, strangely. Which has been kind of a shock to me, because I'm in this place where there are people who are outside this industry: people who are death midwives, people who do home funerals, people who do green burials, people who do want to go back to a much simpler time of dealing with death; they're usually outside the industry. And then there are people, mortuary science students, who are heavily steeped in the traditional American funeral industry. I went through the whole rigmarole with the traditional American funeral industry. And so, there are these two groups, and for a while it's sort of been "never the twain shall meet..."

CR: You're the bridge.

CD: That was the idea, that I would be the bridge. But - and I feel a little devious here - both sides for the most part seem to be okay with me. They are like, "Let's see how this goes." Neither of them probably totally trust me, but so far I've managed to get some really enthusiastic, genuine support from both sides. I think there's a lot of people in the traditional funeral industry who know that we could be doing a better job, who know there's much more out there, and who aren't so set in their ways. Then there's people outside the funeral industry who know that it's difficult to exact change from the outside, that in some ways, you need to rehabilitate from the inside. We're not going to burn down the entire death system in America, and start anew like an old-growth forest. You have to make some change from the inside.

“”

I THINK THAT WHAT YOU WOULD CALL GOD IS PRESENT WHEN THERE IS LOVE AND COMPASSION AND KINDNESS AND CURIOSITY AND CREATIVITY. **AND GOD IS NOT SO MUCH PRESENT WHEN THERE IS DESTRUCTION AND JEALOUSY AND ENVY AND WARFARE.**

CHAPTER 9

STANLEY KRIPPNER

EPISODE #5 (NOVEMBER 8, 2012)
&
EPISODE #24 (APRIL 14, 2014)

Stanley Krippner is a psychologist and parapsychologist, currently serving as a faculty member at Saybrook University in Oakland, California. He is best known for his pioneering work on dream telepathy as well as his research into altered states of consciousness and shamanism.

MIND-BODY CONNECTION | WESTERN MEDICINE | SEX | SOCIETY | PSYCHOLOGY

CHRIS RYAN: I wanted to tell people who you are very briefly first, people who aren't familiar with your work. I guess your first scientific prominence came about because of your research at the dream lab at Maimonides in New York. Is that right?

STANLEY KRIPPNER: Yes, that's right. Back in the early 60s. I graduated from Northwestern University in '61, and I spent three years at Kent State University. Then I came to Maimonides, and stayed there until the middle 70s. And at that point we ran out of money. I came to San Francisco because my friends were just starting a University devoted to humanistic and existential psychology, Saybrook University, and I have been there ever since.

CR: Yeah. Lucky for them. You're the North Star of Saybrook.

SK: Well, lucky for me too, because at Saybrook people can explore different human behaviors and experiences that they can't really explore anyplace else. Everything from ayahuasca, the mind-altering beverage from South America; to telepathic dreams, which was the topic of our research in the Dream Laboratory; to mate selection among early humans.

CR: For example, to pick one at random.

SK: Yes! It was turned into a bestselling book.

CR: The research you did at Maimonides is still referred to in most books; it's the most solid investigation of psi – telepathy, and paranormal experiences and events. You were looking at whether or not people were more receptive to telepathic imagery... was this during a REM stage, or was it hypnopompic/hypnagogic states?

SK: We checked out all three. And of course most dreams come in Rapid Eye Movement sleep. But we also checked with people as they were drifting into sleep, which is the hypnagogic state, and when they were coming out of sleep, which is the hypnopompic state. And, much to our surprise, we found that they were even more telepathic in the hypnagogic and hypnopompic state. The place where they were not especially telepathic was during the small dreams that they had outside of Rapid Eye Movement sleep. Those were very down to earth, very simple dreams - they didn't have a lot of metaphors, or a lot of symbols in them. And so we ran the gamut in terms of that particular investigation; we published close to 100 articles. And now that work has been repeated, mainly in the United Kingdom at various universities, and most of the results are robust; they're as strong as ours - not quite as strong - but still strong enough to demonstrate this is more than chance.

For example - just so your listeners will know a little bit about the experiment - we would have a volunteer participant come in and have dinner with one of our psychologists, who established a rapport with the volunteer. Then the volunteer would go into a soundproofed room, and have electrodes attached to his or her head so that we would know when they were asleep and dreaming, and when the Rapid Eye Movement would occur. The psychologist would throw dice, and the dice would direct the psychologist to a double sealed envelope. Why double sealed? Because if it's single sealed you could look up at the light and see the image inside of it. Anyway, he took that to the other side of the building, opened it up and there was an art print. By Picasso, Van Gogh, Gauguin, you name it.

CR: And he's choosing from how many possible envelopes?

SK: If we were going to do a 12 night study, it would be 12 or 13 possible envelopes. And so, on one night for example, the image was George Bellows's painting *Both Members of the Club*, about a boxing match. And the dreamer, who was an artist, had a series of dreams in which he went to Madison Square Garden to buy tickets to a boxing match and there were posters of the boxing match all over the walls of Madison Square Garden. The psychologist would look at the picture, trying to send the picture and the sleeping subject was trying to receive the picture. Then the dreamer's account of his or her dream were typed out word for word, tape recorded, and then outside judges, who were experts on dreams, would try to match each picture with each possible target.

CR: So they would look at all 13 of the pictures.

SK: Not only that, they'd look at pictures from the whole study. If we had 12 nights of the study, there'd be something like 12 x 12, or 144 matches, and they would match every one of those. And then we were able to compare the correct matches with the incorrect matches, to see if the correct matches produced a rating, at a scale from 1 to 100 above chance or not.

CR: Right, right. And that's why this research is still being cited. The methodology is so strong. You've said this to me many times: that the methodology for research in parapsychology has to be iron-clad because there's so much skepticism.

SK: Oh yes, and it's a good thing. It has to be ironclad. Ray Hyman is a professor at the University of Oregon; he is probably the most outstanding skeptic and critic of parapsychological research. He has examined our dream research and has said in a published interview, "There's no smoking gun." In other words, he could not find any flaws in the research. The only problem he cited was that you don't get results every time you do it. I would agree with him. We don't know why we don't get results every time we do it. But if you look at the overall pattern, and let's say you have ten direct hits - like the boxing match hit - out of twelve possible trials... well that's way above chance. Six out of 12 would be chance.

CR: Right. One of the many things that makes you a unique figure is that you've done this research, but you are also a skeptic. You're someone who's respected by both sides of the parapsychology debate. You've told me about how you've been on a talk show with the Amazing Kreskin, and your job was to try to uncover the *tricks*, right? To give some scientific validity, or not, to what these people were claiming.

SK: And I was also on a show with James "The Amazing" Randi. He was recently interviewed about me, and he paid me a nice compliment: he said that he had met me several times, and he could find no bias one way or the other toward the topic of parapsychology. So that was a nice compliment.

CR: It's the *highest* compliment.

* * *

CR: I remember you telling me a story about a Brazilian mystic that you had taken into the jungle with Michael Winkler. And you were measuring electromagnetic fields around the house.

SK: Amyr Amiden was, for lack of a better term, a mystic or a psychic. But he was also a secretary of his trade union; he had a day job. And when he came to the attention of Pierre Weil, the president of the City of Peace Foundation in Brasilia, Pierre thought Amiden would be just the type of person I would like to investigate. The only problem is, I didn't have equipment or the money to get a video camera and bring it down. And so an interesting thing's happening: things like polished stones falling out of nowhere, or medallions appearing on a table. In one incident, one of the psychologists said, "My daughter is turning twelve this week. Do you have a birthday present for her?" And immediately, out of nowhere, popped this lovely ring with 12 little rhinestones set in it. It seemed to fall out of nowhere. We heard a pop, and there it was, flying through the air and landing on the ground. Yes.

CR: And you're sitting at the table with this mystic and some of the other researchers, and it wasn't coming from Amiden; he wasn't throwing things.

SK: Not as far as we could see, because sometimes these things happened in another room or even in another building.

CR: Right. And you were outside on the driveway, and stones were falling from the sky.

SK: Dozens of stones falling down while he was in the house having dinner... and I patiently went around, picked them up, and looked at the timing. Because you mentioned the geomagnetic field: yes, this was very important, because Michael Winkler spent much of the time with a geomagnetometer, the only one in the city of Brasilia, that we borrowed from the university. Every two minutes he would notice what the readings were. And when it ran out of juice, he would come back and join us in the offices. But whenever the geomagnetic indexes were high, this is when the phenomena were extremely intense. Now, geomagnetic readings are high when there are electrical storms, when there is sun spot activity, and when there's a lot of electricity going through the atmosphere. And we got the truly statistically significant results when we paired the time of these paranormal phenomena against the geomagnetic index at the time. This is something that had never been done.

CR: Did the geomagnetic field precede the event? In other words, was there already a change when the stones fell from the sky?

SK: Yes, I'd say it preceded the events.

CR: Right. I remember a conversation in which you and I were talking about your general conclusions regarding people who claim to have paranormal abilities. And I remember you saying that your sense after so many years - how many years have you been researching this, 50 years or something? - was that some people do have an inborn ability to see things the rest of us can't see, and to predict things. But that ability comes and goes, and it's out of their control. And so a lot of these people - because they get ego investment - they learn tricks to compensate for when the ability's not there. So even if someone's caught doing a trick, it doesn't necessarily mean they're a complete fraud. It might just mean on that particular day, the vision wasn't there; so they did a trick to compensate for it. I've found that to be very interesting, because we have a very black or white vision of these things.

SK: Yes, well, it causes severe problems for researchers.

CR: Right, sure. Because once someone's caught, then there's no coming back from that.

SK: Yeah, they're anathema. Nobody will do research with them.

CR: Right, right. Now, at what point did you get interested in altered states of consciousness, and shamanism?

SK: I got interested in altered states of consciousness by observing my dreams. I started a dream diary when I was in high school, and have recorded literally thousands of dreams throughout the years - keeping up this interest ever since. When I got this offer to join the research team at Maimonides Medical Center, I literally jumped at it - even though there was no guarantee that it would be a permanent job. Well, the money lasted for ten years, which is longer than it usually lasts in such endeavors.

Oh, you asked how I became interested in altered states of consciousness and shamanism. Some of your listeners might not know what a shaman is - a shaman is a very special type of healer in indigenous and native societies who claims to be able to talk to spirits, and to animals - and who uses extraordinary means of not only healing, but weather forecasting, mediating disputes in tribes and among families, and passing on the mythology of the culture. I was interested in shamanism because I had a long-standing interest in Native Americans. When my father would plow the field, he would sometimes plow Indian arrowheads. I found out that the Potawatomi Indians used to live in our territory, and so I began reading about Native Americans.

When I was at Maimonides, I was once on a panel with a well-known shaman from upstate New York, and this was my first contact with a real-live, honest-to-goodness shaman. So I listened attentively. Her name was Grandmother Twylah Nitsch, a Seneca shaman. Later, through a serendipitous series of events involving the Grateful Dead, I met Rolling Thunder, an inter-tribal medicine man. My latest book, which I wrote with his grandson, is called *The Voice of Rolling Thunder*. But I have taken the opportunity to learn from shamans, and visit them, and work with them over the decades - and have had some remarkable experiences, especially with the South American shamans and Native American shamans from North America.

* * *

CR: Some people view experiences with psychedelics as educational, others as recreational. How would you classify them?

SK: *Learn* is not quite the right word; I would say they reinforced things I already knew. I'd read a lot of Alan Watts' books, a lot of philosophy, a lot about Native Americans... so I already had a worldview which was quite different than the general American worldview - with its emphasis on materialism, possessions, competition, and rivalry. So the psychedelic experiences with peyote, with LSD, with ayahuasca... each taught me something, and reinforced and re-emphasized what I already knew. But it was often put it in a different context, something that I could put to use. So for me, the experience was basically an educational one. It was spiritual in the sense that I became closer to the earth, I valued relationships more, and I valued love and kindness more. I wouldn't have considered taking anything like that for recreational purposes; because if anything is sacred to me, it is the special experiences like this that you do not violate.

CR: I agree. Hear, hear. Let me throw an idea past you, something I've been thinking about recently: An animist (and I think all hunter-gatherers are essentially animists) looks at the world and sees it as being alive in all aspects. There are spirits of the clouds, and spirits of the river, and spirits of the rocks, and everything is imbued with spirit. And one of the things that seems to be an almost universal aspect of a psychedelic experience, is that you get this sense of life all around you. And inanimate objects that had seemed - or that we were taught - are dead, suddenly seem as living things. Rocks have some sort of spiritual substance that you're (depending how you look at it) tricked into seeing by some toxic chemical, or your mind is opened up enough that you see something that is actually there but has been hidden. And so I was thinking... I wonder if the day-to-day life of an animist is, in a sense, kind of trippy from our perspective. Obviously the brain reaches equilibrium and adapts to imbalances, so that would be the normal state of being for these people: being aware of this mesh of life that people often report from psychedelic experiences. I wonder if that's similar to the daily experience of an animist. Have you ever spoken with anyone about that, or do you have any comment on that?

SK: I have run across that idea from time to time; it's mentioned in some of the descriptions of what life was like among the Mayans and Aztecs before the Spanish invasion. And of course, these people consumed mushrooms, morning glory seeds, peyote, etc. But even aside from that, they were so close to nature, and felt that animals and birds were siblings - brothers and sisters - not something that one harvested or took advantage of. Yes, they ate them, but they gave prayers before they ate them.

CR: Another aspect of this question, of whether or not psychedelics give us a window into normal states of an animist's consciousness, is the fact that there's now research being done showing that psilocybin and LSD are very effective in helping people deal with the fear of death, and are being used in terminal cancer patients. People are reporting extreme alleviation of the fear and anxiety surrounding death. Not necessarily because they suddenly believe in heaven or an afterlife per se, but merely because they feel embedded in a web of life. So whether or not they transform from one state to another seems like less of an issue. But I'm putting words into peoples' mouths, which I shouldn't do.

SK: You're not, because just a few weeks ago I was talking with one of the participants in the Maryland Psychiatric Consortium's research with psilocybin. He has cancer, and he had an absolutely ecstatic experience. He just went on and on about it for almost

THE MOST FAMOUS EXPERIMENT WE DID WITH DREAM TELEPATHY WAS A LITTLE PILOT STUDY THAT JERRY GARCIA OF THE GRATEFUL DEAD SUGGESTED TO US.

an hour. Among other things, he completely lost his fear of death because he found himself as part of this matrix, this latticework of the universe. He realized he had played his role, and that after his death, there would be a part of him that would still be part of it all. And this oneness is something that permeated his whole being. In addition to perhaps having some health benefits, it certainly had a spiritual benefit for him. And I think it's simply criminal that more of this research, and more of this therapy, has not been done. Literally tens of thousands of people could have been helped to have a more pleasant and more meaningful death, had the research not been terminated back in the 60s.

CR: Do you hold Timothy Leary responsible for that?

SK: Leary gave an excuse for the Food and Drug Administration and the Nixon Administration to put the whole research project on hold. So I think that Leary played his role. But official medicine and official psychotherapy was so strongly against this type of treatment, that if Leary hadn't gone off the deep end, somebody else would have. Or they would have found somebody else to blame. Remember that Nixon called Leary the most dangerous man in America.

CR: And Elvis was his drug czar!

SK: Elvis went to visit Nixon, and came away with a badge. The poor guy became an honorary deputy at the time he was pumping himself full of legal drugs – which ultimately did him in, and made him fat and bloated. Of course, that was no strike against him, because it was prescribed by a physician, and it was legal.

CR: A couple of weeks ago I was interviewing a friend of mine, Pete McCormack, who's a documentary filmmaker. And he mentioned he had heard from someone, on solid ground, that Elvis often came in his pants during concerts. That he was so into the music, he would ejaculate on stage and have to go backstage to change pants.

SK: Oh, yes, yes. This is not only true of Elvis.

CR: Enlighten us. Who else? David Byrne?

SK: Oh, I have seen it in person, through my contact with the Grateful Dead and being backstage. I've heard about it from groupies and members of the entourage: that they get so hyped up that (we're talking about the male singers here), they get erections. Tom Jones is noted for his erections, and people would actually watch out for it. And some of them would ejaculate during the performance. The women also got wound up, but we don't know as much about them, because their ejaculation is not quite as obvious.

CR: Right, right. And they're all wearing black on stage anyway, so how can you tell? I should mention that you've also done a lot of research and published a lot of work on sexuality. So, this talk about ejaculating rock stars is not outside your area of expertise.

SK: No, not at all! The most famous experiment we did with dream telepathy was a little pilot study that Jerry Garcia of The Grateful Dead suggested to us. At six of their concerts in Long Island, about halfway through the gig, a sign flashed on the main screen displaying these instructions, "You are about to participate in an ESP experiment. Malcolm Bessent is in the Dream Laboratory at Maimonides Medical Center in Brooklyn, New York. You are going to see an art print. Look at this art print and try to 'send' it to him." Then, onto the screen, came this super-big art print of an emotional portrayal by some famous artist. The Dead would talk about the art print, and by that time the audience was under the influence of one substance or another – so they went along with it. The Dead started the music again, while the picture remained up for about half an hour. Then our dreamer, whose name was Malcolm Bessant and was an English psychic, would try to incorporate that image into his dreams. He was quite successful; it took only six attempts, but he got what we call "borderline statistical significance" for those six nights.

CR: Oh, excellent, from a bunch of trippers at a concert. That's alright.

SK: And now there's a Grateful Dead's archive at the University of California Santa Cruz, and they want to have a special exhibit devoted to that experiment. I just found out that our laboratory assistant saved all 12 of those slides! So we know exactly what pictures were used, and he is going to donate them to the archives. In the meantime, the article was printed in a dentistry journal, and one of the great regrets of my life is I didn't have the Grateful Dead sign a few copies. Those are collector's items; I could be retired by now!

* BEGIN TS #24 *

SK: The idea of a shaman is a sort of social construct; it's cobbled together from Siberia, from both the Yakut and Bayaut tribes. The translations, "singer of songs," "inner heat," "flying to the sky," all apply to shamans. They supposedly rouse the inner fire to heal people, go out of the body to the upper or lower worlds, and sing songs; narrative, myth, dance are all part of their repertoire.

CR: You mentioned upper and lower worlds. As I understand it, that doesn't refer to heaven and hell; it's just two other realms through which these shamans can move. Is that something that's common in shamanic traditions: that there are three realms, and we're in the middle?

SK: Anthropologists apply the term shaman to practitioners in various indigenous cultures, because they all did similar things. One writer and enthnologist called them technicians of the sacred. I often refer to it as spiritual technology. And part of that technology is knowing how to navigate between different states of consciousness, and different aspects of reality. One common aspect among shamans of different cultures is that of traveling to different worlds. In many traditions there are upper, lower, and middle worlds – but some have as many as seven that they travel to. It's not as bizarre as you might think, because we have some physicists talking about multiple universes coexisting at the same time. Why can't shamans traverse these hypothetical or actual universes in search of knowledge and power, to serve their community? This is the one unifying theme of shamanism. They use their skills to gain knowledge, power, and information that can help members of their community live better, live longer, live healthier, and to do better in their world.

CR: What, if anything, do you see as the connection between psychosis and the shamanic experience?

SK: Back when I studied shamanism in the 50s and 60s, the leading psychiatrist at the time who knew anything about shamanism considered them schizo, or manic depressive, or pathological. But this was before the psychologists came in, started to study them, and to give them psychological tests. They came out with surprising findings: shamans were the best functioning people in the community! They had less pathology than others, they were imaginative, they were much more in touch with their body processes, and much more creative. They told more fantastic stories: sometimes they took ink blots and linked the blots together to tell a continual story.

So that is one thing that began to change people's opinions of shamans, from the academic point-of-view. Some of the anthropologists actually undertook training so they could study shamanism from the inside-out, rather than from the outside-in. Michael Harner is the most well-known, with his book *The Way of the Shaman*. What Harner did, was to go through initiation into the Jivaro tribe of Ecuador. He and his wife set up a foundation for shamanic studies, and got funding to travel around the world. They find people who still remember what the shamans did, to help them bring shamanism back. They did it in Finland; Finland had a long tradition of shamanism that sort of disappeared during World War II. They did this in Siberia; the communists wouldn't allow shamans, and killed them off because they were a threat to Marxism and materialism. The shamans who survived simply buried their drums.

What we've forgotten is that Shamans aided evolution. They did ceremonies that, from a strictly rational point-of-view, don't make sense, but which worked. They worked because they activated a person's inner healer, the innate intelligence of the cells. People *believed* it worked, and visualized it removing bad spirits. Only a special type of person could do this: people who were suggestible, who had good visualization skills, who were amenable to placebo. It didn't work for everybody, and for the people it didn't work for... they died early and their genes dropped out of the gene pool.

CR: What psychologists call hypnotic ability would've been much higher in shamanic cultures, because with that ability, you have more leverage with which to be cured.

SK: We still retain some of that legacy; hypnosis and placebo *do* work.

CR: But in our society that doesn't work for everyone, because our society doesn't favor that particular trait.

SK: Our society uses drugs and surgery; they don't believe they need hypnosis, and powers of the mind.

CR: Also, if you *do* have a lot of imagination and visualization, you're kind of screwed unless you can make it as an artist. In school you'll end up being diagnosed with ADD and then drugged to death. Fascinating, though; I'd never considered how the favoring of hypnotic ability in shamanic societies would lead to this runaway, evolutionary effect.

SK: Yes... the placebo effect, the ability to be hypnotized, an active imagination... they were all very important from an evolutionary point-of-view.

CR: For people who think this is sort of woo-woo, think about this: you're working with the placebo effect

“” SHAMANS AIDED EVOLUTION. THEY DID CEREMONIES THAT, FROM A STRICTLY RATIONAL POINT OF VIEW, DON'T MAKE SENSE, BUT WHICH WORKED. THEY WORKED BECAUSE THEY ACTIVATED A PERSON'S INNER HEALER, THE INNATE INTELLIGENCE OF THE CELLS.

all the time – every time you go to a doctor. Doctors always have that stethoscope around their necks, but depending on what type of doctor it is, they might not use it. They wear the traditional surgical scrubs. All of that, whether the doctor knows it or not, is there to trigger and amplify the placebo effect.

SK: One of the stories we tell in our book, *The Voice of Rolling Thunder*, was about his first encounter with a Western physician; it took part at Mickey Hart's ranch (drummer for The Grateful Dead). I had a friend by the name of Doctor Irving Oyle, who was an osteopathic physician, and he really wanted to meet Rolling Thunder. We thought Mickey's ranch would be a good place for them to get together, so we sent them off to the barn. After about two hours, the two of them came out of the barn arm-in-arm, smiling from ear-to-ear. Then Doctor Oyle says, "You know, we were a little suspicious of each other, but then we realized we knew pretty much the same things. A patient comes to me, I listen very carefully, and I do a diagnosis. I go through a little ritual called writing a prescription, give the prescription to them, and then they go and get some medicine. Then they usually get well. Rolling Thunder's ritual includes maybe some drumming, maybe some prayer, maybe some smudging... then he gives them some herbs, with directions on how to take the herbs, and they usually get well. But what really helps them get well is if they really believe in what they're taking, and have faith in the person who's doctoring them."

CR: Right. One of the things I find so fascinating in shamanism occurs in many traditions: that it's the shaman who takes drugs as opposed to the patient. They take drugs to facilitate moving between worlds: traveling to the upper or the lower world to uncover the source of the problem. And then they come back and share that information with you. It's interesting because it subverts the Western model of the doctor as medicine giver. But also I found a resonance with the early days of LSD, when it was marketed by the pharmaceutical company Sandoz as psychotomimetic for psychiatrists who wanted to gain deeper insight into the experience of their psychotic patients. They would take the LSD in order to understand what it must be like to be psychotic. Since then, of course, scientists have determined that there are many dissimilarities between the two. But I find that noble and beautiful, that a doctor would take acid and go through this eight or nine hour experience to gain compassion and insight into a patient's condition and suffering.

SK: Well you're absolutely right: the shaman would do the drumming, take the substance, do the chanting or singing, go into the lower or upper worlds, into the past or the future, and would come back with the answer needed for his patient to get well.

CR: Right. Well, listen, we're running out of time, you've gotta pack for your trip to Vegas. I was wondering... your friendships span cultures, they span the world, they span generations. Do you have any conclusions? About the big issues: what happens when we die; where we come from when we're born... What's your vision of the world? Would you consider yourself an animist? I know you're not a practicing Christian, but you were raised in a Christian environment.

SK: When you say practicing, I believe in practicing one's religion through daily actions: through compassion and kindness, through spreading and accumulating knowledge, etc. I think that God resides in everything, making me an animist. But I'm somewhat of a heretical animist, because God resides in some things more so than in others.

CR: I like that; a selective God, a God who chooses where he lives.

SK: Right. And I think that what you would call God is present when there is love, compassion, kindness, curiosity, and creativity. And God is not so much present when there is destruction, jealousy, envy, and warfare. So I'm not one of these people who has a value-free view of the world; I can be very, very judgmental. I don't know what happens after we die. All I can say is that since we part of everything while we're alive, we will continue to be a part of everything after we die; just how aware we will be of that, I don't know. But it wouldn't surprise me that there might be *glimpses* of awareness, and that from time to time, we might appear to those who are still living. Because consciousness is on a continuum; it's a flow, and it goes in and out like a Mobius strip, with no beginning and no end. I think that life is a flow. Death is part of that flow, and evolution is certainly part of the flow. I think that despite all the objection to evolution by the fundamentalists of various religions, evolution really gives us a wonderfully spiritual view of how matter and non-matter, life and nonlife, have survived and have adapted over the years. And if humanity makes the terrible mistake of blowing itself up, life will go on. The insects will outlive us all. And the evolution will trend toward more simple forms of life, rather than more complex forms of life – to survive the radioactive blasts. I think evolution, and the adaption that evolution ensconces, is extremely spiritual. I don't mean spiritual in the sense that the creation scientists mean it... I mean spiritual in the sense of being something that evokes wonder, and evokes awe. I hope this is what I have done with my students at Saybrook University and other psychology venues that I've been part of. One can appreciate science, one can appreciate psychology and the other sciences; but in this appreciation, there's an extremely fulfilling sense of beauty, of wonder, of awe. For me at least, that keeps me going: it sees me through the tough times, which I've had several of and am *still* having; and it helps me to enjoy the good times, which, thank heavens, I'm also still having.

“”

I FIND THAT NOBLE AND BEAUTIFUL, THAT A DOCTOR WOULD TAKE ACID AND GO THROUGH THIS EIGHT OR NINE HOUR EXPERIENCE TO GAIN COMPASSION AND INSIGHT INTO A PATIENT'S CONDITION AND SUFFERING.

CHAPTER 10

AJ LEON

I MADE IT.
MONEY, COMFORT.
THE ONLY PROBLEM
WITH THE SITUATION
WAS THAT I WAS A
FUCKING FRAUD
AND I KNEW IT.

EPISODE #222 (JANUARY9, 2017)

A.J. Leon walked away from a corner office on Wall Street after realizing that his life was inauthentic. Since then, he has founded Misfit – one of the most enigmatic, admirable hunter-gatherer enterprises around (and publisher of this book). AJ's life is full of travel, love, passion, and positive energy. Plus, he's brilliant, good-looking, quotes Shakespeare from memory, and dances like a Cuban. Fuck that guy.

TRAVEL | RELIGION | SOCIETY | U.S. SOCIETY

CHRIS RYAN: I'm in Vancouver, Canada with AJ Leon. What does AJ stand for?

AJ LEON: Alberto Juan.

CR: How did I meet you again?! Matt, who's a mutual friend of ours, and whom you work with, listens to the podcast. You guys were in Portland two years ago.

AJ: We were having some beers and hanging out. And he really wanted to meet you, because he loves the podcast.

CR: It was one of those situations where I'm travelling through somewhere, and a fan will message me something like, "Hey man, I'm in town, let's get a beer or whatever." I have friends who are famous, and they're surprised that I ever accept that. But as you and I were talking about last night... you and I were out last night 'til quite late.

AJ: 'Til two o' clock in the morning.

CR: And then I went home and you stayed out.

AJ: So if I mutter for the next hour please forgive me for getting my hangover on your podcast.

CR: He's drinking a lot of water. And I'm not drinking this month, so I've got this unfair advantage here. I'm all spry. Plus, I had plenty of coffee before I showed up, so I'm wired.

Anyway, Matt was like, "Hey, I listen to the podcast, can we get a beer?" And then you were there. I had so much fun with you guys, and was so interested in your business model – that's a shitty phrase for what we're talking about, but we'll get into that soon – that one thing led to another, and I had had this idea: I'm conversing with all these interesting people on the podcast; there should be another way to reach out and share this material. So it turned into this whole business thing, and now we're going to publish *Tangentially Reading* together through Misfit Press.

* * *

CR: So you're from the Lower East Side of New York. That's home, that's where you grew up, you know your way around there. So what age did you arrive there?

AJ: I arrived there pretty late – my late teens. But because of my upbringing, I never felt home; I always felt misplaced. The name of my company is Misfit, because I always felt like a misfit for a variety of different reasons.

CR: Both your parents are Cuban?

AJ: Yes. They left during the revolution. My dad was particularly complex. He left Cuba at thirteen and later became one of the ringleaders in the Cuban mafia in southern California. He ended up going to prison. I've met lawyers who know the United States vs. Leon Supreme Court case, because his case changed Miranda Rights laws.

CR: It went all the way to the Supreme Court?

AJ: It went all the way to the Supreme Court.

CR: What was the charge?

AJ: He was drug running; it was an entire operation the DEA had been watching for a long time.

CR: Importing into the US from Columbia?

AJ: Actually from Baja, California. Famously, my dad was nuts; he'd go out and shatter people's windshields if they looked at his sister wrong. But prison is kind of where I met him. Some of the earliest memories I have is visiting Arizona Maximum Security Prison. He would make piggy banks for us kids, and we'd end up visiting him. He ended up reforming himself when he got out, and cut ties with those guys. Which is something you don't do. But he never ratted. He never said anything. They were trying to get the people higher than him, and although he was fairly up the chain, he didn't say a word. Luckily, the case went the way it did, and he ended up getting out far earlier than he should have.

CR: Right. Because if he doesn't rat, how the fuck does he get out?

AJ: Exactly. It was because they didn't read him his rights properly or something. I've never gotten into the specifics, because it wasn't something we talked about a ton. The important thing was, he reformed and became a good man. He tried to build his life back up, but then right at the peak of building his life back up – right in the eighties – there was a recession in California, and he lost everything. Two million dollars in debt, went bankrupt... we had to move a bunch of times.

CR: : So he lived with your mom again?

AJ: She's a good woman, she stuck with him. And then

“” MY DAD WAS PARTICULARLY COMPLEX. HE LEFT CUBA AT THIRTEEN AND LATER BECAME ONE OF THE RINGLEADERS IN THE CUBAN MAFIA IN SOUTHERN CALIFORNIA.

he ended up passing away. It was crazy, the things he lived through. He was in the army in Germany where he was dishonorably discharged, because somebody stole his wallet and he stabbed the guy in the street. He was a prisoner of war in Germany. The things he survived... only to end up passing away from a blood clot in his knee after he broke his leg, and the doctor didn't prescribe him blood thinners. Which they should have done. So that's what I mean about the ebbs and flows of a young life; that's up until the age of fourteen..

CR: How old were you when he got out of prison?

AJ: Five or six.

CR: What was his story leaving Cuba? You said he was thirteen when the revolution happened.

AJ: Well, the whole history around the Cuban Revolution is interesting because of Che and Castro... they took the Granma boat from Mexico City to the east of Cuba, and gathered their army on the way. They only had a couple hundred guys, but ended up taking over the government. This was '59, but finally took over in '61.

CR: And they took over in '61 from Batista, who was a motherfucker.

AJ: Yeah, he was a piece of shit.

CR: Like all the Central American dictators: propped up by the Americans, taught how to torture, taught how to throw people in prison. "We're defending democracy." Everyone around the world laughs at that. The Americans are the only people who don't know the true story.

AJ: The thing about Central America is, it doesn't have the sex appeal of Africa. So people actually know less about the politics, the history, the strife. Because it doesn't have that NGO sex appeal.

CR: And also because we're the ones who fucked over Latin America. It's easy to talk about the atrocious situation in Africa, because that's the Brits, the French, the Dutch, and the Belgians.

AJ: It's funny. That was more overt, but we still do it through economic hegemony. Just fucking awful.

CR: United Fruit Company controls the country... and the fuckin' CIA. Well, you just got back from Guatemala. I mean, holy shit, the stuff that's going on there...

AJ: Jacobo Arbenz, man? That whole era of Edward Bernays, hired by the CIA?

CR: I was just about to mention Bernays! For people who don't know what we're talking about, Bernays was Freud's nephew; he basically invented the art - if you want to call it an art - of modern public relations, of thought-control of the masses. He's the guy who coined the phrase, "We're fighting them over there, so we don't have to fight them over here." It was a phrase about World War I; he was justifying it. He was behind the idea of putting fluoride in the water supply, because he was hired by the Aluminum Company of America, who had all this fluoride byproduct from their aluminum manufacturing. And they didn't know what to do with all the fluoride because it's so hard to dispose of. And he found a way to sell it. He convinced the government that this was good for people's teeth; just dump it in the water.

AJ: And American Tobacco? "Cigarettes are healthy." That's Bernays' handiwork.

CR: He's the guy who linked feminism with tobacco in order to convince women to smoke. Because it was uncool and taboo to smoke. He was the guy who hired all these suffragettes to march down Fifth Avenue in Manhattan, smoking cigarettes. He called them "torches of freedom." What else? Bacon and eggs for breakfast. He was hired by a conglomerate of pork companies, and he came up with this idea of bacon and eggs. Anyway, in addition to polluting the body politic with all this commercial shit, he was also hired by the CIA; and one of his projects with them was to overthrow the democratically-elected government of Guatemala in the fifties.

AJ: The story reads like a fucking novel. He planted a story saying that Jacobo Arbenz was a communist. He absolutely wasn't a communist; it's on record that FDR was one of his favorite leaders.

CR: But he wanted to help poor people, and redistribute a little money to help.

AJ: The big reason was that Arbenz was on record saying the United Fruit Company would have to pay taxes. That's what his deal was. He wasn't saying he was going nationalize it, or take the plants back - he just said, "You have to pay taxes, guys. Come on." Because they owned 85% of all private land - the ports, the railway system... I mean this one company basically owned the entire country of Guatemala. And all he was saying was that they had to pay their taxes. So United Fruit hires Bernays, and Bernays plants a story in *The New York Times*, which then creates this entire episode. It alerts the CIA - who was newly minted and had only been around for several years at this point - and they were looking for communists.

And then, all of a sudden, they hire a militia on the streets of New Orleans, arm them, and sail them in United Fruit boats to the shores of Guatemala. It's like twenty guys, but because they had all these newspapermen on them, they made it appear in the media like there were hundreds of people. The entire population of Guatemala turned their attention to it, because of this media. What do we know? We know what we hear, and what we see. And the final scene of this Quixotic episode is with fucking Jacobo Arbenz in the Presidential Palace, listening to these sonar things the CIA installed that were playing these fake sounds of war, in what they called terror broadcasts. So he thought he was being encroached upon. They planted these all around downtown. So you're getting this in the media, you're getting this on the radio, so you're hearing bullets firing, newspapermen are reporting it. But it's all bullshit. So in the end he's hunkered in his presidential Palace. The very next day he rides down with his motorcade to the airport, and leaves the country of his birth for the very last time. And that all happened because a company in the United States wanted to maintain its profit margins. It's fucking insane.

CR: But the thing is... people listening to this who aren't familiar with the true history of American policy will think this is some outlandish story. But the same thing happened in Chile, in Honduras, take your pick - it's been happening all over the world. Which is why the world fucking hates America. They love American culture and American people, but what people who haven't traveled abroad don't understand, is that America is seen as an enemy by a lot of the world. But what's cool is that they distinguish between the people and the government. They won't hate you because you're American, especially if you're aware of this shit. My favorite compliment I get when I'm travelling is when I'm in a conversation with someone, and they'd say, "Ah, okay, well you're not a typical American."

AJ: That's right. You kind of breathe a sigh of relief. I don't

MY GRANDFATHER TELLS THIS STORY OF HIM ON HIS PORCH, WATCHING ANTS CRAWL UP THIS COLUMN AND REALIZING THOSE ANTS HAD MORE FREEDOM TO MOVE AND TO LIVE THAN HE DID. THE VERY NEXT DAY, HE TOOK OFF. HE LEFT CUBA WITH NOTHING.

know where your listeners land on this, and I don't want to be too political on your program...

CR: Let it loose, buddy!

AJ: Well, when Trump got elected... to travel with an American passport had everybody like, "What the fuck is going on over there?"

CR: You're old enough to have traveled under the Bush administration. And there was this same thing. They'd say, "Are you kidding?"

AJ: Yeah but Bush was never like, "Oh, women? Yeah, let's just grab 'em by the pussy." Say whatever you want about George W. Bush. Politicians are all their own individual breed of fucked-up because of whatever it is they have to do to achieve that kind of power. But this? This is ludicrous.

CR: This is nuts.

* * *

CR: Now where the fuck were we? Your father, and the revolution. He was thirteen.

AJ: After Castro took over the government, he announced the communist intentions a year later. So famously, there were people in his inner circle who didn't know this was a communist takeover.

CR: He was on *The Tonight Show*. He was popular, he was charismatic.

AJ: He was all over. And so was Che. And once that got out of the bag... it's an interesting thing, because on the one hand, the idea of socialism is a beautiful idea, but I don't think it works in practice because people are greedy. What happens is a guy like my grandfather, who was the age I am now, living in Cuba... he worked his entire life, was a doctor, had his own land, had a life he put together. Then one day this cat comes out of nowhere. My grandfather actually went to university with Fidel, so he knew Fidel personally. As the guerillas were going through the towns, they'd gather up the leaders of the towns. My grandfather was one such leader in his town. Che came and said, "Hey, let's all get together and debrief. Let's talk about this revolution, and see if you guys want to join us." Attorneys, doctors, etc... they all go, but my grandfather doesn't go. The guys who went were his best friends, the guys he grew up with. Bullet to the back of the head, every single one of them.

And then the next day, everything is taken from my grandfather. His land no longer belongs to him, his little practice now belongs to the government, and by the way, "you're now only earning five dollars a month." My grandfather tells this story of him on his porch, watching ants crawl up this column and realizing those ants had more freedom to move and to live than he did. The very next day, he took off. He left Cuba with nothing.

CR: So your grandfather's in California. What did he do? Did he get his medical degree recognized?

AJ: He went through medical school again.

CR: No shit!

AJ: Dude, this guy is made of titanium steel. He's one of those individuals who, in the end, is going to get what he wants. That level of defiance... saying, "I'm not going to let this destroy me." Yeah, after Cuba they went to Spain, and then they went to the United States. So he had to kind of reengineer things for a while. He was the age I am now; I'm young, but I'm not like twenty or whatever. You gotta work hard.

CR: Starting over after turning 30. It gets harder every decade.

AJ: And if you get my grandfather going on the Cuban revolution, he takes no prisoners. Because to him this is a personal fight. He was one of the Cubans who had been waiting for Fidel to die, and who consider it a badge of honor to have outlived him. That's, at the very least, the one last "fuck you" to the guy who ruined their lives – in their minds. He's one of those Cubans. Which I get. I don't have that vitriol personally, but of course, I'm generations removed from it. But I tell you, man, if someone took everything that I have right now, and everything my wife has, and ruined the lives of our kids... I don't know if I'd ever be able to let that go.

CR: Now I don't know narratively if this is going to work, but I see as you're telling this story... there's so much reflection on this whole Cuban thing we're talking about, on your grandfather's life. I see it reflected it in your life. I see a theme of defiance. You told me last night that when you were in school, your guidance counselor told you, "Forget about university; just try to stay out of jail."

AJ: Yep. "Don't even think about university."

CR: I want you to talk about all this stuff, but I want to plant a flag here. I see defiance. I see socialism. You say socialism doesn't work, but you set up a company where everyone makes the same amount of money; you have less money in the bank than your employees.

AJ: It doesn't work out there. It doesn't work in a large society of strangers.

CR: It's a scale issue.

AJ: Yes, exactly.

CR: It works when we know each other. When we're looking at a face of someone we love... that's when it works. When it's an abstraction, it doesn't work. That's what I always say: the impulse towards socialism is rooted in our evolution as a species. We hate injustice. We hate it. It makes us sick. And as I said to you last night, it doesn't matter if you're rich – if you're the top or the bottom – it's a vertical system that's uncomfortable for us as a species. We're a horizontal species.

AJ: Exactly.

CR: We like to share. We don't like to see someone suffering. It's why dentists have a high suicide rate – they're around people who are suffering all the time. It drives us crazy. I have a buddy who's a tattoo artist, and he says it's the same thing with tattoo artists. It makes you sick to be in a cloud of pain.

AJ: Of course. But the only way that it works, at all, is if you have a tribe. The term "tribes" has been used by Seth Godin to talk about online followership, but that's an understanding of it that I don't identify with. I would call his concept a "crowd," or an "audience."

CR: Sort of randomly gathered.

AJ: Well it's not anthropological. When you say "tribe," you're not talking about a hundred thousand people who follow an idea or a figure; that's a religion, that's a congregation. A tribe is like, "We live together, we love each other, we would die for each other."

CR: "We raise each other's kids. Breastfeed one another's babies. Take care of one another when we're sick." It's an intimacy.

AJ: And in my case, you can use free market capitalism to create an economic structure to change the world. And relinquish the profits. And relinquish the benefit of money that's supposed to come to you as the founder. Most people start a company to cash out, that's it. That's the entire premise. But you can use that same system to enact the change you want to do in the world, while sharing proceeds among the people that are there with you. People look at Misfit, and they're all like, "Whoa, what a great company!" But that's not quite the right term. I mean, we use the principles of that, but we also imbed the tribe mentality. That's why I identify so much with what you talk about. I'm the leader of this outfit, and you were talking about leadership last night in a really interesting way: where historically, in hunter-gatherer societies, the leader is known for what he gives, not what he attains.

CR: It's your generosity that makes you the leader, not your wealth.

AJ: Yeah, exactly! Think about the systems around us – government, companies – the leadership structure is completely the reverse. So our systems are at odds with our heritage.

CR: With our nature. Somebody should write a book about this!

AJ: Exactly! I'm waiting for it.

* * *

CR: You were saying last night that defiance can lead you astray. Because it leads to defining yourself against other people. So let's talk about that.

AJ: There were a lot of ups and downs in my life. My father passed away, and it was rough; nobody saw it coming. It really wrecked my mom. Her dad had committed suicide just a few years earlier. Her husband had gone to prison for the cocaine thing, then they started doing very well, then they went bankrupt, then they're building their lives up again, and then he dies. I had two sisters, and entire sequence of events fucked us all up in different ways. For me, it led to the same kind of suffering that affected my dad, which was just anger. And not the healthy, defiant, righteous indignation. But just being pissed off at life. I ended up getting really into basketball. But I was kind of like this guy who always got into fights. I was *that guy*, you know? I was still the guy you know today, but I was willing to fight every guy in the street. That whole basketball subculture. So anyways, I didn't do very well in school. I wasn't considered an academic.

CR: Were you moving around a lot?

AJ: We were moving houses; things were still volatile. And when it came time for me to graduate, my high school guidance counselor, Miss Mitchel, said that a guy like me shouldn't think of going to college. That I should commit to maybe being a mechanic. And she hands me a pamphlet to trade school. No offence to mechanics – I have friends who are mechanics. But that's certainly not what you want to hear when you're a teenager – when you want to change your life and move on. In that moment, I was like, "Well fuck you, Miss Mitchell." But it was actually more like, "Fuck all of you who have told me for my entire life, that I was going to be a fuck-up and amount to nothing." So for me, to get into university, it was a fuck you to everybody. And I remember after every semester, I would send a letter to Miss Mitchell, unmarked, with just my grade report.

I did that every semester. She became the personification of everybody who ever said that to me. I graduated Summa Cum Laude, top of my class, with a 4.0. As I'm graduating in finance and accounting (and philosophy), I'm thinking, "What are you going to do? At this point I'm on top of the heap: went from the bottom all the way to the top." But I'm still stupid, still young. "I'm going to get a job at the biggest firm I can, get a huge signing bonus. I don't give a fuck who I'm working for, or what I'll be doing." All I cared about were the zeros. A lot of kids take that track. I worked at PricewaterhouseCoopers, which is a big name; from there you can go anywhere else. I ended up in New York City working in finance from 2003 to 2008. I was making an obscene amount of money and had a corner office overlooking Manhattan.

CR: You made it!

AJ: I made it. Money, comfort. The only problem with the situation was that I was a fucking fraud and I knew it.

CR: In what sense were you a fraud?

AJ: In every sense. When the impetus of the entire narrative of your life is polluted, every decision after that is polluted. That life wasn't *me*. The irony of all ironies is that I was letting Miss Mitchell beat me – by trying to prove her and everyone else wrong, without thinking about who I was. There was no *me* in the equation. It was theatre at the grandest scale. You realize that not only are you a fucking fraud, but that you are the fraud of all frauds: when you're trading away the hours of your one and only life for money, at every turn. There is nothing that will drive you into as deep and as profound a depression as that; I was enveloped in sadness. During the day I was cutthroat, doing my thing. I wasn't hurting anybody, but I would do anything to win. But at night? You can ask Melissa... I was crying.

CR: Melissa is your wife?

AJ: Yes, she's known me since I was kid. And she was young too; she didn't know what the fuck was happening or what to do about it. And what do you do? I was doing well, and that's the whole problem with this. If I were to talk to anybody I knew... you can guess what the response would be, "What are you talking about man? You've got the corner office, you've got the money." Nobody stops to think about that, and I didn't either. Until this one day... December 31st, 2007 – days before Melissa and I got married. I was pulled into my boss's office; I knew this big promotion was coming. And he said, "Here you go." At that point, I'm minted. With this promotion, I became third in the company. So I get the promotion, and it should be the moment where you look back at Miss Mitchell through the pangs of your own history and say, "I fucking did it." But when you climb this precipitous mountain, and you get to the top of it, and you realize that the whole fucking thing was horseshit, and that you climbed somebody else's mountain... and you're young and you don't know how to restart. It's easy to go from failure to success, or from one failure to another failure, and to keep trying. But when you start from success – where do you go then?

CR: It's all downhill from there.

AJ: It's all downhill from there, exactly. So I walk out of his office and I walked into my own – I remember it like yesterday – and I started bawling. Because I realized they had fucking *got me*.

CR: Wasn't there something about your honeymoon? What was that?

AJ: That was another aspect of it. I blew all my money on the honeymoon and this stupid ring. And one of the things that the boss said is, "You're going to have to curtail that honeymoon a bit." And I thought that was even more depressing. I sign this deal, and then I have to swallow the fact that I have to cut my honeymoon short – cut the whole thing down to a weekend. So basically not even have a honeymoon. Just because this guy says I'm important to this company, to make him money. I'm making fat, rich, white dudes in New York more money; it's not virtuous, it's devoid of virtue. So I'm sitting there at the top of this whole thing, weeping, because I realize I'm going to swallow this. I'm a fucking chump, a fucking fraud, a liar, the worst type of person there is. It's corporate prostitution. You know you're trading your life for money, you know it in your bones.

CR: Another theme running through your family's story is reinvention. So you're twenty-seven at the time, you have this crisis, and then what?

AJ: I sat in my office that day, and I wept. Because what do you do when you realize you're *done*? Your life is scripted, and you hate the script, but it's *done*. After I had that thought, another thought came in, "You always have a fucking choice. You always have more choices than you think you have." I thought, "I could walk out right now!" Of course, I'd be taking my degrees, lighting them on fire, and pissing on them...

CR: Everything you worked on in the last ten years is gone

AJ: Done. But if I hate it, and it's not me anyway, then what the fuck? I inherited these thoughts, and I can kick them out tomorrow. Maybe I live on the streets, maybe I live under the Brooklyn Bridge... but at least I'm fucking free.

CR: So what'd you do?

AJ: Immediately after I had that thought –

CR: Because you can't pause.

AJ: You can't pause. It's the momentum of those moments, the brief moment of audacity... I'm smart enough to know that if I go into this office tomorrow morning, I'm done. If I wait an hour, I'll talk myself out of it. That's what would happen. So I immediately grabbed a box, put my shit in the box, walked past my boss' office, and gave him the tail end of a Shakespearean-like soliloquy about the fuckin' system, the rat race...

CR: Seriously?!

AJ: He called a security guard to take me out. Everyone was all, "What the fuck happened to AJ? Is he drunk?"

CR: So you freaked out, you gave your boss a bunch of shit, and you were escorted off the premises.

AJ: Yep. With my box happily in tow. I took the 28 stories down, and hit the street. It was the first time in my adult life that I breathed a breath of free air. It was a really profound moment. There and then, I made the decision that I was going to live my own life, and that all of my decisions would be deliberate and intentional. I had to figure out who the fuck AJ was. And that's what led me on this path that I'm on now, eventually starting Misfit. But I wasn't leaving to start any company or to do anything specific.

CR: Now we're up to the point in the story where you've got this wedding coming up. And you tell Melissa you quit your job.

AJ: I told her. And what she said – this is probably almost verbatim – is, "AJ, I would rather live with the real you under the Brooklyn Bridge than an impersonation of you anywhere else. I'm so glad I have you back." Melissa and I have a refrain, the last cheers of the night no matter where we are, and that refrain is: *to the bitter fucking end.* Come hell or high water, no matter what, that girl knew that moment was true for me. It wasn't practical or pragmatic but it was true. And she could hear the harmony of it, and she was going to be with me, and help me figure it out.

CR: She's cool, she's like, "This is you." It's fascinating Here's the thing. I think a lot of the men who listen to this podcast are young men. And they're afraid to make a move like this. They're intimidated, and they think, "What is my girlfriend going to think?" I think we men underestimate women; we're worried about what they'll think about money, about our dicks, about how we do this, or how we do that. I can't speak for all women, but the women who've been in my life, who are meaningful people – without exception, the trait they value the most is sincerity. Be real. Everything else is secondary.

Back to your story, what did you do next?

AJ: So Melissa and I got rid of everything and took to the road. I taught myself web design. This was 2008. And I was thinking, "Well, what am I going to do with my life?" I didn't know what, but I knew enough about history, and I was trying to think of the early builders, the industrialists. How did they gain the power to build buildings? It seemed like if I could figure out a way to build websites, and these things called web apps... then if I have an idea, I have the power then to enact the idea. I don't have to go to somebody else. Think about the way it is today: if you don't have a web presence, you can't do the things you want to do. And the barrier entry to all this was *zero.* All I had to do was read a few books. So Melissa taught herself WordPress, and I taught myself web design, and we cobbled together websites. And it wasn't for the money; we weren't good enough, and people weren't paying enough. We traveled around the world trading web design for bagels and for places to sleep. And that was it.

* * *

CR: Now we haven't even talked about Shakespeare. I know he's a huge part of your life. How'd that come about?

AJ: From 14 to 16 I was really angry and stuff. And then I had this one moment where I'm in the gym shooting baskets. At the time, I thought I was some big shit. I was kind of a basketball thug; that was sort of my existence. So I was in the gym shooting baskets, and this one teacher I had – this one guy who I still love to this day – really changed the trajectory of my life. He was a 21-year-old substitute, and he was into theatre

“”

IT WAS THE FIRST TIME IN MY ADULT LIFE THAT I BREATHED A BREATH OF FREE AIR. IT WAS A REALLY PROFOUND MOMENT. THERE AND THEN, I MADE THE DECISION THAT I WAS GOING TO LIVE MY OWN LIFE, AND THAT ALL OF MY DECISIONS WOULD BE DELIBERATE AND INTENTIONAL.

and stuff like that. But he was a rough guy himself; kind of like this teacher you didn't know if they'd kick the shit out of you or not. And he saw me shooting in the gym, walked up to me, and said, "I know you think you're hot shit, but about ten years from now, when you're working at Walmart, that's not going to matter anymore." Nobody talked to me like that. Sure I was an asshole to him and to everybody else, but nobody talked to me like that.

CR: What was his motivation?

AJ: His motivation came to the fore later on. He comes up to me, and he's wagging this book in my face. Basically he said, "I bet you don't have the balls to walk on this stage." And then he threw the book in my face; it was *Henry V*, my favorite play to this day. That little Misfit emblem is a Japanese anime rendition of Henry V at the Battle of Agincourt. That was a key moment, because I was going off the rails. I was going to be a bad kid possibly. That teacher is sitting there like, "Yeah, I bet your don't have the fucking balls" and I'm like, "Fuck you." So then I did it. And what I found out was that there were no theatre kids. So he was starting this thing, and was basically going around school type-casting people whom he wanted for various roles. And one of these roles in Henry V was Fluellen, a general who's close to Henry and fought in the Battle of Agincourt. A real rough cat, you know. Fluellen was gritty, and talks like me, like some piece of shit who thinks they're better than they are.

CR: And it spoke to you?

AJ: It changed my entire life. Shakespeare changed my entire life.

* * *

CR: Before we go: You have a book, a collection of essays; you were sort of writing in those days. Trying to figure out what was going on.

AJ: Yeah, I was just writing letters to a younger version of myself. I never thought I would publish any of them... how the fuck would I publish them? Basically I wrote to learn what I think. It was very cathartic, because I thought, "These are my ideas," and I started creating a life deliberately around that. And once we started doing these web-barter deals, I realized that when you do something 100 times, you get good it. When you do it 1,000 times, you get very good at it. So we got really good. It was 2008, and no one knew how to do this shit. I thought maybe we could do this for money. And

“” IT CHANGED MY ENTIRE LIFE. SHAKESPEARE CHANGED MY ENTIRE LIFE.

I had this vision of building a digital creative agency where we could build world-class campaigns, and apps, and websites – but where we would redistribute all the profit to social and humanitarian work around the world, or to fund another business that can do the same. The deal was this: anytime we made a profit, Melissa and I would take it, meet with people fundraising in sub-Saharan Africa or wherever, and partner with them to do pro-bono campaigns connecting the beneficiaries with the donors, in real time. We were like, “Oh fuck, we're nobody, yet we can change the world.” I want to die penniless. I don't want a big yacht. I'm just the founder; this isn't about me. I have to give more. That was the vision. One thing led to another, and as we met more and more people, those people started seeing the campaigns we were doing – and these campaigns were raising $15,000 a week. People were like, “Who are these kids? They're flying out to Africa, using their cellphones to connect villagers to people on the other side of the world.”

CR: And meanwhile you're always getting better at it.

AJ: Yep. We built Misfit, Inc., and then parlayed that into Misfit Press. Jess and I were talking about not so much the idea that things are broken in the publishing industry, but that we could do some cool stuff. And we can do this differently. Every time we sell a book at Misfit Press, a kid in India gets a pair of glasses through a relationship we have with one of our friends who's the CEO of the Sankara Eye Foundation. From there, we started another company called Studio Misfit. Our profits there help fund cataract surgeries again in northern India, again though a partnership. And that's how we look at business; it's sustainable. Also, if we meet somebody who is doing something cool in the world, we can help them out. We meet so many people. I just met some cat in Guatemala, and we're gonna build a website for him, we're going to run a campaign, we're gonna do this whole thing because I'm like the industrialist: we can build shit; we aren't powerless. That's when I feel like I've crossed the enemy lines. I studied their schools, I know the game. Make money? I can make money: these are legit companies with fifty different people working for them. And I've got about twelve core team members who are like family, who are the tribe. We share everything; that's the message of Misfit as an enterprise. So, why can't we take the keys back? It's the greed we inherit that forces us to think, “A business is supposed to make money.” No, you're supposed to make it sustainable. If there's virtue in the organization's business, then wouldn't there be virtue in keeping it alive? Misfit Press will never make a profit for me, and I'm the owner. Same goes for Misfit at large. If there's profit at the end, after the family are taken care of, you plow it right back in. That's how I want to live; that's how the Misfit crew wants to live. And that's how we'll do it.

CR: To the bitter end.

AJ: To the bitter fucking end.

“ ”

AS LONG AS YOU DON'T STEP ON ANYONE ELSE'S TOES, YOU SHOULD BE FREE TO DO WHATEVER THE FUCK YOU WANT. END OF STORY.

DANIELE BOLELLI

CHAPTER 11

EPISODE #18 (APRIL 19, 2013)
&
EPISODE #60 (MARCH 6, 2014)

Daniele Bolelli is a writer, history professor, martial-artist, and podcaster. He is the author of several books, including On the Warrior's Path, *and hosts the* History on Fire *podcast.*

HISTORY | U.S. SOCIETY | ACADEMIA | DEATH | EUTHANASIA | FREEDOM

CHRIS RYAN: Why did you come to the States?

DANIELE BOLELLI: The thing about Italy is - as much as there are some things I like about Italy - it is very old culturally. It is very conservative, not so much politically, but in terms of attitude. If you come up with a new idea, or a new project about anything, you're going to have ten people sitting at a bar telling you why it can't be done. They'll have very good arguments, but the attitude is always "no." I like the fact that in the US, it's the exact opposite: where sometimes even ideas that shouldn't fly sometimes fly, where people are more willing to take risks, even stupid risks - but at least it's exciting. It can be a lot worse in Italy, but it can also be a lot better. Italy is sort of middle-of-the-road: neither this nor that, no risk, no chances, nothing too horrible or too amazing is going to happen. It's great if you don't really care that much about creating anything, or care for amazing new ideas. Then it's great. For vacation, Italy is an awesome place. But in terms of getting anything done with your life, not so much.

CR: I assume Italy is similar to Spain. You were talking about friendships... I experienced what you were talking about, that there is an ease of connecting with people in the States, but it's much harder to develop any depth. And a lot of that is because people move so much; you end up making friends with someone, and then they move away or you do - which is a common thing in America. In Spain I've found that a lot of people are friends with the people they grew up with, so it's harder to integrate yourself into people's social circles. Because those circles are set and they've been that way for so long. Even if they are very friendly, everybody around this table has known each other since they were three years old... and then there's me. Is Italy like that as well?

DB: Yes.

CR: It's very static, people don't leave town.

DB: Which is both good and bad, because on one end you get that which is very tribal, and there is something very cool about that. And on the other hand

WHAT GOOD ANTHROPOLOGY AND GOOD HISTORY SHOULD BE ABOUT IS STUDYING THE DEEP PAST, AND THEN TAKING THE GREAT IDEAS AND INSIGHTS FROM THOSE ERAS AND ASKING HOW WE CAN REUSE THEM TODAY.

it's why nobody ever gets anything done – because you're always stuck in the same three miles radius. It's changing though. If you grow up in big cities, people tend to experience life outside of it more.

CR: What part of Italy are you from?

DB: Milan. Big industrial city, but at least the metropolitan aspect of it makes it easier to connect with the wider world, otherwise people tend to stay put a lot longer. To me the problem was that Italy wasn't friendly enough; I needed more out of human relationship. Coming to the US was a big shock because there was a lot less than that. Eventually I realized that what I want doesn't quite exist, I am sure it exists somewhere but not exactly what I expect.

For example, I've hung out at some American Indian reservations where life sucks in a lot of ways: extreme poverty, high rate of alcoholism, lots of the negative statistics. The plus side is there is the idea of the tribe, this sense of community so damn strong that it's beautiful; there is something really amazing about it. But at the same time the price to pay is so nasty in other ways, that it's not exactly like anybody wants to sign up and be part of it either. So it's tricky. My ideal would be to have globalized tribes, in a way: containing a tribal aspect that I deeply love for its intensity of human relationships that it creates, but at the same time not containing the aspect of tribe as in "stuck with the same thirty people all your life and you never leave your valley." You know, connected with the bigger world.

CR: A lot of my next book, *Civilized to Death*, is a critique of civilization. And a big part of it is community and how community has been so fragmented, and fractured, and commodified, and so on. If you look at the science of happiness, there is this whole positive psychology. The number one predictor of contentment, of life-contentment, is whether you feel embedded in a community, and if you've got friends who care about you, and love you – and where you feel protected by that social network.

But you're right: the other side of that is that you're limited by those relationships as well. I don't know whether we are sort of ping-ponging back and forth between this romanticized sense of prehistory where everybody was happy and life was great, and then the modern world – back and forth, not being able to decide which is better. Or if maybe we're actually at a point in human history where it's possible to take some control of our destiny, and with this understanding of where we came from in a prehistoric and historic sense, we can integrate the most important elements of that into our lives. Are we kidding ourselves to think we can have some sort of tribal community in the 21st-century?

DB: No, I think that is what anthropology should be. What anthropology is sometimes is a whole different game. What anthropology should be is a creative aspect of this: taking what we know about the human past (and in some cases even the human present in other parts of the world), borrowing from different cultures and different time periods – borrowing in the sense of taking things from it that can work now. You can read the best book about what life was like 10,000 years ago, or what life is today in a different place, but it doesn't really matter because you are not going to be able to live in the exact same circumstances. So it's just entertainment, do you know what I mean? It's fun, you can fantasize about the cool stuff, but of course, there are the other things that were not so cool that go along with it. But to me what good anthropology and good history should be about is studying the deep past, and then taking the great ideas and insights from those eras and asking how we can reuse them today. To take the best out of these aspects and be able to repackage them in a way that works in a globalized context – and not only work, but work even better because we can take the best from it and leave the worst from it behind.

CR: So you're proposing a kind of applied or prescriptive anthropology.

DB: Right. It's about elevating the quality of human life. If it's just about some academic crap, studying something that has no relevance to how you live outside the classroom, then who cares? That's just purely a weird masturbatory exercise. Actually not even that, because at least masturbation leads to a good orgasm giving it a redeeming quality. A lot of academic stuff is purely for its own sake; there is no point.

CR: So is this what makes you a badass historian? If so, I want to be a badass anthropologist!

DB: You are! But yes. I've been kind of all over the place, which is the ultimate crime in the eyes of academia, because you're supposed to specialize in one thing and one thing only. If you're a historian, you're supposed to know everything that happened on that street corner on that Wednesday in 1712, and that's all you're ever going to do. That's really not the way I work. I thrive on connections. I thrive on applying this stuff to life. Because ultimately, to me, that's what it's all about. I don't care about anthropology, about history, about psychology, about philosophy, about martial arts. Or, rather, I care about all of these things, but I only care about them in the measure that they serve life, the way they make life more fun, more enjoyable. To me, that's what it's all about. The specific field in isolation? Whatever. It gets old really quick after a while.

CR: Right. I guess there is some value in knowledge for its own sake. But I agree, life's short – so if it doesn't have some practical value and application to life, there's something very masturbatory about it.

DB: Yeah, and by practical, we're not just saying, "Hey, study business or something." Practical can include poetry too, you know what I mean?

CR: It's about bringing meaning and coherence into to your life. I studied literature for that same reason. It's like, what am I going to study? I'm young, I'm eighteen, I'm passionate and interested in the world... so I'm going to study literature, because it talks about life, what life is – so I read Henry David Thoreau. My real intellectual passion in those years was the American Transcendentalists, who were sort of like Buddhists but they didn't know anything about Buddhism. They were all about "God is in nature." They were almost animists. I remember reading an essay by Robert Frost called "The Figure a Poem Makes." There's this beautiful image in that where he says, "Like a piece of ice on a hot stove, a poem must ride its own melting." I remember thinking, "All right, I'm going to ride the melting of my innocence until I'm thirty!"

DB: That's the way to do it! There's something that Frost says, I forget the exact quote, but it's basically criticizing philosophers because it says, "These are not philosophers, these are people who talk about philosophers, who talk about other people's ideas; they never had a single creative idea in their life." That's basically what all of philosophy is. His point is that philosophy is not only something you think, but philosophy is also something you live; it's in your muscles, in your joints, it's something you sweat. I can very much relate to that because, again, it boils down to being real to life as opposed to living in this abstract bubble. I mean, I'm a little weird nerd and I do like my intellectual stuff, but if that's the only stuff you ever know, how sad.

CR: There's a Chinese saying: To know and do nothing is to not know. Having the thought is essential, but then you have to do something with it. If you sit around thinking about traveling, but you never go anywhere, then sorry, you haven't been anywhere.

* * *

CR: Now, I know you're working on a project about taking history out of the stuffiness of the ivory tower. Tell us more.

DB: I'm calling it badass history. The whole plan is to take a very edgy take on history shows, because the problem with history shows is that most of them are boring as hell. Some even do it in a suit and tie, lecturing in front of bookshelves... It's painfully boring. Make it edgy, with a more Anthony Bourdain-type of take, where you travel to places and also have its content and delivery be edgy – far from shying away from the blood, sex, and gore of it all, but jumping into it. Not just for the sake of show – which, granted, entertainment is good: sex and violence not only sells, but they sell because we like them, because they are fascinating to us as humans – but also not shying away from real authenticity when it comes to human experience, when it comes to historical characters that are extremely controversial, like one of my idols, this guy Ikkyū. He was the illegitimate son of the Emperor of Japan at the end of the 1300s. He became one of the giants of Zen at that time. His main passions were Zen, sake, and women – and that's all he lived for. To him they were part of one and the same. Working on characters like that, that defy expectations, gives you a deeper appreciation for what it meant to be this crazy Japanese dude in the 1400s.

There's storytelling involved, it's not just some random stuff about who was president at the time. Real human experience with passion, with sweat, with blood, with all of it. That's how you make history come to life. That's what I lecture in school. All the time people are telling me, "I hated history but I'm having the time of my life in this class." And it's not just because of my lovely good looks, it's because you make it for what it can be. Real life to us is interesting. We like storytelling, we like wild tales; the more real they are the better.

CR: The problem is that the good stuff often gets lost because it's so sanitized. One of my favorite interesting figures from history, one of the people I would most love to meet is Richard Burton. He was Irish, 19th-century, spoke 27 languages or something, and was the first person to translate the *Kama Sutra* into a Western language. He spoke Arabic so well that he dressed up as a Bedouin, I think, and was the first westerner to travel to Mecca! Undercover! Can you imagine? You have to have some real confidence in your Arabic linguistic skills to put a fucking turban on your head and walk into Mecca.

DB: And he got busted, didn't he? As far as I remember the story, he got busted and then they were about to chop his head off. So he was there with the royal

THERE'S A CHINESE SAYING: TO KNOW AND DO NOTHING IS TO NOT KNOW. HAVING THE THOUGHT IS ESSENTIAL, BUT THEN YOU HAVE TO DO SOMETHING WITH IT. IF YOU SIT AROUND THINKING ABOUT TRAVELING, BUT YOU NEVER GO ANYWHERE, SORRY, YOU HAVEN'T BEEN ANYWHERE.

whatever, the local lord who would decide his fate. In the course of this philosophical conversation, he gave this answer that stunned everybody and so the local boss said, "You know what, you're too cool! It would be a waste to chop off your head because there is such good stuff coming out of you, so you can go free!"

CR: Wow, he talked his way out of it! Good luck with that. Wow. He is such an interesting figure. He was in the Foreign Service. He was in India for years, what's now known as India. He went all over in Africa. All over the place. And wherever he went, he studied sexuality. He was very interested in sexuality, and he wrote about it. And after he died, as I'm sure you know, his fucking wife burned his papers! Threw them in the fireplace to protect his reputation! What the fuck, man!

DB: That makes her the mother of all historians, basically, because that's what we do.

CR: That's what we do! We destroy the good stuff. The stuff that's *human*.

DB: Calling it badass is funny because that is just what history *is*, you know. The reality of it is badass in itself. But it's funny that we even have to consider it badass. As opposed to what? The dry, lifeless stuff that the normal, professional historians turn history into?

* BEGIN TS #60 *

CR: Oh, my God. America, get your shit together, will you? I mean they are starting to, a little bit. At least with the drug laws and the same-sex marriage. It seems like we are sort of over that hump.

DB: Do you think prostitution is ever going to become legal here? Kind of like the half of Nevada that has a legal brothel system.

CR: I don't know. This country is so fucked up about sex. As I used to say with my Spanish friends: America is like a country ruled by fourteen-year-old-boys. They are fascinated by guns and cars and tits, and yet they are also very ashamed of much of what they are fascinated by. So there is this deep, weird adolescent conflict at the center of our culture.

Maybe it is possible that countries have a sort of life cycle, and if so, it does kind of feel like maybe the United States is coming out of its adolescence. It's like a 19- or 20-year old, because there do seem to be a lot of people in some position of power now saying we can't really afford this drug war anymore. We are spending a lot of money on things while our country is falling apart. These old assholes in the Senate and Congress, they are stopping anyone from really doing anything about the infrastructure. And what happened to the peace surplus we were supposed to get? Clinton

“”

AS I USED TO SAY WITH MY SPANISH FRIENDS: AMERICA IS LIKE A COUNTRY RULED BY FOURTEEN-YEAR-OLD-BOYS. THEY ARE FASCINATED BY GUNS AND CARS AND TITS, AND YET THEY ARE ALSO VERY ASHAMED OF MUCH OF WHAT THEY ARE FASCINATED BY. SO THERE IS THIS DEEP, WEIRD ADOLESCENT CONFLICT AT THE CENTER OF OUR CULTURE.

balanced the budget, which was pretty cool, and worked down the deficit. Anyway, I don't want to get lost in all that shit. Maybe America will change, but it will probably be awhile. There is a dude on hunger strike against same-sex marriage in Utah. Why would you starve yourself? Why do you give a shit man? It's so strange.

DB: It's bizarre.

CR: Anyone who gives a shit should just automatically be labeled a closeted homosexual. But maybe he's not. Maybe he has some other hair up his ass, but there is no reason to care unless you have some imbalanced weirdness in you.

DB: There is something to be said about the fact that so many people are totalitarians at heart. It's not just that they want to organize their own life the way they want to, they want everyone to go by their dogma. It is amazing because, in the US especially, we talk so much about freedom: freedom this, freedom that. Everybody uses the word, everybody is for freedom. It is just what they define as freedom which is completely different.

CR: Right. You are free to do what I tell you.

DB: Precisely. It's funny when you point to the inconsistencies of this stuff. I remember having this discussion with this guy who was all about freedom, and dying for freedom, and freedom being the core value. He was going on and on and on. And he was clearly super conservative. I wasn't judging, I wasn't arguing, I wasn't antagonizing. But I was saying, "Oh, so that means you want to legalize drugs, you want free prostitution, and you are clearly for euthanasia."

CR: Like a libertarian position.

DB: No. That's not what I mean. I am like, "Sorry, I am confused here because you said you are for freedom. Those are individual rights where you are not hurting another person. So if you are for freedom, that means you are supporting that." I saw a brain meltdown happen in front of me, because it is not like he could say anything, but he suddenly was like, "Oops." You could hear the circuits burning as he went.

CR: It is so strange. Yes, individual freedom as far as guns go, right? And with Obamacare, "Get government out of my life." Okay but then force women to get vaginal ultrasounds before they can get an abortion. So you want government out of your life but in her cunt. What the fuck? There is no consistency there. David Brooks from *The New York Times* recently wrote a column about the legalization of marijuana, and he is against it. And, interestingly, his reasoning was that when he was in high school, he smoked pot with some friends, had a lot of laughs, but then grew out of it. He went to college. He discovered more mature pleasures like love, and literature, and science, and blah, blah, blah. Which is interesting because some of the greatest scientists, like Carl Sagan, said that smoking marijuana gave them a greater insight into science, and certainly into art and music and so on. But, anyway, David Brooks: fuck David Brooks. He wrote this column, and the point of the column was, "Yeah, marijuana is for kids, whatever, I grew out of it, so should everyone else." And that is exactly what you are saying. By making marijuana legal, Colorado is creating what Brooks called an "immoral ecology" where it is more difficult for people to grow out of it, thereby making legalization harmful because it makes it easier for people to waste their lives lying around smoking dope, right?

DB: That's because *I* get to decide what wasting somebody's life means, versus enjoying their life.

CR: Also, it completely ignores the repercussions of arresting people and putting them in jail: they now have a felony on their record, they can't get student loans, they can't vote, they can't this, they can't that. It completely ignores that entire aspect.

DB: That improves their lives, clearly.

CR: Right. Because Brooks is a privileged white kid. Now I don't know where you were, but I smoked a lot of weed when I was in high school and college – but I went to a private, very expensive college and there were no police busting down any dorm doors anywhere near there. If they did, daddy would have been calling the chief of police. Well, not my daddy but a lot of other daddies, and that guy would have been out of a job. So we were in this protected bubble because we were rich white kids.

So, back to the story, Chris Hayes, this young intellectual who just got a new show on NBC with Rachel Maddow, did this thing on his program the other day where he talked about when he and his girlfriend were twenty-one, his girlfriend decided to go to the Republican Convention just to check it out – and there are all these security checks. When they got to the last security check where they actually open your bag and go through everything, he realized he had a bag of dope in his glasses case in his bag. The cop took it out, shook it, opened it and immediately turned his back to Chris Hayes and his girlfriend. Two other cops came over – not security guards – to look at it. They talk, and after a few minutes he closed the glasses case, put it back in the bag, gave it back to Hayes, and said nothing. He said something like, "I have no idea why that happened, but my only guess is that they thought I might have been some Senator's son or something, and it wasn't worth the trouble." Their job was to look for weapons, so they decided it wasn't worth the trouble. He said, "It was because I was a white kid with a tie and glasses, but what if I would have been a black kid with cornrows? I would have been in jail."

And it's not like you just spend thirty days in jail, it derails your life. You aren't going to college now, you aren't getting a job. You are fucked, and it is because you are black. And then he showed this graph of whites versus blacks in terms of marijuana usage, and usage is very similar. But marijuana arrests – Boom! – four times more for blacks.

DB: But that's the thing... I love it when people say, "I don't think it's a good choice, so no one else should be allowed to make that choice either." It is the most anti-freedom argument that anybody could make. And people are willing to restrict the most fundamental freedoms. The fact that you don't have a choice regarding how you want to terminate your own life – that is insane.

CR: You're right, euthanasia is a huge one. If you don't have the right to determine your own death, what right do you have?

DB: Exactly. Are you going to talk to me about any other freedom? There is nothing left to talk about.

CR: This is my body. This is my game. I decide when it is over.

DB: The fact that anybody could have the courage or hypocrisy to ever use the word freedom again when they deny someone else the right to do what they want with their own body, they should just be kicked in the balls – metaphorically if they don't have any balls, or in reality if they do. Are you kidding me? You really dare to use the word freedom again? You evil son of a bitch.

CR: I love the arguments they come up with like "human life is sacred." Oh really, human life is sacred? So what about all the lives of people you threw into prison for life, and you don't even know if they are guilty, and if they were, being in prison isn't going to help them. What about the kids all over the world who don't have a dollar for a fucking vaccine? This idea that human life is sacred? Bullshit, no it's not. There is no consistency in that argument, whatsoever. You know, it is sacred as long as it's an American fetus apparently, but then once it becomes a baby you don't give a shit anymore.

DB: And also the word *sacred*: what does it mean? Sacred means that we should force you to continue your pregnancy when you don't want to – that's what sacred means? Sacred means, if anything, that it should be about individual empowerment. Sacredness should mean that somebody gets to design their own journey, gets to choose how they live, choose how they die. As long as you don't step on anyone else's toes, you should be free to do whatever the fuck you want. End of story.

CR: I was thinking the other day... the American way of death is like basketball games. You ever watch basketball?

DB: Oh, where they put like seventeen thousand commercials, so it takes like two hours for the last minute?

CR: Right, but it's not that they are putting in commercials. It's how the rules are set up: you foul, we have to stop and do foul shots. Foul, timeout. Foul, timeout. That takes all the excitement out of the game! Nine-tenths of the game was a lot of fun. There is

“” THE FACT THAT YOU DON'T HAVE A CHOICE REGARDING HOW YOU WANT TO TERMINATE YOUR OWN LIFE – THAT IS INSANE.

rhythm, and there's flow... but at the end there is just interruption, interruption, interruption.

DB: You know why they do that.... It's so they can throw in a lot more commercials at the end, where more people want to find out who is going to win. So it makes more money.

CR: Yeah there is a collusion between the rules and the commercial interest, as there always is. "Follow the money," as Deep Throat said years ago. The basketball metaphor really works, because of what you say: the reason for the interruptions have nothing to do with improving the quality of the game. In fact, it destroys the quality of the game, but people make money from it. Same thing with the American death industry. Prolonging death is not the same as prolonging life. Prolonging the process of dying does not prolong life. I hope I have the courage to follow through with this, but if somebody tells me I can live three months with good quality of life, or a year with all these chemicals and all this horrible shit, I sure as fuck hope I am the guy who says, "Give me three months and let me out of here!" I do not want to die that way.

DB: There is this thing that we do in the US called a "hospice." It is weird because everybody knows that "hospice" is essentially the management of your death. The way it is done, because euthanasia is illegal, they can't just give you a big shot of morphine and be done with it. The way they do with hospice is that first, you have to qualify for hospice. But even if you do, then they start increasing your morphine intake over days or weeks. The idea is that it will eventually kill you. They are killing you, and you are asking for it. But because euthanasia is illegal we can't do a clean euthanasia where it's over in a few minutes. We will drag it on for a few days or weeks, giving you a little more and more each time. Not enough to kill you. Just enough to start slowly moving in that direction. And it eventually kills you. The point is what? Let somebody die the way they want. It is that simple - why is there even an argument there? It's your life, that's what you want, here you go, self-help kit, done.

CR: Yeah, yeah. Strange world. It's funny because so much of this is a first world problem. I was just in Mozambique a few weeks ago. My wife worked as a physician for years, and you go to some place like Brazil, or even most of the world, and nobody is watching this stuff. It is only in America where everybody is looking over everybody's shoulder, and there are all these committees. They are not paying any attention to the food supply apparently, and they don't notice all the radiation leaking into our rivers, but they sure are watching the morphine use of physicians. And the explanation is so amazing: because we are so paranoid about drugs, morphine is this highly controlled substance. There are - this is in writing, this is US medical policy - limits on the amount of morphine that can be prescribed to patients with terminal illnesses, because we want to avoid getting them addicted. You are going to be dead in four months, but we can't risk you getting addicted. You would be a drug addict, and drug addicts are bad.

DB: No addiction... if I'm dying, just give me enough for a one-time shot.

CR: I'll be a *dead* addict. Okay, how about that?

DB: It's actually kind of crazy the power doctors wield, when they're really just technicians.

CR: Most people in the world don't even see a doctor. My wife, Cacilda talks about how, when she was a young doctor in the countryside of Mozambique, if someone came to her with an issue, she would do

“” IF YOU REALLY DIG INTO THIS STUFF, WHAT YOU FIND IS THAT MOST OF THE MAJOR KILLERS OF HUMAN BEINGS DID NOT EXIST BEFORE AGRICULTURE. WHETHER THAT BE HEART DISEASE, OR DIABETES, OR TUBERCULOSIS, OR MOST KINDS OF CANCER.

her best, but a lot of times people died. But nobody was suing anyone. There is no malpractice, because they know you are lucky if a doctor will even see you. Especially if you don't have any money, as these people didn't. And people die. They know people die. They have seen people die. Death is part of their lives, so when someone dies, it's not immediately assumed it is a great tragedy and that justice is missing; that's an American thing. Elsewhere it is like, "Yeah, I am sorry. It didn't work." Sometimes it doesn't, and paradoxically that allows doctors to learn. Cacilda was trained by Cuban physicians, and she has incredible respect for them. American physicians not so much. Because American physicians never get to fail. They never get to try things and learn things. With American physicians it is all about, "Cover your ass and order fifty different tests because somebody will sue me if I don't. Even if it is a virtual certainty the person doesn't have whatever this test would indicate, I am going to give them that test anyway. Because if there's the one-in-a-million chance they have the disease, I am going to get sued, my insurance will go crazy, I won't be able to work anymore, I will lose my license."

DB: That is the acronym CYA.

CR: Yeah, cover your ass. That is America.

DB: Insane really.

CR: My feeling is that the overall quality of life really has not improved one iota for human beings ever since fifty-thousand-years ago. A lot of half-educated nitwits are going to say, "Oh, wait a minute, people were dying from tuberculosis and cancer." Tuberculosis did not exist fifty-thousand-years ago. If you really dig into this stuff, what you find is that most of the major killers of human beings did not exist before agriculture – whether that be heart disease, or diabetes, or tuberculosis, or most kinds of cancer. So it is a moot point to say, "Now we have medicine." Ah, fuck, we didn't need medicine before.

That's not to say people didn't die. But the question is: how did they die? Generally they died pretty quickly, and they died without a lot of suffering. What we were talking about earlier is central to this question about the quality of human life, because so much of our society is built upon the illusion that we can avoid discomfort and pain, and ultimately even death. It's the denial of death. If you call bullshit on that, then suddenly most of what we are spending our energy and resources on no longer makes any sense. Ultimately you are not going to succeed by avoiding the basic stuff of life.

THE THING THAT I'VE LEARNED MAKING THIS MOVIE IS THAT THERE ARE A MILLION APPROACHES TO LOVE AND TO SEX – AND WHAT WOULD BE NICE IS IF PEOPLE REALIZED AND ACCEPTED THAT THERE ARE A MILLION APPROACHES.

CHAPTER 12

TAO RUSPOLI

EPISODE #3 (APRIL 19, 2013)
&
EPISODE #115 (MARCH 9, 2015)

Tao Ruspoli is a documentary filmmaker and the son of an Italian prince. His latest project, Monogamish, explores the failings of the common relationship paradigms of the 20th and 21st centuries.

ADDICTIONS | MONOGAMY/POLYAMORY | FILM-MAKING
RELIGION | MARRIAGE | RELATIONSHIPS

TAO RUSPOLI: We are sitting in a 1976 GMC motorhome. They are classic collector items that have a whole cult around them, because it is the most perfectly designed RV, in the history of all RV making, so they say. And we have been traveling since Los Angeles, and we've made to Vancouver. There are five of us living in here, and we cook, and we have an editing studio. Patrick is in front of us, editing our new documentary called *Monogamish*.

CHRIS RYAN: It's pretty sweet, it's like a production studio on wheels.

TR: I actually lived in a school bus for two years. Now that was a production studio on wheels because I gutted all the seats out and put in three editing systems, this is back in 2001 when digital editing was still a bit new. You couldn't do it on laptops like you do now so we bought all these solar panels and put Radar-ray with two terabytes which at the time was the biggest hard drive you'd ever heard of. And we had this old school bus that had this high tech roving digital film studio and it was called the LAFCO bus, which stood for Los Angeles Filmmakers Co-Operative. It was great because it helped people make films and introduced artists who worked in other media to the wonders of digital film-making.

CR: So you were truly mobile? You didn't have it in the backyard and take it out occasionally?

TR: No, I lived in it for two years, traveling around and making documentaries just as we are doing now.

CR: Let's talk a little bit about your family background because I have to say when people ask me what sort of wild characters I am meeting in L.A. these days, your name comes up, just because you have such a fascinating background. Your father was an Italian prince who hung out with Fellini?

TR: And Dali and Bridget Bardot and Cocteau as well; these were all his dear friends. My father was born in 1924 and his father was a military man born in the one year where he had to fight in both World Wars. He was a devout fascist from an old aristocratic family tracing back a thousand years in Rome. And my father rebelled against that very early. Imagine: he was 16 when World War II started and he was suddenly hanging out with the wrong crowd and doing drugs, being very rebellious. As soon as the war ended he was 21 and he had a huge inheritance and suddenly he just started his exuberant life which then became known as 'La Dolce Vita.' They say Fellini based the film in part on his exploits. He lived very extravagantly. He said everyday was like the last because he had lived through World War II and knew that everything was fragile. So my father lived very exuberantly and extravagantly because he loved life, and he squandered a thousand years of family fortune in a few decades. But he did it in style!

CR: He did it in style. That's great because my parents also squandered my inheritance but it wasn't a thousand years. They earned, they squandered it. Good for them. So, how does that feel to you?

TR: I am lucky because my mother is American, and she is like a hippie artist so I wasn't raised with this sense of entitlement that a lot of people with my type of family in Italy might be born with. I came to the United States often where there is this do it yourself frontier mentality which I hoped to have inherited and hope I am living by going on adventures like this.

CR: I can confirm that we are not in what you would call princely surroundings here. It is comfortable and wonderful.

TR: I couldn't fail to disagree with you less.

CR: How did your parents meet? How does a prince meet a hippie chick from the States?

TR: Well, he was living a very extravagant life in the 60s. Gunter Sachs said that there were only twelve real playboys in the history of the world and my father was one of them, right up there with Casanova.

CR: Two Italians? Who else qualifies?

TR: There was Rubirosa, another big 1950s playboy. The idea was that Hugh Hefner – who everyone associates with word "playboy" – actually killed the notion of "playboy." Made the idea of The Playboy impossible because he muddied it by making it something accessible to everybody. There were all these prerequisites to being a "Playboy." My father said every time they asked him, "What do you do?" he would say, "About what?" The idea of working didn't even occur to them. My father was one of the twelve great playboys of history and lived outside of the realms of normal possibility, even of intelligibility to the rest of the world. He partly had no ambition. In America, the word "ambitious" is used as a compliment. In that old Italian world, to call someone "ambitious" was an insult.

CR: Because it implies that you are missing something...

TR: That you are upward climbing, that you are opportunistic. This lack of ambition endeared him to

> **SO HE LIVED VERY EXUBERANTLY AND EXTRAVAGANTLY BECAUSE HE WAS ABLE TO AND HE SQUANDERED A THOUSAND YEARS OF FAMILY FORTUNE IN ONE LIFETIME, THEY SAY. BUT HE DID IT IN STYLE!**

IN AMERICA, THE WORD "AMBITIOUS" IS USED AS A COMPLIMENT. IN THAT OLD ITALIAN WORLD, TO CALL SOMEONE "AMBITIOUS" WAS AN INSULT.

a lot of very interesting people, whether it was Orson Welles -my father taught him magic tricks supposedly - or Roman Polanski - another great friend of his, another controversial and scandalous figure, of course. He was with Polanski at a party and my mother had moved to Italy because her father had become a spaghetti western actor and he was friends with Polanski also. She met my father: she was 15 and he was almost 50. He was older than my grandfather, my mother's father. Then they went to Thailand. My father was an opium addict and so he spent a lot of time in the Far East. So he took my mother to Thailand when she was 17. They conceived me -

CR: Oh that's where you were born?

TR: That is where I was born. That is how I got the name Tao.

CR: What did her parents think of your father?

TR: They liked him because he was such a great guy, a great character.

CR: A charmer, huh? If you can charm your way into the hearts of the parents of your 16-year-old girlfriend, when you're 48 or something, that's climbing charm mountain right there. That is a tough gig.

TR: It wasn't a frivolous affair. They stayed together ten years and they had my little brother. He already had another son. His wife, who he was separated from, lived in the same building. My father lived in the main apartment and his wife lived above. Then you would see the paparazzi pictures of him, and it would say, "Here is prince Ruspoli with his wife, his lover, his son from his wife, his son from his lover - and the lover is pregnant with the second son." I was raised with this kind of very expansive view of what family can be.

CR: And here you are all grown up, a full-grown man making a film about monogamy and its discontents. To me it sounds like this has been a long time coming. Is there an autobiographical element to this?

TR: Yes, of course. I've always used film-making as a kind of therapy, a way of processing what is going on in my life. So my first movie, my first documentary that I am proud of, was called *Just Say Know*. It dealt with drug addiction in my family. My father was an opium addict for 45 years and before that he had been a heroin addict for many years. My mother was a heroin addict for many years. My little brother was a heroin addict for many years.

So there is a dark side to all of this. There was a lot of drug addiction, so I made this movie interviewing these three generations because the ages were so wildly different. At the time my father was 78, my mother was in her early 40s, my brother was in his early 20s, and the three of them are talking about their struggles with addiction. So it was this look at how they dealt with it: a 78-year-old prince in Rome; a 20 year old kid in L.A.; a single mom - and how that affected their addictions. So that was one of my first films. And then I made that into a feature film called *Fix*, which was a fictional account of a guy who has to rescue his brother, bail him out of jail, and get him to rehab – but it was based on a true story. Then I was married for nine years and went through a divorce, and I found that it brought up a lot of interesting issues on the state of marriage. What does it do in our culture? What does monogamy mean? What do we look for in our relationships? So I started this project.

CR: Was monogamy an issue in the divorce, if you're open to talking about it?

TR: No, it wasn't the reason for the divorce. It was a more subtle thing, which I think everybody experiences in a long-term relationship. It can become platonic and people can feel like they've become great friends but the passion goes a different direction.

CR: You become siblings.

TR: Yeah. So I think that was part of it, and of course it's complicated. More complicated than I probably can explain. Not that I am reluctant, but ... the idea with the film was that I just wanted to figure out monogamy. Obviously it used to mean having one wife, right? As opposed to polygamy. Then people thought that to be monogamous meant to be with one partner for your whole life, whether that's natural or even ideal. Then, of course, it's changing a lot, very quickly. If you look at the history of it, it changes a lot. All the time! People like to project backwards to whatever the ideal of their time is, to be how it's always been – and of course, you don't have to dig very deep to find out that's not true.

CR: Yeah, I love this phrase: "Traditional marriage." Which fucking tradition are we talking about here? Traditional marriage, gimme a break.

TR: Right? It's been really interesting to look into this, and find out about the unspoken ideals and unspoken assumptions around relationships, about where we are as a culture. And I do feel that we are in this state of transition. I don't think it's just me. I think there's a seismic tectonic shift happening in our culture about what matters, what we look for in a relationships. And that maybe there is a new kind of reconsideration around these assumed values.

CR: I think you're right. With monogamy, the basic illusion is that loving someone means your interest is focused only on them, that you have no interest in anyone else. That's exhausted. Everyone knows that's not true.

TR: I'm pathologically optimistic, and even with my films about drug use, I've often looked at the bright side of everything – and I love the way people's struggles can turn people into individuals. We don't want everybody to have a safe, banalized existence – a trend that is especially prevalent in American culture – when you see so many places look exactly like every other place, and you know exactly what to expect from the Denny's, or the Starbucks. Localized things are being destroyed, but then in other places, there is a resistance to that, right? I like to explore how fucked-up-ed-ness can actually make people who they are or make them unique. So whether that's drug addiction or weird family structures, I don't think we should all be aiming for this one *Leave it to Beaver* ideal. I think that it's kinda interesting that people have multiple relationships and families.

I am still very close to my ex-wife's family. Of course, the tradition would have you say that once you've ended this, then this terrible thing has happened, so let's just push it into this dark corner and move on to the next thing. I like these new models that people are looking at, this tribal idea with open-

“”

I'VE ALWAYS USED FILM-MAKING AS A KIND OF THERAPY, A WAY OF PROCESSING WHAT IS GOING ON IN MY LIFE.

mindedness around monogamy – which can create this new tribal sense of the extended family. One of our producers is divorced and has three kids from that marriage. She is now with somebody else who has kids, and her ex-husband is also with somebody else who had kids. And all of the sudden these four different families are all vacationing together.

CR: Beautiful! I love those stories.

TR: It's an alternative to saying that it's an awful thing that happened and that divorce is a failure of marriage. It's like these are cycles, and maybe we can just relax about it all, and we can all be friends. We can all acknowledge this deep connection that we have.

CR: That's the thing. It changes but it doesn't go away. My ex-girlfriend and I were together six years, and now she's like my best friend. She's my sister and her husband is a great friend, and there is nothing that makes me happier than hanging out with them and their kids. That's as close to a kid as I'll ever have: my ex-partner's child that she has with another guy. Margaret Mead, the famous anthropologist, was once giving a press conference and she was talking about relationships and some journalist asked, "You've had three failed marriages, who are you to opine on relationships?" And she said, "Excuse me, I've been married to three wonderful men, all of whom are still great friends of mine. None of those marriages was a failure." Fuck you, journalist! That should be said in more press conferences.

TR: People ask why we are doing this trip. We filmed for this in Europe and New York, but now we are doing the Pacific Coast. I like that we are on this margin of this land, the final frontier in America, the West Coast. Without dissolving boundaries altogether we can nudge people, and explore that edge of what they find acceptable. We are looking into people who are trying new things, often successfully.

CR: You were talking about addiction and now we are talking about sexuality and monogamy. Do you have any opinions on sex addiction? You think it's a real thing?

TR: No, I think it's yet another attempt to create a box and pathologize what makes people alive and human. Even though I use the word addiction with my family, I would like to see the individual path in each of their stories, rather than to just label them all as addicts.

There was a great Jungian psychologist named James Hillman who wrote *The Myth of Analysis*. Someone said to him, "My son is in L.A. and he's a heroin addict. What should I do?" And Hillman, who was also wary of the idea of jumping to the conclusion that somebody is sick, said, "Well, imagine it was 500 hundred years ago and your son wanted to go on a boat to America, and there was no way you could communicate with him for years. And he might die, but, at a certain point, you'd have to just accept it; that's his journey, right? You could just love him and hope for the best." I thought that was a great way to view it, because you're not going to tell somebody to stop using drugs for you. If they need to go through this, they'll figure out when they need to stop. And then they'll come and ask you for help, which my brother did eventually. I was happy to help him out in my own humble way, but that's very different from imposing what you think is best for somebody. I think it's the same with sex addiction.

* * *

CR: So we opened with this beautiful flamenco guitar playing. How did that come into your life?

TR: That's another passion of mine. I love the music, but more than anything I really, really love the lifestyle associated with it. The gypsies in the south of Spain have a philosophy of creativity that's embodied into their way of life and their approach to their music. This really resonated with me since I started playing 18 years ago. It's this idea that the boundary between life and art is blurry, especially between commerce and art. In the modern world there's this sense that if somebody is really, really good at what they do, then they must do it professionally for money. And if they have some other work then they must not be that good.

CR: Keep your day job.

TR: Right, right. And in Spain I remember reading the liner notes of this CD of this very famous flamenco family, and they said they were all butchers. When asked why they remained butchers when they could so easily be making money with Flamenco, they said, "Well, only the most desperate person who doesn't know anything else would prostitute their music for money!" Right? So, they much rather preferred to create their art when it sprung up naturally, when it was part of their culture, when it wasn't being paid for, and being put on a stage. I loved that, and I love it in the way I play music, and hopefully to a certain degree in the way that we make films. Here we are, 5 of us living in this RV, traveling, and there's not a set rigid agenda. There's not a primarily commercial film we've done. It's an exploration of life and art, blending together.

CR: Right, I could see that yesterday, you had a big heavy tripod on your shoulder and we had sound guy with a big backpack full of stuff, and we were just walking around talking to whoever we found. It was very spontaneous and sort of hunter-gatherer approach to film-making.

TR: And of course, the gypsies... everyone thinks of the gypsies as being nomads; although in the south of Spain they aren't so much nomadic. But I've always loved that nomadic spirit. That adventurous spirit mixed with a rich tradition and roots - and that's what the gypsies have. I joke that this RV is a phallus and a womb, because we're out there adventuring and finding a resolution to the conflict that Esther Perel talks about: between safety, home, and predictability; and between the unknown, adventure, and passion. And those two things seem to be incompatible, and in some senses they are, but in other senses... here we are in this wonderful, nurturing, home-like environment while at the same time exploring new lands.

CR: I can see that. You've got all the comforts of home in here, and yet you can just start up and go somewhere new. That's like having an open marriage. A lot of people I've spoken to with open marriages, that's exactly what they say: "the two of us are adventuring together, but at the end of the day or night, we've got each other." They've got their marriage, intimacy, long term stability, comfort...

all the things that people love in marriage, but they also have the excitement of having these sexual adventures together.

TR: Again, yes, it's about pushing these limits. I don't think we can push too quickly beyond our comfort zones, but the idea that it is possible to have both a sense of adventure and a sense of safety and security, is something worth looking at very seriously. I don't think this there's anything inherently wrong with serial monogamy. The fact that we have these 5- and 10- year-long relationships, we exhaust all possibilities within them, and then we move to a new cycle in our life. That's definitely something I don't think should be stigmatized. If you said, "I just want to be with this one person for now, and we'll see how it goes," that is another possibility. The thing that I've learned making this movie is that there are a million approaches to love and to sex – and what would be nice is if people realized and accepted that there are a million approaches. Not in the sense that I want to categorize everything... but if we can really respond to the situation in a way that's right for us... It can expand people's sense of possibility, which is not a bad thing.

CR: Yeah, and also by realizing there's so many different approaches to these things, people can make smarter choices as to whom they get involved with initially, and who they stay with as well.

* * *

TR: The Wal-Mart-ization and McDonald's-ization of culture extends to everything. My father, even in the drug issue, distinguished between cultured drugs, like drinking wine at the table in Italy or France, or hashish in North Africa, or chewing the coca leaves in South America, or the opium in the Far East. These are rituals that are thousands of years old, that are integrated into the practices of a culture. And we should preserve those practices, because if you don't, they're replaced with something much worse: the coca leaves becomes cocaine, the opium becomes heroin.

This is the result of divorcing a practice from its culture, and you instead look for efficiency. Let's step outside of drugs and think about food. A great meal is not efficient: it takes time to cook it, you sit around and eat it, and it has all these great benefits of bringing people together, and making you grateful for the land, and grateful for your tradition and your culture, and all of these things. McDonald's tastes the same all over the world, and you know what you're going to get. It's safe, and efficient, and fast, and cheap; it's all of these things that you think might be good. What I think I inherited from my father's family and my mother's family is a sense of wanting to fight the banality of a life lived according to safe expectations.

CR: Milan Kundera called it "the uglification of the world."

“” WHAT I THINK I INHERITED FROM MY FATHER'S FAMILY AND MY MOTHER'S FAMILY IS A SENSE OF WANTING TO FIGHT THE BANALITY OF A LIFE LIVED ACCORDING TO SAFE EXPECTATIONS.

TR: So that is what brings us into this funky old RV traveling off the coast, five people living in a tiny little space. It's a sense that there are possibilities beyond the very limited scope of what it makes sense for 90% of people, especially those in America. Another nod I'd like to make is to my former uncle-in-law, Alexander Coburn, who just died and had the most incredible funeral I've ever been to outside my father's. We were driving to Petrolia on the Lost Coast of California, where he lived, and it was two and half hours through these curving winding roads into this completely other world, so far from the strip malls. And I realized that, echoing what another great mentor of mine taught me, we have a duty to show people another way to look at things, and another way to live. Just going on this journey to where he lived was a way of stepping into his world and his way of seeing things. I hope that with my work I'm able to do the same thing; that when you look at the photos and films that I make, that you see another possibility, another way of looking at things.

CR: Beautiful. Has it ever occurred to you that your father might have been a closet Marxist?

TR: Well, he was very radical in his politics. He definitely considered himself a radical. I don't know if Marxist would be exactly right, because I guess there would be a certain hypocrisy in a prince being a Marxist... unless he was going to assume a totally different lifestyle. But he believed in freedom and the legalization of drugs. He obviously had compassion, not a sense of entitlement. He felt very lucky for what he'd been born with, but he didn't want to disavow it either.

CR: But he also didn't really to want to protect it and preserve it; he squandered it.

TR: This is true.

CR: So not a real *serious* Marxist but...

TR: A joyful Marxist!

* BEGIN TS #115 *

CR: Well, the movie, *Monogamish*, looks great. I don't know how many versions of it I've seen at this point. You're editing it and changing it, and I have to say: I know you did not want to make the movie explicitly about your experience, that you wanted that to be implicit. But it's become more and more explicitly about you. You've been more personally revealing with each version that I've seen, which I know must be excruciating on some level.

TR: That's one of the reasons it's taken so long, because I've had to work some of these things out myself and come to terms with my own perspective on these things. My ex-wife happens to be a famous actress and so I didn't want to ever be seen as exploiting that, and I still don't. It's a fine balance that I've been trying to achieve between telling my story as a way into this huge subject, which otherwise could seem too big or too academic, and at the same time asking hard questions of myself without putting other people in an awkward or uncomfortable position. Again, I think as a journalist or documentarian, you have to tread lightly and at the same time be persistent in your search for truth, right?

CR: It is hard, and I do a separate podcast from this one called *Talking Out My Ass*, which is where I tell my life stories, travel tales, and stuff like that. I am constantly running into that conundrum of, "Well this is my life, and I'm telling this story – but it involved other people, and in some sense it's their story too – so even though I change the names, how much of this do I have a right to use without other people's consent?"

TR: Film-making is a somewhat aggressive act and that's reflected in the language we use. We talk about *shooting* people and *taking* pictures. I have always been very sensitive to that, because I do think that you're taking something from someone by pointing a camera at them - and it can be somewhat aggressive, but at the same time, being somewhat aggressive is something you sometimes have to do in order to unearth things. I think our job as filmmakers is to negotiate that tension as carefully as we can. Film-making has been so patriarchal and so dominated by men; in Hollywood today it's still this dictatorship of giant male egos. The one role in the film-making process that's been open to women from the beginning is editing, and it's also the most essential because every other part of film-making is borrowing from other media.

When you're shooting something it's almost like theater, you're telling a story like you do in a novel, but editing is unique to film-making, right? So editing is a huge part of the film-making process, a part that the general public doesn't spend much time thinking about, a part that's not glamorized. Again, it relates back to the male ego and its inability to recognize the importance of roles that aren't out there in more obvious ways -where most of the film-making process is actually happening. You're sitting there with this material that you've gathered, it's like paints that you know have to put on the canvas, and you work through it slowly, slowly. There is a hundred different ways to cut the same material, and to give a very different tone and message with it. So I have been struggling with that for a while, more than any on other film that I've made, but that's again because it's a very big subject. It affects everyone; that's been very clear as I've gone forward: that there's nobody who is untouched by these issues.

I'm not pretending to make something totally objective here. I think there's a subjective point of view. There is something broken about the way things are set up now, and we easily look back at other eras and recognize that there were things wrong with the way they had things set up. We can look back at the 1950s, and look down our noses, and say oh these people were so backwards, and so repressed. And that's going back 50 years - but let's go back 100 or 200 years, and we can clearly see that there were improvements made. Obviously some things got worse. I think there's a tendency to think that the way things are today is the right way, and you see it a lot in the marriage debate. "Traditional marriage"... I don't know how people can say that with a straight face. How they can reject gay marriage and say, "We are for traditional marriage. What's next, polygamy?" Well look at the Bible, it's all polygamy.

CR: Well that *is* traditional marriage. I don't want to be intrusive at all, but I really like the fact that with each iteration, the film has skewed more into your personal story. Because it's so fucking interesting you know? I mean, your experience, in some ways, is so idealized from a normal person's perspective. An Italian prince married to a fucking movie star, right? How can it get better than that? You're good looking, she's good looking. You're both brilliant. You're both creative. You both have absolutely everything, and your marriage didn't work out for whatever reason. It's like Zeus and Hera or something like that. If they can't get their shit together, what hope is there for the rest of us?

TR: Going into the family history part of it (because I did go back to my family history), again people talk about traditional: there is this religious side of marriage, obviously, and this political side where religious people want to defend marriage as this sacred institution, which obviously got its title from the pope. It was known as the papal aristocracy; there were certain families that provided military and

“”

THE HISTORY OF MARRIAGE IS ONE OF CONTROL; IT'S ONE OF CONTROLLING WOMEN, RESTRICTING WOMEN'S SEXUALITY – AS I LEARNED FROM YOUR BOOK.

financial support to the Vatican, and in exchange they would get titles and feudal lands.

CR: So they were the Zuckerberg of the 800s?

TR: Right, I think that I'm a unique position to see up-close that there's this co-existence of something that's called sacred, and a public ritual that is acknowledged by the community. These religious institutions are born out of a quest for power and domination. So the history of marriage is one of control. It's one of controlling women; restricting women's sexuality – as I learned from your book. As private property comes into the human sphere, men want to make sure their property is being passed on to their own children, so they need to control who their women are sleeping with.

Religion is a very complex subject, and we could spend a lot of time talking about it, but I do think there's something real about the longing for something that's transcendent. And I do think that's there, even in institutional religion. I think the people on the left often don't want to acknowledge that, right? The idea that there could be something more profound, a practice that stretches back beyond your lifespan, that involves your community and isn't just you alone with your own spiritual whatever-the-fuck-you-want.

CR: There's ritual.

TR: Ritual. It's just an uneasy marriage, pun intended, of these very disparate ideas and practices. You have love, passion, and commitment on one hand and domination and control on the other. You have pragmatic concerns around the pooling of resources; Stephanie Coons, one of the world's authorities on the history of marriage, is one of our main interview subjects in the film, and she explains that marriage was traditionally very little about the man and the woman. It was about the two families coming together. I don't think that should be seen as a bad thing; that's great. When you start to have two people that are on their own, just making their decisions based on flighty emotions... maybe that makes things much less stable.

CR: So at this point, I think anyone who has listened to this podcast is going to see your film, if they can.

TR: Yes! We have a Facebook page for *Monogamish* which we are constantly updating. We have monogamish.us the website. And we appreciate everyone's support.

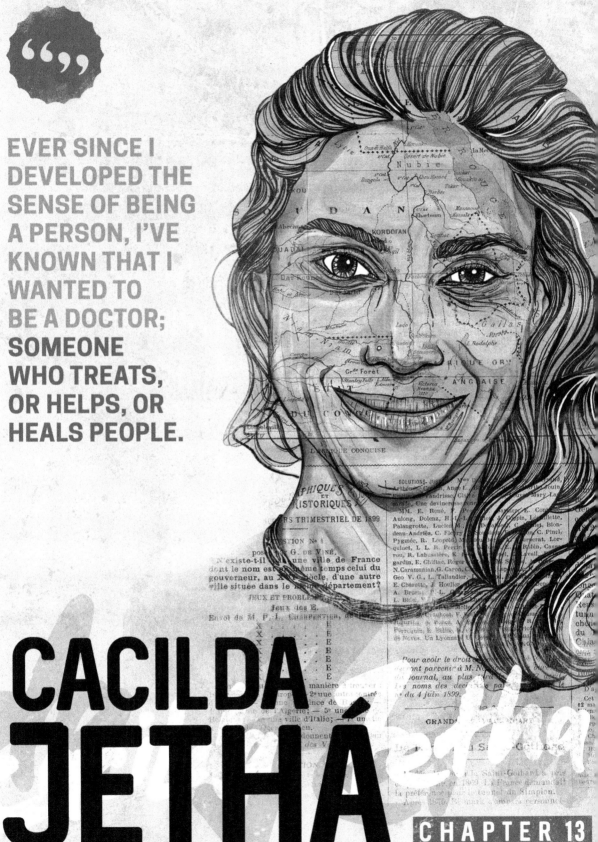

> EVER SINCE I DEVELOPED THE SENSE OF BEING A PERSON, I'VE KNOWN THAT I WANTED TO BE A DOCTOR; **SOMEONE WHO TREATS, OR HELPS, OR HEALS PEOPLE.**

CACILDA JETHÁ

CHAPTER 13

EPISODE #100 (NOVEMBER 17, 2014)

***Cacilda Jethá, MD, is a psychiatrist. She worked as a physician for seven years in Mozambique, and directed WHO-funded research in the development of AIDS prevention efforts. She eventually teamed up with Chris to co-author* Sex at Dawn: How We Mate, Why We Stray and What It Means for Modern Relationships.**

SHAMANISM | PSYCHOLOGY | WESTERN MEDICINE

CHRIS RYAN: I have conversations with people on this broadcast who I find to be interesting, and I trust that most of the audience will find them interesting as well. Cacilda is the most interesting person I know. I haven't had her on the podcast, because it's personal. There is a line between business and pleasure, or personal and public, and I've tried to respect that line. But Episode #100 was coming up, I wanted to do something special, and I couldn't think of anything more special than to have you on. Thank you for agreeing to do this.

CACILDA JETHÁ: Hi.

CR: I don't want to talk about our personal stuff too much. Just to introduce you to people, Cassie speaks seven languages. Her life is unlike any other life I have ever heard about. First of all, being born into a mixed family, your mother was raised in a Muslim family, your father was raised in a Hindu family. They are both primarily, ethnically, Indian. There is some Persian connection – part of your ancestors came from what is now called Iran. That's the Muslim part. Another part came from India, particularly Goa, which is on the west coast of India. You were born in Mozambique when it was still a Portuguese colony. You were born in 1960 into this family that looks Indian, is half Muslim half Hindu, in Africa. Your family had a lot of money. They had a taxi business, they had a chain of general stores, different buildings, and property.

You're 13 years old, and there's a war happening. The war for independence, which became very nasty. South Africa is supporting one side and, of course, Portugal is fighting not to lose their colony. So, you've got white people, essentially, who are fighting against black people who are trying to take their country from the colonialists. But then the black people are also being supported by Cuba and the Soviet Union, so it fell into that whole proxy-war thing that was happening all over the world in those days: in Vietnam, in Latin America. Anytime there was a war, it turned out to be communism versus capitalism. So it was a very nasty war. You're 13 years old, you're locked up in your house with all the shutters closed because of the bombs and the bullets flying around. You're hiding in your house, reading comic books. For two months you're hiding in your house. You're hoping nobody is going to break down the door and come in the house.

“ ” AND BEING THE ONLY NON-WHITE PERSON IN THE CLASS, I REMEMBER THE FIRST DAY: NOBODY WOULD LOOK AT ME, NOBODY WOULD TALK WITH ME.

CJ: And you could see through the window at night, and it would be like fireworks. The rockets and bombs and so on. Luckily, my parents had a lot of canned food, rice, and beans; all the food we would need for those two months. And I would read *Astérix and Obélix*. My brother had a whole collection of them. I had a lot of fun reading those comic books while the war was happening.

CR: So, there is this war going on, then the Communists win, and they take over the country. Samora Machel goes on the radio, and he says the country is now ours. Everything belongs to the state: all the buildings and the businesses... everything belongs to the state. If you want to leave, you have 24 hours to leave, and you can take 20 kilos with you. Your parents put you on an airplane, at 13 years old, to Portugal. Had you ever been to Portugal before?

CJ: No.

CR: Were there a lot of refugees coming from Mozambique to Portugal?

CJ: Yes. Not only from Mozambique, from Angola, from all over the world.

CR: The whole empire was collapsing.

CJ: So all those people were called *retornados*; the "returned." But nobody was returning. Suddenly, a white country became a multiracial country.

CR: So you're in Portugal, where there is also a revolution happening. There are riots in the street, people getting shot, and crazy shit happening. You're in school and you're studying. So, just to keep with this quick summary, you grow up and you decide to study medicine. You always knew you wanted to study medicine.

CJ: Ever since I developed the sense of being a person, I've known that I wanted to be a doctor; someone who treats, or helps, or heals people.

CR: So you got into medical school in Portugal, which was really hard. And then one Christmas you go back to Mozambique, and what happened?

CJ: I didn't leave.

CR: You just said, "Fuck Portugal, I want to stay here."

CJ: Yes, but I wasn't prepared to stay, actually...

CR: Because you were there on vacation.

CJ: Yes. And my parents went crazy because they didn't want me in a communist country. But I was so unhappy in Portugal.

CR: Yeah, but you'd worked so hard to get into medical school in Portugal. Wouldn't it have been easier to just go back to Mozambique, and go to medical school there from the beginning?

CJ: Probably, but I was a very responsible person, I guess. I would follow everything that my parents would say to do, so I stayed. I had very good marks in school, but I was miserable. I remember when I was 13 in high school, and I didn't know anybody. And being the only non-white person in the class, I remember the first day; nobody would look at me, nobody would talk with me.

CR: You were the only non-white person.

CJ: Exactly, the only non-white person in my school. Because I was living in a part of Lisbon that was quite upper-class. One day after a physics test, I had the high score, but I didn't know that. It was interesting, because the teacher kept calling one by one to give the paper with the score. And they were very low scores. So bad. The scores went up to 20, but the scores were like 10 or lower. At last she said, "I'm very surprised about this, but I have to say I'm very proud, because Cacilda has 18."

So, I remember to be in the last row, and the whole class turned their heads back to look at me. I remember at that time, oh God, for the first time, all those people who never looked at me, they turned to look at me. Of course I was very proud to have best marks. So after this day, I started to be the popular girl. I was always a very good student. After that, I felt, at school at least, I could be relaxed. And I nailed it. But I was miserable outside of school. And I didn't like Portugal. It's so different from Africa. You can see from my pictures at that time, I wasn't very happy. I was 20 when I went to spend Christmas and New Year's Eve with my parents. And I decided, I'm not going to go back. My parents were very angry, because that time I didn't go back.

CR: The war was still going on, right?

CJ: Sort of. But the Mozambique Liberation Front (FRELIMO) was the government.

CR: So you were doing volunteer stuff, and you transferred to the medical school there.

CJ: And I do not regret. Because there I had more cadavers, more people, more everything to train with. The first year of medicine we were 60 students, the second year we were 19.

CR: There's normally a pretty big drop off, but that's extreme.

CJ: Extreme! It was a small class, and we had a lot of material.

CR: So, you're back in Mozambique, you finish medical school, and you immediately start working there as a doctor.

CJ: Yes, after finishing medical school there. They put us working there, still with the guerrilla war ongoing.

CR: Right. The war was officially over, but not actually. It went on for years and years, because South Africa was supporting. And also, Mozambique had training camps for the African National Congress, who were going in and blowing shit up in South Africa and agitating against apartheid. And the apartheid thing was also happening in Mozambique. So you're a young doctor. How old were you when you finished medical school?

CJ: I was 25 or 26. The year that Joanna was born, they let me stay in a health clinic, and I stayed there for six months or so, because I was still breastfeeding Joanna. And then, after that, I started to work in that area, an area of 50,000 inhabitants.

CR: I've known you 15 years, we've talked about stuff a lot. I still can't imagine what it's like to be 25 years old and just like, "Here you go, here's your clinic. Deliver babies, amputate limbs."

CJ: It wasn't easy because, first of all, I didn't appear to be a grown-up person.

CR: Right, you're a kid. And you're not African. You're not black, and you're not white. If you were white, they...

CJ: They would even respect more.

CR: Right, because white people know things we don't. But you're Indian. What the hell is that? Indian people are seen as business people.

CJ: Business people. They didn't respect me at all. I remember many times to say to a woman, "Okay, get undressed, and I will do a gynecology exam." People would say, "No, I am not going to open my legs for this kid." So things like that. I had to impose, through my knowledge, and try to work with them. Which I don't regret at all because all that experience made me actually study more, and prove that I can do stuff. And besides that, there was a lot of fighting with some nurses.

* * *

CJ: The most scary day for me was the day that I arrived, and they attacked the village at night, the guerrillas. They literally went to every house, burned the houses, and with the machetes, decapitated the people. They wanted to make a point. I remember arriving that morning, and it was surreal. I can't describe that feeling of seeing the houses completed covered in dark ashes because they were burned. And dead bodies, and others who didn't die from the machetes, with the half of their neck cut. But African people have a lot of resilience and resistance. They were walking, like robots, toward the hospital, toward the clinic that I have, to receive treatment. That was surreal. I can't describe that. But luckily my team, the nurses, were so beautiful, so hard working. Like, they get to work, and do work, work, work, work to try to help everyone.

CR: Do you remember the first person who died in your clinic or your first patient who died?

CJ: No. I saw a lot of dead people or people dying in front of me since I was in med school. And when I was in rotation for pediatrics, you see a lot of babies dying, because infant mortality is high in Africa. After a while it becomes routine, so no, it didn't bother me. I'm not saying that I do not feel, but it happened every day.

CR: It's not remarkable. So you go back to Portugal. You spend a year to get your medical degree recognized there. Then you decide you're going to do psychiatry. Why psychiatry? Because, at that point, you could have done anything.

CJ: I was going to do internal medicine, because I love it. After general practitioner, internal medicine would be the specialization. But when AIDS and HIV education went to Africa and I saw the ads on the street all saying, "Have only one partner," "Use condoms," I thought, are you kidding me? You can't ask African people to have only one partner because of AIDS. It's not going to work. At the time, I was interested in epidemiology and investigation, and I wanted to do research. So, I went to take a course. The World Health Organization provided research courses.

CR: This was back in Africa.

CJ: There were 3-month courses. That's where I met a

great professor. Then I explained my perspective. We have to design a health education plan that is more accurate for Africa.

CR: One that's culturally designed.

CJ: According to the attitude, the belief system, the way they behave. We can't apply the European version to Africa. They agreed with me, so they supported me. I designed a study, and since I was in that village, I already had people that I could research on. So I took advantage of being in my little hospital there, and I started to investigate that. And that was where the interest in doing psychiatry came, from talking with them about their belief system, their attitudes, the way they behaved, their sexual behavior. Talking with them and seeing how their mind functions. And in a person who has lots of casual partners, the mind works completely different than a man who has multiple wives. There is a difference. I put those into categories: multiple casual partners, multiple wives, or monogamy. I decided I want to do psychiatry, not internal medicine.

CR: Because of that World Health Organization study? And that's the same study where you inspected a thousand mens' penises?

CJ: Yes.

CR: You hussy!

CJ: I had to inspect to see if they had gonorrhea, if they had chlamydia!

CR: A thousand of them. That a lot of African penis. And you didn't think about becoming a urologist or something, after all that?

CJ: No, psychiatry was fantastic, are you kidding me?! I love brains...

CR: What about neurology? Did you consider that? Because brain is more neurology, isn't it?

CJ: No. Neurology, for me, is like being a mathematician. Because neurology is like the brain: the circuits fail, it's very mechanistic. It's beautiful. I like that, I really appreciate it. But when I discovered the whole mind behind that belief system, I thought psychiatry.

* * *

CR: One thing we haven't talked about is the fact that you are left handed: And that you were in one of these schools where they made you write with your right hand.

CJ: The primary school, when I was six years old.

CR: What do you think, looking at this 50 years later as a psychiatrist, what kind of effect do you think that has on a kid?

CJ: I think a big effect. On me it was huge. And you know me.

CR: Okay, so we're going to tell a secret here that people don't know. Since *Sex at Dawn* came out, a lot of people have been curious about why you don't do more media. And I tell half the story. I say that part of your condition of being listed as co-author was that you didn't want to do any media, because you're a private person. And all that's true.

CJ: And I am. It's true.

CR: It's true. And we did have that conversation, and

you did say, "I don't want to talk to media," and I'm not lying. But I've never publicly explained this part, which is, as you were just saying, probably as a result of being forced to use your right hand when you were naturally left handed. Our friend, Stanley Krippner, described your condition as "cognitive dyslexia".

CJ: And I think he's right about that.

CR: Just to explain to people what we are talking about... Cacilda has a tendency sometimes, especially when she's nervous, to flip concepts. So, in the middle of winter she might say, "Oh, it's really hot outside," when you mean it's really cold. For me, over time, and knowing you, I tend to listen to what you say in context, and I normally know what you mean. Although, sometimes I get completely confused. So, in an interview, Cassie might say, "Oh, I hate Dan Savage. He helped us so much." And the interviewer is going to be, like, "What the fuck was that?" And the problem is that sometimes you will say things that aren't immediately noticeable ... nobody's going to stop and think about it, because it sounds like it makes sense in the context. And it does make sense in the context, but it's the opposite of what you meant to say.

* * *

CR: We talked about you moving between the worlds of Africa and Europe; between the village where you were the doctor; back home where you were a wife and a mother and a daughter; and the whole Indian, African, European... all these different worlds you move between. Now we're talking about when you finished your studies and started working as a psychiatrist. You found that the people you most enjoyed working with were whom?

CJ: Oh, psychotics. I love psychotics.

CR: Right. So, for people who don't know, psychotics are the people standing on the street muttering to themselves; they hear voices.

CJ: They hear voices. They do not fuse; or they don't recognize this world as fitting in together. So they are outside of this world. Kind of lost in between worlds.

CR: Right. For people who aren't familiar with psychiatry or psychology, they are not people who are depressed.

CJ: No, they're not neurotic.

CR: They are not neurotic. These are people who have lost connection with what we call reality. And, correct me if I am wrong, these are the people I think most psychiatrists don't like to work with because they're intimidated. Because they are scary. Because deep down inside, I think most of us are afraid we're going to catch it from them. We know, I mean, even if you know, you know, psychosis, schizophrenia, is not although now they're talking about how there might be some viral connection.

CJ: I think there could be a viral connection. Because I remember when I was in residency, my professor was doing a longitudinal study, looking at the different months in which the psychotics were born. In the winter months there were more psychoses; it could be related with the flu and the virus.

CR: Right. I've also read there might be some connection with vitamin D deficiency. There are connections with toxoplasmosis, possibly. There are all sorts of things.

CJ: Psychosis is a syndrome. There is no etiology for that.

CR: Right. Nobody really knows.

“” OH, PSYCHOTICS. I LOVE PSYCHOTICS.

CJ: That's the paradigm of psychiatry. Nobody knows what causes it, but we know the times and seasons, right? And the changes in the brain; we can see the difference. But that doesn't explain schizophrenia or other psychotics.

CR: So, these are the people that you feel most comfortable working with, the ones you're connected with.

CJ: They're very authentic, very true. And people are afraid of them because they can be aggressive. No, they're not.

CR: Right. It's very unusual for a psychotic to hurt anyone. And that's not what we hear. We hear, "They lost their mind and they killed everybody." Well, they didn't lose their mind as a psychotic, probably. So, you became a psychiatrist because you're fascinated by the brain, as you were saying earlier.

CJ: I love the brain.

CR: But you're nothing like the sort of normal psychiatrist that a person is likely to meet at the hospital, or even to look them up in the phone book or whatever. I go to the normal psychiatrist, and I say I'm having trouble sleeping, they're going to prescribe pills. That's what psychiatrists do. And you're the opposite of that. You're like a shaman who happens to have a medical degree.

CJ: And they always saw that I was different from them. Maybe because of that, I started to have more patients, particularly patients that would look for me and not for others. And they would say that loudly.

CR: So this is what I find so interesting about your approach to psychotherapy. That you aren't trying to convince people that the voices aren't real. You're trying to help them live with the voices.

CJ: Integration into daily life, normal life. To know a psychotic person, probably, is very difficult for many of us. But, if they feel trust toward someone, if they feel comfortable with someone, they relax. And I think our duty is not to shut down their voices, it's impossible. What are you going to shut them down with, pills only? It's not a way to live. It's to accept and embrace that in a way they can't be afraid. "Are you afraid of dogs? Let's go and confront and see. See, touch the dog." I started to use my cognitive approach to that. I tried to use a fusion of psychoanalysis and integration with their culture and with their religion. So, a sort of holistic approach in that way; but by also confronting their fear.

CR: I remember reading a paper recently that seemed to suggest that people who aren't psychotic at all hear voices, even among different cultures. I guess aural hallucinations are the most common form of hallucinations among these people. We've all had it, we've all been falling asleep, and you suddenly hear your mother's voice, and you hear someone calling you. It happens to everyone.

CJ: Oh yes, normal. Falling asleep or when awake.

CR: The difference is that, for most of us, it's like, "Oh yeah, I heard that voice again, and you forget about it." But for them, the voice is always there, and they can't forget about it. So, anyway, the paper said that the content was different from culture to culture. For instance, the voices telling you to kill yourself or to kill someone else... that's very American.

It's like the voices maybe are created by biology or who knows what? But what the voices say... that is created by the culture.

CJ: Yes. It's *very* related to the culture where they live.

CR: And that brings us to, back to shamanism, right? I often talk about *Black Elk Speaks*. I'm writing about that in this new book. How he was, what we would consider psychotic, or schizophrenic. He heard voices; he thought the animals talked to him. He thought he could control the weather. All in his late teens, at about the same age when a lot of boys have their psychotic breaks. But his society viewed that as an incredible gift. And they decided to help him move through that transition, to come out integrated on the other side, in the same way that you're trying to do with your patients – not to ignore the voices, but listen to what they say, to learn from them. Just because you hear a voice telling you to do something, it doesn't mean you have to do it. But don't give it more power by resisting it, by fearing it, right?

CJ: Exactly.

CR: So, his society helped him go through that, and he becomes a shaman. That's the process of becoming a shaman. Whereas, in our society if you're sick, then you're dangerous; we put you in a padded room.

CJ: Of course, not all of them are going to become a shaman. It's not –

CR: But *none* of them are if we fucking drug them and throw them away.

CJ: Oh yeah. And most of them don't need any hospitalization, or they don't experience any psychotic crisis if the culture embraces their psychosis. Like psychotics in Africa... they were embraced by their own family. They would take to *curandaro* to try to treat it, but that's more integrated. They listen to their voice, "Okay, the voice says that we need to make an offer to our great-great father," so they do. And that is good – you have to follow and help the person be in this life.

CR: It's weird interviewing you, because I know the answer to most of the questions I'm asking you. But what comes next? Because you're not going back to normal medicine.

“”

PSYCHOSIS IS A SYNDROME. THERE IS NO ETIOLOGY FOR THAT.

I'VE NEVER REALLY PRACTICED "NORMAL" MEDICINE. I DON'T WANT TO BE A CONVENTIONAL MEDICAL PSYCHIATRIST. I WOULD LIKE TO WORK, BUT WITH THE WORK AND THE HEALING BEING ADAPTABLE TO OUR LIVES.

CJ: No. In fact, well, I've never really practiced "normal" medicine. I don't want to be a conventional medical psychiatrist. I would like to work, but with the work and the healing being adaptable to our lives. For example, I would like to consult people through internet. I'm not very good at internet, not at all. But I see that people do on Skype.

CR: The other thing I'm trying to get you to do is to write some sort of memoir about your time in Africa, your childhood, some of the things we've been talking about now. Some of the cases that you remember. Because I think it could be such an interesting book. The personal path that we've talked about that people have heard today, the multicultural life that you've led. It's sort of a natural pivot point in your life, right? A certain part is finished. So I think it's a good time to look back and tell that story. And then the new stories will be a different volume. Because, otherwise, you're going to move into the next phase, and you're going to be too busy.

CJ: Yes, I think I should do it now. I think I'm more and more motivated to do it before I start getting big projects or start to work. Part of wanting to do this is because I've already got information, but it's analysis to me. To look through what I did and think about that. To think about my mistakes, and think about my limitations. Mistakes and limitations are things that are very important to me, to see through that. That's what I want to do, because I don't want to pass to a second life doing the same mistakes, or having the same limitations because of my persona. But I need that. Definitely I want to do that.

“”

MY SHRINK ALWAYS USED TO SAY THAT **ARTISTS ARE JUST HEALTHY PSYCHOTICS. THEY CAN'T DEAL WITH THE WORLD AS IT IS,** AND HAVE TO IMPACT IT IN SOME KIND OF OTHER WAY. THAT'S THEIR WAY OF UNDERSTANDING IT.

CHAPTER 14

JOSH FOX

EPISODE #209 (OCTOBER 29, 2016)

Josh Fox is documentary filmmaker, playwright and environmental activist. His 2010 film Gasland was nominated for an Oscar for Best Documentary Feature. His most recent work, How to Let Go and Love All the Things Climate Can't Change premiered at the 2016 Sundance Film Festival.

FILM-MAKING | CHILD DEVELOPMENT | ACTIVISM | U.S. SOCIETY | WAR | COMMUNITY | CLIMATE CHANGE

CHRIS RYAN: Ladies and gentlemen, I'm sitting here with the one and only Josh Fox, a true Renaissance man. It's been a long time since the Renaissance, and so you don't get a lot of Renaissance dudes. You're a writer, a playwright, a director, the star of many of your films, your documentaries. You're a dancer, a banjo player, a drummer, a guitarist. You're a kick-ass cook, which I have seen in action over the last few days, where Josh goes into the kitchen and 20 minutes later, food for thirty people comes out and it is delectable.

JOSH FOX: I think the bottom line is I really enjoy having a lot of people around. And that's a lot of people working on a play, a lot of people working on a film, or it's time to have these weekend parties or dinner parties because there's something in me that not only craves community, but deeply believes in it as a way of life. We are so isolated from each other in our normal lives. I love to create that experience. I remember one Labor Day weekend event, you came up to me in the kitchen and you said, "If I were running this, it would completely fall apart. I could never keep it together." The truth is that I'm not running anything, I'm just cooking. The rest of it is just permission for people to be a community, and this kind of feeling that gets passed on from one person to another. It happens very, very quickly and then you see this natural human arrangement of community.

CR: You allow a culture to create itself, to arise spontaneously.

JF: Which is spectacular. And you know, there are habits that some people might have that you would find annoying after a day, because everybody's a character. Someone might grate on you, but everyone is actually the best version of themselves somehow, because of that generosity. It's like what you talk about in your book. If you were to just feed your own kids in a tribe of 150 people, you'd be ostracized because you'd be selfish. And that selfishness is impossible in a setting like this one. I can't tell you how many times people are like, "Can I help with this? Can I help with that?" And I'm always like, "No." Because I'm very bad at delegating authority, I hope it just happens on its own.

ALL CREATIVE PEOPLE HAVE A BURNING PROBLEM OF SOME KIND.

CR: Yeah, I felt that way but I felt I'd just be getting in the way. You know? There's shit going on here and I'm just coagulating. But if you create a space, and you bring in interesting people, stuff starts to happen. Love, and families, or movies, or whatever it is.

JF: There have definitely been babies born out of the strange parties that I've set up over the last twenty years.

CR: And isn't that on some level responding to the nature of actors? Aren't actors generally trying to work out issues?

JF: All creative people have a burning problem of some kind.

CR: You think so?

JF: I do.

CR: You think there are healthy creative people?

JF: My shrink always used to say that artists are just healthy psychotics. they can't deal with the world as it is, and have to impact it in some kind of other way. That's their way of understanding it. Maybe. As an artist you go through various phases. I started going to the theatre when I was eleven years old.

CR: Why?

JF: Because my home life was a disaster. My parents were in a very violent, abusive, incredibly upsetting divorce that went on for eight years, which bankrupted the whole family and put an enormous amount of trauma into the genetics of me and my younger siblings' upbringing. And no disrespect to my parents – I love them both, they're amazing individuals – but during this period of time they were completely reckless and out of control.

CR: And as the older sibling, I imagine you felt some kind of protectiveness over the younger ones.

JF: For sure, but I don't think I exhibited that very well. I felt it but I didn't know what to do. My route was mostly escape. So I made tons of theatre; I was never off the stage. I went from being a shy, introverted kid who never did his homework to top of his class. Well, that's not entirely true. At one point I was in detention every single day because I tried to set fire to the school. I was a metalhead. I was seeing Mötley Crüe, and Exciter, and Motorhead – I was 12 and smoking pot.

CR: So you were acting out against this craziness at home. What happened?

JF: I ended up getting into a better school where

there wasn't all this violence around me. In my public school in seventh grade, there were a thousand seventh graders, eight hundred eighth graders, and two hundred ninth graders. So that was the rate of attrition. There was a police precinct on the first floor. Fights every single day; I got into a fight every single day, pretty much. I was shorter than everybody so anything anyone would say to me would set me off. Clearly still a fighter in different ways.

But honestly, those were incredibly wild days in New York City too. There were no rules. It was a very different city, you could get mugged on any corner.

CR: I lived in the city in those days. That's when I was here. Early AIDS days, lots of sadness.

JF: I actually went to Act Up meetings as a sixteen-year-old, the only straight sixteen-year-old at Act Up. I got hit on a lot. But I loved it there because there was this sense of us as a community fighting back. And we had every Keith Haring shirt and pin. We used to stick those "Silence is Death" stickers everywhere as high school students. And it was this sense that we were fighting back. I mean, we hated Ronald Reagan...

CR: So was that your first political engagement, you think?

JF: I think the first real moment was in 1985: there was a huge anti-apartheid march. That apartheid divestment campaign educated me. Our little contingent from my school was going to the march, and I was straggling because I was talking to a girl. The two of us were really slow. I was in the 8th grade, the whole high school was up there, and Fred Daley, the English teacher, looked at us and says, "Come on! You have to run fast if you want to smash apartheid!" And we're like "Shit!" and we just ran to catch up with them. I think about that moment all the time.

When we were making *Gasland*, we found that it's a race to get the information out. You know that you want to intersect with this political moment, to run and catch that wave. You have no time to waste; it's this fire, and it's been with me since that day of the march. When the teacher said that, it was like getting this Zen master. All of sudden you realize you have to run to catch this, this isn't coming to you. And that's how I think about political involvement now, to this day.

CR: Yeah, I was in Mozambique when Mandela died, and I know some of the people who knew him. And what a historical figure – what an amazing, beautiful human being.

JF: Well, I saw him in Yankee stadium in '90. It was wild – we were in the bleachers, struggling to hear him. He sold out Yankee stadium.

CR: I heard you talking to someone at the party, and you said you've played with Pete Seeger?

JF: I've played with Pete Seger a couple times. He's not only one of the great authors of folk music in America, he's one of the great authors of America, period.

CR: There'd be no Bob Dylan without Pete Seeger.

JF: No folk revival. But yeah, I put Pete Seeger in *Gasland* because he was a role model. He found a way to campaign for the Hudson River by connecting it to New York City. So he reminded New York that if you pollute upstream, it's coming downstream. And he sailed this Clearwater ship up and down the Hudson, and educated people about this river. His whole river was the Hudson River. My river is the Delaware River on the other side of the valley. It's the pristine river, it's the watershed. What I wanted to do was remind New Yorkers that those waterways are connected, because New Yorkers actually get their water from the headwaters of the Delaware. If they were fracking up there, that would destroy New York. I think New York City is the reason that the tide turned, but it had to do with connecting that to the rivers, and that's what Pete Seeger taught me.

* * *

CR: What do you think of Sebastian Junger? Have you read his stuff?

JF: Oh, I know him. Tim and Sebastian were at Sundance with the film *Restrepo* when I was there with *Gasland*. I don't know him very well, but I saw that film on opening night and I was shaking.

I can't believe those guys – the real war reporters. I'm with Pink Floyd: I'd never go to war, I could never do it. These guys go to report on it, they're real heroes. And they die, they die all the time. I have a friend who's right now reporting in Afghanistan and I'm terrified for her. But if it wasn't for those guys, we wouldn't have the images that teach us not to go to war. We wouldn't have Tim Hetherington's unbelievable reporting or Chris Hondros' photograph of the girl crying at the checkpoint where her parents had just been shot by the US military, and she's covered in blood and screaming. They died alongside each other in Libya. We are in a time of war. All of my work before *Gasland* was about the war. I did ten plays about the war, and I did a film about the war. I was the spokesperson for theaters against the war. We are still in a fucking time of war. And my work right now is about getting people to understand that climate change is happening right now. And it's the things that are happening all around us that we refuse to look at. And we're at war now. When Abu Ghraib happened, I felt that every American was implicated because it was our fraternity, hazing, Girls Gone Wild, beach, date-rape culture that had created that, just as much as it was the FBI and Dick Cheney and the rules. We decided to do a sexual fraternity hazing experiment on prisoners. Only Americans could've done it in the way they did it, and they did it for the camera, they did it because of the camera, and they did it in the same way that the girls "gone wild" will strip on the beach and pull their pants down – because it's this crazy part of American fraternity hazing.

CR: Think about how often on television one of the popular laugh-lines is, "Hey pretty boy, in prison they really like guys like you." That's a laugh-line. "You're gonna get ass-raped in prison. Ha. Ha." What kind of culture is this?

JF: Right after Abu Ghraib, I went on Memorial Day weekend in Ocean City, Maryland and that's a war holiday. Memorial Day is a holiday where we respect

“ ”

WHEN ABU GHRAIB HAPPENED, I FELT THAT EVERY AMERICAN WAS IMPLICATED BECAUSE IT WAS OUR FRATERNITY, HAZING, GIRLS GONE WILD, BEACH DATE-RAPE CULTURE THAT HAD CREATED THAT, JUST AS MUCH AS IT WAS THE FBI AND DICK CHENEY.

and honor all the war dead, not just the soldiers. The soldiers have Veterans Day. Memorial Day is for everyone who died, civilians and soldiers alike. But we've turned it into this jingoistic, American flag, have a barbecue, go to the beach, get fucked up, unofficial beginning of summer. Right after Abu Ghraib in 2004, I ended up at one of these places where there were drunk fraternity assholes throwing up on their dates going, "Support our Troops! America!" And I was thinking, "You don't know what you're saying. You might say that if you know what you're saying, but it's so clear that you don't." The true story of Abu Ghraib is that those dudes were in Virginia Beach right before they shipped out, and they did all the same shit to their friends. They took pictures of them when they were passed out with their pants pulled down. They did it here in America first, and then the CIA, and whoever was running it in Iraq, sent out that memo to the Abu Ghraib people saying, "Be Creative." They said, "These are your approved interrogation techniques. You can hit with an open hand, you can use stress positions, you can do waterboarding," and then at the bottom it said, "Be Creative."

CR: So what are they gonna do? What they know.

JF: They made enforced rape porn.

CR: And their intended audience was their buddies that they had just left. That's who they were sending the photos to. Spectators in the Iraq War.

JF: I felt that the Iraq War was in every conversation. Even more so when you're sitting in a cafe in New York City, and you're listening to two people who don't vote talk about Britney Spears. That was the most intense conversation about the genocide in Iraq because they weren't fucking talking about Iraq.

CR: Right. And that's part of the thing that allows it to happen.

JF: All the people in America who didn't protest Iraq, who just sat around doing their normal lives. I felt they were guilty.

CR: But are we overwhelmed by our implication in all these things? I'm not a vegetarian, but I know that pigs are intelligent animals like this cat sitting between us on the table. Beautiful cat, that we have this relationship with. We call it *The* Holocaust, although there have been so many of them, but that's *The* Holocaust. We're doing that to the animals. The Nazis used cattle cars. The Nazis used the same sort of technology that we use now in our industrialized livestock system. Sometimes I think, "I'm one of those Nazis because I know it's evil. I know it's incredibly evil, and I had bacon for breakfast this morning." Sometimes I feel like there's so much evil in this culture. I feel like Western civilization is fundamentally sick. Deeply sick. It's overwhelming. It's like, yeah Iraq's a mess, Afghanistan's a mess, Central America's a mess, the pumping oil in Ecuador's a mess, the food system's a mess, I'm just overwhelmed.

JF: Guess what else agrees with you? The Bible. I don't know if it's that you can't do anything about it, but you are in a particularly difficult moral dilemma. Adam and Eve is a metaphor for 200,000 years of humans living at peace with nature and hunter-gathering – a time when there were one-million people on the planet, and we were just one species, who hadn't yet invented this thing called agriculture, and the wheel, and civilization. That is what Adam and Eve was. And you describe it in your book very well. When they first came to New York City, they said one shot would bring down 30 geese, the sky was so thick with birds.

ADAM AND EVE IS A METAPHOR FOR 200,000 YEARS OF HUMANS LIVING AT PEACE WITH NATURE AND HUNTER-GATHERING.

CR: And you could walk across the cod...

JF: You had this bounty. The Bible then talks about Cain and Abel, the progeny of Adam and Eve. God accepts Abel's offering, but rejects Cain's offering. I like the explanation that's in this book called Ishmael, where he says Cain was a tiller of the fields and Abel was a herder of sheep. There's a very big distinction. To be a tiller of the field, you need to own and control land. In other words, you're an agriculturalist, you're a civilizationist. To be a herder of sheep... not so much. You can graze and wander around. You don't own land. But The Bible says very clearly: to own land, to believe in the idea of possession, which entails agriculture and civilization, means you are going to be a murderer. You will become a murderer.

So the idea that the world has been a gigantic mess for the last 10,000 years, well, that's the premise of all our major religions, the premise of all our major psychology. And it's unfortunately the deal that we're working out, and it looks like we're moving closer and closer to the prophesies that are in The Bible. They're coming true. We do know that it's a mess right now, and we're thrust into this moment of personal choices and communal choices...

CR: I think that the key to all of this is an intentional, gradual, compassionate reduction of human population. Because every time they say we have to feed the future generations, we have to generate energy for 9 billion people. Well, why do we have to have 9 billion people? Why? Growth, growth, growth. Why is growth fundamental?

JF: Well, development and economic growth bring the population rate to zero. The reason why people have so many children is because it's a form of life insurance. There's two answers to the population problem. One is actually development, but how do you do development responsibly from the standpoint of climate and the environment. And the other one is the education of women. When you educate and empower women, you tend to have less children. So progressive values are actually a great thing. The problem of the guilt, of, "Oh my god I'm doing this" and "Oh my god I'm participating in this" is part of the way that they trap you in their individualism. The individual consumer and the individual guilt-ridden, non-active person are the same person to them, because they're consuming just as much. It's just that one of them feels bad. The big difference is political action, to start to take a communal, group, political direct action. Climate action is a team sport. So is democratic action. And so is action on animal agriculture. These are all about political organizing, political direct action. When we organize, we win. When we don't organize and sit around and feel guilty at home, we don't win. We get sucked into that individual aura. "What should I do?"

This is what Americans always think. Well guess what? You're not that fucking important. If the question was, "What could I do as an individual to stop climate change?" Well the answer is nothing. Almost nothing. What can I do as a part of a movement? Well a lot. An enormous amount.

CR: So if you want to change the world have a party. Get people together, form a community.

JF: A protest is a party, a concert's a party. A party is just a community without a purpose.

* * *

JF: In my film *How to Let Go of the World and Love all the Things Climate Can't Change*, all the things climate can't change are civic virtues. They're community, they're love, they're resilience, they're innovation, they're creativity, courage, democracy, human rights. These are the things that the climate won't destroy.

CR: It might actually cultivate them. Give them space to come out. Every civilization that's ever existed has collapsed. Every one. The only thing that's different is that this time it's global. This is the first global civilization. If it does what every other one has done, there won't be anywhere to go.

JF: The body count on this is higher for sure.

CF: Every time history repeats itself, the price goes up.

JF: That's true. And every century has been bloodier than the last. I worry that this century is going to be bloodier than the previous one because climate change will cause resource wars.

CR: It already has in Syria. That's a water war, essentially.

JF: The United Nations predicts that when we hit 2 degrees of warming on the planet earth, that will cause 800 million climate refugees.

CR: Yeah, the Ganges is gonna dry up.

JF: What that will create is a lot of violence, and a lot of individual choices, and a lot of group choices. I think that there is an infrastructure in New York City, of progressive behavior and values that won the day when it came to Occupy Sandy, and that did not win the day, for example, in New Orleans. The images from Katrina...the mayor said "Go on the bridge. Get out of town." And the people who were mostly poor, mostly black, from the inner city, got on the bridge to get to safety only to be met by the white suburban shot guns of the racist police force on the other side, and many people were shot. At that point, that wasn't a climate change crisis. The storm had passed. That was a total breakdown of human civic virtue, of American values.

And what worries me is that situation being replicated everywhere you go, ad infinitum. Add in half a dozen Fukushimas, because there are a dozen nuclear power plants up and down the East coast that are in the flood plain, and it takes 20-30 years to decommission a nuclear power plant. Think about that, plus, people are relatively easy to move compared to an oil refinery, or a chemical plant - and they're all near the water. You don't want that shit flushing in and contaminating the world's oceans. A single corner gas station costs $800,000 to remediate. Move all that shit before it goes in the water, because otherwise you won't be able to go into the water ever again. You'll have this giant toxic cesspool which used to be the ocean. What kind of ramifications does that have? World hunger, people dying, people scrambling

EVERY TIME HISTORY REPEATS ITSELF, THE PRICE GOES UP.

for resources, and unfortunately a lot of violence. What Bill McKibben says to the question, "Where do I move?" He says, "Anywhere there's a strong community, you have a better chance of survival." So what does the climate movement have to do? Reinvest in this idea of community. There is a chance, that if we follow a little bit of Occupy's example, that the values that were attacking the big banks, and attacking economic inequality, and so politically active, protest and a sense of humor, and of giving. Those values are the right thing to employ when you're in a crisis.

CR: Right. Because they're human values. *Truly* human values, not what we're told are human values. What is that line? Politics is the –

JF: Entertainment division of the military industrial complex?

CR: That's Frank Zappa. But I'm thinking "Politics is Hollywood for ugly people."

JF: Oh my God. Well, I do think that one of the things we're trying to do – both you and myself – with this new moment in American culture, is to burst that bubble that is all about appearances. Which is to say, these are the underpinnings. Let's look at history, let's look at sociology, anthropology, let's look at our culture, let's look at the things that we don't see that are outside the frame.

At the same time we're indulged in the most virulent narcissism we've ever had, with the Facebook and all the social media, and constantly looking at ourselves in pictures. I think that one of the missions that we have as a revolution is to redefine American culture and say, "These are the values that we want to distance ourselves from." Because we are in dire shape right now, politically speaking, and I think art culture is a very important part of fighting that... continuing to make movies and popular works of art, not just works of art that are avant-garde or philosophical, but at least try to make something that a lot of people are going to see. And so that's why I was extremely grateful that *Gasland* and *Gasland II* got released. But I do think there's a symbiosis between a movement and its grassroots origins. I don't think *Gasland* would've made it where it did without that grassroots support. It's because we had done grassroots screenings with every mom and pop anti-fracking group across America, in dozens of states, and built this sense of connection between people. I don't think it was just about, "Oh this was a good movie and people liked it."

"

YOU HAVE TO UNDERSTAND THAT ADDICTION IS NOT JUST A CHEMICAL IMBALANCE, IT'S NOT JUST YOUR BRAIN BEING HIJACKED. **IT'S A SOCIOCULTURAL DISEASE, IT'S AN EMOTIONAL DISEASE, IT'S A SPIRITUAL DISEASE.**

CHARLES JOHNSTON

CHAPTER 15

EPISODE #175 (APRIL 13, 2016)

Charles Johnston is a former heroin addict who currently works to help others find their way to sobriety. He is an advocate of psychedelics as an aid to recovery.

ADDICTIONS | RELIGION | PSYCHEDELICS | U.S. SOCIETY

CJ: I grew up in a really small town, and I wanted to leave pretty quickly. It was a beautiful place, a really beautiful place, there was just no opportunity for me. I wanted to explore and learn. I was always a kind of experiential person, I just wouldn't do drugs, so I tried to experience life in as many ways as I could without doing any of those drugs. I went to Japan for a year in high school, then I came back, then I went to college for a little bit.

CR: What about sex in high school?

CJ: None.

CR: Masturbation?

CJ: Mormons aren't supposed to. That's probably the number one issue that most young men have in that church. It brings a lot of shame and guilt, it was kind of traumatic.

CR: Well, that's what it's for. You don't realize it at the time, but the whole point of that is to set a hook in your cheek so they can drag you around. But in Mormonism... is it seen as something you're going to hell for, like with Catholics?

CJ: No, it's like you're messing up, you're doing something wrong, you're not supposed to do that. They don't take masturbation super seriously, but they do limit you on what you're allowed to do. They have this whole priesthood thing for young men where you do the sacrament; like the priests in the Catholic Church, you are the one that is giving people the bread and the water, and you have to have this responsibility that you're supposed to be clean and uphold that.

CR: It's amazing, isn't it? In addition to the shame and the guilt, what they are doing is ingraining hypocrisy from the very beginning; you become accustomed to pretending to be something you know you're not.

CJ: Yeah, unless you're perfect, unless you're just *right on*, but the majority really struggle with that. I went and served a mission, and I did the whole two-year thing too, and a lot of guys had a really tough time with that. It brought a lot of pain. A lot of sadness revolving around them not being worthy.

CR: Japan - What was that like? You're a young 17-year-old at the time.

CJ: A young, insecure, 16-17 year old. I wasn't the most outgoing. There was a lot of inner turmoil; I had a lot of rage going on, a lot of angst, teenage angst, but especially because the Mormon thing added a lot to that. There were a lot of things, because I wasn't part of normal culture growing up: I didn't drink, I didn't smoke, I didn't watch R-rated movies when I was a kid, I didn't date girls. Those kinds of things left it very challenging for me to feel comfortable in social life.

CR: Did the other kids in your school, who weren't Mormons, give you a hard time?

CJ: Yeah, it was an issue, but they didn't harp on it. They never gave me shit, per se. It became kind of a joke, I was the "Stormin' Mormon," as they referred to me. I was an Eagle Scout, I was a good kid, I had a lot of integrity, but then I kinda did stupid shit, like I'd go break into the school and mess things up in the school, or I'd be outside shooting out light bulbs, starting fires in places. Vandalism was something I really enjoyed as a teenager, running from cops and that sort of stuff. It's a very interesting dichotomy that I had going on with myself, whereas I'm like the good kid, then also I'm not such a good kid when it comes to this other stuff. There were just certain lines I wouldn't cross. Japan, though, was at times a very isolating experience, I was kind of on my own, living with Japanese people, Japanese families.

CR: Did you hook up with any Japanese girls?

CJ: I didn't. I didn't kiss a girl until I was 18 years old. I didn't have sex until I was 23. That was a really weird thing for me too – not feeling comfortable around girls and that kind of a relationship. In the Mormon Church, with the whole thing going on with pornography and masturbation, I think I developed this complex about sexual relationships and females. Since I had no sisters, and my mom wasn't around ever, I just didn't know how to relate or adapt. That's something that's come to me in my late 20s.

CR: How old are you now?

CJ: 30.

CR: There's an old Japanese expression I love, I heard it years ago: "By the age of 30, we become responsible for our face." I heard that around my 30th birthday. What it means to me is that at 30, you can't blame anyone else anymore. You've had enough time to figure your shit out, correct whatever mistakes you made when you were young. I'm not saying everyone should have healed every wound, but you're sort of driving the bus.

CJ: I would agree with that. In my own situation, that's kind of how it's progressed.

* * *

CJ: I came back from the mission and was doing door-to-door sales around the country.

CR: Funny. "What do you do? What is your job experience?" "Well, I can knock on doors and bother people!"

CJ: It's tough. When I was door knocking, doing the satellite thing, I got burned out on that, super burned out. And then I met some people and started to drink a little for the first time. I remember the first time

SO THEN I READ *DUNE*, AND THAT WAS AN EYE OPENER, TO SEE THIS MESSIANIC FIGURE WHO BASICALLY TOOK SOME PSYCHEDELICS AND STARTS LEADING PEOPLE; THIS HERO FIGURE WHO IS DOING HIS OWN THING AND BREAKING THE MOLD.

I drank, I was in Minneapolis and we were driving downtown. And we buy this bottle of Bacardi, and I'd never tasted alcohol. So I just start chuggin' this shit. It's so gross, so vile, and I'm just like, "Whatever," and my buddy asks if I want a chaser. But I just don't care, I'm just going to drink it. So I drank couple big swigs, and I stumble out of the car when we get downtown, and I can't even walk. That was my first time ever being intoxicated, really on anything, and it wasn't that enjoyable.

CR: Well it's funny, it sounds great! And the puking must have been wonderful too!

CJ: I couldn't go to sleep, my head's spinning, and I eventually got arrested for disorderly conduct one time - spent a night in jail. So those were my first kinds of experiences with alcohol. And then I was like, "Fuck, I've gotta lock some stuff in." And so me and my friend just pick up and move to Arizona to kind of rekindle the Mormon thing. We didn't know anyone, we just got in the car and drove down there. We didn't know where we were going to stay. I remember going to church and trying to meet people so I could go back to their house and stay later that day.

That's how I started in Arizona, trying the Mormon thing a little bit more. My whole goal was to get married, because they tell you when you come off of the mission, to go get married. So I met Mormon girls, but they were very different than me. The way they thought and the way I thought was distinctly different. Even though we had the same belief structure, my cognitive level, and the way I sort of see the world, and experience the world, is significantly different. And I think that's probably like most people, but especially in the case of Mormons, there is a huge disconnect because they don't experience much at all. Most of them are just locked into their church thing and that's what they do, and that's the experience they have. That wasn't very interesting to me, so I started studying chemistry and going to school. I thought I wanted to be a doctor, and after about a year in school, I started to drink a little bit and smoke a little pot; I was becoming uncomfortable with the whole Mormon thing. It was really losing its interest. I read Ayn Rand's *The Fountainhead*, and I was like, "This guy, this character lives for himself."

CR: Howard Roark? One of the only redheaded heroes of literature

CJ: But he's just completely autonomous and he does his thing. I was like, "Wow, that's really amazing, my whole life I've wanted to do that, but I've been tied down by this whole religious thing." So then I read *Dune*, and that was an eye opener, to see this messianic figure who basically took some psychedelics and starts leading people; this hero figure who is doing his own thing and breaking the mold. And the thing was, I realized I was tired of feeling guilty, I was tired of feeling ashamed of being me, and feeling sad, and always kind of needing to appeal to someone to feel better. Eventually I was just like, "I'm not doing this anymore."

CR: Now, how old were you at this point?

CJ: Twenty-three.

CR: Okay, so twenty-three, you make a break, and then what happens?

CJ: I did mushrooms for the first time, took about a 1/16th of an ounce of mushrooms.

CR: After you left the church.

CJ: Yeah, right in that same time. And I ended up leaving Arizona, leaving school where I had a scholarship to Arizona State University, where everything was great, but I was like, "I don't want to do this anymore, I'm going to move to L.A." And I always wanted to be an actor, had never taken classes or anything, so I just moved to L.A. with that idea in my head because I liked L.A. I was also exploring psychedelics, I was ordering seeds online, and taking different psychedelics that most people don't take.

CR: Like Datura and shit like that?

CJ: I didn't take Datura, but I took Morning Glory seeds, Hawaiian Baby Woodrose, L.S.A., Salvia, and things of that nature. The more unconventional stuff.

CR: So you move to LA, you're going to be an actor, you're exploring all of these altered states. Is it like a pendulum situation?

CJ: It is. It's swinging. And when I moved to LA, the pendulum is kind of right in the middle. I had this roommate who introduces me to cocaine and ecstasy, and I start doing those. Then I move out from his place, and I start growing mushrooms, doing acid, doing more ecstasy, and really exploring... really starting to swing more and more.

Then I quit the acting thing, which lasted like four months, thinking this kind of sucks. So I got back into school because the whole acting thing was a bust for me. I thought, "I'll do the doctor thing again." I started going to West L.A., which was a little community college. I was at a classmate's house one day and I popped some Norcos. I liked them, so my classmate suggested I try heroin. And, when I started doing drugs, I basically took the attitude of, "I'm not going to listen to what anyone says about what I should or shouldn't do, I'm going to try whatever I feel like trying." And I knew about addiction, but because I'd been raised Mormon, addiction to me was just a willpower issue. I just thought people who are addicts are weak.

So about a week later I bought some heroin and I started smoking heroin off of tinfoil. At first, it's very subtle. At first, it's very pleasurable, it's like this total enveloping of happiness. You're just so at peace and happy. And, I would use it maybe once or twice a week, it was kind of just a recreational thing. And maybe I'd go out to a friend's house, or go out to a party, and I'd smoke heroin instead of drinking alcohol or doing anything else, because I enjoyed that feeling, and it made me more sociable, too. So eventually I was doing it more and more, and found myself physically addicted. I felt like I could get over it... The first little bit of being addicted was tough. I went through withdrawals a number of times, and eventually I kept getting to the point where I kept failing at getting through the withdrawals.

CR: So you went through the withdrawals because you felt like you didn't want to be addicted.

CJ: Yeah. I was like, "I don't want to be addicted, I know I'm doing it too much." I was aware of what was happening. At the beginning you get this idea of, "I can just do it one more time." You have that thought quite a bit, like I did many times, and gradually it got worse. There was one time where I wanted to get off it, so I smoked Meth for a few days, and I ended up crashing the car from my job, then losing my job. So then I had to start selling drugs, figuring out other ways to get money. You're running out of money, right, because you're buying and smoking heroin. You smoke a lot more heroin than you would theoretically shoot. I told myself I'd never shoot heroin, but eventually I had to start to do it as an economic choice. So I started shooting up, and slowly but surely after that happened, things started going downhill.

CR: Is it a very different experience?

CJ: Oh yeah. It's like the difference between making out with a woman and orgasming. That's the difference. Yeah, it's just an immediate rush that is just so extremely pleasurable, but it is very short-lasting. You feel that intense rush for a few minutes, then you're kind of, well, normal. A lot of my friends didn't know I was shooting up in their bathroom. Or when I was at school, I'd walk into class, take my spoon into a stall at UCLA, and cook up heroin. Just ridiculous stuff that you end up doing, because you can't be three or four hours without it. Things were getting really bad. I started to steal to make money, I was stealing large amounts of things, like electronics from Target and Best Buy; I bought tools to do it too, being all sneaky. Thought I was one-upping the system and getting by, but the whole time I'm in this pure cloud of opiate addiction. I would try to go back home and detox. I tried Suboxone a few times, which is a maintenance therapy. I tried to taper down. I tried doing ayahuasca.

CR: So you were struggling against it.

CJ: I was. I was really fighting against it. I would tell people this, "I'm not an addict. I have a bad habit. I'm not an addict."

CR: And what does that mean now? Does that sound like bullshit justification?

CJ: It totally *was* bullshit justification. I was an addict in the sense that I had a serious addiction. It wasn't just a habit, it was a serious addiction.

CR: Where do you stand on the disease model of addiction?

CJ: You can call it a disease if you want, but if you're going to call it a disease, then you have to understand that it's not just a chemical imbalance, it's not just your brain being hijacked. It's a socio-cultural disease, it's an emotional disease, it's a spiritual disease more than anything. Even when I would get clean for a few weeks, I still felt pain, I still wasn't normal. I never felt normal, and that was the problem. Eventually, I just got tired of not feeling normal and I'd end up using again.

CR: Maybe this is a good description of addiction: where your normal becomes being high.

CJ: The real normal eventually becomes so painful, and there's so much inner turmoil going on, that you wake up in the morning and you're depressed and you

I TOLD MYSELF I'D NEVER SHOOT HEROIN, BUT EVENTUALLY I HAD TO START TO DO IT AS AN ECONOMIC CHOICE. SO I STARTED SHOOTING UP, AND SLOWLY BUT SURELY AFTER THAT HAPPENED, THINGS STARTED GOING DOWNHILL.

have no motivation. That's hard to live like that. People who are mentally ill who are dealing with depression have the same kind of experience, except that they don't resort to a medication until they start feeling that way. But it's the same thing.

* * *

CJ: Around the beginning of December 2011, I started looking into places to do ibogaine, a powerful anti-addiction psychedelic, but I didn't have the money to do it. So my goal was to steal enough money, to sell enough stuff, to get the money to go do ibogaine. I spent all of December doing that, but wasn't making any progress. I went to Vegas for 2012, because 2012 was going to be a big year, the Mayan Calendar, that kind of stuff. On New Year's Eve, during the day, I was like, "I'm going to go into Target really quick, and I'm going to steal $1,000 worth of stuff just to make this trip even out financially." I go in there, I do my thing, and as I'm going out, a cop comes in and says, "Hold on!" I try to run from him, and he grabs me and slams me up against a window. So I'm locked up, I'm going through the process, and I'm so scared because I'm going to be going through withdrawals. It's a Friday or something and the courts aren't going to be in until Monday, so I'm going to have to spend four days in jail. So I'm just shittin' bricks, I'm like "Oh shit, this is so bad. I can't believe this is going to happen."

CR: Fucking Mayans.

CJ: Fucking Mayans!

CJ: I tell the counselor, "I need to go into detox because I've been taking prescription meds." I didn't tell them I was taking heroin, I didn't want to pull that one out. So they put me in a detox cell and I'm chillin' with these other dudes, and I'm there for the whole afternoon and the evening. And I remember watching this little shitty TV in the corner, and the ball is getting ready to drop, and I'm just like, "Fuck this." So I just go lay in the corner, take this little Xanax out of the little pocket of my jeans, crush it up on the floor, and snort it. And I just conk out in the corner.

So I conk out. About 2:30 in the morning, they call my name, and I wake up in a complete daze, and I get up and I start stumbling out of the cell. All of the other guys are laughing because they think I'm drunk. The Xanax has got me pretty kinda fucked up. But, I got let out. I get back to LA and realize that I've got to do something NOW, I can't wait anymore. I call up a place that's in my phone from before that answers and that says, "Yeah we'll take you." I'm like, alright, I'll be there in two days.

CR: For the ibogaine.

CJ: For the ibogaine. So I get on a bus at Union Station in

LA and head down to Mexico. I get down to Mexico and walk across the border with these people that picked me up, get in the woman's car, and just start bawling. I'm so distraught. Before that, before I'd even gone down, I had contemplated suicide. It was a very serious contemplation. So I get down there, and for two days I'm kind of laid up sick in a little dingy, dark house in Mexico, withdrawing a little bit. For two days, I'm kind of just with my thoughts, detoxing, laying in bed, not eating, just hoping that this upcoming treatment thing works. They give me the ibogaine on a Sunday night. It makes my withdrawals go away, but I'm expecting this brilliant, visionary experience, and I'm thinking, "Ah fuck, did I just get ripped off? Did I just spend my whole load on something that's not going to work?" I'm laying there for a few hours thinking, "Fuck, I just blew it."

Then, all of the sudden, this thing happens: I call it my epiphany, my moment of clarity, and I just let go. I just release all of the pain, and I forgive myself. I just started weeping and weeping. And all of this suffering and pain that I'd felt, all the inflicting, everything I had caused myself, that didn't come from anywhere externally, but which was all internal – it just suddenly resolved, and I'm just letting it all out in this cathartic moment that lasted maybe a couple of hours. That was the extent of it. I don't remember anything else, except the vomiting that happened, which was kind of traumatic. It was like buzzsaws going through my head. It was like exorcising demons and getting out all of this vileness. And then the next day, I kinda come to. I'm not on the ibogaine anymore, but I'm really wiped out physically. For two days, I'm just wiped out and I can't sleep; I'm just really tired. Finally, after two days, I have to sleep, so they give me some medication to help me sleep. I woke up the next morning at about 6:00am, no one was up. I made some breakfast, took a shower, and felt like I hadn't felt in years. Maybe in my whole life, I don't know. But it was gone. It was a miracle. It was a straight-up miracle, in my book. Because it was gone. At that moment, I was like, "It's over. The addiction is over."

* * *

CJ: So I met this kid down there; we became friends, and I told him how I was so interested in psychedelics, how I was interested in MAPS, which is a great organization for psychedelic studies. So I told my new friend about this, and he goes, "Why don't we just do this? Why don't we start a clinic? What they are doing here – we can do that." Have a little dingy house, and give people ibogaine, have nurses and doctors, and just do it. I didn't even think about it, I just said, "Yes." And so this guy came back to LA with me, moved into my house, helped me clean out all of my needles, all of my paraphernalia, and he helped me start to create my life, and really start to fix my life. I basically started selling everything I had – my guns, all my collections, my car... I started getting rid of everything. Then I built a website and started making this business; we started figuring it out. And I also went back to school. So, I was back in school, and also starting this new business where I was going to take people to Mexico to treat them – it was kind of ad-hoc.

CR: Kind of ad-hoc! That's good.

CJ: After a couple of months, some guys came along and they said, "We want you to help us build a bigger thing." So I started doing that, and I built a bigger thing. After about a year-and-a-half, I separated from that for personal reasons, then started working with a project in Costa Rica for a year, which was a lot of fun. But again, I separated from that for personal reasons. Now, I most recently joined Crossroads with Dr. Palanco. He was one of the first people I met after I did ibogaine, because the nurse that treated me when I went through my experience – the one who picked me up at the border – was one of his best friends, so she connected us. After three years, we've kind of hooked up again, and I've started working with Crossroads because I love helping people go through this. I love being able to teach people the truth of the matter: that they're not some helpless addict whose whole life is gonna be restricted because they made a poor choice somewhere along the road.

So, that's what I do now. I talk with people about ibogaine. I talk with people about plant medicine, and entheogens in general, but for the most part, I talk with them and help them make the right decision to get clean – not just by detoxing, but by actually allowing their spirit and soul to heal with these amazing plant medicines. That's kind of the story of...

CR: And that's your life story. It's been pretty eventful, huh? It's funny how when you look at a life, I mean I remember reading an interview years ago with Paul Newman, in *Playboy* I think it was, and it was towards the end of his life. The interviewer said, "So what was your secret?" And he said, "You know, I look back on my life and I understand that people look at it and it looks like I had a plan - There was no fucking plan." You know? It looks, in retrospect, like a story that sort of fits together. But, when you're going through it, it's just one thing after another. What I tell people is, I say, "The most important thing you can do with yourself is be patient with yourself."

CJ: Be forgiving. Recognize that this is all a process, and that you're not at the end, it's going to keep going. Just be patient with it. It's going to hurt. It's going to suck at times. There's going to be times that will be beautiful, but if you're patient, and you're focused, and you have the right intentions... and if you're curious, you're going to find yourself exploring so many beautiful things coming along into your dream, that eventually you will get to where you want to be. It just takes, sometimes, a lot of time.

CR: Yeah. Listening to you talk, I'm reminded of something I've thought about a lot about over the years: in a way, the people who get hurt the most (and this going to sound trivial now) are the people who are most vulnerable. Right? But their vulnerability is their sincerity, their curiosity. I mean I look at you, and I'm thinking, okay, now that I've heard this whole story, like you really believe this stuff, and as a kid, I'm not just a Boy Scout, I'm an Eagle Scout! You're really going for it, and if you had been a shallower person, you probably wouldn't have gotten into some of the dark spaces that you got into. Which is not saying, "Be Shallow, Kids!" It's saying, that when you see someone who is having a hard time, whether it's mental illness or homelessness or drugs or whatever, a lot of times it's the best things about them about them that led them into that mess.

CJ: Totally. I was just talking with someone the other day, and they were saying, "Oh man, I don't want my boyfriend talking to those people, I hate those people and I want to call the cops on them." She was referring to her boyfriend talking to other people who are addicts, and I told her, "You need to have compassion for those people; they are so miserable, and they hate what they are going through more than you could ever understand." Just love them. It doesn't mean you have to be their buddy, or associate with them, but you need to loosen your grip on that whole stigma of, "This is a bad person", because in reality, we're all good people, we've just all made mistakes. And sometimes we get stuck in the wrong place, and we're feeling pain, and we act out to try to get rid of that pain by doing ridiculous shit, like drugs.

CR: Well listen: it sounds like you are in a great place now.

CJ: I am. I'm extremely happy. I'm happier than I've ever been in my life. I'm fulfilled, and I'm doing

BE FORGIVING. RECOGNIZE THAT THIS IS ALL A PROCESS, AND THAT YOU'RE NOT AT THE END, IT'S GOING TO KEEP GOING. JUST BE PATIENT WITH IT. IT'S GOING TO HURT. IT'S GOING TO SUCK AT TIMES.

something I love... but it sure ain't easy. It's still very challenging. I still face the same challenges and struggles that everyone faces, and I still remind myself the same things that I tell everyone else, "Be patient, breathe, relax."

CR: Is there any undertow pulling you toward heroin or anything else addicting at this point?

CJ: No, I don't really do any addictive substance anymore. I don't drink alcohol, I don't even like smoking weed. I still do plant medicines. I'm a very avid plant-medicine enthusiast, and I think that the practice of using those medicines in a ceremonial and spiritual way has benefited my life and helped my sobriety. Because I do consider myself sober even though other people, the current AA model, might not consider me sober. My own personal take on that is that I'm happy, and I'm sober in the sense that I don't use things that make me unhappy.

CR: Right. You're not using something to get to normal.

CJ: No, I'm using things to grow, and to accelerate my awakening, to accelerate my consciousness and become a better, more loving, more open person. I don't really do any addictive, detrimental substances anymore.

CR: Well good for you, man! You found your way out, and you're guiding other people out.

CJ: It's fun. It's a lot of fun. Life is a lot of fun. You've just got to let it be that way.

> GUYS HAVE THE RIGHT TO LEARN TO BE BETTER AND MORE SUCCESSFUL WITH WOMEN. IF I HADN'T LEARNED ALL THESE THINGS, I WOULD JUST BE THIS TURTLE, NEVER COMING OUT OF MY SHELL, NEVER KNOWING WHO I AM.

CHAPTER 16

NEIL STRAUSS

EPISODE #1 (APRIL 19, 2013)

***Neil Strauss is a seven-time* New York Times *bestselling author, journalist, and contributing editor at* Rolling Stone. *His best known book is* The Game: Penetrating the Secret Society of Pickup Artists.**

SEX | WRITING | MALE SEXUAL FRUSTRATION
CHILD DEVELOPMENT | FAMILIES | MONOGAMY/POLYAMORY

CR: I'm here with Neil Strauss at his kitchen table in Malibu. For those of you who don't know, Neil is most famous for writing *The Game: Penetrating the Secret Society of Pickup Artists*, the super mega bestseller that looks like The Bible. Did all editions look like The Bible, or is that a later thing?

NS: We tried to get it printed at places that do Bibles and five places rejected it as sacrilegious at first. The funny thing is, I was doing a book signing at Barnes & Noble one time, and they told me that it was the second most stolen book at the chain so most stores keep it behind the counter. I asked, "What's the number one most stolen book?" It's The Bible. When they get to the part that says "Thou shalt not steal," they must be like, "Oh shit."

CR: Wow. Yeah, if you steal The Bible... that's a special kind of Christian right there. An example of something like that which comes to mind: my first class in grad school was about addiction and alcoholism. On the first day of class the professor says, "Raise your hand if at least one of your parents was an alcoholic or a drug addict." Half the class had their hands up. "The rest of you, raise your hand if you were raised in a family that you consider to be severely dysfunctional." At that point, everyone in the class but me had their hands up.

NS: You just weren't aware of how dysfunctional your family was.

CR: Either I'm completely un-self-aware, or that explains why I'm not a clinical psychologist.

NS: Do you think your family was highly functional?

CR: I don't think they were dysfunctional, any more than your average family. I love my parents and I like my parents. If they weren't my parents, I'd still hang out with them. They're good people.

NS: What would dysfunction be? Would it be two parents who don't show love to their children?

CR: I think dysfunction can take so many forms.

NS: I'll tell you this: I would not have raised my hand in that class, but now based on everything I've learned,

I think almost every family is dysfunctional on some level. It's like perfection, you can't be perfect. And every family fucks up their kids in some ways that they play out now. I don't want to flip this whole interview, but I'm curious of this about you.

CR: This is what happens when you interview an interviewer, and bullshit a bullshitter.

NS: Want to do an interesting exercise?

CR: Sure.

NS: And by the way, if there's someone that I'm dating and I think that I may or may not want a relationship with them, I'll have them do this exercise to teach them something about themselves, not as a test. And if you're listening, you can do this too.

CR: Am I going to end up in bed with you after this? Is that where this is going?

NS: Yeah, this is step one of the game.

CR: I've agreed to the paddleboarding, but not to the paddling.

NS: That's step two.

CR: I'm being gamed, ladies and gentlemen!

NS: Step three is... that'll be for your videocast. If you're listening, you can draw this too. So circles are going to represent females, triangles are going to represent males. You're going to draw a diagram of your immediate family growing up. So it'll be you, your siblings, your parents, and if you had a grandparent or someone else who was a primary caregiver, you would put them too. And what you want to do is draw them in terms of their emotional closeness to each other. So if your mum and dad never talked, you'd draw the circle and the triangle way far apart, and label each one. Then draw where you are on the diagram, whether you're closer to your mom or your dad, and where your sibling was. So go ahead and draw that out.

CR: For me that would be very difficult because the schema changed during different parts of my life.

NS: I would say that the default age would be somewhere in the 8 to 12 range, say 11. Even in families where the dad is really abusive, they age, and they mellow, and they soften. So go back to that age and how you felt about your family, not how you feel about it now looking back.

CR: Here you go, can you see that?

NS: So there's a circle up top, I take it that's your mom. So a mother-dominated family?

CR: No, it's just that I felt very close to my dad. I think my sister felt very close to my dad too. My mom and my dad were close together, but I think my sister and I both felt more distant to my mom. Largely because of the good cop, bad cop thing. Mom was home, dad was at work.

NS: Mom was strict.

CR: Yeah, she was more strict than my dad was and a little more, "Let's get things done, it's not about just having fun all the time."

NS: And how emotionally close were they? How much did they give you affection, touch, and say "I love you?"

CR: A lot, a lot.

NS: So they were quite emotionally close.

CR: Unconditional love, perpetually.

NS: So you knew that they loved you growing up.

CR: They said it, they showed it; it was wonderful.

NS: And, by the way, I once dated a girl who was a twin, and I had her and her sister do it, and they both drew their family completely differently. So the way you perceive it may not be how it is. And I always ask myself, "Did they have a healthy model of a relationship growing up?" Yours is interesting because with some people if they draw their dad and their mom far apart, and they haven't done work on themselves, they're probably not going to be great at a relationship.

CR: Yeah, that's not actually accurate because I moved my mom up there to get her further away from my sister and I, but she's really close to my dad. In fact, I had a lot of conflicts with my mother because we were very different. My dad would have to be the mediator when he came home from work. I remember him saying to me one time, "Look, I love you, I love you completely. But I love your mom more. Let's not get any confusion here. I loved your mom before you existed. So, you're not going to get in between us."

NS: Wow, that's interesting.

CR: By the way, I just want to note for our listeners, that Neil has now taken possession of my notes and he's seen all the questions I was going to ask him.

NS: I wasn't looking at them, I promise! I'll give them back to you

CR: This was all just a plot to look at my questions.

NS: Exactly.

CR: Gamed again! Watch out for this guy, listeners.

NS: The plot is to not get to them at all. So, we pathologize things and say "dysfunctional," but the fact that you're in conflict with your mom, that your dad had to mediate, and that your dad says, "No, you're mom's more important," that's interesting. I don't have kids, but I would imagine that the kid is more important. I was reading an article about how if you had to save one, you'd save the kid. But it sends interesting messages if your dad says, "I love you, but I love that person more." So where do you stand?

CR: Looking back at it, and even at the time, I felt that I was definitely getting put in my place. But I remember being comforted by that at the time, because one of the things I was most afraid of was that my parents would get a divorce. A lot of my friends' parents were splitting up and I remember having nightmares about having to choose which parent I was going to live with. So, the cohesion, the sense that, "You're important but number one is your mom" was comforting to me. But again, I don't know if my mom was that strict, it's just that it all fell on her and she was so young, and I was such a little bastard.

NS: Right. Well it was kind of mother-dominated, and I don't know if your mom is slightly narcissistic or...

CR: Who isn't? She was beautiful. My mom was like Elizabeth Taylor. Gorgeous.

NS: So that's a yes to the narcissism... note the gorgeous thing, and your lack of a direct response. But Chris didn't say it.

CR: You're a wily fucker aren't you?! I keep feeling like I'm being elbowed into a corner somewhere. It's like fighting Ali. "Stay out of the corner!"

NS: Yeah but it's great. It's intimacy. We're experiencing intimacy right now.

CR: Is that what it is? I thought that was coming after the podcast.

NS: That's physical intimacy, this is emotional intimacy. You may not be used to emotional intimacy because you had very little of it growing up, but this is what it feels like.

CR: Yeah that's true, because my parents abused me. They were so distant. Okay, let me try to get you in a corner.

NS: I'm just here to answer questions.

* * *

CR: Now, admittedly, I'm not very familiar with your work. But it's interesting that people have been telling me about *The Game* since... When did it come out?

NS: The 1950s.

CR: Yeah, Jackie Gleason first told me about *The Game*, as I recall.

NS: No, it was about five or six years ago.

CR: Then as soon as it came out, I was in Barcelona. I remember the guy who told me about it: he's a tattoo artist, a good friend of mine, and we were talking about my book. He said, "Dude you have to read *The Game*, it's fantastic." And this is a really cool, really smart guy. He'd been in prison for gun-running in Canada.

NS: Clearly a smart guy.

CR: A really smart guy, but not a particularly educated guy. And he kept telling me, "You gotta read this book man." But the thing about my friend was that he was a seeker. He was looking for answers. He was looking for someone to show him how to live, I think because of his upbringing. His father was a treasure hunter or something. It was this bizarre family situation. And what I knew about *The Game* was that it's essentially about manipulating women to get them into bed. So that turned me off completely. That's the opposite of what I want to think about. So what do you say to people who say, "You're full of shit. All you're about is teaching losers how to get laid. It's not helping the world and it's not helping them because they don't know how to manage a relationship afterwards."

NS: I like how you couched it as if it's not you saying that. It's just someone else. If someone were to say, "You're a total asshole," how would you respond to that? What I usually find is there are two kinds of people: those who have read the book and those who haven't. And those who haven't read the book have a very skewed perspective of it. But that's okay because that's not what the book is. First of all, the book is a story.

CR: I read little pieces of it, and I really liked that at the end you actually address this.

NS: Oh, you're one of those that just reads the last page of the book. Even the beginning, it begins with the guy who is the greatest pickup artist in the world about to commit suicide over a woman. So this is not an advocacy book. If someone said to me, "What's *The Game* about?" I'd say, "It's about male insecurity." And

IF SOMEONE SAID TO ME, "WHAT'S *THE GAME* ABOUT?" I'D SAY, "IT'S ABOUT MALE INSECURITY."

to me the book was my story, my journey to - even though I didn't know it at the time - searching for self-esteem. At that time it was sort of like, "What's the best way to heal my self-esteem? If this beautiful woman is willing to be naked in bed with me, I must have something going for me".

CR: At this point you'd had half a dozen *New York Times* bestsellers...

NS: At this point I was able to have a career by having no social life or sex life. And believe me, I tried. I did a book with Mötley Crüe. And the whole reason I did the book is that I wanted to be backstage at a Mötley Crüe show. I knew I would have sex then. So I would go backstage, I'd grab all the backstage passes, and I go around giving them to the hot women in the audience. Then they'd say, "Thank you" and walk away. And I'd be like, "Well, when's the sexy supposed to happen?" And, literally, I went on tour with Mötley Crüe and did not have sex or even a makeout.

CR: So those girls were going backstage and screwing Mötley Crüe?

NS: Yeah, or just going backstage. I think at that point most of Mötley Crüe were in relationships. Or with really jealous people who would call them right after the show to make sure they weren't having sex with anyone.

CR: So you were just being a famous author and having all this access to rich and famous people, and going to great Hollywood parties... That wasn't doing it for you?

NS: No, man. And a lot of people think it helps if you're well-known or if you've got money - and I don't think I was well-known or had a lot of money or anything like that - but it's really your behavior more than what you do. I'm sure every woman listening knows this: if she wants to meet some guy and he's a total douchebag, or he's just boring, or he's trying too hard, she will all of a sudden lose interest just like that. So I just didn't get it. I could befriend women, but I couldn't get past that physical point. I would be waiting all day and all night for a moment to kiss, then I'd make that mad desperate lunge and I'd get the cheek turn. It happens so often that there's an acronym for this in the pickup-artist community: LJBF - let's just be friends. So I'd get that, then a week later they'd be telling me about some guy they met at a bar, and slept with, and how he didn't call them afterwards. I'd be like, "I would've slept with you, and I would've called you after, and I would've been your boyfriend. What's wrong with me?" And the truth is, when people go to the pick-up artists seminars, these people are the nice guys. And they're getting nowhere. So for me, it's really a book about male insecurity. But I wrote it half for women, so that they can understand the way men think.

CR: I know this is really unfair. I would've preferred to have read the book before talking to you, just as I prefer that people interviewing me have read my book.

NS: It's cool, there's a lot to read.

CR: What I was going to say is that this is exactly the kind of dynamic I get in interviews – the people who are most pissed off about *Sex at Dawn* are people who haven't read it. They think know what it's about, but then they read it and they're like, "Oh shit, sorry, that's not actually what it is." But what about the whole concept of "negging?" Isn't that about creating insecurity and about leveraging a woman's insecurity?

NS: It's a journalistic thing.

CR: This isn't a thing you developed. You're interviewing guys who do this.

NS: Yeah, but not just interviewing. I went under their wings and learned their stuff. The concept of negging comes from a guy named Mystery. The idea of negging is not like insulting someone like, "Wow, you're ugly."

CR: It's like, "If it weren't for your nose, you'd be really pretty?"

NS: Closer, but I think that's still an insult. What these guys are trying to do is this: if you meet someone who has a lot of guys hitting on them, you have to actively demonstrate that you're not interested in them in order for them to start to be interested in you. To me a neg is the act of actively disqualifying yourself as a potential suitor for someone because, "There's no way he would say that or do that to me if he was interested in me." You're not doing it just for that woman you want to meet. There are a lot of gay guys who read the book who also use negs.

CR: But being gay, you don't need to jump through all those damn hoops, you just have to go to the gym.

NS: You do when you're trying to date out of your league. Negging is also for her friends who are always seeing her get hit on, and they're in protective mode. This helps them feel safe and comfortable with you there. The truth is, you can't walk up and compliment someone. Sometimes you can, with a really sincere compliment that's really meaningful, but for most people who walk up to a woman and compliment her, she just thinks they're hitting on her. So to me, a neg can actually buy yourself the credibility to pay someone a genuine compliment later, that they then believe. But if you're hurting someone's self-esteem, you're doing it wrong. The whole point is that someone's going to have a better experience or interaction, because you walked up and talked to them.

* * *

CR: Maybe I should call this podcast *Interviews With Authors Whose Books I Haven't Read.*

NS: Yeah, exactly.

CR: Have you ever read a book called *Finite and Infinite Games*?

NS: No, what's that?

CR: It's a wonderful little book written by a philosopher named James Carse who's at NYU. Because you're so famous for *The Game*, it reminded me of that book. What he says is that everything in life is a game and there are two types of games: there are finite games, where you are trying to win by ending the game, and then there are infinite games where you're not trying to win; you're trying to keep the game going. And I was thinking how *The Game* – as I understand it from my ignorant, unread perspective – is a finite game in the sense that what you're trying to do is get her into bed.

But relationships are infinite games because what you're trying to do is keep it going, make it deeper. They're both games, but they're sort of diametrically opposed in some ways. I interviewed a woman in San Francisco last week named Tracy Clark-Flory. She writes about sex for *Salon*. I mentioned that I was going to be seeing you and she said, "Oh, *The Game*. I first heard about that from a guy who used it on me successfully."

NS: That's hilarious. I was just thinking during the break, why am I sitting here defending negs? There is some good stuff and some bad stuff in *The Game*. It is what it is. When it came out, I promised myself I'd never allow myself to totally apostatize it, or get too defensive about it. Although I did find myself being defensive about one thing – and maybe that's what I react to sometimes – which is that guys have the right to learn to be better and to be more successful with women. I'm my own case study, but if I'd never done the work to become more successful with women, I wouldn't be here with you speaking eloquently (if I'm speaking eloquently at all, I'm not sure). I wouldn't have my radio show like I do. I just wouldn't be that comfortable around *people*. I wouldn't go speaking like I am this weekend. If I hadn't learned all these things, I would just be this turtle, never coming out of my shell, never knowing who I am. So I know it worked for me. And I also think if I end up having a son who is a 30-year-old virgin – and believe me, some of the guys who come to the seminars are like this – I hope he would learn to become better with women. I feel like it's ethical, if it's honest and if no one gets hurt. It shouldn't be culturally shaming for someone to get better at dating, and become better at interacting. That's my only little soap box about it.

CR: I hear you. And let's look at the industries that are built around helping women attract more men. From cosmetics, to surgery, to fashion. It's *all* about attracting men and wielding some power over men.

NS: And now to flip the script, I do understand people's fear of *The Game*, because when the so-called dominant group within a culture (men) gets together to become even more dominant, that's a threatening and scary thing. So I'm empathic about people's concern there.

* * *

CR: Often when I meet highly successful people – people who have a lot of money, or a lot of power, or a lot of anything – I'm struck by how a lot of their drive is related to some inner wound. And earlier you were talking about –

NS: Your wounds.

CR: Yeah, all the wounds my mother left on my psyche. No, you were talking about –

NS: Your dad's mixed messages.

CR: No! You were talking about feeling that you could speak eloquently and speak in public. If I understood you correctly, you were saying that a lot of this self-confidence came about when you were researching *The Game*. So we're talking five to six years ago.

NS: Right. In fact, I think you can look up a Charlie Rose appearance that I did when I was writing for *The New York Times*. It's just so embarrassing. I just can't get a word in edgeways. If I look at myself then and look at myself now, I'm a completely different person.

CR: Because you were just dominated by Charlie Rose.

NS: There were three other guests on the show at the

THERE IS SOME GOOD STUFF AND SOME BAD STUFF IN *THE GAME*. IT IS WHAT IT IS. WHEN IT CAME OUT, I PROMISED MYSELF I'D NEVER ALLOW MYSELF TO TOTALLY APOSTATIZE IT, OR GET TOO DEFENSIVE ABOUT IT.

same time, and I just didn't make a good showing for myself.

CR: I'm the same way. I mean, I never have trouble talking, but I don't like fighting to get a word in. If they need to be heard more than I do, let them talk. And if he wants to hear me, he'll talk to me. Talk about dysfunctional parenting, I've got a friend whose mother always says to him, "Honey, why can't you be more like Charlie Rose?"

NS: Oh my God, that's funny. "What would Charlie Rose do?" But the thing is, when you speak, you're very learned, you're very eloquent, and you're very smart. I mean, all those intellectual debates with your mother have really paid off.

CR: Oh thanks. One thing that brings a tear to my eye, when my mother got really upset she would say, "I don't know what I did to deserve such bad kids. You treat me like the salt of the earth."

NS: That's funny. For a lot of people, myself included, functional parenting – and this is not about your mom of course, if she's listening – is really about taking care of your kids' needs and your kids' emotions. When the kid has to start taking care of the parent's emotions, that's when it becomes destructive. I'm not trying to pathologize or stigmatize any kinds of relationships, because we are what we are, and there are many kinds of relationships. But I do find that one commonality among people who don't fit well with monogamy, is that sometimes there's a point where they were always taking care of their parents' needs. And so a relationship can feel smothering psychologically, on a subconscious level.

CR: That could definitely be. You know, one of the things I thought a lot about while I was writing Sex at Dawn is how important and yet unexamined the sexual frustration is in men during adolescence – and it extends long beyond adolescence for some people. We become sexual beings at 12 to 14 and it's turbocharged. You can't think about anything else for years. You're getting hard-ons walking by mannequins in a store window. And yet, sexual satisfaction is something that's completely impossible for most kids at that age.

NS: I have a theory about that.

CR: My too. It's like people who are starving when they are kids. They become obese later.

NS: My theory is that naturals – guys who are naturally good with women – lost their virginity at a young age, 10-14. Guys who are uncomfortable with women – and they end up being a lot of my students – lost their virginity at a later age, generally. What happens is, as you said, you go through with this desire for sex, and wanting this thing so bad. And women have this key that will unlock you from this prison of virginity that you are in as a male. And to go through life like that for five or six years, you get this awkwardness.

CR: Five to six really important, very formative years. And for a lot of guys, that frustration curdles into a form of hatred and misogyny. I think if you really dug into a lot of rapists' heads there would be a lot of hatred. Who do they hate? A lot of these psychopaths that kill prostitutes, it's very much related to the victim being a sexual symbol personified.

NS: I think that's true. "What we fear, we hate." You gotta read the book, because I would say only 5% or less is tactical. Most of it is just my thoughts on this stuff. But I do feel that by understanding the opposite sex - which I think is a lot of what *The Game* is about - we start to understand them and not fear them.

CR: And that's one of the things I was trying to do with *Sex at Dawn*: show that this notion of a war between the sexes is a false flag operation. We're set against each other like a dog fight, but we're in this together actually. And there's no reason for men and women to be in conflict. It's that sexuality has been turned into another commodity that the powers-that-be have learned how to withhold from us, and then charge us for in some ways.

* * *

NS: What brought you to Spain?

CR: Well, when Reagan was elected, I started planning my escape; I was in college then. I've never really felt comfortable in American society. The values of American society and my values have never aligned, even since I was a little kid. My first and still probably deepest intellectual passion was studying Native American cultures. And I was super into living in the woods, and what was edible, and what wasn't, and making snares to catch rabbits. I was living in suburban Pittsburgh, but I had rabbit skins tanning in the back yard, and a wigwam that I'd made from tree bark. I made my own moccasins and stuff. A redheaded, pale, Indian kid, sneaking around...

NS: You know what's crazy? A lot of these things are illegal. It's illegal to set your own snares for animals. In a lot of cities it's actually illegal to capture rainwater.

CR: Wow, it's illegal to dry your own clothes on the line. Can you imagine that? This is an embarrassing confession; from age eight to 14 I used to come home from school, take off all my clothes, and put on a loincloth made of pink and purple bath towels. I'd fold it into thirds and put a belt around it. And I'd wear that until I went to school the next morning.

NS: That's hilarious. Little Christopher...

CR: Not so little either, I was 14. I remember being upstairs reading *Bury My Heart at Wounded Knee* or one of these books I read obsessively. And when I read, or write, I get into an altered state like a lot of us do. Anyway, I was tripping out on this book, and I went down stairs to get some water or something, and my parents were having a bridge party. I walk through this room of people and I heard everything go silent. And it wasn't until that moment that I realized I was wearing my loin cloth.

NS: What do you think you were searching for on a deeper level? What did you need? You were missing something that you wanted to feel connected to?

CR: If anyone wants to make a movie of my life or something, it'll be pornographic of course, but the

> “THAT'S ONE OF THE THINGS I WAS TRYING TO DO WITH *SEX AT DAWN*: SHOW THAT THIS NOTION OF A WAR BETWEEN THE SEXES IS A FALSE FLAG OPERATION.”

interesting part would be that there's this big cycle. I felt out of place. I felt born in the wrong place and time; I felt that this Native American consciousness that I was absorbing was animist, embedded in nature, not interested in material wealth – but rather a more spiritual and psychological relationship with the world. All those sorts of things were much more in alignment with what I felt in my deepest being. That's why I left the States, that's why I ended up in Spain. It's a very long story, but I was in Spain on my way to Burma, and I got robbed on my first night in Barcelona. And I ended up living there for 20 years.

NS: That's great, that changed your whole life for the better, in the end.

CR: I've been robbed twice in my life, and both of those occasions wound up making life much better for me.

* * *

NS: I actually have a bone to pick with you regarding *Sex at Dawn*. I did feel like you were too hard on predecessors if you didn't agree with one of their points.

CR: Yeah. Did you read the hardback or the paperback? Because in the paperback there's an extended interview with Dan Savage that they added in later. One of his questions to me was, "What would you change if you were writing the book now?" And that's what I said: I would've been a lot less snarky and dismissive.

NS: Sometimes there was a tonal thing that I felt.

CR: I agree with you. I read it now and I'm like, "Dude, come on. Calm down a little bit."

NS: And I want to be like that. With every book I write, I want to feel like, "Oh I messed that up, I can do it better." When I read a book, I'm like, "Oh my God, that's so much better than the book I'm writing now." That's my fear, I want to learn from each book.

CR: Yeah but the problem with that tonal thing – and I've seen this in your writing as well – every page dances. There's movement, it draws you in from the tone. You're telling an exciting story and you're aware of that; it comes through in your voice. The danger in that is that you can go overboard; you try to be funny but you come across as an asshole... speaking for myself of course, not you. I would like to tone that down a bit in future books without draining any of the vitality.

My father, who taught literature and was a professional writer for a long time, he always said to me, "When you're writing, try to write like you're sitting at a bar with some friends, telling a story you really care about." So when I write I get shit faced first... No, I'm kidding.

CHAPTER 17

CEARA LYNCH

“”

I LEARN A LOT ABOUT THE WEIRD THINGS THAT PEOPLE GET OFF ON – DESIRES THAT FOR THE MOST PART THEY DON’T TELL ANYONE ELSE ABOUT. **IT’S SPECIAL, AND INTIMATE, AND COOL, AND SILLY, AND STUPID, ALL AT THE SAME TIME.**

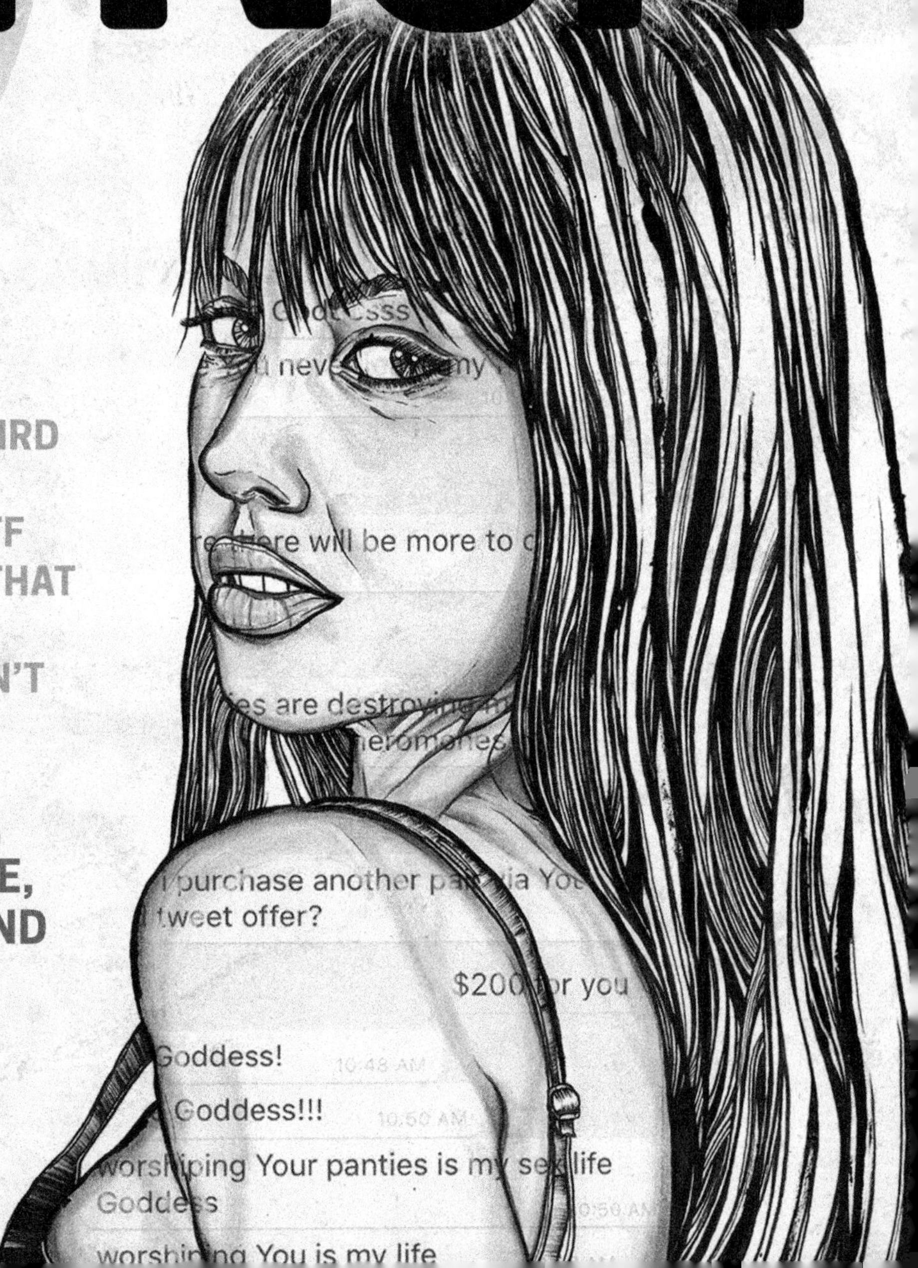

EPISODE #85 (AUGUST 11, 2014)

Ceara Lynch is an online humiliatrix, bringing to life the denigration fantasies of men throughout the English-speaking world.

SEX | PERFORMANCE | PORN | MALE SEXUAL FRUSTRATION

CR: Do you take being a humiliatrix seriously? Do you get creeped out?

CL: I get creeped out if guys start acting stalker-ish; that's creepy. I'm not creeped out by anything that happens in between someone's ears. I don't think we choose what we like, so we are just kind of stuck with it. So no. None of that creeps me out. But as far as how seriously I take it, I take it very seriously - as a job. I see it as a business and a way to make money. That's not to say I don't have fun with it, I totally do. It's great, I get to be creative, I learn a lot about the weird things that people get off on - desires that for the most part they don't tell anyone else about. It's special, and intimate, and cool, and silly, and stupid, all at the same time.

CR: Is there a therapeutic aspect to it?

CL: I think for some guys, yeah, totally. Especially if they are in a situation where they are really repressed. Like in a marriage or something where they couldn't possibly imagine telling their wife what they like. Some guys come from certain cultures where they are sexually repressed. And I think, just dealing with submissive men in general, it is particularly hard for men to admit that they are submissive. I feel like it is kind of a closet, like a coming out of the closet. So, yeah, guys have a hard time with it. But at the same time, I should say, they are okay with it. It goes both ways: sometimes it is therapeutic, and other times guys just really don't want to like what they like, and so they are angry about it. Sometimes the anger is directed at me. So it depends on how comfortable they are with their fantasies. It can take a therapeutic direction; it just depends. Some guys are just looking for an orgasm too.

CR: How often does it get stalker-creepy?

CL: Not too often, luckily.

CR: I ask because it is inherently a power thing going on, right? They are ostensibly asking to submit to your power, and you're exercising that power. But I know from other parts of life, that often when you know

> **“I LOOK OUT FOR THE ANGRY ONES. THERE HAVE BEEN A FEW INCIDENCES WHERE THINGS GOT STALKERY. I THINK IT HAPPENS WHEN GUYS HAVE A REALLY HARD TIME WITH THEIR DESIRES AND WHAT THEY LIKE, AND THEY'RE MAD AT ME FOR IT. ALMOST LIKE I AM DOING IT TO THEM.”**

someone's asking you to wield power over them, the whole top-from-the-bottom syndrome, things can flip really quickly.

CL: I look out for the angry ones. There have been a few incidences where things got stalkery. I think it happens when guys have a really hard time with their desires and what they like, and they're mad at me for it. Almost like I am doing it to them. I don't seek anyone out, everyone comes to me. So that's what I watch out for. I also get the puppy dogs, the adoring guys, who by and large are harmless.

CR: You don't seem like a bitchy undercutting person. Or maybe this is an act, I don't know. You're in character now, so I have to keep that in mind. When I was thinking about this conversation, I thought of some questions, and then I thought, "Well that's not really fair to ask her because some of her clients could be listening to this." I don't want to undercut your persona. From your perspective, I imagine, when you're doing anything like this that's public, if you are too authentic... wouldn't that mess up the gig?

CL: That's something I'm becoming less concerned about as I do this. I seem to make more and more money each year, and I feel like I'm at a point where I'm more willing to open up and say what I really think about things. Like at the beginning, I was black and white: this was my persona online and I wouldn't want any of my customers to know anything about who I really am. But as time goes by, it has blended more; I like opening up, and I think it sets me apart a little bit. I'm sure a lot of guys are turned off by it, but there seems to be a lot of guys who like it.

CR: In a funny sort of way, the guys who don't like it, fuck them. Maybe they like *not* liking it.

CL: Well here's a funny story. So I wrote a blog entry recently that was actually a huge boner killer. The title was "The Product of Your Fantasies," and it was basically me writing about how the reason I'm good at what I do is not because I actually get off on this, it's just that I have talked to so many guys at this point that there are certain patterns that arise; they are not as unique a fantasy as you might think they are. I mean they are pretty weird at first, but after a while you get the idea. And I had a guy comment, "Oh, this was really disappointing, I guess maybe I'll still buy your videos, but I thought that you really got off on your power and inflicting this evil on men." And all this like, "You've really changed, in my eyes." And then, literally within an hour of him writing that comment on my blog he bought two items off my wish list, he sent me a $100 tribute, and then he emailed begging me to make like $600 worth of custom videos.

CR: On a psychological level, how does it shape you to have spent ten years pretending to be this person? Do

> **HE LIKES VIDEOS WHERE I'M ROLE-PLAYING AS THE BRATTY SISTER, AND HE'S MY BROTHER WHO JUST GOT A CIRCUMCISION. AND I'M MOCKING HIM BECAUSE HE CAN'T MASTURBATE FOR SIX MONTHS, SAYING IT MUST HURT SO BAD...**

you ever have an argument with a partner and hear your Ceara Lynch persona coming out?

CL: I hear her coming out when I've been drinking. As far as getting mad, no, because what I do doesn't come from a place of anger. Guys are doing it because they actually like it, they actually get off on it. So if I'm angry with them, what I really want to do is block them, just ignore them because that's really mean. I don't think it's affected me in that way. I've seen it in some girls in the industry, but by and large, I've met some really cool people in this line of work, just down-to-earth women. But I have seen a few that have let this go to their heads, where they really do take it seriously.

CR: Are these women innately dominant? It sounds to me like you stumbled into this thing, and it's almost like your personality was leading you... like the thing that was triggered in your personality was a cleverness, "There's a market here, let's figure out what that market is. This guy likes it, others must like it." An entrepreneurial spirit, as opposed to like, "I love giving guys shit and someone will pay me for it."

CL: It's a mixture of both. I think a lot of girls stumbled into it the way I did. Others... I have a friend who goes by the name of Alexandra Snow; she's fucking cool. If you were to meet her and you didn't know she was a dominatrix, you would totally guess she was a dominatrix. It's just the way she carries herself. She's a nice person but just no nonsense, don't fuck with her. She's always had that in her, a dominant, type A personality. But when it comes to financial domination, a lot of girls just stumbled across it online and thought it was too good to be true.

* * *

CR: Do you think your opinion of men has suffered because of ten years of constant work?

CL: I don't think so, to be honest. Maybe it has though... I don't know what to compare it to because this is the life I've led.

CR: When you meet a guy - like here, talking to me, you hardly know me - are you secretly thinking, "Oh, he's a pervert, he's into the same stuff the rest of them are."

CL: No, definitely not. I don't think that all guys are into this, because if that were the case, PornHub would be littered with videos like this. It's a niche. I don't think it's really damaged my opinion of men.

CR: You ever have any women clients?

CL: Not really. Sometimes men will pretend to be a woman but that's always very obvious to me. I get messages like, "I caught my husband looking at your videos, how should I punish him?" Just overly sexual words that I know a woman wouldn't write. There is this one that I do really think is a woman, mostly because she doesn't make a big deal over the fact that she's a woman. And she buys custom videos for her boyfriend. Her boyfriend has an unusual kink. He likes videos where I'm role-playing as the bratty sister, and he's my brother who just got a circumcision. And I'm mocking him because he can't masturbate for six months, saying it must hurt so bad... And she has ordered videos with different variations of this concept.

CR: Do people send you scripts? How specific do they want it?

CL: Yeah. I ask them to narrow down the script to a paragraph. Some guys will get really detailed, and I'll charge them a reading fee if it's too long. I get away with charging for anything. That doesn't necessarily mean they'll always pay for it.

CR: Aren't you afraid that this will seep into your personality, and you're going to turn into Paris Hilton or something?

CL: I don't think that's been the case for me, I really don't think I'm superior to anyone intrinsically just because I'm a woman. I've been doing it long enough that if it were to happen, it would have happened already. But yeah, I honestly don't think that anyone owes me anything. But apparently there are a group of men who feel that they do owe a beautiful woman something. So who am I to turn that down?

CR: Yeah, well, these sorts of things... I went through a period of my life when I was single and I seemed to be meeting a lot of women whose deepest expression of eroticism was to offer themselves completely: bank account number and insane levels of vulnerability. And the expression of vulnerability for them was kind of an expression of love, or desire, or something like that. I remember being really frightened for them.

CL: Yeah, that's intense.

CR: I was a safe person, and on some level they had decided they would only entrust me with this level of vulnerability, because they had already decided that I wasn't going to abuse them with it. But, my God, some of these women had children, and if I wanted to clear out the bank account and be gone the next day, I could have. And there are a lot of guys out there who would have. I guess I am just saying that what you're dealing with, with men... I think that same hunger exists in women. Not expressed in as fetishistic a way, but still the desire to surrender. Certainly to surrender control; I don't know about the humiliation aspect of it. Although I did have a woman once who wanted me to burn her with cigarettes. That was too much, that was a bridge too far for me.

CL: Damn.

CR: So you said a couple of times that we don't choose what we want, or what we are turned on by. Do you think that that's a blanket statement or do you think it's particularly relevant to men?

CL: I do think that it's particularly men. From the research I've read in terms of sexuality and how it comes about – and there isn't much out there in general – it seems that men are pretty hard-wired. Once they are introduced to something, it gets set into them. I think I've read that there is a sensitive period around the age of 9, and once that gets set in, it seems to be irreversible. Women are a little bit more flexible, a little more fluid, but men seem to be really hard-wired. I think that is the case, especially dealing with the guys that I deal with: they are into some pretty weird stuff. I think if they could choose not be into it, a lot of them would choose to not be into it.

* * *

CR: I'm sure you have limits. What sort of request would you say no to? For example, are people asking you to pretend you're a little girl that they're going to sexually abuse?

CL: That would put me in a place where I wouldn't be dominant. I'm either dominant or neutral. I'm not going to take any requests where I appear submissive. But for the most part, I don't think that fantasies are intrinsically damaging. So I am open to just about anything. I don't like to involve other people that aren't consenting. These guys get off on being exposed and humiliated, and will sometimes send me a picture and ask me to send it to their old girlfriend or something. I think that's a violation so I don't do that.

CR: What's a blackmail junkie?

CL: Blackmail is a fetish, a really popular one in my world at least. Guys will send me their personal information – it's usually fake – with the idea that I blackmail them with it. I tell them that they have to send me X amount of dollars every week or else I'm going to tell their wife that I have this picture of them wearing her panties or something like that.

I made a video one time called "Interactive Blackmail," and it was insanely popular, probably my bestselling video of all time. In the beginning, I told the guy to open up his inbox and create an email and send it to me, without pushing send; write me all your personal information, your phone number, a picture of yourself, your most embarrassing secret, and just leave it there for the rest of the clip. And then throughout the rest of the video I tease him, get him all worked up, and then at the very end I get him to the edge. Then I say I'm going to count you down to orgasm, but here's the deal... when I get to one you have to click send or you can't cum. And so I count them down from ten to one and I tell 'em to send. And if he does he's allowed to come, and if he doesn't he gets to have blue balls for the rest of the day. And from this video I received hundreds of emails with people's social security numbers, people's phone numbers... I think a lot of it is fake, but a lot of guys really have this fantasy of giving up that level of control.

CR: And I'm not sure how much of it is fake, because if you think about it, why is he doing it? He is doing it because it turns him on, and if he's giving you fake information, it's not going to turn him on.

CL: Well that's the tricky thing about that fetish: it's really hot to them when their dick is hard, but after they come, they're just like "Fuck. No."

CR: "What'd I do?!"

CL: Exactly. Men are *very* different people before and after they cum.

CR: Let's not roll past that. Do you think there's a similar thing with women?

CL: No, I don't.

CR: I don't either, I think that's a fundamental difference between men and women.

CL: What's that Louise CK bit about women's sexuality? Women can just decide to stop having sex with their minds. And it's true, we can still think

“” MEN ARE *VERY* DIFFERENT PEOPLE BEFORE AND AFTER THEY CUM.

rationally. I think men very clearly have some cognitive impairments when they're turned on.

CR: Yeah. Priorities shift completely... When you're turned on, what's important is so important, but then the second you cum, it's over, it's gone. And now you're back to normal you. It's like a Dr. Jekyll and Mr. Hyde. It's a really bizarre thing.

CL: It really is, especially being a woman and not experiencing that – but seeing it. I remember it was something very confusing to me early on in my sex life.

CR: Well maybe a similar sort of thing is the whole PMS, hormonal changes, or whatever. I remember as a kid, every once in a while my mother would just be crazy. It got to the point where I could say, "Oh, it's a crazy day." And I recognize that same sort of thing with other women over the years. We both have our temporary insanities, it's just that they are different.

CL: It's very true, a lot of these guys will be talking to me and they'll just be like, "I want to give you all my money, I want to devote my life to you, I'm going to send you all this, blah, blah." All these promises. When you first start doing this, it's like, "Oh, awesome!" But you quickly realize you can't take anything they say seriously when they are in that state of arousal.

CR: Right. Do you get guys saying "I love you" a lot?

CL: Oh yeah, totally. "I love you, I worship you. I'll do anything for you."

CR: Now I'm thinking... you're getting all these emails from guys with social security numbers, bank accounts, their most humiliating experiences. What if your email got hacked?

CL: I never thought about that. But I really do get the impression a lot of the information I'm given is fake. A lot of them will give me just partial information I can't really do anything with. I've had conversations where they want me to seduce information from them bit by bit. So they'll give first 4 numbers of their credit card and I'm supposed to seduce out the rest...

CR: Do you have safe words? You say, "You better send me $1000 a month," and I write back and say, "No I can't, I can only give you $100." How do you know if that's me asking you to make me send $1000 or if it's me really saying I don't have any money?

CL: I've learned that most of these guys are just sending me fake information or what they'll do is they'll send me information in lieu of payment. They'll be like, "Oh I don't need to pay you now, because you have this information and you have me by the balls right now." And to me that's like you're trying to get something out of me for free. So I have them pay up front for a session. For a certain allotted amount of time, I'll get information out of them and basically just threaten them. I don't go through with anything, and once the session is over, it's over: I'm done and they're dead to me until they pay me more money. That's how I do it, basically. And I don't tend to do one-on-one sessions like that in general, just because in general guys are trying to get something for nothing. They're trying to give me information in lieu of payment. I mostly just play-run with that fetish through my videos; that seems to be the way to go for me.

* * *

CL: I have this funny thing when I go out, where if I go out on a date with a guy, I take a picture of the receipt and I send it to one of my cuckolds. And they reimburse me for it. So I'm able to take people out that way. Which is kind of fun.

CR: Have you ever had a partner who participated in your thing, like took a photo of the two of you having sex? Because that would freak clients out?

CL: Nothing quite that intimate. Recently I went out on a weekend trip with this guy I was seeing. I had one of my online cuckolds pay for the cabin; so I took pictures of the bed, the cabin, and the dinner, and stuff like that. Pretty boring pictures for someone that isn't into that sort of thing. But he loved it; he thought it was fucking awesome.

CR: It's like seeing a married woman whose husband pays for the date. On the topic of people who aren't real clear on where they are: do you have any sort of insight into the Anthony Weiner thing? Was he trying to get caught with the dick pics and all that? These senators who take pictures of themselves in the mirror and email them to a stranger... are they that dumb?

CL: I think that just comes back to the idea that men, in general, are kinda dumb when they are horny. They kind of make stupid decisions. And in this day and age it's just so easy to just take a picture, and it ends up online.

CR: You think that these situations, like with Anthony Weiner... that it's just normal male stupidity?

CL: Yeah. That's what I think it comes down to. People shouldn't lose their job for that type of thing; it's not hurting anyone.

CR: Dick pics are funny... how it's become a big deal. And that kids who are sexting are getting busted for child pornography. Do you get adolescent boys contacting you?

CL: There have been a few times when they admitted to it right away, "I'm sixteen, is that okay?" Nope. Block.

CR: Getting back to the therapeutic aspect of this whole thing... my wife Cacilda often says she'd rather – as a psychiatrist, as a counselor – work with young people to help them avoid problems, than work with older people trying to solve problems.

CL: Prevention is easier than cure.

CR: If this were a different kind of society, there would be a place for women online to help adolescent boys to not develop a lot of this misogyny and weirdness around insulting women.

CL: To not develop revenge fantasies.

CR: I think a lot of that comes from this intense sexual frustration that a lot of boys feel from 13 to whenever they start having relationships. A boy from 13 to 30 is constantly horny. It's like being drunk for ten years straight. And that accumulated frustration really poisons the society in general.

CL: I don't know what the answer to that is; we can't even get our basic sex education in check. If we could do that, I think the next step would be to educate boys and girls on porn – a lot of it is very misogynistic and hateful. I don't think that people who have those fantasies are necessarily misogynistic and hateful as a person, but when you're young and you're stumbling across that, it is hard to separate the two.

CR: That's really important and beyond my generation. I grew up with *Playboy*, and *Penthouse*, and that sort of thing. By the time internet porn hit, I was already 30. But kids now... that's some hardcore stuff out there. Do you have any insights into how that is changing the development of people? Is that what's making all these men in Portland so pussified?!

CL: Passive Portland, huh? If I go out to a bar I almost never get hit on, which I like. I think it's really nice, but compared to other parts of the world where I go out, guys are much more aggressive.

CR: You ever read *The Game*, by Neil Strauss?

CL: Is that the pick-up artist stuff? I haven't read it, but I used to watch the show they had with Mystery. And I guess that was all about pick-up artist techniques.

CR: It's sort of a flip of the power dynamic: it's all about getting the upper hand over women, using these proven psychological techniques.

CL: It's about almost tricking them too. Me, I'm pretty up front, I'm not pretending, I'm not luring anyone in a manipulative way. I'm very up front. I think you're a piece of shit, and your penis is garbage, and I'm going to take your money. And if guys like that, they can find me.

CR: Have you any plans to branch out into other realms?

CL: I can see myself getting more into the production side of things. I mean, that's what I do now. I shoot all my own videos, but it's just on a tripod; it's nothing advanced.

CR: So you're in a room alone when you're making these videos. Is that liberating for you, in any way? Like being in character, is that a comfortable place to be? You said you get there when drinking a little bit.

CL: I think it's a lot of fun, I don't know if I would say that it's liberating. I see it as like a performance art. I get a kick out of it.

CHAPTER 18

DUNCAN TRUSSELL

WE HAVE TO KEEP THE SEEDBED, THE PLANET, CLEAN – SO THAT WE CAN CREATE WHAT WE ARE LOOKING FOR, WHICH IS HIGHER AND HIGHER LEVELS OF NOVELTY.

&

THE POTENTIAL OF OUR SPECIES IS THAT WE CAN WAKE UP COMPUTERS SO THAT THEY CAN COME TO LIFE WITH THEIR OWN CONSCIOUSNESS.

DANIELE BOLELLI

EPISODE #30 (JUNE 4, 2013)

Duncan Trussell is an actor and stand-up comic who hosts* The Duncan Trussell Family Hour *podcast.

DEATH | CIVILIZATION | U.S. SOCIETY
PSYCHEDELICS | REALITY | FUTURE

Daniele Bolelli is a writer, history professor, martial artist, and podcaster. He is the author of several books, including* On the Warrior's Path, *and hosts the* History on Fire *podcast.

HISTORY | U.S. SOCIETY | ACADEMIA
DEATH | EUTHENASIA | FREEDOM

CHRIS RYAN: You know, I think Jack Kevorkian is going to go down as one of those people that most of us have already forgot about, but in a hundred years, everyone will know who he is. His idea, "Dying is not a crime." That will seem so obvious in the future. And the fact we locked him up for decades will seem like such a crime. I think there are a lot of people like him; people out on the edge of the radar that, over time, will come to be admired.

DUNCAN TRUSSELL: There are people who can lead us into an actual time where humans stop blowing people up and start working on making fucking spaceships that do interstellar travel, and seeing if we can control the flow of time, and use our technology to develop super-developed sex androids. All these great fucking things that we are just so close to right now that, based on what technology is giving us, are emerging from the technological field. You have these martyrs, and what all these people have in common is technology. They are using advanced communication mechanisms to transmit these stories of oppression to the world, and they are getting thrown in dungeons for it.

DANIELE BOLELLI: Just to fuck with you guys, because that is always good of course... Here you don't blow up babies. It's not polite to do. The thing you hear all the time from people on the left and, by now, even on the right, is that the War on Terror has been taken too far; that drones are killing a bunch of civilians. What do you guys see as alternatives to that? That is the one thing that you hear all the time, that this is wrong. And I agree, but what is the right thing to do instead?

CR: I get this all the time. I tweet something fucked up about America, and they compare it to somewhere else. But you need to compare it to something that doesn't exist. If you say it is illegitimate to compare it to something that doesn't exist, and only compare it to things that do exist, then there is no possibility of progress. Progress is, by definition, moving into a state that didn't exist. We need to go in, and instead of blowing people up, and killing a lot of innocent people, we say, "Yeah, there is a long history of the U.S. fucking with your people. We have supported dictators. We have exploited your resources. Let's start again, let's start new." Instead of sending in a hundred million dollars' worth of bombs, why don't we put in thirty

“ ” IF YOU LOOK AT THE HISTORY OF OUR SPECIES, IT'S A MIGRATORY PATH. WE HAVE TO KEEP FOLLOWING THAT. WE HAVE TO CONTINUE THIS MIGRATION THAT STARTED IN AFRICA BY CONTINUING IT OUT TO THE STARS.

million dollars' worth of schools or health care? It costs so much less, and you are recognizing people's' grievances. They do have grievances. Everyone on this planet has a reason to be pissed off at the United States if they wanted to.

To take your point, you are a big target if you are the biggest, strongest country in the world, but enough with the arms. There was a thing I read recently that says, "Here is what you can do with the price of one F35 that is wrecked during training in the desert." How many schools can be built? It's like what we do with prison. We spend more on one person in prison than we would on education and housing. It is not cost effective. It is not effective on any level, so that is my understanding of foreign policy. Yeah, if you come to this country and try to kill somebody you're going to prison forever. But, we are not going to torture you. We are not going to send you to some prison in Cuba, that really isn't Cuba, without ever charging you with anything, and not knowing if you ever did anything, and leaving you there forever because we can't think of what else to do. That is bullshit.

DT: You know what we are going to try to do? We are going to deprogram your ass and figure out why you tried to kill people, and help you because we are all humans, and we don't know why you wanted to hurt us. Try to shift things *inside* of you, so that you no longer want to kill your species for some kind of a nonexistent death god. If we can't do it, then we will keep you in a place where you cannot hurt any of us. That's it. I think that the war is a war of spreading connectivity, not spreading information. The idea is to try to create the perfect conditions for a person to obtain enlightenment. In other words, we are not going to try and inject you with enlightenment, but we may be able to create a situation where you wake up to what you are.

CR: That is the exact same thing with teaching. They say, "You cannot teach anyone anything. All you can do is create an environment in which learning takes place."

DT: What do tyrants automatically try to do? They try to disrupt connectivity. They shut down the internet. They shut down the information streams. We need to create a climate of connectivity, and in that climate of connectivity, nature will take care of itself because nature is connected. Through that, that is where the real revolutions emerge. The real freedom starts emerging because people are sharing pure information, and pure information is poison to dictators. Pure information is poison to all cults, all tyrants. Maybe I am being naïve. I know information streams can be disrupted, but I know it cannot be disrupted when there are pure channels coming in. It's like any time someone tries to remove a pirated song from the internet... Are you fucking kidding me? You can't do it.

CR: Let's relate this to family styles and raising kids. One of the things that Cacilda tells me about Africa is that everybody raises a lot of kids in rural Africa. If your father is an asshole, it's not that big of deal because you have a lot of adult males in your life. If your mother is a pain in the ass, there are other women that love you and take care of you. So it's like these multiple information streams coming into the head, and if one of them is fucked up and distorted, in some way it's not a big deal. It's crowd-sourced learning and crowd-sourced nurturing, which is much better for us as a species. It is the way we have evolved.

DT: It's this is the problem we have all been indoctrinated into, this form of thinking that is all selfish and based on personal gain. Personal gain is great. It's good to have accomplishment and prosperity, but again, we have to look at potential. What is the potential energy of our species? We can see little sparks of it when information isn't obstructed. It tends to create some of the most insane novelty ever. For example, the free flow of information is what all technological enhancements are based on. The potential of our species is that we can wake up computers so that they can come to life with their own consciousness – and eventually with the help of this new entity, we might be able to create a way to effect the flow of time, or the fourth dimension, so we can travel to any place in the universe that we want to.

CR: Or at least let each other die in peace.

DT: You know, man, that's great. And I think we can get to a place of social equilibrium. But, beyond that, it is not insanity to say that everyone on the planet can work together instead of getting caught up in invisible nonexistent death gods, or invisible nonexistent notions of freedom. If everyone just worked together, and gave up these insane ideas of country, and state, and ideology... then we would be able to create either a time machine, or some form of new interstellar travel, that would allow us to go to other planets. That is not insane. If you look at the history of our species, it's a migratory path. We have to keep following that. We have to continue this migration that started in Africa by continuing it out to the stars.

CR: I am a little more conservative with that, and maybe this reveals my overall agenda, but part of that process is shitting because it's like cats versus dogs. Want to know why you cannot train a dog to shit in a box, but to cats it comes naturally? Because felines in general live in one range, and they stay in that range their whole lives. Whereas dogs just run, and run, and run. It doesn't matter if they take a shit now because in ten minutes they will be miles away from it; so it's a different way of looking at your space. A dog is constantly traveling through space where as a cat is like, "This is my space. I am going to take care of it, stay here, and keep shit together." I kind of feel like humanity – or at least western, capitalist, European, Judeo-Christian humanity – involves the process of living in your own shit until it becomes intolerable, and then finding a new place, and shitting all over that, and then keep moving along. We keep destroying everything until it's no longer habitable, and then we move.

DB: Not to be too ying-yangy, but you kind of need the best of both. The ability to deal with things the way they are right here, right now; the ability to fix the foundations of life where you live in this one spot. At the same time, what's wrong with expanding the range? As long as it's not tied to all the negative crap that you are pointing out?

CR: Expanding the range is fine, but it is almost always propelled by the fact that you either you made a mess where you were, or you are trying to plunder, rape, and pillage where you are going.

DB: But you are talking about beings that are completely neutral by their instincts. Humans are different, and I think in the process of coming to a special enlightenment - which is waking up to the fact that we are all just the same beings, that we are earthlings - that part of it will entail recognizing that we have to keep the seedbed, the planet, clean - so that we can create what we are looking for, which is higher and higher levels of novelty. And part of that novelty is interstellar travel. It's also the telescoping inward that will come from the super advanced, neurologically enhanced virtual reality devices.

CR: Do you think novelty is really the highest value? What I am saying is that, when people ask if you could be born during any time or place, what would it be? For me, it's hunter-gathers in the 1300s or 1100s, before there was any smallpox, or European influence at all, in the San Francisco Bay. So many fish, and food is everywhere. When Columbus got to Española, he said, "This is paradise. People are happy, and healthy, and having sex all the time."

DB: Columbus also added, "so it will be really easy to enslave them."

CR: That's what he said. "With a hundred men, I could enslave the entire population." My point is, that if we can recreate that reality, where there is not a lot of novelty other than every sunset being different, every day the weather is different, and every season the flowers are different.... In other words, is the search for novelty the fall? Is that what ruins paradise? Is paradise boring? I guess that is what I am asking.

DT: I think what you're saying is brilliant, and it is also tragic. The question itself is a tragic question, which is: are we being lured into the future by some evil compulsion?

CR: I think we are being lured ever further away from paradise by the promise of paradise.

DT: Who is making the promises?

CR: The culture. I think Western Civilization is a bait and switch. It is the biggest con game ever. George Carlin agreed with me one hundred percent.

DT: We are in the process of fabricating consciousness in the form of technology. Technology is about to wake up. They call this the singularity. To say that this carrot that you are talking about is being hung by honkies that are desperate to enslave the planet... I do not think that is the case, man. Because I think that this carrot that is being hung is leading more and more to a free flow of information, which is a little bit like what Karl Marx said: "Communism is an inevitability as the species evolves." The notion of property is going to become less and less logical. When you look at 3D printers - these remarried forms of matter-simulators - when you look at the ability to instantaneously transmit terabytes of information in seconds (which is coming), when you look at how we're trying to get to a place where all scientific research is instantly available to everyone on the planet... these are not tyrannical ideas. These are not the ideas of Columbus chopping up indigenous people. These are indigenous ideas re-emerging.

As they say in The Bible, "In the beginning is how it shall be in the end." Only now, in the same way, the child is born and wanders around in a state of complete freedom. Then, over the course of time, is indoctrinated in some nonsense fear mechanism. And by the time they get into their 30s, they can reawaken

I THINK WE ARE BEING LURED EVER FURTHER AWAY FROM PARADISE BY THE PROMISE OF PARADISE.

into the innocence that allowed them to smell a flower purely. I think it is possible that our species has gone through the exact same thing. We have this beautiful innocent childhood where you ran on the banks of rivers, and gathered food, and fucked freely, and children could be raised by many different parents. All these beautiful things... but then we got corrupted by guns, germs, and steel. We went through a dark period, but goddammit, I think it is possible to go back to that original innocence. In a way, we have regained and won it this time. I think that is possible. I think that the carrot is leading us into a very beautiful place. But, it is a bloody place. It could be bloody to get there.

CR: Well that is a beautiful vision ,and I hope you're right. But I tend to think that when you get a conglomeration of a certain number of beings, whether that is a religion or a corporation or a government, an emergent organism arises. And it's a malicious organism. I remember Joseph Campbell said that when you go into a village in Europe, you can tell when that village was built and what the most important intuition was in that point in history by the highest building in the village. Initially it would be a castle, some baron's castle; and later it would be a church steeple; and then after that, it would be a government building, a city hall or whatever; and then after that it would be a bank building or a media building. I think that what happens is we think of ourselves as individuals on some level, but that is part of the con. We are no more individuals as bees in a hive. It's the hive that matters. It's the termite mound that makes decisions that the individual actually has nothing to do with. So in that sense, okay, the internet and this free flow of information is a beneficial emergent property of high-population density. But the problem is that you can have all the scientific studies available immediately, yet people are not going to read them. They are mainly going to spend their time listening to bullshit produced by people who make distractions for a living. So the availability of information doesn't necessary mean that a significant amount of people are going to access it.

DT: I think it only takes one Tesla. One great mind leading to great invention.

CR: But don't you think that the reason inventions emerge is because they make money for the people in power? For example, Darwin being completely co-opted by Andrew Carnegie?

DT: But look what is happening with the Tesla car or Google Fiber. That is going to be an extremely profitable endeavor for them, *and* help people.

CR: Sure, but things that help people, but aren't profitable – we never hear about them.

DT: Weirdly the two seem to be coinciding. And that will continue.

CR: Here's hoping you're right.

> WE'RE ABLE TO WITHSTAND THE CULTURE'S CONSTANT BARRAGE OF DEATH IMAGERY PARTLY BECAUSE IT GIVES US THE COMFORTABLE ILLUSION THAT IT WILL NEVER HAPPEN TO US.

CHAPTER 19

SHELDON SOLOMON

EPISODE #154 (NOVEMBER 22, 2015)

***Sheldon Solomon is a psychologist and professor of social psychology at Skidmore College. He is known for developing Terror Management Theory, which is concerned with how humans deal with our own sense of mortality. Solomon co-authored the book* The Worm at the Core: On the Role of Death in Life.**

MORTALITY | EUTHANASIA | WESTERN MEDICINE | ABORTION

CHRIS RYAN: I first came across your research when I was in graduate school. Must've been the late 90s. Have you been doing terror management theory since then?

SHELDON SOLOMON: Yeah, we actually started, I'd say, in the mid-80s.

CR: Oh okay, so you were well into at that point. I remember Stanley Krippner, who was my adviser in grad school, gave me some of your papers to look at. I was immediately intrigued by the underlying theory. Which basically says that the human awareness of mortality creates all sorts of mechanisms for avoiding that awareness. Is that an accurate summation?

SS: Yep, very accurate! Our work is based on Ernest Becker, a cultural anthropologist who won a Pulitzer Prize in 1974 for a book called the *The Denial of Death*. Becker's basic claim is that what distinguishes humans from all other critters, is that we are smart enough to realize that one day we will someday die, that we can die at any time. And he proposed that this is an incredibly unwelcome realization, and that we go to incredible lengths to deny it. And that underlies just about everything that people think about, and do, and say. All of behavior.

CR: I'm very tuned into this idea at the moment, even more than usual because I'm writing a book called *Civilized to Death*. And right now, just this morning, I was writing a chapter about death. Freud basically argued in *Civilization and its Discontents* that civilization is the product of redirected sexual energy. I'm arguing that civilization, at least western civilization, is a product of the denial of death. That we construct all these institutions out of our fear of our own mortality. So I'm resonating a lot with Becker's ideas and your ideas. Can you give a few examples of the way these things play out in the subconscious?

SS: Sure. According to Becker and our work, what humans do quite unconsciously in response to death anxiety is to embrace a culturally constructed view of reality. We call it a cultural worldview that gives each of us a sense that life has meaning and that we have purpose. And the idea is that, ultimately, what is at stake is immortality. Because every culture, as far as we can tell, offers some hope of immortality - either literally or symbolically - to people who behave

“”

EVERY CULTURE, AS FAR AS WE CAN TELL, OFFERS SOME HOPE OF IMMORTALITY – EITHER LITERALLY OR SYMBOLICALLY – TO PEOPLE WHO BEHAVE IN ACCORDANCE WITH CULTURAL DICTATES.

in accordance with cultural dictates. So from our perspective, people are highly motivated to maintain faith in their beliefs about reality, and confidence in their self-worth. Whenever either of those constructs are threatened, either our beliefs or our self-worth, we will lash out quite defensively.

One example of that – and I think of most of the most profoundly uncomfortable examples – is the way people can't get along with other folks who believe differently from themselves. Because if your beliefs serve to reduce death anxiety, and you accept the validity of someone else's beliefs, then you are undermining the confidence with which you subscribe to your own. And that brings the very anxiety to the psychological foreground. And so in our studies, when we remind people that we will someday die – by asking them to fill out a questionnaire about death, or sometimes interviewing them in front of a funeral parlor, or even flashing the word *death* so fast on a computer screen that you can't even see it – turns out that in response, we like people who share our beliefs a lot more, and we hate people who are different. Not only do we sit further away from them, but if we are given an opportunity to hurt them, we'll do that. We are even more in favor of killing them, if need be.

CR: Yeah I remember some of the research of yours that I read, some years ago. I think they were judges, and they gave harsher penalties when they were subconsciously primed to think about their own mortality.

SS: That's right. In fact, that was our first study, and in many ways, it remains one of the most profound. To the point where when I talk about these ideas, and people are like, "Oh that's bullshit. There's no way that this could possibly be true!", we tell them about this study. It was conducted on municipal court judges in Tucson, Arizona. We just randomly divided the judges into two groups. One half of the judges were asked to think about their own mortality, and then we asked them to set bond for a municipal case of someone convicted of prostitution. And what we found was that the judges who were reminded of their mortality set a bond that was nine times higher than that which was set by the judges in the controlled conditions.

Then we turned that around. We took another group of people, and we had them think about death or something unpleasant. Then we asked them to assign a monetary reward for someone who behaved in a heroic fashion. When that happened, people reminded of death set a reward that was three times higher. So the point we try to make is that it's not that the reminders of death make people unilaterally negative, or unhappy, or extraordinarily punitive, or aggressive. If that were true, it would not be particularly interesting. I think what is more subtle is that these death reminders have effects that go in both directions: we support and like people to the extent that they share our beliefs and values, and we denigrate and destroy those who are different.

CR: And let's be clear for people who aren't familiar with your research. When we say people that are primed - the subjects are primed to think about their own mortality. As you say, it's flashing an image on a computer screen that the conscious mind isn't even aware of. Was it one of your studies where you interviewed people walking down a sidewalk, and you interviewed some of them before they got to the funeral home, and then others when they walked past the funeral home?

SS: That's right. You have a good awareness of our stuff, Chris, I applaud that! I think this was a very clever way to momentarily remind people of their mortality. I say that it's clever because one of our German colleagues, Robert Wicklund, came up with it. We stopped people either right in front of a funeral home, or 100 meters to either side. And we found that when people were interviewed in front of the funeral home, they showed the same defensive reactions that we find in the lab. The point you made is very important: these are subtle effects, and you don't need to know that death is on your mind. A lot of times when people hear about these ideas, they're like, "Well this can't possibly be true because I rarely think about myself dying." And our point, with all due respect, is that yes, you rarely think about yourself dying, because you are comfortably ensconced within this symbolic worldview from which you derive a sense of meaning and value. And if that worldview was to be challenged, then death anxiety would come cascading in like a river flooding your psychological lagoon, as it were.

CR: Okay, let me challenge you a little bit here. First of all, the idea that we're rarely aware of death flies in the face of the fact that a great mass of what comes out of the media is all about death. Whether it's scaremongering news programs in which every shark attack is deemed as some sort of threat to suburban America; or the constant war footage that we see; or the murder shows that we see. Aren't we being inundated with reminders of mortality constantly?

SS: Okay, you got me. Because the reality is, you're right. And a lot of folks say, "I never think about death," and quite frankly our response is, "Open your eyes or your ears. How can you go through ten minutes of popular media without being inundated with these popular images?" So you're quite right, we are being bombarded with these images every day.

CR: But I wonder if that bombardment is in and of itself a method of desensitizing us.

SS: Exactly, nicely done. That's correct, being inundated with these repeated images kind of fortifies us. I think it was Aristotle who said there's nothing more uplifting than when the guy next to you gets hit with the arrow. I think psychologically speaking, that's probably what's at stake. We're able to withstand the culture's constant barrage of death imagery because it gives us the comfortable illusion that it will never happen to us.

CR: That's right. We're the lucky ones. We got away. I think about that a lot when I'm debating civilizational issues with people, and they say things like, "Well, we always survived every calamity. We survived this, we survived that." And I think who is "we" here? 70,000 years ago, there were about 5,000 breathing human beings on the planet, because of a volcanic eruption that wiped out everyone else.

SS: I agree with that. You make a great point that I find myself going back to repeatedly. And that is to remind people, as you do in your discussions, that human beings were a remarkable anomaly, and ridiculously improbable. Every person is descended from this really tiny, and rather in-bred group of proto-humans who made it through this genetic bottleneck. It's quite amazing that any of us are here.

CR: Sort of extrapolating from this: are you familiar with the idea that western civilization is essentially a PTSD response?

SS: Yeah, I like that idea.

CR: Well it meshes nicely with your own work doesn't it? It sort of exposes the engine of these psychological mechanisms.

SS: Yeah, I like that. You know that lunatic Oswald Spangler's *The Decline of the West*?

CR: Yeah, sure.

SS: And I put "lunatic" in quotes, with respect and affection, because I think that was his argument: nowhere do you see death denial more unmistakably clearly, than in the underlying dynamic of Western civilization. Just this idea of an inexorable road to progress, leading to some utopian state where we will abolish death, or at least render it extraordinarily unlikely... I think it is death denial par excellence.

CR: Totally. Which relates to one of my pet peeves: This idea that thanks to civilization we've doubled the human lifespan.

SS: Yes!

CR: Any time I offer a critique of civilization, the first thing that comes back is, "Come on man! We live twice as long as we use to! Of course life's better!" I don't know if you are familiar with the research in this area. But that's complete bullshit. Human modal lifespan is 68 to 75 years.

SS: And has been for quite some time?

CR: Forever. Our species is designed by evolution to live into its late sixties, early seventies. So this idea that we've doubled the human lifespan is purely a statistical trick in which you include all infant mortality in order to come up with your average.

SS: That makes a lot of sense. I never thought about it that way. That would do it.

CR: And you don't include, by the way, abortion, or aborted infants. There was a lot of infanticide in prehistoric societies. A child that was born obviously incapacitated or not strong... you let that baby die, because you don't have enough energy to take care of everybody. If it's clear that this baby is ill or incapacitated, you take it out to the woods and let it die. And in those societies, an infant was not even considered a human being. So we're really talking about a post-natal abortion.

SS: That's right.

CR: So the idea is like this: in an essay, I said that if you live on a vacation island with a bunch of middle class people, and then Bill Gates comes in and buys one of the properties, suddenly the average income on that

> **THIS IDEA OF AN INEXORABLE ROAD TO PROGRESS, LEADING TO SOME UTOPIAN STATE WHERE WE WILL ABOLISH DEATH, OR AT LEAST RENDER IT EXTRAORDINARILY UNLIKELY... I THINK IT IS DEATH DENIAL PAR EXCELLENCE.**

island is a billion dollars a year, or something like that.

SS: Great example.

* * *

CR: Are you familiar with a book called *A Paradise Built in Hell*, by Rebecca Solnit?

SS: No.

CR: It's a great book. I don't know whether you would see it as a challenge to your research or not, but what she does is interview people who are experts in human behavior during disaster scenarios. It's really fascinating. One of the founders of the field of disaster research said that his research - his entire career - led him to the conclusion that the true disaster is "normal" life. It's not the earthquake, the fire, the war, or whatever has caused the disruption in people's lives. Because what happens is, in these situations of incredible stress and disruption, people are kind to each other.

SS: They *step up*. I like that; I'm enamored with that idea. That also occurs in a lot of my favorite novels. A lot of these people make the point that it's the tragedies that bring the best out in us, and that the normality... we just tranquilize ourselves with the trivial. I like that take.

CR: And her evidence is replicated all over the place. Which also goes for your work, right?

SS: That's right. I think that's more important than our work, because if you replicate your own ideas that's an interesting start, but it's not science. It only becomes science when someone else can do it. But you do make a good point Chris, and it's one we think about a lot. And that's to remind ourselves and other people, that in our studies the death reminders are very subtle and very fleeting; we flash the word "death" on a computer screen. When you're seeing the earthquake or the tsunami, you know that's a reminder of death in a very different order. As Plato put it, in the cave people are dreaming while awake. If that's what it takes to wake us up, a glaring reminder of our finitude... if that's what it takes to kind of shake us out of our slumber, then so be it.

CR: For about ten years, I used to work in hospitals in Spain, and one of the reasons I liked working in hospitals was I felt that being in the presence of death is sacred. I don't know quite how to explain it. There's a feeling of being in the presence of the sacred. I especially liked working with oncologists and intensive care physicians, people who were facing death constantly, because all the bullshit was stripped away. And I found that they had a great sense of humor, and the women were sexy as hell! My theory was: they're faced with death, so they're living. They're like,

“”

AS PLATO PUT IT, IN THE CAVE, PEOPLE ARE DREAMING WHILE AWAKE. IF A GLARING REMINDER OF OUR FINITUDE IS WHAT IT TAKES TO WAKE US UP, TO KIND OF SHAKE US OUT OF OUR DEATH-DENYING SLUMBER, THEN SO BE IT.

"Goddammit! I'm alive! I just saw three people die this morning and I'm going to have sex during my lunch break!"

SS: Silliness aside, I could not agree more. Because of the work that we do, I'm at a lot of conferences with palliative care and psychology types, and I just say to those folks, "You're at the vanguard, not only of medicine but of humanity," for the reasons that you say, Chris. They're around death every day, and death is the ultimate challenge. You know, it really threatens people to tear a gaping hole in that delicate, humanly-constructed tapestry of meaning that we all depend upon to stand up every day. And they are the ones that help people die. Not in a way that denies death, but in a way that affirms life. That's my sense when I run into those very special people. They are not around death because they relish it; they are around death because they love life.

CR: And they love people. But I do kind of feel like, especially in America, they're caught in a crossfire between people who need to be helped to die, and a culture that refuses to see death as anything but a failure.

SS: Absolutely. I think the American medical profession is in a terrible existential dilemma, and I hear that from the palliative care people and the hospice people. Of course, this is a grotesque over-generalization, but the American culture is the ultimate culture of death denial. And it does make it very difficult in our country, in ways that I have not seen in, let's say, the UK or Canada, where there is a much more integrated and holistic approach to these matters.

CR: It always blows my mind. This morning I was writing about a case in Florida. A 75-year old man's wife had advanced Alzheimer's, advanced osteoporosis, and arthritis. She was in constant pain, was delusional... the whole thing. The hospital kicked her out, and the nursing home wouldn't accept her, because they couldn't handle her. She would get up and pull the needle out of her arm, wandering around... just a terrible situation. And in a moment of clarity, she begged him to help her die. And he did, he shot her. And they sentenced him to 25 years in prison for first-degree murder. What kind of...? If that had been the family dog, we'd applaud him for his courage and his mercy, right? But if it's his wife of 51 years, we send him to prison for the rest of his life.

SS: I would argue – not surprisingly, with the work that we do – that that is the extent to which we recoil in horror from the prospect of the inevitability of death.

* * *

CR: So we were talking about cultures, and how American society seems to be in a particularly vehement state of denial about this stuff. Have you looked at how doctors respond to the prospect of death? For example, do oncologists, or other doctors who are facing existential issues on a daily basis... do they respond differently than random people?

SS: Great question. The short answer is: we don't know yet, and we sure would like to find out. Now, we have done some preliminary work with medical students. And we did one study a decade or two ago where we took a group of medical students and divided them into two groups. We had half of them think about death, and the other half think of something unpleasant. Then we showed them a case that was written by physicians about someone who was suffering from extraordinary respiratory problems, who didn't want to be kept alive artificially, and had signed a DNR (Do Not Resuscitate) order. We asked the students, "If the person comes into the emergency room in distress, how would you treat this person? How aggressively would you try and keep them alive?" And what we found is that the medical students who were reminded of their own mortality advocated for a much more aggressive treatment, despite the fact that the patient didn't desire it. This was particularly true for students who were high in neuroticism (the proneness to anxiety), and of course our argument was that the med students' own existential concerns were getting in the way of how they were diagnosing and treating their patients.

Of course, we would want to replicate this with physicians. Part of the problem for us has been that it's been very difficult for us to get doctors to participate in these studies. And so – kind of ironically – when we've asked over the years to have access to physicians, the physicians say there's no way that your stupid questionnaire is going to influence how I practice medicine. Which is funny for doctors, who base what they do on evidence, to just declare in advance that they know they wouldn't be prone to these effects.

CR: Well the notion that the American medical practice is based off of evidence is, in itself...

SS: ... debatable, let's say.

CR: I mean, even the bias built into the research process is astonishing. Basically the papers that don't confirm what you set out to confirm don't get published. The reason I was working with the oncologist and intensive care physicians in Spain is that – about the time I first came across your research, actually – I came up with this idea for a doctoral dissertation. I wanted to study the personality profile of physicians who were successfully able to manage the existential challenge of dealing with dying patients. And then the plan was, once I worked out a profile – which would obviously include measure of neuroticism, as you had mentioned – then I would develop a predictive tool that I could use in medical schools to screen medical students who were choosing those specializations, and potentially say, "Look, you've got a very high chance of burnout if you become an oncologist, you might want to consider pediatrics," or whatever.

That was my idea. So in Spain, doctors are much more relaxed than they are in America. I approached a couple of hospitals there, and told them what I was interested in doing. Without exception, they said, "Sure, come in, we'll have a meeting, and you can introduce your research." And so I ended up becoming friends with a lot of oncologists and intensive care physicians in Spain. But I ended up not doing that research because I ended up getting so damn depressed. You know, just reading about death all the time. I think I don't have the right personality for that. I liked being in that environment, but I got very blue thinking about it, dealing with it constantly.

SS: Yeah I think I react the same way, frankly.

CR: My wife is a physician, and she can't remember how many people have died in her hands. She worked in Africa for seven years in the bush, during a simmering war in Mozambique. So she's seen it all. Which I really admire – but it's not something I can do. Talking about physicians... did you happen to catch the article that Ezekiel Emanuel published in *The Atlantic*, "Why I Hope to Die at 75"?

SS: Yes.

CR: Wasn't that great? Makes the argument that societies and family will be better off if nature take its course swiftly and promptly.

SS: I like how he qualifies it, when he says, "I'm not going to shoot myself the day I reach 75; I'm just not going to do anything to perpetuate myself." And at first I thought, "Crap, you know... I don't know if I have the fortitude to do that." But then when he went on, and was a little more explicit about what he had in mind, I thought it was commendable.

CR: He was essentially just saying, "I'm not going to get chemo, I'm not going to get prostate exams, I'm not going to do things that are designed to sort of perpetuate life beyond the point where it's really worth living." He says that many of us seem to resist the idea that living too long is also a loss. It renders many of us, if not disabled, then faltering and declining – a state that may not be worse than death but is nonetheless deprived. It robs us of our creativity and ability to contribute to work, society, and the world. It transforms how people experience us, relate to us, and most importantly, remember us. We are no longer remembered as vibrant and engaged, but as feeble, ineffectual, even pathetic.

SS: Yeah, I thought that was – that was compelling to me.

CR: You probably also saw in *The New York Times* a series of articles called "How Doctors Die"? That series really showed that these procedures – like the ones you described where doctors recommend to their patients CPR, intubations, and all sorts of aggressive procedures – they themselves choose not to accept.

SS: Yeah they don't want to; again that's revealing.

CR: They know the reality. It's not what you see on TV.

* * *

CR: So, continuing the story of Terror Management Theory... what other cultures or peoples have you or other people studied for these sorts of effects?

SS: We've been, I would say, limited in terms of our own research team. We've done work in Canada with our students, we've done work with our German colleagues, done some work in the UK. My buddy Tom has worked in Poland. But all of these are European cultures. More recently, we've branched out, and importantly there's a lot more work that's being done in Asian countries like India. A colleague has done work in Australia where he had Australian Aborigines think about their mortality. And he found that they were more eager to go to war against the white people (I'm sympathetic with them, by the way). But the point was that most of these effects have been replicated in non-western cultures, to the extent that we've looked into it.

CR: That's interesting. What did you find in India?

SS: In India there was a group of researchers who went Varanasi, where a lot of bodies are burned ceremoniously, and they studied the people that handled the bodies every day. They wondered whether or not someone in that condition would be chronically in a state of, what we call mortality salience. If so, they predicted that those people would consistently be prone to disliking folks who were different, not just when they are reminded of death... because they are *constantly* reminded of death. And that's precisely what they found.

CR: Interesting, then that would argue against what I was hypothesizing earlier in light of Solnit's *A Paradise Built in Hell*.

SS: I don't think so, though. Here's where it's tough, Chris. I think that for the body handlers, it just becomes routine, to the point where it's kind of fleeting. As opposed to what all of the theologians and philosophers have been urging us to do since antiquity: to be über-conscious, hyper-aware of the frugality of life and the reality of death. To the point that every moment just feels sweeter.

CR: Do you think that's possible? To hold that awareness?

SS: Probably not. Great question. By the way, Ernest Becker refers to Abraham Maslow, who made the point that we would kind of psychologically implode if we were perpetually in a state of either fear or awe... that we really couldn't remain in either psychological condition.

CR: Right. It kind of feels like both conditions only makes sense in the context of their absence. If you're constantly in a state of awe, then... are you a dog? Is that why we love dogs, because they are like, "Wow, that guy's back again! Food! I get food again! Amazing!"?

SS: And you know what, it would be alright to be a dog. But that dog doesn't have that meta-awareness of *dog-ness*, like we do of our personhood. So it might be okay to be a dog in terms of being hyper-enthusiastic, but that would be exponentially compounded, in a self-conscious creature like ourselves.

CR: Yeah, *Homo sapiens sapiens*, the hominid that knows it knows. So what is it that we know we know? Is it that we're mortal? Is that the defining characteristic?

SS: That's in our book. We have a chapter that we call *Homo mortalis*. Our point is that there's been a lot of designations on what it means to be human. You got *Homo sapiens*, meaning we're wise, rational creatures; then you've got *Homo ludens*, meaning we're playful creatures; *Homo fabers* means we're tool makers; and *Homo aestheticus* means we're aesthetic creatures. And all of those are good for heuristic purposes. But we like what the Scottish essayist Alexander Smith said: "It is our knowledge that we have to die that makes us human." We would argue that *that* is ultimately our defining characteristic. *Homo mortalis*.

CR: It's interesting to think about these questions, questions of whether other animals are aware of death in any sense. Apparently elephants and chimpanzees seem to have a sort of grieving processes around death.

SS: Absolutely. It would be surprising if there weren't rudimentary hints of this kind of awareness, at least in primates. I think the difference is this capacity to think abstractly, combined with what is sometimes called mental time travel. So, an elephant might be aware of mortality at the time it occurs, and even go back to the pre-verbal scene of a tragedy. But you're not going to see a five-year old chimp sitting on a rock thinking, "I'm going to die someday." But there is ample evidence that children as young as two are aware of, and concerned about, the fact that they will someday die.

YOU'RE NOT GOING TO SEE A FIVE–YEAR OLD CHIMPANZEE SITTING ON A ROCK THINKING, "I'M GOING TO DIE SOMEDAY." BUT THERE IS AMPLE EVIDENCE THAT CHILDREN AS YOUNG AS TWO ARE AWARE OF, AND CONCERNED ABOUT, THE FACT THAT THEY WILL SOMEDAY DIE.

CR: Really? Two years old?

SS: Yeah, we were surprised when we started thinking about these things. We're just egghead researchers, so we started doing all these studies, and those produced interesting effects. Then we did something unusual in our field – and this is nothing to be proud of – we started reading books. We came across one book by Irvin D. Yalom, an existential therapist. There's a chapter about death and childhood, and in that chapter he writes about a book by a British woman named Sylvia Anthony called *The Discovery of Death in Childhood and After*. Anthony did these remarkable interviews with kids as young as two, as early as they could talk. More kids than you would think have these existential concerns at an extremely early age. In fact, there was one study that I found phenomenal. They interviewed kids and then they interviewed the kids' mothers. They asked the mothers, "What are your kids afraid of?" And the mothers said, "My kids are afraid of snakes and getting bad grades in school." What the kids said they were afraid of is: getting ill and dying.

CR: Wow! That's interesting. As you were talking, I was thinking about Elisabeth Kübler-Ross and her book *On Death and Dying* – which of course introduced the whole idea of the five stages of grief: denial, anger, bargaining, depression and then acceptance. Being reminded of our own mortality induces a sort of micro-grief process. Your research seems to be uncovering the anger stage.

SS: I think that's a nice way of putting it.

CR: Right? There's a lot of aggression in what you are finding.

SS: Yes.

CR: This is sort of unrelated, but we were talking about India. Are there differences in cultures where people believe in reincarnation or symbolic afterlife – as it was with animist hunter-gatherers, as it was with most of our ancestors?

SS: Good question. We need to do that research. Because that would be a critical test. Is this a universal proclivity – which we argue it is – or is it some manifestation of modernity or civilization?

CR: Right, because if we are living in a society that inculcates the idea that death is sort of unnecessary, then we're frozen at an immature psychological stage where we think we are going to get away from it.

SS: I like that imagery. One of my phrases I use in my talks is, "It's time for the human race to grow up." Because if we don't, we are going to be in deep trouble.

CR: I'm reminded of a scene in, I think it was *Catch-22*. The Americans finally land in Italy, and one of them finds this old Italian man sitting in some ruins, and they have this conversation. And I remember the old Italian guy is like, "Come on! This has been going on here forever. Armies come, and they destroy things, and they kill people, and they leave..." And the American is like, "No, this is unique. There's nothing like this!" It's such an interesting world view. I live in Spain; I've lived in Spain most of my life, and so when I'm back in the US, I feel like a visitor. I grew up here so I get it, but it's still foreign to me in so many ways. I think that, not consequentially, the American attitude towards sex and death is very adolescent.

SS: Absolutely.

CR: So I guess my instinct would be that it is cultural. I'd be very interested to see where your research goes when you get into more, sort of *pure* subject pools. If you could work with hunter-gatherers, for example. That would be so interesting. But it's hard as hell to do.

SS: Yes it is, but it needs to be done.

CR: Well, if there are any anthropology graduates students or psychology graduate students listening right now, this is a ripe area for research.

SS: Yep. Give me a call!

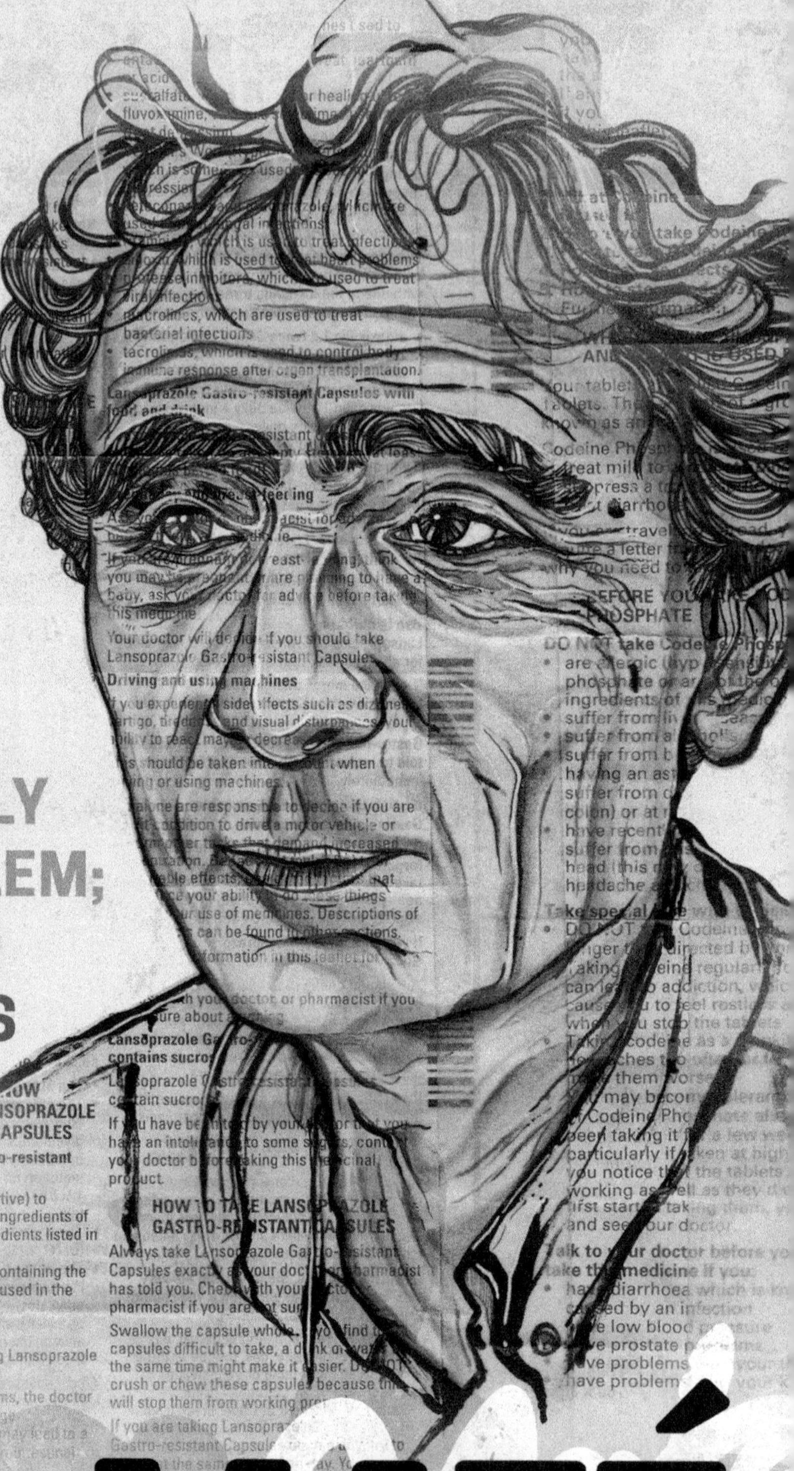

> **ADDICTIONS ARE ACTUALLY NOT A PROBLEM; THEY ARE AN INDIVIDUAL'S ATTEMPT TO *SOLVE* A PROBLEM.**

CHAPTER 20

GABOR MATÉ

EPISODE #39 (OCTOBER 16, 2013)

Gabor Maté, MD, is a Hungarian-born Canadian physician and renowned addictions expert. His book* In the Realm of Hungry Ghosts: Close Encounters with Addiction *explores the nature and causes of addiction.

MENTAL HEALTH | ADDICTIONS | CHILD DEVELOPMENT
MIND-BODY CONNECTION | PSYCHEDELICS | WESTERN MEDICINE

CHRIS RYAN: Thank you for making the time to do this and having me over, this is fantastic. I saw you most recently on... was it called *The House I Live In*?

GABOR MATE: The film on addiction.

CR: Yeah, fantastic film. But as I was watching that film... there's something you said, and I stopped, went back and wrote it down. And it's in my notes for this book that I'm working on. You said, and I'm paraphrasing, something like, "The question is not when people are in pain..."

GM: The question is not "Why the addiction?" but "Why the pain?"

CR: "Why the pain?" Because they have to soothe the pain, and the addiction is just a way of soothing the pain.

GM: That's right.

CR: Yeah, that was very beautifully put, and I know it's an obvious point for someone like you, but I think for –

GM: Sorry to interrupt – but it's not an obvious point for someone like me, because among a thousand addiction doctors, you might find three or four who'll point that out to you. And the other 995 or more will think that they're dealing with some genetic disease, or some choice, or some brain disease – without looking at the antecedents of that in a person's individual life and multi-generational history. So the idea is: Addictions are actually not a problem; they are an individual's attempt to *solve* a problem. That's not so apparent to most addiction physicians.

CR: Yeah. That's what I was going to say. To someone like you, it is. To someone like me, it is. But I think you're right: for most physicians and most therapists, it's not obvious – especially with the disease model, which is an issue you raise. What's your stand on the disease model of addiction?

GM: Well, there's truth in it. But the danger of something that has truth *in* it, is that we mistake it for *the* truth.

CR: So it's dangerous and seductive.

THE QUESTION IS NOT WHY THE ADDICTION BUT WHY THE PAIN?

GM: Well, exactly. It has the dangerous and seductive appeal. Because it says the addicted brain is a diseased brain.

CR: Right.

GM: And in a sense that's true; there are pathological changes in it that you can see in brain scans and assays of neurotransmitters, and receptors, and so on. And the more people are engaged in addictive behaviors, particularly with substances, the more damaged the brain can become. So it's appropriate to speak of it as a disease. Also, the disease model at least ought to give us pause when it comes to blaming people for their behaviors. Because if somebody's heart is diseased, and isn't pumping oxygen as efficiently, that person develops blueness of the fingers. We're not going to blame the person. We're going to say that person has a diseased heart. Well, the brain motivates and generates behaviors. So if we understand that this is a diseased brain, then we're not going to blame that person for the symptom that the behavior represents. So there's some validity to it.

The problem is that the disease model does not ask the question, "What causes the disease?" The assumption is that it's genetics. So the American Society of Addiction Medicine defines addiction as a primary brain disease. Primary means that it just arises on its own, or perhaps is genetically programmed. Not true. What actually happens – and this is far more complicated than most people like to accept – is that the human brain develops an interaction with the environment, and when the environment does not meet that brain's need for the optimal conditions, that brain does not develop optimally or properly – and the biochemistry, the circuitry, the receptor activity, the connectivity of important brain centers and brain systems will be impaired. And that's what sets up the template for addiction. And that impairment. If you look at its environmental causes, it is rooted in the nature of the child's relationship with the adult world, and the more trauma introduced into that relationship, the more likely the kid will become addicted, and that his brain will be receptive to the addictive substances and behaviors.

So yes, there's a disease aspect to it, but disease itself is not primary. And just to reduce it to a disease is oversimplifying, because it has other aspects to it that are not disease based; they're based on the fact that people who were traumatized or hurt have a lot of emotional pain, and when they have pain, they want to soothe that pain. And so that's why I ask not, "Why the addiction?" but "Why the pain?" And from that perspective, the addiction is not the primary problem; the addiction is actually the person's attempt to solve a problem. This goes for anyone who has addictive behaviors – whether it's shopping, or pornography, or gambling, or cocaine, or crystal meth, or whatever.

CR: Making money is an addiction in our society.

GM: For sure. And I would argue that there's a broad range of addictions in our society that are not substance-based, but which employ the same brain circuits, and the same emotional dynamics, and are designed to soothe the same pain as drug addiction.

CR: So then from an evolutionary perspective, the story you're telling about how the brain interacts with the environment – the insufficiencies of the environment, or the trauma introduced by the environment – leads to the very good point that trauma can be either the presence of a traumatic event or the absence of a normal, healthy event or influence in someone's life. So a distant parent who never beats you can still be traumatic in a way.

GM: Exactly. So a Harvard article in the journal Pediatrics last year put it this way: that brain development depends on what they call "the mutual responsiveness of adult-child relationships."

CR: Right.

GM: So that when the parents are too stressed, too emotionally absent, too distracted, too caught up with all kinds of economic concerns, too blocked in their own emotional expression, haven't dealt with their own childhood trauma, or whatever it is... If the parents are not able to be engaged in that mutually responsive relationship with the child, then that child's brain will suffer. Even though they never lifted a finger to hurt their child, and even though they love the child.

CR: So when I'm thinking in this sort of grand evolutionary way... in the same way that warlike society creates frustrations that mold young men into warriors, is it possible that our society is introducing these traumas into us as a way of perpetuating itself? As a way of making us workers, as a way of making us hungry to run on the wheel to keep the society running, to go to work every day, to make more money, to get the status, to... you know what I mean? It creates itches in us that we can never really scratch, but that perpetuate the society itself, almost as if we were parts of a larger organism.

GM: Well, this is where it's so tempting to come up with conspiracy theories. Because if I had to design a society that would create people who have to soothe their pain and fill their emptiness with all kinds of meaningless activities and meaningless goods, I'd come up with exactly what we've got right now. There's actually no conspiracy. It's not that there aren't conspiracies out there; as we know, the corporations know very well how to conspire to sell us stuff we don't need, to make us eat food that is bad for us and all that. So I'm not dismissing conspiracies. But overall, there's no social conspiracy. This is just how this society works. But how it works is that it's a materialistic society.

What does that mean? It means that the control, possession, and consumption of material goods is the highest value. And so people are valued to the extent that they can produce, or consume, or possess. That's it, that's how we value human beings. And the successful ones are the ones that can control and possess the most. And then once people lose their capacity to produce or consume – or if they don't have it in the

IF I HAD TO DESIGN A SOCIETY THAT WOULD CREATE PEOPLE WHO HAVE TO SOOTHE THEIR PAIN AND FILL THEIR EMPTINESS WITH ALL KINDS OF MEANINGLESS ACTIVITIES AND MEANINGLESS GOODS, I'D COME UP WITH EXACTLY WHAT WE'VE GOT RIGHT NOW.

“”

THE DANGER OF SOMETHING THAT HAS TRUTH IN IT IS THAT WE MISTAKE IT FOR THE TRUTH.

first place – they're considered useless, they're outside the pale. So that means that people's actual needs – to be accepted for who they are, and to express who they are as human beings, unrelated to material considerations – are completely frustrated. And that means there's a terrible itch there. Because we all want to be accepted, we all want to be contributed to, and we all want to contribute. Those needs, for the most part, are frustrated by this society. And then we compensate for that. And how do we compensate? By working more, by buying more, by possessing more, by X number of ways. But again, we've become the perfect members of a society that's geared to maximize profit. So yeah. It does work that way without an overall conspiring intelligence.

* * *

CR: I know your work has not only been around addiction, although that's probably what you're most well-known for. I know you've also written books about ADD (Attention Deficit Disorder). What's your take on that?

GM: As a medical doctor, I've worked in many different areas and I became interested in Attention Deficit Disorder when I myself was diagnosed with it in my early 50s. I was the coordinator of the palliative care unit here at Vancouver hospital, working with terminally ill people. Then I went to work with drug addicts in a heavily addicted area of Vancouver for 12 years. And I have a great interest in mind-body health, the relationship between stress and health, and the relationship between emotions and physiological illness. Part of that is when people have the right environment, they'll stay healthy; and when the environment is lacking, their development will be distorted, and so will their health. And that's true whether you're talking about cancer, whether you're talking about rheumatoid arthritis, multiple sclerosis, or ADD. Now, my take on ADD was that, again, it's considered to be a genetic disease by most people who deal with it. But it's A: not a disease, and B: not genetic. The difficulty in paying attention – the tuning out, the absent mindedness – is not a disease. It's actually a defense mechanism.

CR: Against what?

GM: Overwhelming stress. If I were to stress you right now, your natural and healthy response would be to fight back, to escape, or to seek help. But what if you were in a position where you couldn't do any of that? Then how would your brain deal with the overwhelming stress or whatever I was imposing on you? One way would be to tune out. And so when people are helpless, they'll typically just tune out.

CR: Dissociative state.

GM: Dissociative state. That's just a natural brain defense, necessary in some cases. If you have a severe wound, but collapsing means that the enemy will

THE REASON WE SEE SO MUCH MORE ADD NOW IN OUR SOCIETY IS BECAUSE THE CONDITIONS HAVE BECOME SO STRESSED, AND PARENTAL CONDITIONS HAVE BECOME SO DIFFICULT, THAT KIDS ARE DISSOCIATING AS A WAY OF DEALING WITH THEIR ENVIRONMENT.

kill you, then you better tune out the pain and keep running. But if there's help available, you would not tune out, you'd just collapse with the pain. That's the first point. The second point I found out almost by accident because ironically it is still not taught in the medical schools. It relates to the stuff we were talking about earlier, about the human brain developing under the impact of the environment. And it's this: those brain circuits that develop and those that do not has to do with what happens *in utero* and what happens particularly in the first few years of life. There are times in the first few years of life when, every second, there are millions of connections being laid down. But what if a kid is stressed during that time?

For example, I was as a Jewish infant under Nazi occupation in Budapest, Hungary in 1944. And my mother was a terrified, grief-stricken woman whose parents had been killed in Auschwitz, whose husband was away in forced labor, and she didn't know if he was dead or alive. And she didn't know if she and I would be dead or alive. What was her state of mind? And therefore what was my state of mind? I was under constant stress. How does an infant deal with it? Escape? Fight back? Seek help? No, tunes it out. Tunes it out when? When the brain is developing. That tuning out becomes programmed into the brain. And the chemistry of the brain, like when we treat ADD with Dexedrine, or Ritalin, or Concerta... what we're doing is we're increasing the level of a chemical in the brain called dopamine.

Now, dopamine is a motivation attention chemical. Incidentally, cocaine, nicotine, and caffeine all also increase dopamine – which tells us a lot about self-medication and addictions. But the point is that when young infants are stressed or absent from their mothers, or their mothers are stressed, their dopamine circuits don't develop. Therefore ADD is not a disease that you're born with, it's actually a response to the environment. And that means that to simply consider it as a disease and say, "Here's a pill," rather than recognizing that we're dealing with suboptimal development... the question becomes: how do you not just deal with the symptoms, but more importantly, how do you promote development in an older child or an adult? That was the subject of my first book, *Scattered*.

So, in other words, ADD is a response; it's a dissociative response to the environment when there's stress. Now stress does not have to be Second World

“” PARENTS ARE STRESSED OUT DEALING WITH KIDS BECAUSE WE ARE NOT A SPECIES DESIGNED FOR ONE OR TWO ADULTS TO RAISE KIDS.

War and genocide.

CR: Economic stress? There are many sources...

GM: *Many* sources. Relationship stress, economic stress... Stressed parents don't love their kids any less, but they're not as able to be attuned to their kids. Not because they don't want to be, but because they can't be.

CR: Getting back to something we were talking about earlier, the nuclear family... there is this society-wide assumption that the nuclear family is a natural, sort of eternal structure in human organization. Parents are stressed out dealing with kids, because we are not a species designed for having only one or two adults raise the kids.

GM: No, it was never like that. The nuclear family is a historical aberration, you might say. Very recent.

CR: And even in the *best* nuclear families, where the parents aren't stressed, and they are attentive and so on. Kids aren't meant to be raised by one or two adults, they're meant to be raised by lots of adults.

GM: I know, but at least if the parents are attentive and emotionally present, they can do a lot. But ideally, parents need the support of the village, the extended family, the neighborhood, the clan, the tribe. There are millions of American kids being medicated for ADD now. This is not because of some genetic explosion of the disorder, which is totally implausible. The reason we see so much more ADD now in our society is because the conditions have become so stressed, and parental conditions have become so difficult, that kids are dissociating as a way of dealing with their environment.

CR: I agree with you on the developmental environment. But isn't it also a response to the stultifying, ridiculously boring environment of most schools?

GM: That will cause attention problems and boredom problems, but it would not cause ADD.

CR: But ADD is a name we throw at kids who aren't paying attention in class.

GM: I know, and so that is the problem of ADD is as a concept: it doesn't explain anything, it just describes something. It describes a certain set of traits or behaviors. But it doesn't ask what is underlying that set of behaviors. Let's say a kid doesn't pay attention in school. It could be that they learned to dissociate early because of stress in the family, or it could be that they're gifted and thereby bored in that stultifying environment.

CR: Could be that the teacher sucks.

GM: Could be that the teacher is just non-vital, and non-exciting, and non-connected. It could be that their emotional relationship has transferred to their peer group to such an extent that they don't pay attention to what adults say; they'd much rather pay attention to what their peers are doing. There could be any number of dynamics. Just because a kid is not paying attention does not explain anything about that kid. So among that subset of kids, there'll be a smaller subset whom I'd say will have genuine ADD, in the sense that their brains are tuned to dissociate and probably lack dopamine. And the question then is what do you do with those kids? What do you do with any kid, for that matter? The solution, no matter what the source of the problem, is to create environments that are vital, to create environments that meet the kids' needs and where kids are connected to adults – nurturing adults – so they can feel secure in themselves.

Now, it's totally unnatural for a kid to sit in a desk for six, seven, eight hours a day and pay attention to a blackboard. It's got nothing to do with human needs. What that has to do with is what we were talking about before about the needs of the society. Because if I had to design a school system that'll turn out people that don't know how to think for themselves, that follow authority, that swallow meaningless facts, and engage in meaningless activities so that they can go to work in factories and jobs that don't reflect who they are, then I would design the school system we have now.

* * *

GM: There's a psychiatrist called Bessel van der Kolk who's a world expert on trauma. He's a professor of psychiatry at Boston University. He says that virtually every single inmate of the criminal justice system was a traumatized child. So we're punishing people for having been traumatized, basically. I would argue, and I do argue in my book *The Body Says No*, that cancer, rheumatoid arthritis, ALS, multiple sclerosis, colitis, Crohn's disease, chronic fatigue, chronic asthma... that these are all symptoms. In other words they are diseases, but they're not discrete, they're not accidental, they're not unexplainable. They have to do with what happened in people's lives, and how they've had to compensate for early childhood loss. For example, cancer typically happens in people who've emotionally repressed themselves, particularly their anger, because they had to do that to survive their parental environment. And then that becomes a coping style. We now know that the mind and the body are inseparable, that the emotional system, the immune system, the nervous system, the hormonal apparatus, the cardiovascular system, the intestinal apparatus... these are not separable; it's one system. And again, these are things that nobody breathes a word about in medical schools, but which scientifically aren't even controversial.

So when you're suppressing one thing, you're affecting the other parts of the system as well. So when people are emotionally repressed, they're actually repressing their immune system. Therefore, they are more likely to develop some disease related to immune suppression. And that's clearly related to what happened to them in childhood, to what happened to their brain development, to the kind of emotional patterns and self-concept they developed in their early years. So that by the time you look at the cancer, or you look at the colitis, or any one of these other diseases... they're symptoms of a lifetime. Now they have to be dealt with, but with more than just physical modalities.

CR: And I think it even goes further than that. I'm sure you're aware of the recent research in epigenetics that shows that even a grandparent's stress levels are reflected in –

GM: Physiologically in the child, and not genetically. Fascinating. And so that when you look at the science of psychoneuroimmunology, which studies the relationship between the psyche –

CR: I spoke with Robert Ader at a conference years ago. His research started the field of psychoneuroimmunology. He showed that your mental state could affect your immune system.

GM: He actually wasn't the first one to show that. There was a Hungarian-Canadian physician called Hans Selye who actually coined the world stress.

CR: Oh, really?

GM: Yeah, he almost won the Nobel prize.

CR: Well, that's what I'm thinking: Ader should have won the Nobel Prize. Somebody in that field.

GM: Selye began his work on these theories. His father was a Hungarian army officer, his mother an Austrian, so his Hungarian name is Janosz Selye, but he's better known as Hans Selye. He's the one that showed in the laboratory that when you stress rats, it'll cause hypertrophy of the adrenal glands. When you stress rats, their immune systems become suppressed, their adrenal glands enlarge because of overuse, and they get ulcers in their stomachs.

CR: I think I was mixing up Ader with him.

GM: Ader was the one with the saccharine.

CR: But the rats escaped from the cage, and whoever it was chased the rats around. And for weeks he couldn't find the rats. Finally he found them, and put them back into the research. When they did the autopsies at the end, he noticed that there was a difference between the brain structures of the rats who hadn't escaped and were given the stress, and the rats who had escaped; although I'm sure they were stressed too, in different ways. Which brings us to Rat Park, the fantastic research that was done here in Vancouver.

GM: Which has to do with addiction, again. The rats were given differential environments: some were given more room to play, more companionship, a more interesting environment, and so on. Contrary to the belief that drugs in themselves were addictive, you couldn't make these rats addicted if you tried. Whereas the ones in all these studies in the laboratory, where you put the rats in cages, attach electrodes to them, and so on... and then you show how they become desperate for drugs... well of course they become addicted! How would you react if you were put in a cage and had electrodes placed all over you?

CR: It's like if we did all our research on prisoners, and then extrapolated that to general society. That's absurd. Unbelievable. Have you ever read a book called *Lives of a Cell*?

GM: No.

CR: It's by Lewis Thomas, who was the President of Memorial Sloan-Kettering Institute in New York. So he was a very traditional, very successful medical doctor. It was written in the seventies; it's sort of a classic of the genre where the medical doctor writes about patients and his thoughts – before Oliver Sacks and all that kind of stuff. It's a beautiful book of essays. And essentially what he's offering is sort of a Gaia hypothesis, that the earth is a living thing, but he says it's a cell: it's got a membrane, it's got these different elements that are interacting. And one of the essays in there relates to how science is like a flashlight: it only sees the illuminated area, with the assumption that that's all there is – while ignoring the darkness around it. In this essay he talks about folk traditions for dealing with warts. And how societies all over the world have these... traditions. In Ireland, you have a wart, you cut a potato and you rub the wart with the potato and then you bury the potato out in the yard under a full moon, and in three days your wart will be gone.

This is an oncologist. He says, "Okay, these traditions work. What's happening there?" What's happening is that through this arbitrary ritual that we've designed, the mind learns to distinguish the wart cell from the non-wart cell.

GM: That's right.

CR: And while you're sleeping, it eliminates the wart cell.

GM: It's the immune system, yeah.

CR: So he says that's what we're trying to do with radiation, and chemotherapy, and all these other things... to distinguish one set of cells, the malignant cancer cells, from the cells that are surrounding them – and to then eliminate the bad cells. But we already have this mechanism *within* us. And yet we're not spending a dime researching this. Why? Because pharmaceutical companies won't make any money from it.

GM: Partly it's because the pharmaceuticals have a huge and overweening influence on medical practice, but it's also more complex than that. It's also that we as people are so cut off from ourselves, from our own emotions and our own unity with our bodies, that we actually don't know how to do it. We don't perceive that there's a real healing potential inside every person. We don't know how to enliven it, and invite that human capacity into our lives. So then that leaves us with coming at it from the outside and either killing it, or cutting it out, or poisoning it.

CR: And we're trapped in our metaphors. You see this with the brain, which today we frame as a computer, with memory and processing, blah blah blah. People get trapped in that. It used to be that the brain was a steam engine, and we sort of applied these mechanistic metaphors to the body.

GM: And, of course, the truth is that when you look at the modern research on the brain and the mind, they're largely emotion-based. A computer is not emotion based. They're program based; you can say that they're mechanical analogs of the brain in some way, but really, the human capacity to function, and to learn, and to develop, and to grow is largely based on emotion. And you got Antonio Damasio who says that the importance of the emotional apparatus is as a substrate for the intellectual apparatus. So those models, those metaphors for the human mind, they just don't work.

* * *

CR: You have to hit a wall at some point. There's a line we quote in *Sex at Dawn* from the playwright Arthur Miller, speaking about Marilyn Monroe, and Kennedy, and all that. He said, "An era can be said to end when its basic illusions are exhausted." I feel like we are living at a moment, a historical moment, when virtually every basic illusion of Western society is exhausted. Whether it's the trust in the banking sector, or government, or the church, or medicine, or American foreign policy as a defender of freedom and good, or the integrity of sport... I can't think of a major institution that isn't discredited. Not to mention the inaction on climate change.

GM: That's true, but that leaves people depressed and apathetic and alienated, and not more enlightened and more impelled to search for some humane and positive solution. And that's the key question: where do we go from a place of massive apathy? It's fine for you and me – as university-educated, socially engaged, and successful people – to have these insights. But really,

"SUPPORTING THE TROOPS" MEANS WAVING A FLAG AT A FOOTBALL GAME. IT DOESN'T MEAN ACTUALLY SUPPORTING THE HUMAN BEINGS THAT COME BACK BROKEN.

when you look across the social spectrum, a lot of people are more hurt, more disempowered, and much less capable of turning their lives around than you and I might be. And they're not seeing through everything. They're just resigned to everything. And that's the problem. I mean, if people actually saw through stuff, that would be a position to move forward from. But there's not too much that people see through; they just think that's how it is, and it can't be any other way. They're just resigned to it. And that's the biggest buttress of this system: this resignation that people have. That learned helplessness that people have acquired.

Look, I grew up in communist Hungary. Everything was propaganda, everything was party-controlled. And most people saw that. The system of control and propaganda here is infinitely more sophisticated, and more pervasive, and more successful. I mean, those commies, they knew nothing. Compared to the control and propaganda apparatus that functions in this society.

CR: The best way to control someone is to convince them they're free. It blows my mind when I hear Americans talking about freedom, and you know, "Our heroes over in Afghanistan, protecting our freedom!"

GM: And then those heroes come back, traumatized, and how are they treated? "Supporting the troops" means waving a flag at a football game. It doesn't mean actually supporting the human beings that come back broken.

CR: Or not sending them out in the first place. To do things that...yeah. Listen, I know you've got stuff to do, and you're a very busy guy. Before we finish, one of the things I wanted to ask you about *The Realm of the Hungry Ghosts* – it's one of the coolest titles. It's so evocative; it just feels like I enter another world when I listen to that phrase. What's the origin of that?

GM: It's a Buddhist phrase. In Tibetan Buddhism, people cycle through a series of realms: the realm of the human, which is our ordinary selves; the animal realm, which is our drives, instincts; the hell realm, which is unbearable emotions; the realm of jealous titans; and the god realm. Each of these represents really different states that we all know. The last realm, the realm of the hungry ghosts, has creatures depicted with large empty bellies, tiny or narrow scrawny necks, and very narrow gullets. So they have these large empty bellies but they're small mouthed, so they're incapable of filling that emptiness. And that's the realm of the addict.

CR: Wow.

GM: And my contention is, as I say in the book, in the realm of hungry ghosts and addiction, that we're in a hungry ghost realm to escape the hell realm of unbearable emotions. We're actually stuffing it down all the time trying to get something from the outside to deal with what's unbearable, and so that's what the image comes from.

CHAPTER 21

ANDREW WEIL

"I'M FASCINATED BY CASES OF SPONTANEOUS HEALING, AND I THINK THE MORE WE FOCUS ON THEM, THE MORE THEY'RE LIKELY TO HAPPEN."

EPISODE #6 (APRIL 19, 2013)

Andrew Weil, MD, is a well-known American physician and champion of integrative medicine credited with changing the national approach to wellness preservation.

BODY SCIENCE | PARAPSYCHOLOGY | PSYCHEDELICS | EUTHANASIA | CHILD DEVELOPMENT | FAMILIES | DEATH

CHRIS RYAN: Did you ever meet Aldous Huxley?

ANDREW WEIL: No, but I corresponded with him. I got a letter from him shortly before he died.

CR: In '62 or so?

AW: He died on the same day that Kennedy was assassinated in '63. So reading his book *The Doors of Perception* – which I think I did the summer before I entered Harvard – had a major influence on me, and it was one of the things that awoke my interest in experimenting with mescaline and other psychedelics.

CR: I mention him because I think a lot of people who are familiar with the whole psychedelic movement in the 60s see Aldous Huxley on one side, and Timothy Leary on the other. Huxley was arguing that these substances were so powerful, and so sacred, and so important, that they should really be reserved for people who were ready for them.

AW: So he envisioned a kind of priesthood of shamans that would dispense them and control them. And Leary wanted them for everybody.

CR: Leary just thought the whole world would be better if everybody tripped.

AW: The other polarity was between Leary and Albert Hofmann, the scientist who invented LSD, whom I also knew. A very proper Swiss chemist (but also quite twinkly) who did a lot of self-experimentation. He felt that Leary had essentially done-in psychedelic research – he had so poisoned the atmosphere – that it made it impossible for these things to be studied in universities. That's changing again, finally.

CR: Thanks to MAPS, the Multidisciplinary Association for Psychedelic Studies, and our mutual friend, Rick Doblin. And other people like Julie Holland who, like you, are extremely academically qualified and have put in the time. Rick Doblin was at the Harvard Kennedy School of Government; Julie Holland is a psychiatrist; and lots of other people have really risked their careers to stand up and say it's absurd that these substances are not available to qualified, practicing physicians, psychologists, or psychiatrists. Stanislav Grof said that psychology without psychedelics is like biology without a microscope.

So it seems, from my perspective, that the politics

have finally come around. Not to get too cheesy here, but you really blazed the trail. When I look at people who trod that path, who said, "I'm going to go to Harvard. I'm going to check every box on the curriculum that anybody could possibly have, and then I'm going to stand up and tell the truth and risk it all," you're the person I think of first in that line. And Leary, from my perspective, was about ego and taking shortcuts. His personal biography is very interesting: his wife committed suicide on his 40th birthday. He had a lot of tough things going on in his life, so I don't mean to be blaming him for anything or judging him, but he did seem to be more about himself. Whereas you, and the people who follow behind you, seem to be more about bringing these very important substances and experiences back to an accessible place for people. Because they are incredibly healing. Correct me if I'm wrong, but I believe every society that has ever had access to psychedelics has considered them to be the greatest gift from the gods. And here we are throwing people in prison. In the U.S., you get more prison time if you get caught with a hundred hits of acid than for second-degree murder.

AW: And that's nuts. Very irrational. It's crazy that we've denied ourselves the positive uses of those. Same with cannabis. The medicinal properties are so great, and the safety is so great... it's foolish that we don't use that in medicine. So I think that we are in a time when things are changing.

CR: Why?

AW: Maybe it's just time. Maybe it's a result of a new generation coming up that is more comfortable with all of this.

CR: Do you think that psychedelics have a place in development and education? Do you think they should even be included in an ideal educational curriculum? Is that even a possibility?

AW: I don't know. Maybe. I think one of the questions that raises is whether there's an age below which it would not be appropriate for people to experiment with these?

CR: Good question.

AW: And I think the answer is probably yes. I don't know what that is, but I think that taken too early in life, they may interfere with normal development. I think that they can be very useful tools, and I think the main caution is that they be used under the supervision of people who are qualified by their own experience to know how best to use them, and how to shape the set and setting to produce positive experiences.

* * *

CR: Have you had psychic experiences yourself?

AW: Well, I've had a lot of experiences of what I would call *synchronicity*. Either thinking of a thing and then meeting it, or thinking of a person and then they call. I like to focus on that, and I think that by focusing on that, it happens more frequently. And I find those experiences very reassuring; they reveal a bit of the hidden connectedness out there. So I have those kinds of experiences a lot, and I make use of them. I'm very intuitive, and – I don't know if you would call this psychic – but I think by using intuition, I'm sometimes able to understand people and events, and predict them by understanding them on a deep level. And that may look like some kind of psychic ability. I don't see ghosts, I don't have experiences with spirits, or anything of that sort. But this sort of *synchronistic* *awareness* and what many people dismiss as being coincidences, those are very important in my life.

CR: Since I read your book, *The Marriage of the Sun and Moon*, your image of the sun and the moon has been a touchstone for me. I bring that up to people, I've used it in classes I've taught, and I try to pass it to people as a gift. And it's interesting to see how many people are so quick to dismiss it. And what I'm talking about of course is – which blew my mind when I first read it in your book – is the idea that the sun is many times the size of the moon. We know all this information, but we don't think about it. The moon is a fraction the size of the Earth. But the distance of the sun to the Earth, relative to the distance from the moon to the Earth, makes them appear to be pretty much the same size, within one percentage point depending on what time of the year it is.

AW: And if that were slightly off, there wouldn't be total eclipses of the sun. And here we are on the one planet where that happens.

CR: The one planet that happens, which happens to be the one planet with life. And I even spoke to an astronomer, asking if this were the case on other planets. They can calculate all this, and apparently from the surface of Jupiter, even with all the moons around it, this doesn't pertain. There's no mathematical necessity, this isn't an epiphenomenon of gravity or planetary formation. Walt Whitman talked about "leaves of grass," and he says something about how a leaf of grass is like a handkerchief dropped by God so that we'll note his passing. And I always think of that in terms of the sun and the moon.

AW: Well I think there's a lot of stuff like that out there in the world that, if you pay attention to it, is just remarkable and makes you aware of the specialness of things. The other kinds of experiences that I've had are what I would call *subtle energies*, were when I worked with a number of energy healers. I have one woman who was extremely good, when she put her hands on you, it felt like motors, and energy would go through your whole body. And it wasn't subtle.

CR: Is this Reiki?

AW: No, this was her own form of energy work. But that's stuff that regular science dismisses as being unreal, and to me it's quite real and obvious.

CR: Talking about these experiences, I wonder what you think of Jack Kevorkian, and the right to die, and euthanasia – which is also a direction the culture seems to be moving towards.

AW: Over the years I've been asked, by so many older patients especially, if I would help them die – would I be there to assist them? I think this is such a strong need, that people really don't want to be in situations where they're out of control and are unable to end their life if they want to. I think you have to credit Kevorkian with raising this issue to a level where there is real public discourse about it. We can argue about the methods that he went about doing that, but he's solely responsible for it, and it's very good to see that debate happening. A lot of this is done anyway, under the table, and is quite routine. The hospice movement in this country has been a really good thing, but I still think there are a lot of doctors who think their mission is to prolong life at all costs.

CR: A warfare approach to medicine.

AW: Yeah. I agree, we are seeing things change somewhat.

ISN'T IT FUNNY HOW WE'RE TERRIFIED OF WHAT COMES AFTER LIFE, BUT NO ONE TALKS ABOUT WHAT CAME BEFORE BIRTH?

CR: Do you have an idea of what the best way to institutionalize this would be? Because you said it's a good thing that we're having this public discourse. But having lived in Europe a long time, sometimes I wonder whether it's better to just let things happen without the big discussion. Which is sort of how it happens in Spain.

AW: In general, in many situations where patients are terminal and in pain, the way it's commonly done is to increase doses of narcotic medications until breathing stops.

CR: But then that can get the doctor in trouble, right? Because then they're monitoring their use of opiates.

AW: So that shouldn't be the way. But I don't know. I agree, it may be better not to have all the discussion about it. And the big issue is: do we need criteria for this? It's one thing if the person is in intractable pain or has an incurable illness; it's another if they're depressed, for example.

CR: It's like what you said about doctors seeing their job as being to preserve life at any cost. I've seen people in horrible situations where I think they would have been better off if they had taken control. But the reason they didn't was because of an intense fear of death. Do you have any personal sense of what to expect?

AW: I think the human mind is incapable of analyzing that. Death is the ultimate mystery; it's something that we're going to experience but we can't understand it.

CR: Isn't it funny how we're terrified of what comes after life, but no one talks about what came before birth? Nobody says "Thank god I got born, that was horrible!" It's a non-issue and yet where we're going seems to be such a huge problem for people.

AW: Maybe birth is the hard part and death is the easy part, I don't know. Maybe there is no one thing that happens, maybe there is multiple realities that are possible.

CR: Ever heard of Ian Stevenson?

AW: Yes, of course.

CR: His work is very interesting.

AW: Fascinating. And I've read a lot of those case studies of kids that spontaneously remember past lives. Very, very interesting.

CR: And that certainly ties into what you're saying, that maybe different things happen to different people. Ian Stevenson, for listeners who aren't aware, is a psychiatrist who teaches at the University of Virginia. He's done very scientifically sound studies of reincarnation in Lebanon, Brazil, India, and the U.S. He finds three , four, and five-year-old kids who are telling stories about who they were in their previous lives Things like: "in a village with a river and a brick factory, and I got hit by a bus riding a bike." And Stevenson and his grad assistants would find that town and figure out who that kid was. The stories would match up.

AW: And often these memories are then forgotten as the kid gets a little older, after a certain period. And often in the previous life, there was a violent end to it.

CR: An accident, or a murder, or something like that. And sometimes birth marks correspond to the point of injury.

AW: Of course in India, all this is accepted as commonplace, but in the U.S. it isn't. It's fascinating. I'm always interested in anomalies, things that don't fit, and how people deal with them.

CR: In a culture where a kid talking about something like that isn't considered absolutely nuts, people are more likely to listen. Those cases are more likely to be uncovered and so on.

AW: That also ties in with one of the main themes of my work in healing and medicine: I'm fascinated by cases of spontaneous healing, and I think the more we focus on them, the more they're likely to happen. And that's why I wanted to draw people's attention to them.

CR: Sort of like the way you focus on synchronistic events, and how that brings more of them toward you. There are ways of affecting the field of reality around us, without getting into what I consider to be pure bullshit like *The Secret* or that Paulo Coelho crap.

* * *

CR: Here's a question I've been wanting to ask you forever. A lot of your later career involves helping people find healthier ways to live. Do you sometimes feel like you're trying to help fish living in a poisoned lake live healthier?

AW: I think we are living in a toxic world. But I think that there's still a lot of things that you can do to protect yourself and minimize harm. Even if you're stuck in a big city with polluted air, you can spend time in parks where the air is better, for example.

CR: You can have plants in your house.

AW: You can have plants in your house, exactly. So the things that you can control, you want to exercise control over. What's most annoying is when society is structured in such a way that makes it harder for people to make better choices. For example, with food, the government tells you to eat more fruits and vegetables. But at the same time it's subsidizing corn, and soy, and wheat – and this is one of the reasons why these very unhealthy ingredients like refined soy oil and high fructose corn syrup are in all the junk foods. There are no subsidies for fruits and vegetables. So the most expensive calories you can buy in a grocery store are fruits and vegetables, and they're out of reach for some people.

“” THE ESSENTIAL AIM OF PALEO – NOT EATING REFINED AND PROCESSED FOODS – THAT'S THE SAME KIND OF THING I TEACH. THAT'S WHERE ALL THE TROUBLE COMES FROM.

CR: And you can't even get them.

AW: Right, if you're on an Indian reservation, or inner city neighborhood, you can't get them. But all junk food is available and cheap. So that is very bad. But the only way those things are going to change is if there's a collective increase in awareness about that. If people get angry enough, they could change the politics of it.

CR: Paleo diet. How do you feel about the Paleo diet?

AW: Well, the Paleo diet might be a fad, we'll see. And in its extreme form I think it's rather silly: people eating raw meat and exercising themselves to death. But I think the essential aim of Paleo – not eating refined and processed foods – that's the same kind of thing I teach. That's where all the trouble comes from. One of the big questions is around grains and one of the principles of the Paleo diet, is to go back to pre-agricultural times and eat what hunter-gatherers would eat. I think there's a lot of mischief that has come from grains, let alone the whole ecological consequences and economic consequences of it. But I think that the way we have handled grains has made them really unhealthy for us. Most people don't really understand the difference between a whole grain and a pulverized grain. There's a huge difference between flour and products made from flour, and eating a seed or a seed that's cracked into a few big pieces. It's okay to eat some truly whole grains. I think that products made from flour are a huge problem. The Paleo diet is very negative toward sugar, which is good; the latest research makes sugar look very problematic for us, especially the fructose content which our bodies can't handle.

One of the issues that I'm not so sure I agree with is, a lot of the Paleo people won't eat any legumes. And I think they can be very good sources of protein for people, especially if people don't have animal foods to eat. So I think that in basic principle, not in its extreme form, I probably eat that way myself. I eat mostly fish and vegetables. I don't eat a lot of fruit, unless it's berries from my garden, or things that are in season that are very wonderful. And I, for the most part, don't ever eat refined or processed foods.

CR: Yeah, the Mediterranean diet has a lot in common with Paleo. I find I agree with you, the extremists make it silly. And even the idea that there is such a thing as a "Paleo diet" – I mean, you're talking about hundreds of thousands of years of many different environments, and clearly there has been some evolutionary change in the digestive system of people who have been digesting milk for a long time, and grains, and so on. But what do you think about the rise of celiac disease?

AW: That is interesting.

CR: All these food allergies... Are they real?

AW: There's a rise in allergies in general, and a rise in asthma. My guess is that has to do with general overload of human immune systems. The wheat stuff is very interesting. Celiac disease is a well-known disease entity you can test for. We can test for wheat allergy with skin testing. But now we have all these people who are gluten sensitive, and that's not testable. These are patient-driven diagnoses. So people are coming in saying they have headaches, and itching, and are bloated, and they've heard that gluten is what is doing it. And you put them on a gluten-free diet and they're remarkably better. But there is such a huge placebo effect with dietary change, it's very hard to interpret that.

I made two trips to China in the past year. In China, gluten is served as a protein. In any restaurant you go to, you get things like sweet and sour gluten and

WHEN I WAS IN MEDICAL SCHOOL, THE IDEA OF TAKING PROBIOTICS WAS SOMETHING FOR FOOD-FADDISTS. NOW THIS IS VERY ACCEPTED IN MAINSTREAM MEDICINE.

gluten with black bean sauce. I asked a lot of people, and gluten sensitivity is unknown there. People have never heard about it. Same is true in Japan, by the way. So that's very interesting: where is that coming from here? I've heard a few interesting explanations, and one of them that I give some credence to, and I think you'll find fascinating, is that we've bred strains of wheat that make higher gluten content possible. Another is that, until recently, bread used to be all made by a long sourdough fermentation process that may change the chemistry of wheat, and then when instant yeast was introduced, that didn't happen anymore. So bread may be chemically different than it was in the past. But here's a very interesting possibility: it may have to do with gut flora and changes in gut flora. And the rising incidence of cesarean delivery, which has now reached a shocking level in our society. I think something like one in four or five births are now cesarean.

CR: Driven by profit, not medical necessity.

AW: When babies are born vaginally, the microorganisms that they pick up that colonize the gut come from the mother's vaginal tract, the birth canal. And that establishes the gut flora for life. When babies are born by cesarean section, the organisms they pick up come from the mother's skin, which is a totally different population. And in China the incidence of cesarean section is very low.

CR: And breastfeeding very high.

AW: Right. So that is a possibility. And we're seeing more and more things about how gut flora will determine your allergic responsiveness. So that's an interesting possibility.

CR: This gut flora is one of the areas of medical research that I'm looking most closely at now.

AW: Good! When I was in medical school, the idea of taking probiotics was something for food-faddists. Now this is very accepted in mainstream medicine. And not only for things like traveler's diarrhea and being on antibiotics, but we're finding it's beneficial in things like ADHD and autism.

CR: I'm sure you've read about fecal transplants. Apparently they work very well. Do you know what I'm talking about?

AW: One use for it is if the gut flora has been completely wiped out by antibiotics.

CR: I was reading recently that they've been investigating its usefulness for *Clostridium difficile* infection, which is chronic and which there is no real way to satisfactorily treat. It was a small study of half a dozen patients or so. I'm sure they'll be following up, but they did fecal transplant from people who were feeling fine, and within a couple of days the condition had completely resolved itself.

AW: The whole issue of gut flora and probiotics has come into its own.

CR: That leads directly to a topic I've been wanting to talk to an esteemed physician about, which is: how human beings shit. In the West, we shit wrong!

AW: A lot of people have argued that we should be squatting rather than sitting.

CR: Like Asian toilets. Cassie and I have an Asian toilet in our house, and everyone in Spain thinks we're nuts. It was kind of an issue when we were renting our apartment; we had to find the right person to rent it. But once I'd been to Asia, coming back to the West just seemed too backward. Pardon the pun.

AW: There are serious articles written on that.

CR: There's a whole book called *The Big Necessity* by Rose George, which I've just finished reading. It's quite interesting.

AW: That's going to be a hard one to get people to change.

CR: Well, there's going to be a chapter in this next book on how to take a shit properly. And to give a shit: to give a shit about taking a shit. Reminds me: Have you read a book called *Born to Run* by Christopher McDougall?

AW: Yes. Great book.

CR: Another example of how we take a natural, biological activity and make it traumatic. Learning to run wrong and then selling expensive shoes that partially compensate. Birth is another one. An ex-girlfriend of mine had a baby, she said everyone was scaring her, telling her how much it was going to hurt – and then it was one of the most pleasurable experiences she'd ever had.

AW: Wow.

CR: We're confused about so many things.

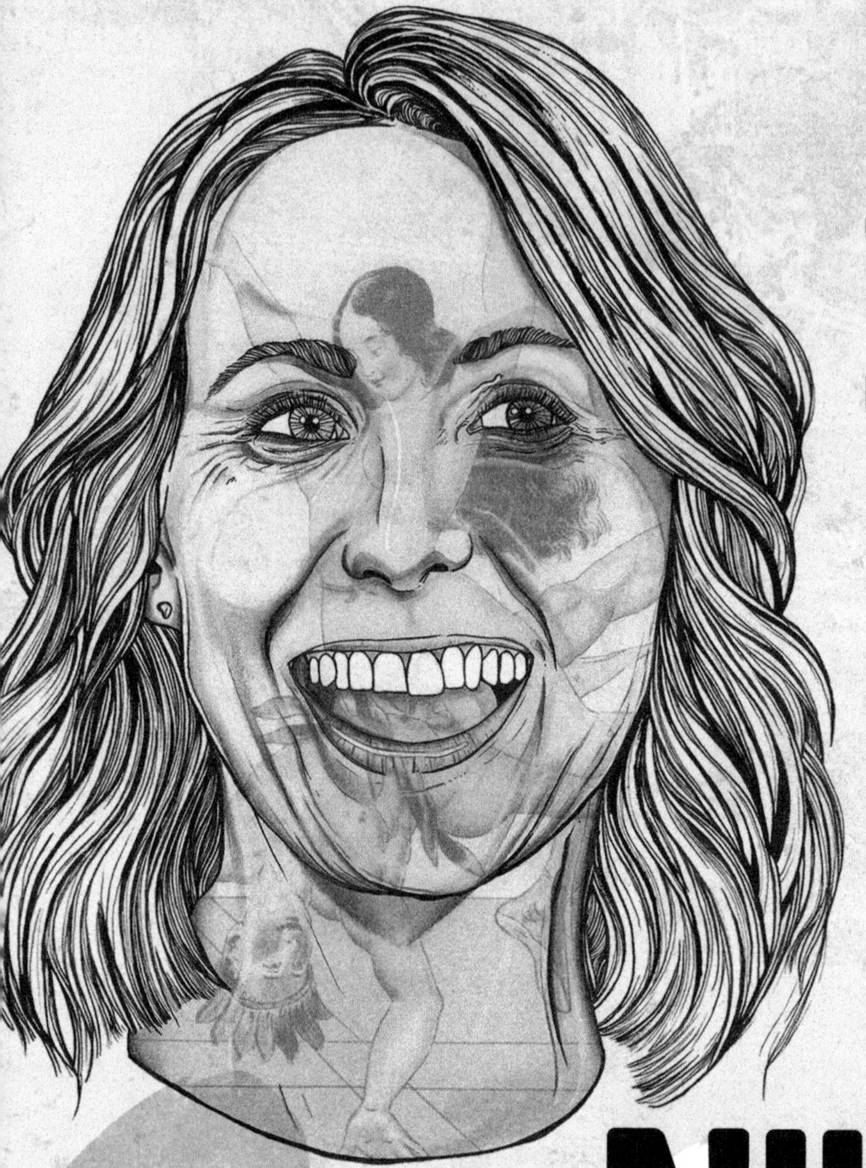

“”

ONCE YOU GET THAT JOKE RIGHT, AND IT HITS, AND YOU HEAR PEOPLE LAUGHING WITH YOU ABOUT SOMETHING YOU THOUGHT YOU WERE ALONE WITH... **IT'S SUCH A FREEING FEELING.**

CHAPTER 22

NIKKI GLASER

EPISODE #122 (APRIL 22, 2015)

Nikki Glaser is a stand-up comedian, television host and podcaster. From 2011 to 2014, she hosted the podcast* You Had to Be There *with fellow comedian Sara Schaefer.

SEX | COMEDY | PERFORMANCE | MIND-BODY CONNECTION

NIKKI GLASER: I have this thing called ASMR: Autonomous Sensory Meridian Response. It pretty much means brain orgasms, where you get this tingling sensation in your brain when someone whispers to you, or they show you something. There's all these videos online.

CHRIS RYAN: We're going to do the rest of this podcast whispering.

NG: People are going to get off to it.

CR: You should have the headphones, because I sound really good in headphones. "Yeah, coming at you late night, this is Dr. Ryan." She's about to have a brain orgasm ladies and gentlemen!

NG: Yeah, okay, here's the thing... a lot of people don't know that they have ASMR, except they do know. Here's how you know: if, as a kid, you got a haircut or someone was talking to you softly, and showing you something, and you got this feeling of euphoria...then it was ASMR. I used to get that, and I thought I was a lesbian because it was women who always did it to me. It's not sexual, it's just the most relaxing feeling ever; it goes down your spine, and it's just so calming. I was very ashamed of it because I thought it was sexual, and I thought there was something wrong about it. But then for a while, like five years ago, I became obsessed with watching YouTube videos of people giving massages, with soothing music, and I was like, "I guess I'm into massages, I don't know what this is about." But I'm not. Then I found out that there was a tag on one of the videos that said "ASMR," and I was like, "What's this about?" So I Googled it and there are just so many videos. These people on YouTube make videos to elicit this response in people because tons of people have this thing. These videos have millions of hits, but it's just someone taking a bottle and just tapping it like this, or taking a book and just slowly flipping through it like this. And it just calms people. I watched them as much as men watch porn, up to three times a day, like I'm addicted to them, and I need them to relax; it's very soothing. If anything I just said made you feel stuff, you gotta search it on YouTube; it's gonna change your world.

CR: Change your world. You know, I can relate to that. I get something like that from getting my hair cut. And you're right, it is confusing, because in America we associate all bodily pleasure with sex because we're so fucked up in this country. It can be confusing. It's like, "Wait, this dude is touching my ears and manipulating my head, and I'm feeling really happy. Am I gay? What's up here?" It's a weird thing. And then you look at black American culture where the barbershop is where the dudes go to hang out. And there's no shame associated with it at all, and it's just cool. They're not as tight-assed as most white aspects of American culture are, and it's funny because since I was probably in high school, of the probably 20 girlfriends I've had (official girlfriends), only one has been white. And she was French. It got to the point where my mother sat me down once and said, "Honey, why don't you like white girls?"

NG: Wow!

CR: And you know, nothing personal. It's just white American women are not very sensual, by and large, because there is all this shame.

NG: So much shame. I didn't have sex until I was 21, and I was terrified of it until then. And now I've gone the other way, because I was so repressed as a kid. As soon as I started drinking, I was able to do it. And now I'm sober for three years and I can do it now without drinking, but yeah, I totally agree with you on that. I was so nervous all the time, and scared, and my mom had me convinced that men just rape you. So I was always just so scared.

CR: Oh God.

NG: She was insane. I didn't get my period until pretty late, and I remember one time she and I were taking the dog for a walk in our neighborhood, and I was like, "I just want my period!" I was just being open about it, and she was like, "You don't say that out loud. If people know that, they'll rape you." As if she thought that's what men would think. "Oh, she can't get pregnant? I'm gonna rape her." Crazy. So I became terrified. I didn't know about masturbation until like 24. I had no idea.

* * *

NG: I'm reading this book right now that someone told me about, about how repressed anger, fear, and trauma leads to pain, and especially back pain.

CR: Dr. John Sarno, *Mind Over Back Pain*?

NG: Yes! It's just so good. I'm reading it now. I'm halfway through, and I'm already feeling better, just acknowledging the fact that this isn't a bulging disc and it's just me being stressed. I remember once I was getting a massage and my butt just hurt so bad, and the masseuse asked, "So what's going on in your life?" And I'm like, "Well, I just got broken up with" and he's like, "He's a literal pain in your ass." It really manifests itself as pain, so I'm so into that.

CR: He used to be an orthopedic surgeon at NYU. What he found was that a lot of the people who were coming in for surgery had a slipped disc, or bulging disc, or whatever, but then a lot of them didn't. So he did studies that showed that a lot of people with these same slipped discs or anatomical irregularities had no pain at all. There's this weird thing where the pain does seem to manifest wherever you've got the disc issue, but there's a correlation, not a causation. And so what he found was that the people were expressing psychological distress in the part of the body that is weakened. So it's almost like the subconscious is saying, "Okay, we're going to cause pain, let's do it there, because there is a weakness there, a physical weakness." So doctors think that the physical

> **“” I THINK A GREAT DEAL OF MISOGYNY IN WESTERN SOCIETIES IS DUE TO TEENAGE MALE SEXUAL FRUSTRATION.**

weakness is causing the pain, but it isn't. Just the understanding of that helps resolve the pain for vast numbers of people.

NG: Yeah and I'm already feeling it working. I gotta get through the whole book because he really gets into how it's manifesting itself. But he also talks about how there's been a sharp decline in people getting ulcers since like the 80s. And it's because now everyone knows that ulcers are a stress-related, stress-induced problem. So just by knowing that it's stress, you don't get them anymore, because it's not a physical issue.

CR: Ulcers are a complicated example, because there's a lot of evidence that gastric ulcers are caused by a particular bacterium, but there was an ongoing debate about this. And finally it was resolved by this Australian scientist who stood up at a meeting with a vial full of this bacterium and drank it. He said, "If I have an ulcer within 30 days, or 60 days, or whatever, we'll know I was right." He did, and so they started testing people with gastric ulcers, and found that they all had this bacterium.

NG: Whoa.

CR: But again, that could be a thing where they've got the bacterium but it's the stress that activates the process. So everything is like that. It's complicated even in genetics now: the latest epigenetic research is showing you can have a gene for x, y, or z, but if things in your life don't trigger the activation of that gene, it doesn't matter at all. So you could have a very high genetic propensity for certain kinds of cancer, for example, but if you lead a low-stress, chilled-out, happy life, that gene never gets activated. So you need the gene plus some environmental trigger to make it happen.

* * *

NG: It's just like a theory I have, but I think if we did some research, a lot of teenage male suicides would have tiny penises.

CR: Alright, I think that's true, and I'm serious about this: I think a great deal of misogyny in Western societies is due to teenage male sexual frustration. And not just sexual frustration, but a sense of inadequacy and helplessness that teenage males feel in a society where their brain, their body, their entire being is 100% pussy-focused, and very few of those guys are getting anywhere near a pussy. And so they end up blaming women. All these fucking serial killers, who do they kill? Hookers.

NG: Yep.

CR: So, yeah, there's a great paper by James Prescott, an anthropologist who looked at, I think 27 societies. And he did a meta-analysis saying there is a relationship between, on the one side, bodily contact between mothers and infants (so how long women breast feed, if they carry the babies or set them down, whether they sleep together, or if they put the babies to sleep separately), and on the same side, acceptance of teenage sexual behavior (so when kids start feeling sexual, are they allowed to experiment or is it "oh my God, don't do that, don't touch yourself"). On the other side was violence. What he found was that of the 27 societies they studied, 26 (which is a super significant correlation) had indirect correlation between the measures of bodily contact and sexual tolerance, and violence. So the more bodily contact between mother and child, and the more relaxed they were about adolescent sexuality, the lower the levels of violence – both within the society, and between that society and other societies. We're talking war as well as murder.

NG: Wow!

CR: So if you have a society where you're trying to inculcate the mental structures of violence and war, what do you do? You create huge classes of sexually frustrated people. You make the babies, you tell them breastfeeding is ugly, you tell them babies have to sleep alone.

NG: "Don't touch yourself," "That's gross," "You do that in private," "You don't do that."

CR: "Your body is disgusting, you need to hide it." Right? Everything! So everything's ugly and dirty. Original sin and all that.

NG: Oh my God.

CR: You end up with people willing to go fight and kill people for no fucking reason.

NG: Wow, I love that. I'm a big Redditor. I like going on there. It's a very male-dominated messaging board system. I subscribe to the sex thread, and there's always a kid posting on there about, "I have a small dick and I'm going to kill myself." The anger is there: this kid's going to shoot up a school because he thinks he's inadequate. And I think you're absolutely right, it causes so much anger. Then it leads to people saying women comedians aren't funny.

CR: Before we leave the penis, though –

NG: Yeah, I don't want to leave it.

CR: Ever, ever. But one thing I've been meaning to say on the podcast is that when people say, "I've got a small dick," there are growers and show-ers. Do you know about this?

NG: Uh-huh.

CR: A lot of guys don't know that. The thing is: your dick can look small, but when you get an erection, it's completely normal. But when you're taking a piss in a public bathroom or a shower at the gym, you're the guy with the little dick. But you don't actually have a little dick when you're erect; it's just as big as anyone else's. That means you've got a grower. With a show-er, it just gets hard and soft, hard and soft, but it stays the same size. They are two completely different classes. It's like sativa and indica, there's two different worlds here.

NG: One puts you to sleep and the other makes you want to clean your room. But then there's the micro penis, though, and those guys...

CR: That's a different subject. I think a lot of these teenage guys think they have an unusually small dick because they get harassed at gym class, or they go swimming like George Costanza in that famous *Seinfeld* episode.

THE *KAMA SUTRA* IS REALLY INTERESTING BECAUSE IT BREAKS DICKS DOWN INTO THREE SIZES NAMED AFTER ANIMALS. THERE'S LIKE THE RABBIT, THE DOG, AND THE HORSE, OR SOMETHING. AND IT ALSO DOES THE SAME WITH PUSSIES. SO IT'S NOT ABOUT HOW BIG YOUR DICK IS, IT'S ABOUT THE MATCH OF YOUR DICK TO THE PUSSY TYPE.

NG: Shrinkage!

CR: The *Kama Sutra* is really interesting because it breaks dicks down into three sizes named after animals. There's like the rabbit, the dog, and the horse, or something. And it also does the same with pussies. So it's not about how big your dick is, it's about the match of your dick to the pussy type. And it's true: there are lots of pussies.

NG: There's lots of girls who can't take a huge dick.

CR: Or even an average dick. It's not like your dick is too small; the woman's pussy is too big for your dick.

NG: That's so great!

CR: Here's another interesting dick thing: in several African societies that I've studied, including the !Kung, an insult for a man is "you have a big dick." That's insulting. "You and your big dick, get out of here. Take your big dick and go away!" It's an insult.

NG: Wow. You know, I used to have deep shame about it. I thought I was a freak. I would see porn and be like, "I don't look like that. Is that what I'm supposed to look like?" And I used to research and say to myself, "Oh, as soon as I save up that money, I'm gonna snip them off." There are girls that do this! They just want that flatness. Now I fucking love what I've got and I've learned that some guys really do too. I've tried to talk about it on stage because I really want girls to know, "Don't do that." Because I was on the verge of doing it.

CR: Again, there are societies in southern Africa where women hang weights from their labia to make them bigger. When it comes to sex and food, things are so arbitrary and culturally defined. Instead of trying to change your body, which is hard, and dangerous, and expensive...

NG: ... and doesn't cure what you're trying to fix...

CR: Right. Learn, learn, and change your mind. You ever read Joseph Campbell? He was a mythologist and a really interesting man. He wrote a book called *The Hero with a Thousand Faces*, which basically argued that every culture has the same story about the character: normally a man or boy, who goes out on a quest and has all of these experiences. And he's looking for something, but he has experiences along the way. Then he comes home and finds that what he was looking for was at home the whole time. But he had to have those experiences in order to recognize it. He also talks about de-tribalization. He says the first stage of the Hero's Quest is to recognize that you come from a tribe. The rest of the process is going beyond your tribe, and learning how to be something bigger than your particular tribe. You do that by recognizing that your tribe has particular set of beliefs that is arbitrary and limited to your tribe, like "A pussy should look like this," and "A dick should be like that." Then once you realize that, and get beyond that, then you can accept things the way they are, and finally start to be happy.

NG: And realize it doesn't matter because none of it matters. That's fascinating. It really is about just educating yourself, and that's way more freeing than trying to fix it surgically.

* * *

NG: It's that thing where "You just haven't met the right person." It's like no, it's because I don't want that.

CR: Yeah, and also, "the right person" sets people up for guaranteed disappointment, possibly for years.

NG: No such thing.

CR: They think the bells are going to ring. The thing is, there's either no such thing, or there are many such things. I think that there are many people that you could love and share your life with happily, assuming you can negotiate stuff. The one thing I try to tell people is to figure out as early as you can, what the non-negotiables are for you. And then don't negotiate. Because I wasted so much time trying to have a relationship with a woman because we clicked in bed. But sometimes that's all there is. And that's okay! That's a good fuck; let it be a good fuck. And if she's happy and you're happy, get together and fuck occasionally, but don't try to pretend that that's your girlfriend or boyfriend. Let it be that, don't call it something else. People get married and have kids, and then 15 years later, they're like, "You know what, we don't even really like each other, we never did, we just liked fucking."

NG: Non-negotiable, that's a great idea. I would generally just think of things I wanted in someone. But thinking of things I can't deal with and won't settle on... Don't negotiate; that's great advice.

CR: He doesn't go down on you. That could be a non-negotiable.

NG: Yeah, oh yeah.

CR: I was with a woman once who was like, "Oh no, I don't like blowjobs. Actually, no women really like blowjobs." No women likes blowjobs, are you fucking kidding me?

NG: Yeah, no, that's true.

“ ”

A LOT OF TIMES GIRLS GET GOOD AT BLOWJOBS BECAUSE THEY'VE BEEN SAVING THEMSELVES FOR MARRIAGE, AND THAT'S ALL THEY CAN DO.

I WASTED SO MUCH TIME TRYING TO HAVE A RELATIONSHIP WITH A WOMAN BECAUSE WE CLICKED IN BED. BUT SOMETIMES THAT'S ALL THERE IS. AND THAT'S OKAY!

CR: Do you think guys give better blowjobs than women?

NG: They probably would, absolutely.

CR: They say lesbians and bisexual women are much more likely to have an orgasm with another woman than they are with men.

NG: Interesting, probably because you know just what to hit. I always think about being with a woman... would they like the same thing I like? I talk to my girlfriends and a lot of them are like, "I can only cum on top." I can't cum on top at all, so I don't know. I might be doing some weird stuff down there, and need a ton of pressure... I like massages that are very deep. So I don't know, but I bet guys suck dick at least better than I do.

CR: Some women, it's amazing, some girls just know.

NG: A lot of times girls get good at blowjobs because they've been saving themselves for marriage, and that's all they can do. So they've had a lot of practice. Whereas I was terrified to suck dick because I've always had big teeth and I would always hear, "Girls with too much teeth." So I've always had kind of a complex about it. I watch porn, I read all these things like new tips, but I'm just not very coordinated, so I think I'm probably like a B-plus with a blowjob at this point. But it took a lot of work to get me there, it's not an innate thing for me.

CR: Do you have a gag reflex?

NG: No.

CR: You just got an A-minus.

NG: Really? I just got bumped up? Sweet!

* * *

CR: I really like what's happening in comedy now, the focus seems to have shifted from that sort of simple, observational, Seinfeld-like comedy to a real courageous, vulnerable, intimate bearing of the soul. Like what Amy Schumer's doing, and Louis C.K. There's something really beautiful about it, it's almost shamanic.

NG: I agree.

CR: It's that person on the edge of the village that everyone thinks is weird, but who tells the truth.

NG: Comedy *moves* me. With Amy Schumer, Bill Burr, Louis C.K. – when I walk away, I've learned something about myself and the human condition. Something that I didn't realize before, and I'm like, "That's it!" And I think that there's a lot of that going on. And podcasts have kind of steered comedy and stand-up in that direction.

You listen to podcasts, and comedians aren't just making observations, they are sharing intimate details of their lives. And you get to notice these people, so that is now expected of us on stage.

CR: That's a good point, like the whole Marc Maron phenomenon. Where this failed "comic" is talking about how resentful he is about the people who made it, and just baring his soul. And it became this huge phenomenon.

NG: Him and Louis, I feel, really changed everything. Louis on stage talking about how he hates his kids... people were like, "What?" This refreshing honesty, I love it, and it's a really exciting time in comedy.

CR: Exciting, but also, fuck, you've got to take off all your clothes every time you go on stage, because that's now sort of expected, as you said.

NG: Yeah, and sometimes there's nothing more painful than trying a new joke in which you reveal something dark and shameful about yourself, and then no one laughs. What a waste. It feels like they're laughing at you. But once you get that joke right, and it hits, and you hear people laughing with you about something you thought you were alone with... it's such a freeing feeling.

SEX IS THE HOSTAGE TAKER WITH EVERYTHING ON ITS SIDE – AND YOU HAVE TO NEGOTIATE A DEAL WITH SEX THAT'S WORKABLE FOR YOU, THAT'LL MAKE YOU HAPPY WHILE MITIGATING ALL YOUR RISKS. BUT YOU'RE NOT STRONGER THAN SEX.

CHAPTER 23

DAN SAVAGE

EPISODE #41 (OCTOBER 25, 2013)

Dan Savage is an author and prominent LGBT activist. His internationally-syndicated advice column, "Savage Love," blasts through boundaries in its exploration of love and sex.

SEX | LGBT | U.S. SOCIETY | TELEVISION | EDUCATION

CHRIS RYAN: You mentioned how much times have changed since you started down this strange, winding road. Do you feel like you've come to the end of a road?

DAN SAVAGE: Oh god I hope not, I've got a mortgage!

CR: Not to say there aren't lots of other roads, but I imagine an animating motivation in your career has been the recognition of the dignity and legal equality of same sex marriages and relationships. And it seems like that has been a dam that's burst.

DS: Well, we still have 37 states to go, 36 states after New Jersey. And the LGBT rights movement has more on its agenda than just marriage.

CR: Right, what else is there?

DS: There's trans rights, there's trans kids, there's the rights of trans adults. E.J. Graff wrote a terrific piece called "What's Next?" and it was a lot about gender non-conformity. And a lot about making a space in the culture for people who are gender non-conforming, whether they are trans or not. Trans people are subjected to a whole lot more violence and have far fewer civil rights organizations. They still can't serve in the military here, so there's a lot of unfinished business there as well. And I'm really passionate about the rights of queer kids, and the rights of queer elders. You know, we have the Stonewall generation getting up there in their 70s and 80s, and people are getting shoved back into the closet because they're entering retirement homes that are religious or served by the religious. I've been very passionate about the rights of marriage but there's also the right to protect our own next of kin.

CR: Well then forget that... the idea that you've done what you've come here to do.

DS: Queer kids are still being brutalized. And then there's the whole international focus of the LGBT rights movement: you look at Jamaica, you look at Russia, you look at the plight of gay, lesbian, bi and trans folks in the Middle East, Nigeria. How right-wing Christian bigots - the Bryan Fischers and Brian Browns of the world - are exporting homophobia to places like Uganda.

CR: It's unbelievable.

“” BECAUSE IT’S A SHORT JUMP FROM ARGUING THAT GAY PEOPLE DON’T HAVE TO EXIST TO MAKING SURE THAT WE DON’T.

DS: It is unbelievable and it has to be fought. And it has to be fought here in America because it’s coming from here, this murderous homophobia. “Eliminationist” homophobia, to borrow Daniel Goldhagen’s phrase.

CR: Eliminationist homophobia.

DS: In that book *Hitler’s Willing Executioners*, he talked about anti-Semitism, but he talked about a particular sort of Germanic strain that he called “Eliminationist Anti-Semitism.” And what the religious right has really shoved into the discourse in the last 30 years is an eliminationist homophobia. Not that gay people don’t deserve rights, but that gay people don’t deserve existence. This whole “ex-gay” thing and “gay is a choice” and the more-than-a-suggestion that the world should be...

CR: Gay-free.

DS: Right. And this has to be combatted and we have to call it what it is: murderous, eliminationist homophobia. Because it’s a short jump from arguing that gay people don’t have to exist to making sure that we don’t.

CR: Yeah it’s amazing to me how often in interviews I still have to explain that human sexuality isn’t about having babies, you know?

DS: I constantly cite your “thousand sex acts for every one live birth.”

CR: Yeah, it’s insane. It’s the most inefficient biological mechanism in existence, if that’s what it was for.

DS: It’s an awesome inefficiency.

CR: Thank god for all that wasted effort.

DS: “Goddamn all these bonus orgasms, when is Terry going to get pregnant, for fuck sake? How many times do you have inseminate a guy?”

CR: Speaking of Terry, I put out a thing saying I would be talking to you and asked if anyone had a good question for you. And one I got from several people is hearing you say the word “husband” in a normal tone of voice.

DS: You know, I can’t believe I get to say “husband,” so I comment on it, I’m ironic with it. My husband. Just because I thought it was a word I’d never have the legal right or authority to use legitimately. And in a way I’m winking at it, and embracing it, and celebrating it, and drawing so much attention to it because it is odd that we’ve come so far so quickly. Terry, here in Washington state or in Canada when we’re snowboarding... he’s my husband. There I said it, there it is.

CR: Terry Miller is right up there with George Michael and who else? There are like three or four gay guys who make me think “You know, maybe I’m doing this whole thing wrong." I listen to a good George Michael song and I'm like, "Why am I so limited?" He's so sexy.

DS: Because you're straight. It's a tragedy for you, but you're straight.

CR: It is a tragedy for me! It is! What do you think about this... I had a professor in College, Andrew Harvey, kind of a famous guru-type guy... and he always argued that we're all bisexual, but that some of us are just blocked in one area, and some in the other area. You don't buy that? Dan just rolled his eyes, listeners.

DS: No, it erases the lived experience of so many people who are 100% straight, like you or my brother Billy. Or who are 100% gay, like Terry. Terry has never laid a finger on a woman. Terry is a lot of things, but Terry ain't "blocked." If Terry wants to do something, he'll do it. So I just don't buy this, "We are fundamentally bisexual."

CR: That's what I've always felt like. I've put stuff in my ass; it's not that I'm uptight about whatever. It's just not there. I wish it were!

* * *

CR: In Spain there is a certain class of people, like dudes who work on their own cars and have a lot of tattoos and stuff. You know who their favorite band in the world is? Queen. They don't know.

DS: Still? To this day?

CR: To this day. Spain's weird. I mean, they have mullets and stuff... I don't know what's going on. But they don't know that Queen has anything to do with...

DS: There are little old ladies who went to the grave thinking Liberace was a nice straight boy. And that's a product of a generation where being gay was literally the worst thing you could think about someone. And there's something wrong with you if you'd think that of somebody... because it's the worst thing you could do. So you didn't think that, you didn't allow yourself to think that. And you can see that vestiges of that have survived in the culture. And so all these people looked at Liberace and thought, "He couldn't be gay. He's too nice, too talented, too charming."

CR: "I like him too much."

DS: "I like him too much and that exonerates him." You know, I was a little weird gay kid. But my parents didn't think I was gay. So they ask me what I want for my thirteenth birthday. I said, "I want tickets to a chorus line." And then five years later I come out to them, and they're blown away.

CR: I've got this theory that there is like a samizdat in American TV, particularly in the 50s and 60s when the censors couldn't conceive of certain things, and so the writers that could slipped it in right by them. Like Batman and Robin... gay couple?

DS: Yeah, hope so.

CR: Always seemed so to me.

DS: Yeah, I always thought there was another door in that Bat Cave behind which is all the bondage gear and the rack. That's where Robin spends his nights.

CR: Or Gilligan and the Skipper. And then there's the drug-related stuff like Scooby Doo. They're all stoned, and they've got the munchies, and it's like... how are they not getting that this is about a bunch of stoners, you know? Or the Beaver, *Leave it to Beaver.*

DS: I actually got a dirty joke into *The New York Times.* I wrote an op-ed about a gay actor playing straight in this movie about missionaries that upset these Christians. And then I just pivoted to, "They want us all to play straight, that's what they tell gay people to do: choose to be straight, live a lie, be ex-gay," and I said, "You can call somebody out on that; anybody who says that they believe people can choose to be straight or gay, and then to not be gay anymore, just look at them and say, 'Would you want your daughter to marry one? Would you want your daughter to marry an ex-gay guy?'" The answer is always "no" because they don't believe it, not for a second. They know that guy is not capable of being in love with their daughter. So then I talked about – oh god this is so digressive – but "Tangentially Speaking," I shifted it to Brokeback Mountain and I just said, "Since Jake and Enus were pitching tents on Brokeback Mountain..."

CR: Pitching tents?!

DS: And there's a dirtier joke in the previous sentence that *The New York Times* were like, "Nope."

CR: But they missed the pitching tents.

DS: They missed the pitching tents because they literally pitched tents on Brokeback, you saw them putting up tents. Two times I've gotten really dirty jokes in *The New York Times.* And I want that on my tombstone with Santorum and "It gets better." I've got two really good dirty jokes in *The Times.*

CR: What was the other one, do you remember?

DS: The book review I wrote for Jeff Chu's, *Does Jesus Really Love Me?* He argued that those of us who were raised in faith, and came out as gay, and then walked away... we are all up there sulking. And if the Church would just come around on the gay issue, we would all file back into the pews because we're just ready to believe; we just stay away 'cause of the hatred and the bigotry. I said, "No, I didn't sulk away, I walked away. I'm done. I saw through it. I'm not angry. Now I spend my Sunday mornings on my bike, or on my snowboard, or on my husband."

CR: Wait, you said this in *The New York Times*?!

DS: In *The New York Times.*

CR: And they let that one fly?

DS: I had to fight for it. The editors were great; they were really thoughtful. They were just like, "The whole issue with the Church is with gay sexual expression." The Catholic Church, my faith, acknowledges the existence of people who are homosexual; it just doesn't think we should be sexually active. So me invoking sexual activity isn't gratuitous at all in an argument about religion and the conflict with people who are queer. It goes right to the heart of it. And the clincher in my argument to the editors was, "And I bet if I start dicking around the archives, I will find references as explicit and humorous regarding the existence of heterosexual sex."

CR: Ah, yeah.

DS: "That you don't have a problem with. That nobody flagged."

CR: Do you think with this new pope, Pope Francis, that there's any chance this pope is going to actually...

DS: I think there's a chance this new pope's going to be shoved down a flight of marble stairs.

CR: That's what I was thinking, yeah. There was one, way back in the 1300s, who was very openly cool about sex and all that. And the library roof was being retrofitted, and he was in there, and it collapsed on him, and killed him.

DS: And nobody else.

CR: And nobody else, yeah. It was after he'd been in for about six months.

DS: I get into arguments with people about their theology around sex – not just about gay sex but about all sex. Because the problem with the Church is that they just can't reconcile themselves to non-procreative sex, because of this Judeo-Christian bullshit. So I try not to argue about theology. But I have no illusions that the Pope is going to say, "Gay people are awesome" and "Gay people are part of God's creation" and "Gay relationships should be blessed too." But it would be great if the Pope could bring himself to say, "Christ himself emphasized caring for the poor, caring for the sick, housing the homeless... but he didn't emphasize homosexuality."

So even if our faith teaches that this is wrong, or that God doesn't love it the most... God obviously didn't want it to be our sole focus. But the Catholic Church's sole focus, and Christianity's sole focus in the U.S. over the last 30 years has been two things God didn't talk about: beating up queer people, and knocking the morning-after pill out of the hands of women. And the religious right nutbags will say, "Jesus didn't condemn other things that are obvious he would condemn. He didn't condemn child rape but, of course Jesus wouldn't be down with child rape." And the argument with that is just like, "Okay, but dude was omniscient, and so if Barney Frank's marriage was the most important thing on Earth that had to be prevented, then Jesus would've known that was coming, and would have coughed up a few lines in the Sermon on the Mount."

CR: Right.

DS: "Thou shall not marry Barney Frank," right? If you're a dude. But he didn't, and that's the game you get into with people who are looking to this Bible. As you have to tease out intent, and meaning, and what God wants from this jerry-rigged collection of train-wreck stories, and allegories, and metaphors. But if the Pope can get there and say, "You know what, we can disagree about same-sex marriage"... and there are some faith traditions that allow for it; it's just Orthodox that doesn't. And some of these are Christian churches and traditions that now bless same-sex marriages, so obviously there are disagreements; people of faith can disagree. We can all agree about taking care of the poor, and housing the homeless, and providing health care for the sick: everybody of every faith, people of no faith, we all agree on that. So why can't we work together? And if the Pope can change that emphasis, God bless him.

CR: Literally.

DS: Figuratively, because I don't believe in God.

CR: But I mean, what do you believe? Do you believe in any sort of omniscient spirit or logic underlying the Universe?

DS: I believe in the limits of human knowledge. That we don't know

CR: Right, there's always something beyond the flashlight.

I'M ALWAYS ENCOURAGING COUPLES TO DO WHAT WORKS, AND TO TINKER, AND TO MAKE IT WORK FOR THEMSELVES. AS OPPOSED TO BEING TORTURED BY THESE IDEALS.

DS: Because where does it end? There's time, there's space, it goes... you start to think about that and your brain instantly shuts down. We don't know. And typically, people who pretend to know are not people you can trust. Anybody who tells you they have the answers is obviously lying to you.

CR: Well this is when people write to me for advice and they're disappointed I'm not giving it. I always hit them back with this quote. I don't remember who first said it, but it was, "Admire those who seek the truth, but flee from those who claim to have found it."

DS: But how do I reconcile what I just said and what you just said with my prescriptive impulses? I will tell people what to do, I just won't tell people what I don't goddamn know.

CR: I hate to disagree with you on what you do, but I never see you as someone who tells people what to do. I see you as someone who gives your honest opinion about things. And that's the value of what you do - that people know what they're getting from you is sincere. It's informed by years of experience in dealing with this stuff. I see you more as a really clean mirror than an advice-giving machine.

* * *

CR: Gabor Maté is a doctor in Vancouver who works with addicts, and he's written several books on mind-body stuff. He's a really interesting guy. He said to me, "What you and I have in common is that we've both made a living out of stating the obvious." At a certain level, that's kind of simple and true.

DS: Yeah, who you going to believe? Me or your lying eyes? The way sex works, the way relationships actually work... there are the ideals that everyone falls short of. And then there are the compromised, complicated relationships that involve a lot of accommodation, and compassion, and permissions, and understandings, and work-arounds, and patches. And those relationships work, but the idealistic ones don't. And I'm always encouraging couples to do what works, and to tinker, and to make it work for themselves. As opposed to being tortured by these ideals - ideals that even people you think are living up to actually aren't. Because on the outside you can't see the patches, and the workarounds, and the accommodations. So people look at their parents' perfect relationships, but you don't know if your mom gave your dad permission to see a pro-dom every once and a while, because they're not going to tell you that.

CR: Yeah, and it happens in every realm of life, not just relationships. Like work. You see people like Peter Gabriel, Dan Savage, whoever... and you're like, "Oh my god, you are in the promised land." And then you meet these people and you're like, "No, they're struggling

“ YOU ARE NOT STRONGER THAN SEX; SEX IS A QUARTER OF A BILLION YEARS OLD. ”

with the same bullshit everyone else is." There is no end point. But to get back to your fame... I do want to hammer on this a little because I respect your self-deprecation and all that - but I've got to say... when people ask me about you in interviews or whatever, I say that you will be seen as a historical figure.

DS: Only because we're running out of historical figures.

CR: I know that seems really pompous to you.

DS: The American Humanist Association gave me their Humanist of the Year Award. I looked at other winners and I'm just like, "Oh you must be running out of people to give this to." I hope I'm not going to be a historical figure. I'm a fan of history, I like to read history, and I know I wouldn't want to be reading about myself in two hundred years.

CR: Well here's what I think: I think that when you started out, you were a fringe figure; you were only in the back pages of fringe publications. And you are now mainstream, and you haven't changed. You haven't changed your jeans, your shirt, your message, your language... you haven't changed anything. What's happened is the stream has shifted.

DS: And I think I've helped that shift, particularly now, because I meet all these people in their twenties and thirties who grew up reading me. And I seem to have this ripple effect, this impact on a lot of people's attitude towards sex in ways that have improved their ability to be in relationships. And to talk to each other. And I feel like that helped shift. I don't think I sold out or I changed. I was a part of this dialogue that I think grew out of the AIDS epidemic and the lesbian and gay civil rights movement - and we entered this moment where we had to actually learn and talk about people in bed.

* * *

DS: The thing is if I brought anything up, it was in a sort of user-friendly, joking about sex kind of way. Sex makes people nervous, but people want to laugh when you talk about sex.

CR: Exactly.

DS: Because it implicates us all. We all feel a little indicted by it. We're powerless. I always say to college students, "You were lied to. You were told you were gonna grow up and have sex. No. You're going to grow up and sex is going to have you."

CR: That's a good line.

DS: That is the way it works. You are not stronger than sex; sex is a quarter of a billion years old, and we are a couple hundred thousand years old.

CR: Especially not when you're in college.

DS: Right. *Sex* built *us*; we didn't build sex, and God didn't build sex. And you have to come to some sort of negotiation with sex. Sex is the hostage taker with everything on its side – and you have to negotiate a deal with sex that's workable for you, that'll make you happy while mitigating all your risks. But you're not stronger than sex.

CR: Although, did you read this recent research out of Japan? Japanese people are not into sex. They're into their dolls –

DS: Well did you read into that though? The economy can't support people partnering up and coupling up. There's no support for women who might have babies. Everything else that sex that comes bundled with – relationships, children, family – is almost too economically unfeasible in Japan, rightly or wrongly. I'm sure people are jacking it.

CR: Then again, I just read an article about a pick-up artist who writes a series of travel books, like "Fuck France" or "Fuck Greece"... he got to Denmark, and nobody would fuck him. He was smart enough on some level to recognize the reason women were impervious to his charms, dubious as they may be, is that they don't need men because the government takes care of single mothers and child care. Single mothers aren't left to fend for themselves.

DS: Is that it? Or is that just his theory?

CR: That was his theory, and it was confirmed by some of the Danish journalists who were writing about this book. And then I saw today that Denmark is the happiest country in the world.

DS: But people are getting laid in Denmark. I've been to Denmark. It's not that if you give women child care and an economic safety net, that they stop sucking cock. People are fucking in Denmark – not this guy, obviously – but people have decent sex education. Maybe all that pick-up artist, undermining, sabotaging, making someone feel weak and insecure... that won't work in Denmark. That'll work in the States because we have lousy sex-ed. Women are slut-shamed, women are stripped of their sexual agency, they're not supposed to act on any desires of their own. But if they're not desired, they're damaged somehow. And a man can come along, and leverage all that baggage against a woman, and get his dick into her mouth. I don't think you can do that in a country like Denmark or Sweden successfully.

CR: Hear, hear.

CHAPTER 24

DANIELE BOLELLI

&

THADDEUS RUSSELL

IT'S THIS BIZARRE BUBBLE, MODERN EDUCATION AND KNOWLEDGE PRODUCTION. I DON'T KNOW IF IT'S GOING TO POP, BUT IT HAS TO SHRINK.

HOW CAN WE PROMOTE WAYS OF LIVING THAT ALLOW US TO BE PLEASANT WITH EACH OTHER, AND THAT KEEP US FROM KILLING EACH OTHER?

EPISODE #163 (JANUARY 25, 2016)

Daniele Bolelli is a writer, history professor, martial artist, and podcaster. He is the author of several books, including On the Warrior's Path, and hosts the History on Fire podcast.

HISTORY | U.S. SOCIETY | ACADEMIA
MORALITY | KNOWLEDGE | FREEDOM

Thaddeus Russell is a history professor whose book A Renegade History of the United States challenged traditional narratives of American culture, lauding those who lived on the fringes of society.

MORALITY | CIVILIZATION | U.S. SOCIETY
KNOWLEDGE | ACADEMIA | FUTURE

CHRIS RYAN: Where do you guys stand on Bill Maher's whole thing: not all Arabs are terrorists, but most terrorists are Arab? Is it a legitimate thing to say? A lot of these Middle Eastern cultures are fucked up because they oppress women...

THADDEUS RUSSELL: Well, they're not places I would want to live in.

CR: They're not places a lot of Arab people want to live in either.

TR: Right but I don't live there. I have no say over how they live their lives. Clearly many people in those cultures, including the women, choose to live those lives and live according to those values. Not all, but many, or else they wouldn't exist.

CR: But to what extent do you *choose* to live according to your culture, especially under threat of death?

TR: I mean, people are leaving all the time, right?

CR: Well, from Afghanistan, leaving means walking. So it's kind of a tough decision.

TR: Right, but you can't force people to be pious. You can't force people to be true believers. No matter what the Taliban do, they cannot force people to adopt that religion, that way of thinking, that ideology. It is a fact – we know, according to polls I saw about five years ago – that a significant percentage of women in Afghanistan agree with the Taliban. Not a majority, but a significant percentage. So then what do you do? If you insist that it's evil and must be eradicated, then the only option, of course, is to get in your tank and roll your way in there. And that's what Sam Harris is talking about all the time. Bill Maher, I've noticed – I've been watching him pretty closely – has not taken that position. He's been pretty clearly anti-war, consistently, at least lately. But Sam Harris is talking about things like pre-emptive nuclear strikes, and he's all about intervening against ISIS – as if that's going to do anything.

DANIELE BOLELLI: So what's the Bill Maher position then?

TR: I don't know exactly, but he hammers away at how

“” WELL, THAT’S THE BIG QUESTION: ARE THERE THINGS THAT ARE INDISPUTABLY GOOD, VERSUS INDISPUTABLY EVIL, OR BAD?

Islam is inherently violent, right? That it’s inherently jihadist, which I disagree with also. But then he’s also anti-war, but his position is sort of contradictory. Because if your argument is that Islam necessarily produces terrorism, then yes, we must go to war. Because that takes the onus entirely away from American foreign policy. So if they’re going to be independent actors, if they’re going to do bad things independently no matter what we do... if that were the case, I would agree with him: we’re going to have to kill these crazy people, right?

CR: I would question that step. Let’s say it does produce terrorism.

TR: Well, I don’t agree with that premise. I’m just playing devil’s advocate.

CR: Okay, but let’s *say* that it does. I don’t think it necessarily follows that we then have to go to war.

DB: The way I see it, on this religion thing, we get so caught up in these debates. Like I saw one video with Sam Harris and Cenk Uygur from *The Young Turks*, where they debate this topic for more than an hour. And every point everyone makes is good, but rather than saying, “Okay, you make a good point,” and then proceeding to temper that point with something from the other side that also makes sense... it becomes a complete exercise in missing each other’s point. The stuff they’re talking about is correct, in and of itself, but it just lacks the context. To me that’s one of the things that we’ve been talking about in regard to whatever religion we’re talking about, whatever ideology, whatever philosophy: what inherently it is. The question, “What is the truth about?” is a bullshit question because there is no one truth about it. Take the wars... take the Nazis, take Stalinism, take stuff that objectively is hard to justify, that is hard to see in a good light... it’s not like a hundred percent of people who subscribe to Nazism were all equally evil with the same mindset.

TR: They even disagreed about what to do with the Jews, even in the highest command within the Nazi party. Many of them just wanted to expel them, and others wanted to kill them. So even there, there was disagreement about what Nazism was.

DB: Which is in everything, right? There is disagreement about what Islam is, disagreement regarding Christianity, disagreement regarding every single religion, disagreement regarding different forms of communism... all of them. So to me, the debate about which one is the true one, is a silly one. Because the reality is, that there are all sorts of options. To me it’s interesting: how do we strengthen the ones that make you be a nicer neighbor? If your being Muslim means that you pray to your God, and you’re nice to your neighbor, and you bring them food when they run out... then believe in whatever the fuck you want. You want to believe in pink unicorns? I have no problem if it makes you bring coffee to your neighbor in the morning. I’m fine with it. We get caught in some weird shit when we say things like, "The violent, nasty things are a misinterpretation of the doctrine," because when you actually look at the doctrine, some passage support that representation very strongly. Not all of them do; that's why there are other interpretations.

TR: But you can interpret even those passages in many ways.

DB: That's what my point is. Trying to establish "the truth" is a hopeless undertaking that helps nobody. What counts is those messages that help us get along, and those that make us want to kill each other. If you support the messages that make us want to kill each other, then sure, we have a problem. But if you don't... then what the hell do I care if you're Muslim, or Jewish, or whatever? It doesn't even matter. I'm non-ideological in that way, I guess. Or, rather, I'm very ideological when it applies to practice: how does it translate into your behavior?

CR: And what's interesting about the application of what you're saying is... when you look at cultures around the world, the culture that I'm aware of that's most famous for its hospitality is probably Afghanistan. They're incredibly welcoming, and it even used to be on the hippie trail. There are so many stories I've heard about people traveling through there with no money, their car breaks down or whatever, and locals just invite them into their homes and feed them because there's this cultural belief of protecting others. It's a sort of, "I'm responsible for you" mentality. It's just amazing and beautiful.

DB: Even within the most right-wing propaganda: *The Lone Survivor*, you know that book? The guys who save his life are these Afghans who are also hardcore about hospitality. That's why to me, the problem is that we've got these people saying, "Everybody who comes from that religion, or from that part of the world... they're all equally evil, and they suck." That kind of thinking is simple-minded. Then you have the other guys who say, "We need to understand everybody, it's cultural, it's not good or bad," and that starts becoming absolute relativism.

TR: But what do what do we get from judging the Taliban? What do we gain by claiming that they're bad or evil?

DB: I agree, judging is bullshit. What matters is: how can we promote ways of living that allow us to be pleasant with each other, and that keep us from killing each other? And how do we wage a sort of ideological war against those mindsets that induce people to squash those that have a different point of view?

TR: So are you talking about engaging the Taliban with language? With ideas?

DB: I don't know if it's the Taliban, but it may be everybody else who's sitting on the fence trying to figure out which way to go. Because you are not going to convert a guy who is hardcore, 300% fundamentalist – however you want to define fundamentalist. You're not going to say, "Let's reason together." That's not going to work very well. But it may work well with everybody else who is sitting on the fence.

CR: Okay, so getting to your point about judging the Taliban... Are there universal human qualities that we can all agree are good?

TR: No. I mean... who's we?

CR: Okay, so let's go with, "Girls have a right to be educated."

TR: Well, that's the kind of society I want to live in, but I don't want to say that's the society that everyone should live in. There are many women in the Middle East who disagree with that statement, who think it's terrible that women go to school. What do you want to do about that? Convince them that they're wrong? I can't decide for other people how they should live their lives and what they should value. Should you? Should we? Should we tell them what they should value?

CR: Well, that's the big question: Are there things that are indisputably good, versus indisputably evil, or bad?

TR: So you're talking about moral claims. Whether we can make moral claims.

CR: Daniele has been saying, "I support things that make us kind to each other, and not kill each other." So let's start with that. Is that something that we can say? That everyone should not be killing each other?

TR: My thought is that you have to differentiate between moral claims and self-interested claims. So I say, "I want to live in a society where women go to school, or are able to go to school." I don't want to say, "It is good for women to go to school" or "It is bad to disallow it."

CR: Why don't you want to say that?

TR: Because I don't want to make claims for other people, about what you or anyone else should value, or how you should live. Because what happens is – as we know, from hundreds of years of very nasty interventions – as soon as you start making those claims, then you have to back them up.

CR: Well, you don't *have* to.

TR: You don't have to, but there's a contradiction if you don't. If you're going to say that those women over there are being oppressed, and they don't even know themselves that they are being oppressed... well, isn't it your obligation to do something about it?

CR: No. See that's the same step that you took a few minutes ago. I think you could say, "Well, we won't trade with you" or "We won't send arms to your government." Take Saudi Arabia. I think we should just say, "Fuck you guys, we don't want your oil, we're not sending you any more missiles or whatever, because you are inspiring the sort of behavior that we find repulsive." It doesn't mean we have to go bomb them, right? You can pursue non-engagement.

TR: But nonetheless, you're still giving a major justification – one that has been used for military intervention by every imperialist who ever lived. Even if you hold a hardcore, Marxist economic interpretation of imperialism... people have won a lot of public support for interventions based on that justification.

CR: I'm with you there... This idea that, "We need to

“” **YOU HAVE TO DIFFERENTIATE BETWEEN MORAL CLAIMS AND SELF-INTERESTED CLAIMS.**

bring them civilization!" But what if they don't want civilization? "Well, they're just too stupid to know they want it. Therefore they need it."

TR: It's just so arrogant, too.

CR: But is it really arrogant to say girls shouldn't have clitorectomies? Is that really arrogant?

TR: Yeah! Because you're saying our culture is superior. "My idea is superior."

CR: Or you're saying that children should not have pieces of their genitals cut off.

TR: But clearly a lot of the people in those societies including women and girls disagree with you.

DB: But I think that's the key point that you're making right there. The issue that you're hammering on about is that of *choice*. The fact that people should be free to do whatever the fuck they want with their lives, and it's not up to anybody else to tell them how to live their lives. You completely agree, right? I think that's the one basic thing that we can agree on. That means I can be grossed out by something, but then that becomes my own personal issue; I can't establish it for everybody else. I can be grossed out by somebody else's choice, but as long as I allow them to have that choice, everything's fine. On the other hand, it does becomes an issue when your choice squashes somebody else's freedom of choice.

TR: Somebody else's choice? I don't know about that. You're speaking on behalf of others there. When your concern is about other people, shouldn't that be between them, the oppressor and the oppressed?

DB: Well, there are issues of power sometimes. If you see a four-year-old kid who's running from some dude whipping him in the middle of the street, and the kid is saying, "Save me!" are you going to say, "Oh it's just between the two of them, I don't want to have to deal with it?"

TR: No, I would stop it because I want to live in a society in which my son can run freely in the streets. So that's about self-interest; that's not a moral claim.

DB: Mine is about zero morality, and no self-interest.

TR: But what we're talking about is people who we've never met, never seen, never will see. People we know nothing about except as abstractions.

CR: Okay, so then let's bring it home. By the way, I'm open to every interpretation here. I don't really know where I stand on these things. But here's one area I do feel strongly – and I think this connects with what you're saying – when some Moroccan family comes to London or to LA, and then the father refuses to let the daughter date anybody, and beats her when she does, or insists that his little girls get clitorectomies... do we have a right to say, "Wait a minute dude, you moved to our culture, so fuck you and your beliefs. You came here, you're going to behave the way we insist, according to our values?"

TR: Yeah I've been thinking about this with the refugees; you've seen the stuff in Cologne. And it's forced me to think through this stuff more carefully again. Let's speak in terms of self-interest: I lived in Germany, and yeah, I would insist they behave the way I want them to behave. Because they're essentially living with me, so it's in my self-interest. I'm all for that. I'm all for people speaking out of self-interest. By the way, I do think it's totally criminal that the left has basically apologized for those sexual assaults. It's been disgusting. Not just the German left, which has been really bad... I mean, what the mayor of Cologne said about women? It's incredible. But especially after close to three years of hammering away at rape culture, and sexual assaults in this country, many of which never happened... to now say, "Oh well it's Muslim men, so now we can't talk about it."

DB: No, fuck that. That's the kind of relativism that grosses me out. This whole politically correct, "I can't criticize cultures that aren't mine" type of stuff.

TR: It's a relativist argument, but it's in the service of something else that's even more nefarious: Maintaining the hierarchy of victimhood, which they're always doing. It's like the Olympics of victimhood on the left.

* * *

TR: So I'm establishing the Renegade University. I'm going to launch probably in the middle of this year, and it's going to start with online lectures that you can download or watch as videos.

CR: And it's focused on history?

TR: It will be history, American history. Stuff I've written on, and lectured on, and taught about for twenty years. And political philosophy, which I've also taught in universities for twenty years. And I'm probably going to do some interactive seminars. And if there's sufficient interest, I'll probably do in-person seminars in West Coast cities.

CR: That will be great. So you'll get a bunch of people in one hotel or something?

TR: Right, exactly. It's already happening; people are doing it and it's amazing. There's a school in Brooklyn that offers these courses – it's totally unaccredited – and they charge three hundred bucks for four sessions with some PhD. And check this out: the courses are about things like the philosophy of Jacques Derrida, and Kantian Ethics. Really obscure academic stuff, and they charge three hundred bucks.

CR: And the teachers probably make more from that than they do at the universities.

TR: Oh yeah, and there's no middle man. So there's clearly a major market for this. And I'm hoping, politically, that it serves to subvert the higher education system, which needs subversion.

CR: I've been saying for a couple of years that I think the educational system is ripe for a fall, and this is the way to do it. It's the same as Uber or Amazon: remove the big middle man that's taking a big cut. With education it's amazing. Because young people write to me all the time saying things like, "Oh I don't know... should I go to grad school?" And I'm like, "You don't need to pay for knowledge!"

DB: I think we're all on board with this plan; I think what Thad is doing is brilliant. But my question is this: let's be real, why do ninety percent of the people go to college? Because they want to acquire knowledge? Fuck no, that's not it. It's because they need the stupid paper at the end that allows them to get their job. So the point is, as long as these guys have a monopoly over the paper machine that releases the diploma, then even in the best case scenario – and the best scenario is not a bad one – you're still only talking about a fraction of the whole game of education willing to spend three hundred bucks to go visit this place four times to go listen to philosophy.

TR: But I think the power of the credential will be subverted.

CR: That's what I was going to say. It already is. The B.A.... who gives a fuck?

TR: Well, yes and no. There's differences of opinion on that. I actually think that employers will increasingly look at something on a resume from a non-accredited school, like this Brooklyn Institute for Social Research, and say "Oh wow, that means something to me. That means you're smart." And that will be one point in your favor, even though there's no accreditation, even though it's not Harvard or Columbia. And I'm hoping that Renegade University will serve the same function.

CR: Also, along with the certificate or piece of paper or whatever they'll get from Renegade University, there's potentially also a letter from Thad Russell who wrote *A Renegade History of the United States*. And they'll be like, "Oh, this guy is well-known in his field, and you've studied with him." So it becomes a mentorship model. A lot of employers don't really give a fuck. They know that you just punch the clock at whatever school you got into because your dad went there, versus: you got off your ass, made contact with this guy who has done work that you find interesting, and you went to help him or her. That demonstrates all sorts of things that are far more valuable to an employer than the fact that you and 20,000 other people went to UCLA.

TR: I think you're right, and I *hope* you're right.

DB: You agree, I agree, Thad agrees... and maybe I'm too negative on this – because I do think there is a market for that, and I do think it's increasing, there's no argument there – but I think that you're still talking about tiny exceptions to the rule. So if you go to work at Aubrey Marcus's company Onnit, he's not going to look at which university you graduated from; he's going to do exactly what you're talking about: look for something that makes you special. But realistically, how many places do that today? Or will even do it in ten years?

CR: I would say the places that you want to work are thinking that way. The places who aren't thinking that way... who the fuck wants to work there? That's some warehouse job, you know. They're looking for drones.

TR: The economics of it works in our favor too, because the price keeps going up, and student debt keeps going up and up. And I think the value of those degrees is going down.

It's this bizarre bubble, modern education and knowledge production. I don't know if it's going to pop, but it has to shrink. I think it already has. There are already inexpensive and even free massive online courses that sit within the university system, and there's tremendous demand for it. There are thousands and even millions of people taking these courses. The Khan Academy, Coursera, Udemy and edX, are all through universities I think. But in the worlds the three of us are in, outside of academia... I learned that there's this massive interest in ideas, in talking, in thinking, and in reading about stuff.

“” I'VE BEEN SAYING FOR A COUPLE OF YEARS THAT I THINK THE EDUCATIONAL SYSTEM IS RIPE FOR A FALL, AND THIS IS THE WAY TO DO IT.

I just mentioned all this to Joe Rogan; he's a great example, right? Did he even go to college? Did he graduate from college? Clearly he's not an academic in any way. But he's clearly fascinated with the world, and he's really curious, and interested in big ideas, and small ideas, and science, and philosophy, and politics, and all the rest of it. And he reads, and reads, and reads, and talks, and talks, and talks. I think he represents a lot of people. Clearly that's why he gets so many downloads.

DB: You're right. If you look at how many Rogan listeners are out there, it's like a city pretty much. It's bigger than most cities. And yet at the same time when you're talking about the economic aspect of, say podcasting... we put it out for free with the idea that, "I'll do things for free, and people will donate because they are nice." The reality is that if 0.2% of your listeners donate, you'll say, "Damn, it went well! That's amazing!" But in reality, that's just not how it works. The economics of the game don't add up. The majority of people don't pay for shit. You can have three gazillion listeners, but how many of them are going to buy your book? Unless that book goes culturally viral, like *Sex at Dawn*. Or you release things for free, and then suddenly you decide to charge for something else... we have a culture now where we get just about any kind of entertainment we want for free - through YouTube, through free downloads.

TR: The economics of it... none of us really know, do we? I don't know the statistics on this, but there is a certain percentage of people that pay *some* amount of money for these things, for knowledge alone. What is it? I don't know. How many people are there in the United States that are willing to pay five dollars for an interesting podcast? Or one dollar? Or ten? Or 100 dollars for an interesting lecture? I don't know.

CR: And as I said before, I think a lot of the value comes from the personal contact with someone whose work you admire. If you're 22 years old, and you love history, and you've read this guy's books... it's like, "Wow I get to hang out with this guy, and tell him this idea I have, and get his feedback?!"

DB: Chris, you did something with some of the events around the launch of *Sex at Dawn*, where you made it into a kind of community. I think there's something to that. The idea of creating something not just for somebody to download online from their keyboard. But also doing things like running a five-day summer course on a combination of topics. Where people show up and hang out. And the point is not only to learn stuff from the presenters, but to also meet other people who are into the same kind of fields, or interests, or passions.

CR: *Plus*, that's the best place to meet a partner, you know? That's the best way to meet somebody, not in a fucking bar, people! In a place where you know they share your passion. Whether it's history, or anthropology, or whatever the fuck it is.

DB: That to me is the future, because those types of activities will always thrive. And they will become even more valuable. Because with technology, we're staying home more; you don't even need to go out these days. But then you still need go out and meet people at some point.

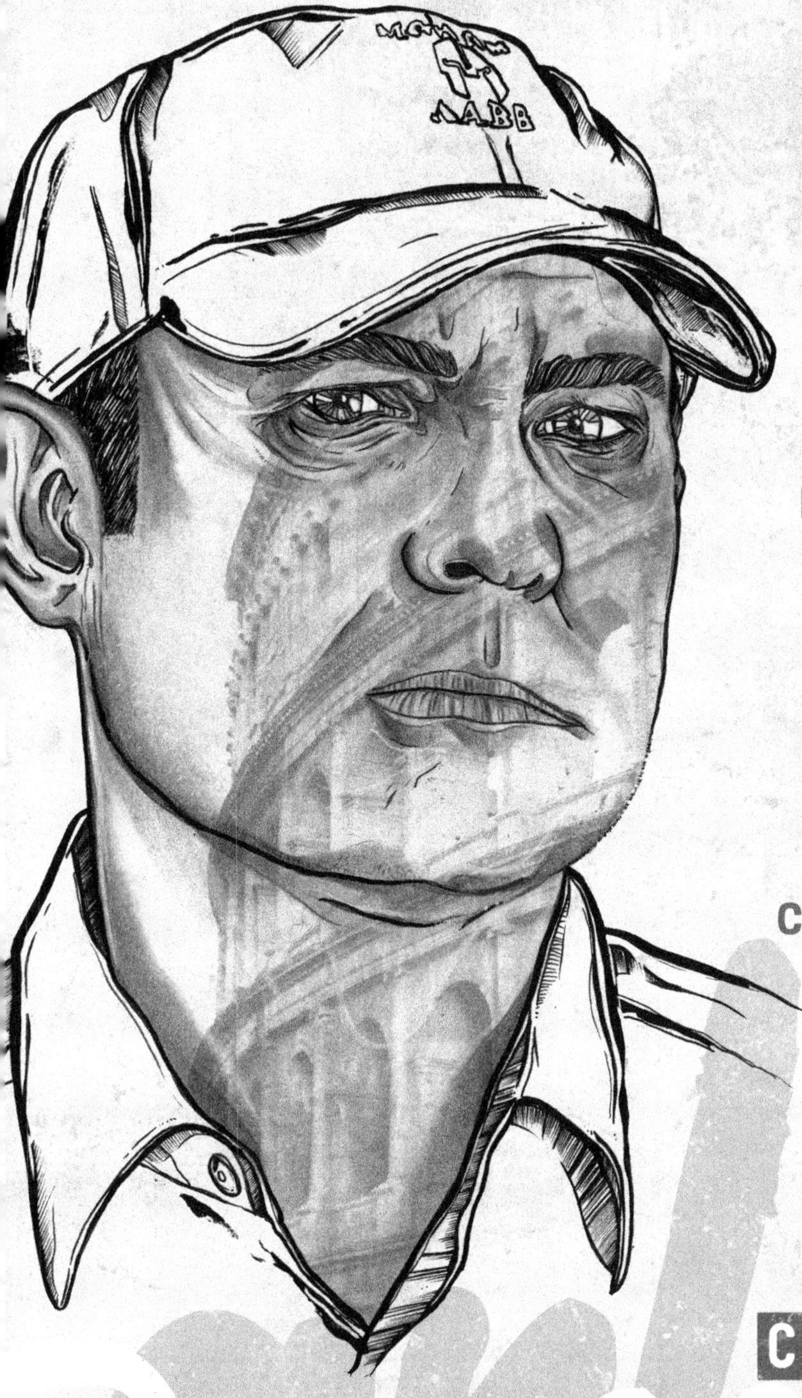

"

IMAGINE IF WE FELT EVERY HORRIBLE PERIOD IN HISTORY AS STRONGLY AS WE FEEL THE HOLOCAUST TODAY. **WE'D STILL BE LIVING WITH A FORM OF CULTURAL POST-TRAUMATIC STRESS DISORDER FROM THE ROMAN DESTRUCTION OF CELTIC CIVILIZATION.**

CHAPTER 25

DAN CARLIN

EPISODE #119 (APRIL 3, 2015)

Dan Carlin is an American political commentator and podcaster. Formerly a professional radio host, Carlin now hosts two popular independent podcasts: Common Sense; and Hardcore History, which is downloaded millions of times per episode.

HISTORY | PREHISTORY | WRITING

CHRIS RYAN: The thing that's so wonderful about your podcast *Hardcore History* is that your passion for your subject comes through loud and clear. I'm sure that's an explanation for a lot of the popularity of the podcast. What is it about history that gets you so riled up?

DAN CARLIN: I'm one of those people who just gets my mind blown on a regular basis by history, and I think that people who love history have a stronger and deeper ability than most to mentally project themselves into imagined scenarios. I've always been a halfway decent communicator, so maybe what I'm able to do on the podcast is to share that feeling with people who can't do that, and give them that same experience. But that's really where I get my enthusiasm from. I really have the ability to at least imagine – as well as anyone not living in these time periods can – what it's like living in some of these stories. We can never really get into the shoes of people raised in different cultures, in different environments, and with different expectations... but I do think that if you couldn't imagine it somewhat, then it would be hard to get very enthused about history.

CR: So it's informed by imagination. And I know exactly what you're talking about; I have the same feeling. I studied literature in college, and I think my passion for literature was similar. When I was reading a Joseph Conrad novel, it was very easy to imagine myself going up the Congo River on that boat, and I think for a lot of people – maybe due to a difficulty reading, a cognitive glitch, or something else – it's much harder for them to put themselves in that "out of body experience" where you can sort of project yourself into that world. But then, of course, it also involves imagination, because we're filling in all these missing gaps. Do you ever worry that your capacity to project yourself may include some sort of bias that you're unaware of?

DC: Oh, absolutely. And I think this is the number one thing that historiography, which is the practice of writing and making history, tries to teach the people who are doing it: how do you filter out first, your own biases and second, the biases of your sources? One of the things we try to do in the podcast is to use analogies, and metaphors, and things like that – so you can say something like, "This story is a little like this," and then people can say, "Oh, I see what you're saying." But right there you're already introducing something that's not quite the same as something you're already worrying about transmitting incorrectly. So yes, obviously you have to be careful. I think the first thing that helps you be careful is admitting right off the bat that, for example, trying to get in the shoes of a Republican Roman from 2,200 years ago is impossible. Now that we've gotten that out of the way, let's try to understand a little bit what it might be like... knowing that it's impossible.

CR: Yeah, definitely. I don't know how much you know about my work, but I'm writing a book largely about prehistory right now, so every day I'm trying to project myself five times further back in history than Rome – a time where there's nothing written, which makes it even trickier. So the reason I ask, is that it's something I'm dealing with all the time: I'm constantly wondering to what extent my own biases are misinforming my interpretations of things.

DC: Isn't DNA evidence starting to make a huge difference in that field?

CR: Well, it sheds light in some limited areas. For example, mitochondrial DNA, which passes only through the females, can demonstrate that women seem to move much further away from their place of birth than males do. So that confirms the idea that our species is female exogamous, meaning that when we reach sexual maturity, the female leaves the natal group rather than the male – which is something we share with chimps and bonobos, our two closest primates.

DC: I was reading something along those lines, that was suggesting there were changes in DNA that occurred when people started using language – so

“”

I THINK THAT PEOPLE WHO LOVE HISTORY HAVE A STRONGER AND DEEPER ABILITY THAN MOST TO MENTALLY PROJECT THEMSELVES INTO IMAGINED SCENARIOS.

they could now begin to figure out some sort of rough estimates of when language began. Are you finding that kind of stuff helpful for what you're doing?

CR: Well, I'm not aware of the particular research you're talking about, but that would be very interesting because the advent of languages is a much-debated topic, as is the advent of culture. They look at things like jewelry, and the adornment corpses during burial, or burial itself, as signs of the advent of culture. But it's a very contentious area.

DC: Because prehistory's tough – the primary sources aren't there, are they?

CR: No, and also you've got the distortion of the secondary sources... as you referred to earlier. You've got people who have very clear agendas that come through in what they choose to highlight or to ignore. This connects to your work, because one of the main debates is violence. Is violence something that's innate to our species and we've been in a state of constant warfare forever? Or is it something that's more a result of cultural changes, and it's actually a distortion in our behavior? Where do you come down on that, Dan? I remember you quoted someone – I don't remember who – but they said, "History is the autobiography of a madman." I love that quote.

DC: That's Alexander Herzen, the playwright. He put it in the mouth of one of his characters, and how obviously Russian is it to look at it that way? It's wonderful. The book is called *Before the Dawn*. I read it and I remember just being fascinated. When you study history, you realize that people begin with the written record and maybe with what we would today call urbanization. As you know, you move from what we call history, into more archaeology and anthropology, and you start getting into things that haven't traditionally fallen into historical expertise. I'll give an example: I've always wondered... when you read someone like Tolkien, and then you find out Tolkien was discussing a world that existed before our current world – almost like it's history, but it's history "before the flood," if you will – I always find it fascinating to wonder... is it possible that there could have been urbanization, say, before Ancient Mesopotamia? At what point do the things that we would use today, to confirm that, disappear from the historical record? Look at what ISIS is doing in the Middle East, bulldozing ancient Assyrian cities... how long does that, or the weatherization, or anything else, have to happen before you lose any sort of evidence that it was even there? It does get you wondering whether sometime between the dinosaurs and Mesopotamia... was there something interesting going on that we don't know about?

CR: Yeah, and another factor in all that is the fact that the sea level has gone up, I think, about 400 feet since the out-of-Africa migration 70,000 years ago. It's quite clear that people would have moved out of Africa and spread around the world along the coastlines. Because that's where the food is, that's where you've got good visibility to hide from predators or see them coming... there are a lot of reasons for people to be on the coastline, and all those coastlines are way underwater now. So what happens is, we find these archaeological sites that are outliers because they're away from the former coastline. They might be hunting parties, or they might be people who were driven into the mountains for some reason. In any case, they're atypical, but that's all that's available. So we extrapolate from them and, I think, end up with a completely distorted vision of the whole world.

DC: My senior thesis professor in college is an underwater archaeologist, and he has this wonderful world available to him. When you go underwater and you dive at these sites, you're seeing things that would be out in the open if they were on land. And they would have been picked over for hundreds and hundreds of years, or the stones would have been reused, or what have you. So I remember him telling us that there's just this wealth of stuff literally right off the coastline that's just sitting there waiting to be discovered. If you could drain the coastlines a little bit like a bathtub... what would you find just sitting there?

CR: Yeah, it's really amazing. I've got this idea for a book about things we know we don't know. Sort of playing off that Rumsfeld quote.

DC: The "known unknown."

CR: Exactly, and that's one of the prime examples I always think about. We know we don't know. We know that we don't have access to that knowledge from all these sites that are along the coastline, and we know that's really important, and yet you rarely hear anybody talking about it, and you don't read about it in popular

WE'RE LIKE FREELOADERS AT A DINNER WHERE WE DON'T HAVE TO PICK UP THE CHECK. IT'S A TYPICAL DILEMMA THAT WE FIND IN HISTORY ALL THE TIME.

science books. It's like the guy looking for his keys under the streetlight because that's where the light is, not because that's where he happened to lose them.

DC: I like that analogy!

CR: Speaking of analogies, I remember in the introduction to the Mongol series, you said something that really made me admire you. You said, "If you want to write a best-selling book, I'll tell you how to do it..."

DC: I know where you're going with this – I've already got people pretending that they're going to write it and put me in the dedication, so I think my safety would be at stake!

CR: But you were right. You were referring to some recent scholars of the Mongols who have said, "Well actually, they weren't that bad; there are a lot of good things they did. They established trade routes, and they made it safe for caravans to travel through Asia, etc." And you can talk about cultural innovations that Mongols brought to the world. And your point was, "Well, the Nazis did a lot of interesting things too, and advanced a lot of sciences, weaponry, and tactical things. But it's verboten to talk about that because it's so recent." But history has a way of removing the messiness. As things become more distant, we're allowed to look at other facets of these historical epochs that we're not really allowed to look at when they're close to us.

DC: I think you made it sound a lot more positive than I did. Basically, it's the trade-offs of empire that have always been cited. If you were on the other side of the Roman Empire you would say things like, "Rome created a wasteland and called it peace," but if you were on the Roman side, well, look at the trade routes that developed, look at how life got better, and incomes were raised, and more people were literate, and you could go on and on. My point about the Nazis and writing a book was: time tends to make us forget the price you have to pay for those benefits of empire if you're a contemporary living through those eras. Yes, the Nazis made great strides in rocketry, for example, which contributed to certainly one of the top ten human achievements of all time: landing a man on the moon. There's a direct connection between that and German-Nazi rocketry programs. But if you'd have asked the people who had to die in the Holocaust as part of that, if that was worth the cost, they're going to say no. But of course we, who are benefiting from the moonshot and everything that will come afterwards, it's totally worth the cost to us.

We're like freeloaders at a dinner where we don't have to pick up the check. It's a typical dilemma that we find in history all the time. The point of the Nazi thing was to suggest that if you actually wrote a book today, where you suggested that, they would be picketing outside your book-signing, and I think probably rightfully so. At the same time, in 500 years I imagine you can write that book and get away with it. And I find it fascinating how, once everyone's dead and

I'M FASCINATED BY THE IDEA THAT SOCIETY MAY TAKE A STEP BACK AGAIN SOMEDAY. IMAGINE NOT UNDERSTANDING, OR NOT BEING AS ADVANCED TECHNOLOGICALLY, AS YOUR GREAT-GREAT-GREAT GRANDPARENTS.

once everyone who knew anyone is dead, and once the passions have cooled, they will reexamine the awful period of the Holocaust the same way we've examined or reexamined every other awful period in world history. I don't know if that's sad or not, but maybe it's a defense mechanism. Imagine if we felt every horrible period in history as strongly as we feel the Holocaust now. We'd still be living with a form of cultural post-traumatic stress disorder from the Roman destruction of Celtic civilization.

CR: Well, you know there are psychologists who argue that we are living with a cultural post-traumatic stress disorder.

DC: History: the autobiography of a madman.

CR: There you go, that might be what drove him mad in the first place. You know, what you're talking about really brings me to a big question that I'm dealing with in the work I'm doing now, which is how we define "progress." For instance, we're talking about the Mongols doing good things, so did the Nazis, so did settling the Wild West and killing all the Indians, etc. But we're seeing those things as good largely because they contributed to where we are now. But is there anything inherent in where we are now that's necessarily good? In other words, do you believe in progress? Are we progressing as a species, or is it more of a cyclical thing as the Buddhists would say?

DC: This may be an eye-of-the-beholder sort of question. I'm going to suggest that yes, if you're talking about progress in terms of the ability of more people to live their life to the fullest – however they deem that – then I think there's no question that more people have more of an impact and more choices. There are people who live in what we used to call the Third World that are just as isolated from opportunity as people were in the past, but I would suggest that in the past those numbers were infinitely higher as a proportion. When you read history books, as the great science historian James Burke told me once, you're reading the top 0.00001 percent of people who had the ability to go to school, or get any literacy, or make any difference. What we've done as a species over time is increase the pool of people who get to share in the glory. It's still a small percentage, I think, if you take it on a global level, but it is an ever-increasing percentage.

Now what fascinates me is that if you look at the past, it tends to have an almost bunny-hop sort of rhythm to what we would call progress. Two-steps forward, one step back. If we were looking at civilization like a stock market, I think you could say that we've been on a constant uptick since the Renaissance without any real downturns. Does that mean that it's a little like trying to start a cigarette lighter, and the first couple of tries you just get a spark, and it doesn't start, and one spark that doesn't start represents the Bronze Age, and then that falls, and then another spark starts, and now we finally got the flame lit? Or are we just so far from the last time we took any steps back, that we don't remember that taking a step back is a standard thing that we're going to see again? I don't have an answer to that, but I'm fascinated by the idea that society may take a step back again someday. Imagine not understanding, or not being as advanced technologically as your great-great-great grandparents.

CR: Well, we're in a moment now where we're seeing a step back in terms of quality of life, certainly in the United States – in terms of retirement security, income disparity... all these sorts of measures of progress since World War II that were increasing into the '70s and the '80s. But a lot of them are now receding; even expected lifespan is starting to edge downward. So again, as you say, it's an eye-of-the-beholder thing. When you were talking about this uptick since the Renaissance, I was thinking that, seen from the European perspective I'm sure that's accurate, but seen from many other parts of the planet, that's probably not so accurate.

DC: But again it depends on how you define it, because the way you just defined it, from an economic standpoint, you're taking a massive society and saying, "Okay, within this mass, people aren't doing as well as their parents." Well, that's a percentage of the population that isn't, but some people are. On an individual level we've got people doing better and people doing worse. When I think about it, I look at it from a technological and "building" standpoint, you could say. If you look at it from an economic standpoint, I don't know that we could notice any patterns over the long haul of all history ever, because those are going to vary from one individual to another. If you're taking a subset of the American middle class, for example, and measuring their upticks and downticks like a stock market... absolutely I think you see the ups and downs. But then you cease to see the giant historical trends, and now you're working within a smaller timeline – does that make sense?

CR: Yeah, you're definitely slicing it up, but you can look at things like infant mortality rates, or how many active years of life versus how many years in a nursing home in the end stage. As you say, there are many different ways to measure these things, but I do think it's interesting that we're at this time where – for really the first time in recent history (in North America anyway) – there is this sense that the wave has crested, and it's starting to recede a little bit in some of these measures. In talking about technology, I'm playing with this idea of the difference between what's good for the individual and what's good for what I'm calling the super-organism. Human beings are part of something – the civilization – that is so much bigger than themselves. So the civilization can progress, even though quality of life for individuals is receding.

DC: Absolutely. I think we see examples of that all throughout history.

CR: That, I think, is a fundamental difference between prehistoric foragers and the agricultural civilizations that arose 10,000 years ago or so... where you get the rise of this super-organism that is larger than the human scale. That's the first time we moved beyond the human scale, with incredible repercussions. Have you studied prehistory at all, or do you keep it all within written history?

DC: I've absolutely studied prehistory. I don't know it like I know history, but I'm a big fan of ancient history and it doesn't make any sense unless you go a little farther back and see the conditions that make ancient

I'M GETTING A REALLY WEIRD FEELING AS I'M APPROACHING 50: I'M STARTING TO SEE THE LIMITS OF WHAT I'M GONNA BE ABLE TO DISCOVER. I'M SEEING THAT I'LL NEVER LIVE LONG ENOUGH TO READ ALL THE THINGS I WANT TO READ.

history somewhat different than prehistory. What I always liked about history compared to something like math, is I found history to be finite and math to be infinite, and I had a hard time grasping the infinite. History ends at some point; it's constantly moving, but I can get my mind around an endpoint. The beginning point is what's so interesting because part of what makes the old historians from 60, 70, 80 years ago so wonderful to read now, is that they're so much more sure of themselves, and happy to go out on a limb to say things. For them, history begins in Mesopotamia, and it begins with writing, and it begins with urbanization. Now we're constantly moving that timeline earlier, and as I said, I would not be shocked if somewhere, somehow they find a sophisticated civilization that precedes Mesopotamia that just happens to be a very dry place. It would be fascinating if, for example, in the middle of the steppes of Russia somewhere, they find something that predates that which has been buried in sand forever.

CR: Are you familiar with these discoveries in the Amazon that they're finding now with ground-penetrating radar? They're finding what seem to be urban centers.

DC: It's a perfect example; it's almost a variation of what we were talking about with the ocean covering up a lot of things. It's easy to find ancient Sumeria. You know it's out there, it's a giant mound in the middle of a place with not a lot of foliage. Go and try to find some of these ancient Mayan or Toltec ruins, or the peoples that were even earlier than that; sometimes they're covered by dense jungle.

CR: And as the technology improves, it opens that stuff up. It's fascinating. When we started talking, you were talking about how you get fascinated by things, and I was thinking, "If I could live 500 years, I can't imagine getting bored if I still had the ability to learn." There's so much fascinating stuff out there, I can't understand people who get bored. Do you get that frustration sometimes?

DC: I'm getting a really weird feeling as I'm approaching 50: I'm starting to see the limits of what I'm gonna be able to discover. I'm seeing that I'll never live long enough to read all the things I want to read. There's a bunch of things I would still like to do that are far away from what I've spent the last 20 or 25 years creating a foundation for, and I'm not going to live long enough to create another foundation. The more you think about that, the more you realize how that limitation also affected the people from the past. One of the questions I always wonder about – I always describe it as a vampire-like situation, because the thing that always fascinated me so much when I read Bram Stoker's *Dracula* was not the vampire-like qualities of the central character, it was the fact that he was so old – if you were able to encompass the learning, not to mention the wisdom that comes from analyzing the learning... if you could take a person and let them live five or six hundred years and still be essentially in the prime of life, imagine what an advantage that person would have over all of us now. If you imagine that societies in the past had far fewer people living as old as people live now... does the accrued experience of a society with so many more people with so many more years under their belt play into things? Does it matter? I have no answer for that, but I constantly wonder about it.

* * *

CR: Do you have any opinion on Howard Zinn and *The People's History of the US*?

DC: Yeah that's a strong influence for me. Howard Zinn, for people who don't know, his motivation was to try to write a counterpoint to what I always call the "1950s high school history textbooks," the rah-rah, American flag, sanitized sort of history. I think Zinn said in the introduction that he was not trying to write a balanced history, he was trying to fill up the other side of the scale with evidence to balance things out. But when you read Zinn, it's profoundly unbalanced. If Zinn is all you read, you're getting a very one-sided view of things. That was Zinn's goal. So when I read him, I do think he's profoundly unfair, but he's not trying to be fair. The facts that he pulls out are true facts. And yet when you read it, you get this feeling by the time you're done, that all these people in history were evil, and that these cultures were awful. Instead of the red men being the savages and the white men being the civilizers (à la the 1950s history book), the red men are the noble savages and the white men are the rapers and destroyers.

And truthfully, what I love about the more modern histories, is that they're doing such a wonderful job of reminding you that everybody on all sides of the story are people, and that these people are responding in ways that people tend to respond. But when Zinn wrote that book, that was not the norm, and so I cut him a lot of slack because I understand what he was trying to do. At the same time, I personally find it difficult to read him. But that's my own bias, and he's perfectly justified in trying to do what he did.

CR: That's a very fair-minded assessment; I'm glad to hear you say that. One of the things that Zinn was addressing, and a point you raised earlier, is that history as it's presented to us is really only representative of a fraction of the top percentage of any given society. And usually, that's the educated people, who by definition are almost always men and almost always white. So I think his enterprise - which was to say, "Hey, let's look at this from the perspective of women, blacks, Indians, slaves, and the poor," was an important thing, and an important corrective. And I think you're right, he wasn't setting out to be balanced; he was setting out to create balance in some sense.

DC: The other problem is to look at the mass of it. I try to explain to people that they're interested in history but they just don't know it. I do this by pointing out that history is everything, everything. Even if you're interested in dentistry, there's a history of dentistry; if you're interested in motorcycles, there's a history of motorcycles. The problem with that, if you're writing a history book, is how do you decide what's important?

In the far past, it's easy to exclude women, for example, because you just don't have a lot of sources on them. That's why a diary here or there is so important sometimes, because all of a sudden you can hang a whole history book on a good diary from some woman in a time period where you don't have a lot of input from women. In the old days, the job of a historian was to search through haystacks and try to find needles; future historians are going to have the opposite problem. They're going to have haystacks everywhere they look. There's going to be everybody's Facebook... there's gonna be so much stuff that the

HISTORY IS EVERYTHING, EVERYTHING. IF YOU'RE INTERESTED IN DENTISTRY, THERE'S A HISTORY OF DENTISTRY; IF YOU'RE INTERESTED IN MOTORCYCLES, THERE'S A HISTORY OF MOTORCYCLES.

historians are just going to be overwhelmed trying to figure out, "My goodness, what's important? How do we determine what, out of all of this, is important?"

I'll give an example. When I was a news reporter, I did some work on the assignment desk, and I started off in Los Angeles. When you open that file at four in the morning to decide what you're gonna cover that day, it is absolutely filled with material. There's more than you could ever get to, and so my job was to go through all this material and go, "No. No. No. No...." Nothing was good enough, and you'd end up at the end of the day with a pile of stuff worth covering, out of the hundreds of things that were originally in the file. Then I moved to a small market – a little town where I had that same job – but you'd open up the file in the morning, and there would be three things in there. Practically nothing! And you had the exact opposite task: you had to sit there going, "Well, how do I find something?" The way it was for me in the small town, is how it is for historians, for example, trying to write about some of these very early societies. There's just not enough stuff; you're working with a jigsaw puzzle and they have four pieces. Whereas in the future it's going to be an impossible task to try to figure out how to cull all the material you have and figure out what's valuable. I don't know that you're gonna be able to write the kind of all-encompassing histories that some of us grew up with in the future.

CR: Well we're already seeing that in social media. Look at Twitter... who knows what's important?

DC: I remember when the whole internet started, there were a few historians who worried that people had stopped keeping diaries. And they said publicly, "What on earth are we going to do in a hundred years without diaries? We're not gonna have any information on how people viewed the world." And now you think, "My God, everybody's keeping a diary."

CR: Yeah, just publicly accessible.

DC: That's right – historians have a lot to work with.

CR: As does the NSA.

DC: Yeah – they may be one and the same down the road.

CR: Indeed.

* * *

DC: I don't like the people who say things like "the Ancient Egyptians could not have built the pyramids," and they'll base a whole theory on how they must have had extraterrestrial help because we couldn't possibly get those measurements that precise, and that they had to have some form of higher technology. And you think to yourself, "Well, if they're wrong about that, what they've really just done is denigrate the cleverness of the people back then." The Persians, for example, during the wars with Ancient Greece (they were known as the Achaemenids)... those people could put armies in the field of forty, fifty, sixty-thousand people. All with no computers, no modern devices. The fact that they were clever enough to pull that off, to me, is absolutely mind-blowing.

One of my teachers had to remind me once when I was in school, that one of the things we have that our ancestors didn't always have, is that we're able to build on the knowledge of previous people better than any other civilization. You can read the works from 50 years ago, 100 years ago... and he said ancient peoples didn't always have that advantage, but that they were always as clever as we are now. I think people forget that there are other ways of accomplishing the same goals than how we do it. Go back and look at Babylonian medicine, which looks practically like witchdoctor stuff to us today... it was built on centuries of observation and record-keeping. So for its day, they were utilizing the best mechanism that they had to accomplish their goals. Obviously it doesn't stand up to even rudimentary stuff today, but it's fascinating to see how those people got around their limitations. And it shows our innate cleverness as a species.

CR: And in fact, it could be argued that we're again receding. The human brain has shrunk in size since the advent of agriculture. Our body has atrophied. Hunter-gatherers are far stronger than most modern people, and in stature, hunter-gatherers were about six inches taller than the farmers who came directly after them. Again, it relates to this question: is the species thriving or is the individual thriving? That's not always in alignment.

DC: The historian Charles Austin Beard had a great line... he said something along the lines of, "To be considered a dangerous radical these days, all you have to do is walk down the street spouting the sayings of the founding fathers." And when you go read the founding fathers today, they sound so radical, and yet that's who we are. As Franklin Delano Roosevelt said that we are the descendants of revolutionaries. And yet we're now as anti-revolutionary a society as we could possibly be

> THE WORLD IS MY HOME. ANY PLACE WHERE I KNOW SOMEBODY AND I FEEL FAMILIAR WITH THE AREA FEELS LIKE HOME TO ME.

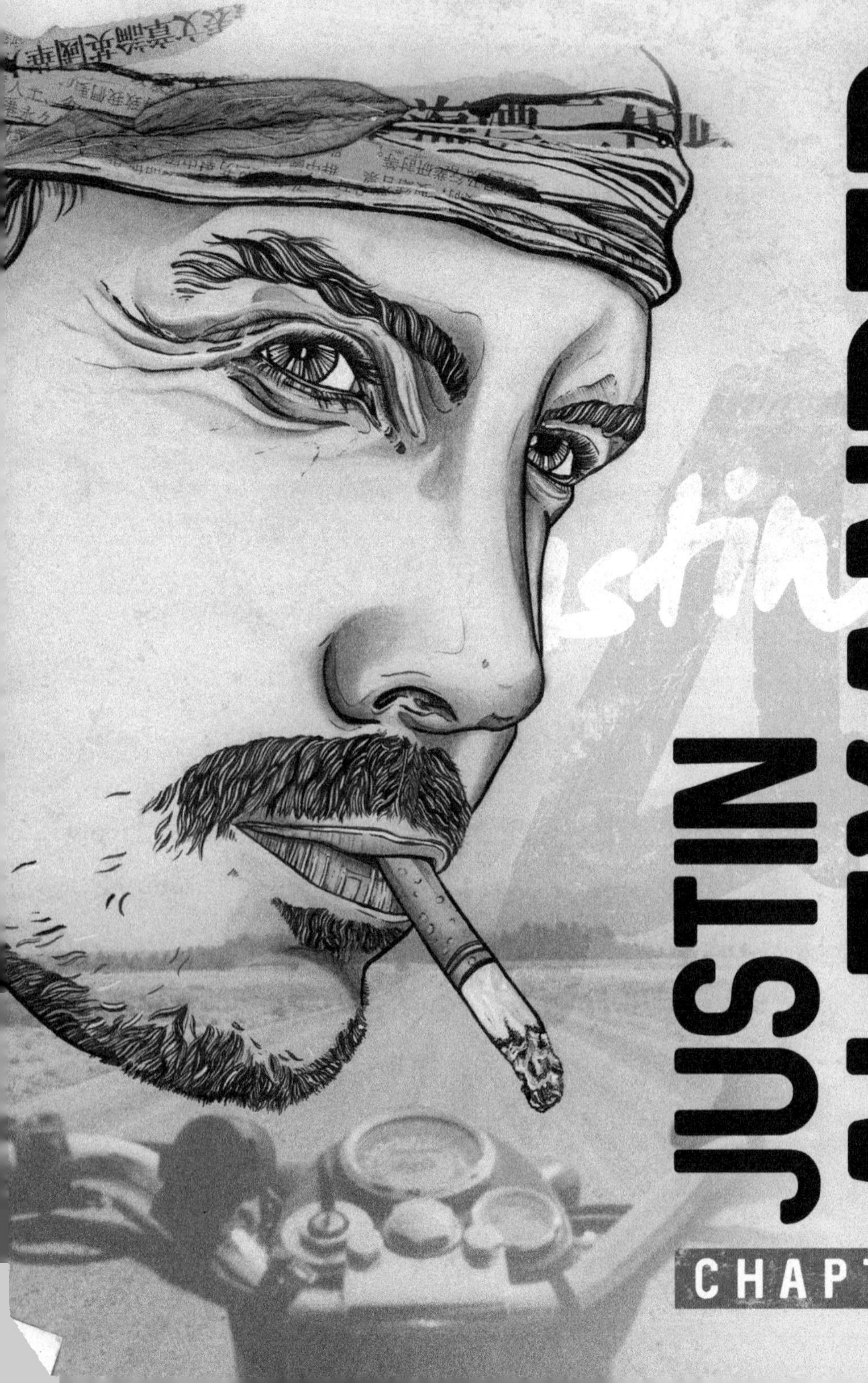

JUSTIN ALEXANDER

CHAPTER 26

EPISODE #143 (SEPTEMBER 13, 2015)
&
EPISODE #167 (FEBRUARY 18, 2016)

Justin Alexander was a modern nomad. His blog and Instagram account (@adventuresofjustin) chronicled his experiences around the globe. In September of 2016, just a few months after he and Chris recorded their third podcast together in Chiang Mai, Thailand, Justin vanished while traveling in the Indian Himalayas. The man suspected in his murder apparently committed suicide while in police custody. Justin's body has never been found.

TRAVEL | RELIGION | SOCIETY | ADVENTURE

CHRIS RYAN: Justin Alexander... who the hell are you? You're a travel blogger?

JUSTIN ALEXANDER: Well, no. I mean, I do have a blog. I rarely post, only when there's some interesting story to tell. But over the last year and a half I think I've posted three times. So I'm not a travel blogger by any means, and I'm not looking to monetize it or anything like that. I just kind of use it as a space, along with social media, to share who I am and what I'm doing with people that might be interested. So when people ask what I do, I generally say I'm just a nomadic world traveler, exploring the world and telling stories...

CR: I like the "just." The humble brag there, "Oh me, I'm just a lowly world traveler, retired at 24."

JA: 34, but yeah. I've been traveling since 2006 but not full time. I sold everything I own, and quit conventional life when I was 32. I fell in love with traveling back in 2006 when I went and helped out with a documentary film-making expedition in Nepal for a month; I caught the travel bug really hard.

CR: Mmm, Nepal is great.

JA: The thing about travel that I love so much is the ability to not just see places, but to also feel like I'm able to time travel – like when I lived with a tribe in Indonesia called the Mentawai tribe (also on my blog), and lived out in the jungle for ten days with a couple families. They do all the traditional tattoos, like with the lines and stuff like that. I stayed with a couple of shamans, and they hunt with poison-tip bows and arrows. This is a small cluster of islands that is famous in the surf world because they have some of the most consistent surf. It's a beautiful tropical island off the coast of Sumatra.

CR: I was in Sumatra for three months and I... ran into some surfers.

IT FELT LIKE IT COULD HAVE BEEN 1,000 YEARS AGO. THEY HAVE ONE OR TWO PLASTIC UTENSILS, AND OCCASIONALLY THEY HAVE A GAS LAMP, BUT BESIDES THAT EVERYTHING IS ANCIENT.

JA: Siberut Island is the one that I went to. It's the most southern island in the cluster, and the whole interior is a kind of reservation where the natives live. They have government housing and stuff like that, but all their elders still live out in the old ways – and you end up taking a five-hour, motorized, dugout canoe ride up these muddy rivers to get out to this place. And I had hired an interpreter there, and he took me up and, man, it felt like it could have been 1,000 years ago. They have one or two plastic utensils, and occasionally they have a gas lamp, but besides that everything is ancient.

CR: And the thing is, as you've experienced, everything is the flip side of what we're told it is. We're told "They're so poor" because they only live on $1 a day or whatever bullshit it is... They don't have a money economy! So a dollar a day doesn't mean anything, and they don't want to join civilization! They're dragging their feet, fighting tooth and nail not to join this fucking party. The propaganda is, "Oh, it's so great, everyone wants to be with us." No, they don't! None of them want to be with us! These are the last vestiges of these amazing cultures and none of them want to walk away from their culture to join ours!

* * *

CR: So, let's' take this back, because I get a lot of emails from people who say, "Dude, I love these travel stories. I want to do that." How do you do it?

JA: How do I have money?

CR: Right. What were you doing before?

JA: So I got obsessed with travel in 2006 and then read *The 4-Hour Workweek* by Tim Ferris and a couple other books about lifestyle design. His whole thing was about starting a company and outsourcing all the work so you have lots of free time. But he wrote that book while he was traveling the world. I would say it has to do with putting your priorities in order, and really being mindful about the decisions you make, and the responsibilities you take. Once you have a kid, and get tied into a house, you fall into the whole freedom vs. security spectrum. The more secure and locked-in you get in your life, the less opportunity you have to do other things. There's pros and cons to both ends of the spectrum. Not everyone really wants to be living with everything they own in a backpack on their back. It's not very comfortable... I've never really had a sense of home. I've always been kind of a nomad. My family moved around a lot, so I've probably had more houses than I've had years of life. So it just feels very natural for me to continue on like that. I feel like the world is my home. Any place where I know somebody and I feel familiar with the area feels like home to me.

But to go back... In 2009, a friend and I started a technology company based out of Miami, so I ended up transferring to Miami. We did anti-counterfeiting tracking and marketing for luxury goods – did a lot of stuff with wine – but it definitely was not my passion.

And I wasn't really proud of who I was and what I was doing. When you introduce yourself and they ask you, "What do you do?" I would always sigh and say I was a tech entrepreneur. I didn't think it was very cool. None of my heroes are entrepreneurs, they're all adventurers. So the company did well enough-and I contributed enough that I was able to step back and still have a passive income coming from my ownership position. So I've got a small passive income that supports the type of lifestyle that I really value.

CR: That's fantastic.

JA: Yeah, like you said, it's luck. I was born in a country where I don't have to worry about getting killed every day, and I don't have to worry about where my next meal is coming from.

CR: So did you feel from a young age that something was just wrong about American society?

JA: Yeah, just with civilization in general. I was really against it, and I definitely have come back around the other way. I spent ten years living in the normal world, and learned to appreciate things from it... and I feel like my life is about walking that razor's edge: learning what types of important things to put value on, not just putting value on things we're told to put value on.

CR: We live in this mass production society, and one of the things that's mass produced is identity. And most people are choosing their identity off a rack, the same way you choose your clothes. It's just like, "Well, yeah... That's more or less my size, I guess."

JA: Default life.

CR: And often it's being defined in contrast to your parent's generation. Everyone thinks they're doing something original, but when you look at it, it's like, "What the fuck, man? What's original about this?" So I feel the same way. I can't be normal, because I don't have friends, I don't have a community, I don't have a home, I don't have an identity that's tied to a particular region, or country, or whatever. I can't be normal, so I'm sort of forced to figure it out on my own. And it ended up being this incredible blessing.

JA: I feel like *belonging* is a real basic human need. With the internet I'm able to build and sustain a sense of being social, and creating my own community, because I've never really had one. So the people I choose to associate with are very, very purposeful. I choose to associate with people who have similar values, and most of them happen to be nomads who live alternative lifestyles, and who don't have any sense of real community either. But also people who are healthy, and have a healthy psychology. As opposed to going off the deep end and becoming some total sociopath who never belonged and therefore, "Fuck everybody. I'm going to go be a hermit, or be a crazy person on the street that no one wanted to give money to, and who people spit at..." and shit like that.

CR: Yeah. You're right. And that's another thing I try to talk about on the podcast: that there is a very steep price to pay for living the kind of life you're living.

JA: Yes. And most people don't realize that. When I tell people what I'm doing, everyone - especially older men who see my motorcycle and hear about what I'm doing - say things like, "Ohhhh, you're living the dream." And it's like, "Yeah, but there's a lot of day-to-day shit like, 'Where I'm going to sleep, or where I'll have my next meal?' Every day."

CR: And the loneliness. I can't begin to calculate how many hours I've spent sitting in restaurants, cafes, park benches, hostels, bars, whatever… around the world, alone, wishing I wasn't. Wishing I was with a friend, desperately wishing I was with a woman. But, if you're moving all the time, you don't have time to really develop those kinds of relationships. You're in flux the whole time. And when I was *really* traveling a lot, there *was* no internet, so I couldn't even do that kind of thing.

JA: It's my favorite thing. The internet and having a smartphone has enabled my life in so many ways. A lot of travelers really reject everything modern, including the internet and technology. But it just enables me in so many ways. I went scuba diving in Thailand in 2007, and I met some Swedish dudes in my dive class. We ended up becoming friends and partying, and then we became friends on Facebook. The next time I'm in Sweden I hit them up, and it's like we're still friends – because we've messaged each other occasionally, or commented on each other's photos; it's like we were able to maintain that bond over those 2 years. Otherwise you never see that person again. This way, I ended up staying at their place, we go out to some great parties in Stockholm, and they take me up to their family's place up in Uppsala.

* * *

JA: When I'm in the US, I love the fact that I can talk to everyone. Traveling around the US, there's a lot that I can really appreciate. The conveniences of being able to go into a grocery store and have all variety of things that I can eat, and knowing consistently where I can do certain things. It's not the same as, say, exploring Kazakhstan by motorcycle. But I want to do *that* kind of stuff too. But for now, the US is one of the most beautiful countries in the world for nature. You've got such a variety.

CR: Especially out west.

JA: Exactly. I'm not that excited about, necessarily, riding around on the East Coast. But there's some really beautiful nature up in the mountains, up through the Virginias and North Carolina, and up into Maine and stuff like that. But there's something very raw and authentic about riding through deserts in the American West… just parking the bike when it gets dark, pulling over somewhere off the main road onto a dirt road, starting a fire, and sleeping next to your motorcycle under the stars. It feels like I'm riding a horse.

CR: That's what I was going to say, it's very archetypal and I do think it's got some deep resonance. I've always felt that. I remember when I first got a motorcycle when I was a kid. And I remember my uncle, an adventurous guy, saying, "I like your ride." So it's kind of like a horse. This is something I didn't even notice until I had a bike… but when you're cruising around, other motorcyclists wave at you as you ride by; there's some respect.

IF YOU JUMP, YOU'LL FIND WINGS. AND THAT'S ONE OF THE THINGS YOU CAN'T ANTICIPATE. IT'S NOT IN YOUR FUCKING *LONELY PLANET*, IT'S NOT ON YELP, AND YOU CAN'T PLAN FOR IT. JUST GO.

JA: It's like a cool little club of people who *get it.*

CR: People who haven't been on motorbikes don't know this, but you're always almost dead. You feel alive, because all day long that lethal road is buzzing by, and it's right there. It's not outside a big metal box, it's right there. You can put your foot down and touch it, and you can't help but be conscious of the fact that you are at the edge of the cliff all day long while you're on that bike. And that makes you feel fucking great. And the other thing about being on the bike is that, because you're aware of the danger, your monkey mind is really focused: "Is there something on the road? What's around that curve? Is that a rock? Is that a pothole? Is that an animal? Is that kid going to run out here? Is that guy going to turn left?" You learn to watch the wheels, not the turn signal. You learn to look in people's eyes. You learn all these survival things that keep your conscious mind so occupied. Do you get into altered states?

JA: Yeah, totally, especially out on open stretches of road. It's very meditative. When you're in and around cars, you're having to be very mindful, so it's like meditation in a way. It's almost like hiking in a way. When I was in Nepal, I had a lot of free time exploring the mountains there, smoking a lot of hash, and going on a lot of walks. I hiked a lot by myself – sometimes going 20 miles in a day. I'd start remembering things in my past, and *really* thinking about things. Really thinking about these memories, and pouring through my own psychology. *Really* digging into important things like values, the type of experiences I've had, and then reinterpreting them. It was very therapeutic, and I find that those long stretches where you're out, especially riding motorcycles through nature... there's something very natural about it. It feels very therapeutic.

* * *

CR: I tell people that if you jump, you'll find wings. And that's one of the things you can't anticipate. It's not in your fucking *Lonely Planet*, it's not on Yelp, and you can't plan for it. Just go. Buy your fucking ticket to Bangkok. Go to some island and hang out, be friendly, be open, have a smile on your face... and you're going to meet people who are going to tell you about amazing places that they just came from, or about places that they're about to go to, and they'll invite you along. That's how it works. That's the difference between travel and fucking tourism. And the other thing is, don't get two weeks off and think this shit's going to work. You've got to quit your fucking job. I've done both. The one kind of traveling lasts until the money runs out. Or until you just get tired of it. But the other kind of travel happens until your time runs out because you've got a month, or two months, or whatever it is. With one kind, you're adding experiences in a cumulative celebration of freedom, and life, and travel; and with the other kind, you're counting down. The whole tone of the trip is different.

JA: Especially when you over-plan something. But planning to some degree can definitely be important. I've shown up in places, for example, in Colombia, where I went to Tayrona National Park, which is a beautiful park on the Gulf of Mexico – and it just so happened that the first two weeks of January is their spring break. So it was madness. I was out in nature but I couldn't get a photo without people playing volleyball in it. So doing a little research is good, but there's something about having an open-ended, unplanned... going *towards* something rather than *to* something. It certainly seems like, in a lot of cases, it opens you up to things that feel like synchronicity. Where occasionally you have this run where stuff feels like magic. Everything works out so incredibly, and if you had planned it, you'd miss all kinds of opportunities. If you got your next plane ticket for a week earlier, but you meet some cool people, then you can't go, you know? You can't follow your Swedish friends down to New Zealand to go whitewater rafting, because you've got to get back to California to get back with your rock band – something that was so frustrating for me at the time. I had commitments and a regular life to maintain. And this type of traveling feels like freedom in its purest sense – which is one of my highest values.

CR: Yeah, just being able to float on whatever current pulls you. That is such a wonderful fucking feeling.

* * *

CR: The thing about the modern warrior... I feel like it's been corrupted like so many other things. It's like fighting dogs. A dog will fight to protect its pack, but today we have dogs that are fighting in a ring for fucking drunken idiots to bet on. That's how I sort of see the military these days. These guys have noble intentions, they think they're going to defend their country... but then they're out there killing somebody to make sure the price of oil doesn't go up. It's just all corrupted. Sebastian Junger... do you know of him? He was embedded with the Marines in Korengal Valley in Afghanistan. I saw this interview he did – it was really moving – and the interviewer asked him, "Why? Why are these guys out there? They're getting shot at every day. They're going through this incredible hardship." And he said, "Well, they do it for love. They do it for each other."

JA: For their brothers. They're fighting on, for their brother on their shoulder.

CR: Exactly, yeah. But that's why the *other guys* are doing it! So we've got all these great guys shooting at each other, and the fucking assholes who send them into it are just laughing.

JA: Yeah. I like the idea of the warrior, in the sense that those skills can be used to protect people – when it's done on a very independent level. You're making moral decisions.

CR: Right. You're not following orders.

JA: I almost became a SEAL. When I was about to turn 29, right at the cut-off, I was wanting something else in my life. I ended up starting a company, and now I am where I am, thank goodness. But I wanted adventure, I wanted brotherhood, I wanted the skills to be able to protect people. My goal was that once I got out, I could get into contract work and do things I really felt good about. Turns out that's not how it works. I've got friends who do that, and they're still not doing it the way I would want to do it. But I still want the training, I still want the skills, I still want the capabilities. Because everywhere I go, I want to be safe and I want everyone else to be safer because I'm there. That's a warrior to me.

CR: Do you ever feel that you're training for situations that never arise?

JA: Yeah. My whole teenage life was about training for an apocalypse. And then I was like, "That's kind of a fucked up way to live!"

CR: And then you get disappointed because the world didn't end.

JA: Yeah. And the thing is, I love people. There's a lot I like about this world that were living in. Granted, you watch zombie movies, or post-apocalyptic movies, and everyone's like, "What would I do? What would I do?" I think it's great to have skills that can work in these situations, so that you're not afraid of it. But I still don't want it to happen. It sure would suck, and I don't know if I'd make it. Almost everyone I know that knows me is like, "Yo, if shit goes down, I'm with you alright?" and I'm like, "I can't make that promise to everyone!" And who knows where I'll be? Who knows if I'll make it?

CR: Shit might go down, and you might step on a rusty nail. I always think of my wife as my post-apocalyptic ace-up-the-sleeve. She's a doctor who knows how to be a doctor without technology, which is exactly what you need.

JA: Well you need a team. You need a warrior ninja scout who can set up booby traps, who can track and counter-track, who knows how to not leave a trail, who knows how to build invisible camps if there's other people hunting you. That's crucial.

CR: And you need someone who knows how to set up a garden. And you need someone who's good with basic technology who can set up a wind thing... And you need money! And a big piece of land! The problem with all this post-apocalyptic planning is if you set it up, and you actually get a good thing going, then you're going to have fucking lunatics coming in with their guns to take it all away. There's no way to plan.

JA: That's kind of how my life is. I'm just dealing with things as they're coming. I think being prepared, or having the mentality to be able to handle it is important, but I don't want to spend a lot of my life energy – same with the warrior stuff – contemplating destruction. And these guys, that's what they think about all the time. I don't want to say they're paranoid, because they're in real situations all the time. But they're always carrying; whenever we're going into a public area, they'll be like, "Hey, just so you know, I'm carrying here. If I go down here's my weapons. The keys are here..." All of this stuff is always in their minds. And if something *does* go down, that will save your life. So that's great. But living that way all the time is just not the mindset I want.

CR: When I was a teenager, I studied martial arts. I carried a knife everywhere, and I had all these fantasies of how I was going to survive in the post-apocalypse. I knew what plants to eat, how to snare rabbits, and all this kind of stuff. And I can't help feeling that it was a manifestation of me feeling vulnerable as a teenage boy who moved a lot and didn't have friends. So I could take care of myself, you know? It was bullshit. If the world ended I would have died as fast as anybody else. But it made me feel better. I feel like in America, the gun thing is sort of the same psychological mechanism. People are telling themselves, "If the government tries to take over, me and my buddies..." No, you're not! You're not.

JA: There is that group, definitely, but there are a lot of people, like old women, who should be allowed to carry guns because they can't defend themselves from people who are trying to hurt them. It is an equalizer. So in that way, I think that a gun can prevent a rape better than screaming will. I don't necessarily think that everyone should carry a gun. I see both sides, I see a lot of sides to the gun thing.

* * *

CR: So where are you going from here?

JA: I have a ticket booked to the Philippines; I'm going to Cebu for maybe three weeks, then I'm going to visit my adoptive Thai family up in northern Thailand. My little brother is going to become a monk on November

2nd, and I'm going to spend some time out in a village with family, then stay in Thailand for a little bit. I don't know what I'm going to do after that. Either go down to the islands, or explore up north more. Maybe do some motorcycling. Then the real thing I'm looking forward to is getting into India. I'm gonna get another Enfield and explore India.

CR: Any idea where?

JA: I've seen a lot of documentaries recently, and I really like the west and the north. I love the Himalayas, and I want to ride over the highest highway in the world. The highest pass.

CR: Up to Leh?

JA: Leh, yeah. I want to do that. There's a good two months that's perfect timing. I'm going to go up into Nepal. I've got kind of a family there: I've got a brother that I want to take out and do some trekking with into a real remote area. He's Nepali, and we've been friends since 2006. He's real family. So we'll go out, and get out somewhere really far. No tour guides, no trekker trail... and just go visit some really out-there areas in Nepal. So I'll probably go there for maybe two months in the summer... ride the Enfield up into Nepal.

* * *

CR: So we aren't traveling together, but you just happened to be in Thailand for your brother's monkhood ceremony. And you *were* a monk.

JA: Yeah. The first time I came solo to Thailand was in late 2006. The story is more about how I was adopted into a Thai family than it is about the monk thing. I didn't come here to become a monk, and I wasn't coming here to seek spirituality or anything. But I previously spent the summer in Nepal, and really loved the form of Buddhism I saw there while up in the mountains visiting monasteries and hanging out with these very peaceful red-robed monks – sitting up in the mornings while they're reading their mantras by candle. I had a big curiosity about that form of Buddhism, so I went back to the U.S. and studied a lot. I was reading a lot of books, and learning a lot, and doing a lot of meditation. When I got to Thailand, I was kickboxing, and I broke my foot in my first fight so I wasn't able to train anymore. I was kind of bummed out about it because that's why I came here.

But I ended up meeting a Thai guy who's my age, and he was like, "Well I know you're bummed out because you can't train, but I'm going to take the bus a few hours away up into a rural province down south of Chiang Mai to visit my family. If you want to see what real Thai life is like, this is a great opportunity." And I said, "Oh, hell yes." So I did that and showed up around the end of 2006 in December. I can speak enough Thai to be... charming, and I think there's a lot to that. I can be very polite, being able to tell them that their food is delicious. And I think there are some other habits that really help garner the friendship of locals. But his family really, really liked me. And one night we were sitting around (as we would) by a fire in the backyard. And grandfather, and grandmother, and uncle, and auntie, and a couple cousins, and brother, and mom, and dad, and I... we're all sitting by the fire grilling pork and drinking Leo beers. I was asking him about Thai Buddhism, and he said that traditionally all Thai males become monks. And that it brings good luck to the family; it's kind of like good karma. I was told that if the son becomes a monk, then the mother and father are assured to go to heaven. So it's a big deal. And I asked him, "Have you done that?" They said, "No, it's not as popular any more, and we just don't really want to." And I said, "Man, if that was a part of my culture, I would definitely do that, because that would be so

> **PEOPLE WHO HAVEN'T BEEN ON MOTORBIKES DON'T KNOW THIS, BUT YOU'RE ALWAYS ALMOST DEAD. YOU FEEL ALIVE, BECAUSE ALL DAY LONG THAT LETHAL ROAD IS BUZZING BY, AND IT'S RIGHT THERE.**

interesting. I'm very curious about it." And that was the end of the conversation. And no one else in the family understood what I was saying because they don't speak English. And the next morning, my friend came up to me and said, "I had a talk to mom and dad about what you said last night, and they said they want to adopt you, and that you can become a monk, and then it will be a blessing on the family."

CR: "And it will get me and my brother out of it."

JA: And I was like, "I can't really say no to that." So there was a bunch of stuff I had to learn. It's a very long story, I'm going to write a blog post about it at some point. I had to learn all of these blessings in Pali, which is the language that Buddha spoke. It's a dead language, like Latin. It was a huge production.

CR: So how many times have you been to Thailand?

JA: I've been going there for ten years, and I think probably eight, nine, maybe ten times? There's been a couple times where it's been a year and a half, or two years since I've visited, but I've also visited twice in some years. The shortest trip has been two weeks, and the longest has been three months.

CR: Would you say it's your favorite country?

JA: Yeah. Well, it feels like home to me. Any place that I recognize, and know how to get around, and can speak the language... it's familiar. So it feels like home. My favorite countries are based on the experiences I've had there, and the people I know. I really love Japan because I was in a rock band there, and I was in an incredible relationship there. So all my experiences of Tokyo have been just peak life-moments, so of course I love Tokyo. But Thailand is definitely one. Nepal is another one.

CR: Yeah, Nepal's lovely. I've only been there once, and it was a long time ago, but I had a really good feeling about the place. The mountains were just so amazing, so otherworldly; you can't believe how big those mountains are. And they're just always *there*. It's pretty cool.

JA: Yeah, when I was up in the kingdom of Lo, there was one point where I'm basically standing above a slightly less grand Grand-Canyon-type thing. And then you turn around and behind you, you've got another 5,000 feet of mountain right behind you. And you're already at 12,000 feet. I've got some pictures of it on my blog, but you can't really tell the magnitude of it. And it's like, "Oh my gosh, the scale of everything!" And you're out there, a full day's walk between villages. It's just you... and then nothing. You know?

CR: Have you been to Pakistan?

JA: No, it's really hard to get into. I would have to go to the US to get a visa, and I don't really plan to go to the US at all this year. I just found out that it's apparently the same situation with Iran – so that sucks.

CR: My buddy Viram, whom maybe you'll meet,

lives in southern Thailand. He's had so many crazy adventures, but one of them... he bought a donkey in Pakistan, and he and his donkey walked for something like 4 months through the Himalayas. And at one point along the way, there was a huge mudslide followed by gunfights... I can't remember all the details of the story. But he was out in the middle of nowhere, and there was this massive mudslide that wiped out the road he was walking on. And he would have had to walk through the mud; it was this huge nightmare. And the president of Pakistan flew in on a helicopter to this little village where he was trapped. And I guess he saw Viram sitting there during the little press conference, and said, "Hey, foreigner! Do you want a ride out?" and Viram was like, "Uhhh, yeah!" So he gave the donkey to somebody, jumped on the helicopter, and flew out.

JA: That's cool man... renting a donkey and exploring Pakistan for four months.

CR: Pretty cool, huh? Just walking along with your donkey. You don't have to carry all your shit.

JA: Yeah, it's like riding a really stubborn motorcycle.

CR: You would've been better off on a donkey, man! That's where you and I part ways. I mean, I'm down with you on the long motorcycle trips and all that, but I would be getting the easiest-to-fix motorcycle. The most reliable, no bullshit motorcycle.

JA: I'll take the donkey. Bukowski had this quote that I've always loved. He said: "To do something dangerous with style; that's what I call art." I like that.

BUKOWSKI HAD THIS QUOTE THAT I'VE ALWAYS LOVED. HE SAID:

TO DO SOMETHING DANGEROUS WITH STYLE; THAT'S WHAT I CALL ART.

I LIKE THAT.

ACKNOWLEDGMENTS

TANGENTIALLY READING was made possible by the generosity, enthusiasm and commitment of the *Tangentially Speaking* community. Podcast listeners' collective contribution to this project amounted to hundreds of hours of work. Without their efforts, you would not be holding this book in your hands. Both Chris and Misfit Press offer our deepest thanks to everyone listed below. (And our deepest apologies to anyone we may have left out.)

Adam McDade
Stephen Cook
Glenda J Wyatt
Cora Venus Lunny
Nick Santos
Na Snow
Jared Johnston
Joey Yip
Jessica Howard
Vinni LaCava
Matt Shumski
Alistair Chalk
Jorge Alzate
Amanda Rice
Eric Doan
Brad Buzzard
Kate Bard
Nate Atwood
Jon Waterlow
PJ Hernán López
Toby Harper
Renee Witehira
James Gibbins
Matthew Frommer
Nicole Leon-Campos
Bev Galster
Hector Pahaut
Ryan Price
Jack Fisher

The Man Behind the Illustrations

ADAM MCDADE

adammcdadeillustration

adammcdade.weebly.com

CPSIA information can be obtained
at www.ICGtesting.com
Printed in the USA
˜˜OW04n0556171217
˜˜˜ES